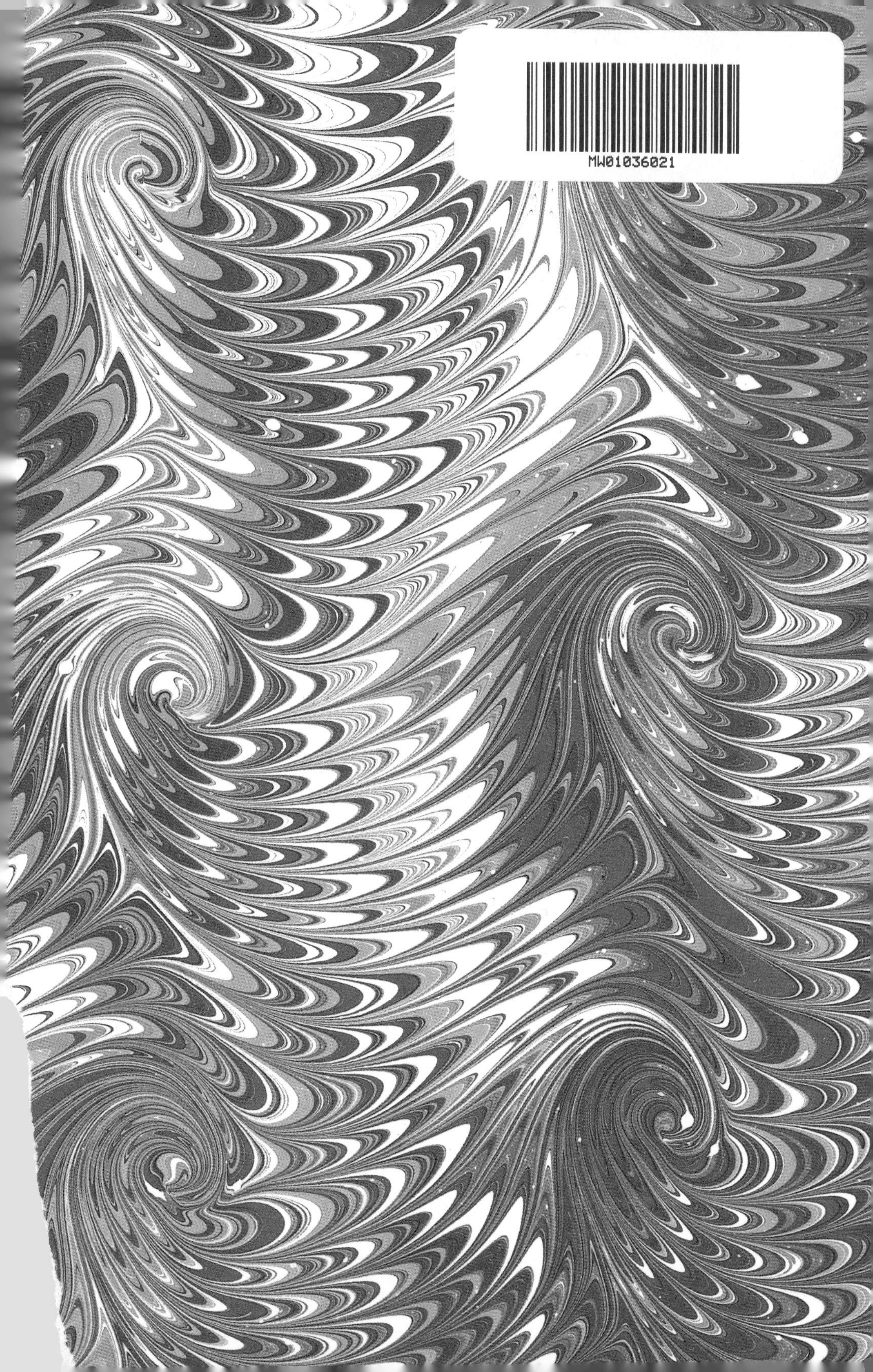
MW01036021

ARMY GROUP SOUTH

The Wehrmacht in Russia 1941-1945

By Werner Haupt
ARMY GROUP NORTH
ARMY GROUP CENTER
ARMY GROUP SOUTH
ASSAULT ON MOSCOW 1941

ARMY GROUP SOUTH

The Wehrmacht in Russia 1941-1945

WERNER HAUPT

Schiffer Military History
Atglen, PA

Book Design by Robert Biondi.
Translated from the German by Joseph G. Welsh.

This book was originally published under the title,
Heeresgruppe Süd,
by Podzun-Pallas Verlag, Friedberg.

Copyright © 1998 by Schiffer Publishing Ltd.
Library of Congress Catalog Number: 97-67600.

All rights reserved. No part of this work may be reproduced or used in any forms or by any means – graphic, electronic or mechanical, including photocopying or information storage and retrieval systems – without written permission from the copyright holder.

Printed in the United States of America.
ISBN: 0-7643-0385-6

We are interested in hearing from authors with book ideas on related topics.

Published by Schiffer Publishing Ltd.
4880 Lower Valley Road
Atglen, PA 19310 USA
Phone: (610) 593-1777
FAX: (610) 593-2002
E-mail: Schifferbk@aol.com.
Please write for a free catalog.
This book may be purchased from the publisher.
Please include $3.95 postage.
Try your bookstore first.

Contents

1

1941

THE FIRST SIX WEEKS

The Second World War was barely nine months old when Hitler decided to attack the Soviet Union. This enormous state to the east of the German Reich had exploited the overall world political situation and reinforced their military, especially on the western border. These measures were interpreted as meaning, that if the Allies weakened the Wehrmacht, the "Red Army" would have an open route to Southeastern and Northeastern Europe. German radio and agent reconnaissance reported that, shortly after the termination of the Western Campaign, approximately 90 rifle, 22 cavalry divisions, and 22 motorized brigades from the "Red Army" deployed into the border area.

It was on 21 July, 1940, that Hitler ordered his Wehrmacht High Command to work out the first plans for the eventual attack against the Soviet Union. After many weeks, the first plan was turned down – the one that was drafted by General of Artillery Marcks, who died in 1944 – so Major General Paulus (the Senior Quartermaster in the Army Group Command) had to work out a second offensive plan, which was approved by Hitler on 18 December, 1940, as "Order Nr. 21 – Plan Barbarossa."

This plan provided for, among other things, an army group to operate in the south, with its emphasis on the right "to quickly occupy the important industrial region of the Donets Basin." The left boundary for the de-

Geheime Kommandosache

Der Führer und Oberste Befehlshaber
der Wehrmacht
OKW/WFSt/Abt.L(I) Nr. 33 408/40 gK Chefs.

F.H.Qu., den 18.12.40

Chef Sache
Nur durch Offizier

9 Ausfertigungen
. Ausfertigung

Weisung Nr. 21

Fall Barbarossa.

Die deutsche Wehrmacht muss darauf vorbereitet sein, auch vor Beendigung des Krieges gegen England Sowjetrussland in einem schnellen Feldzug niederzuwerfen (Fall Barbarossa).

Auch bei der südlich der Pripetsümpfe angesetzten Heeresgruppe ist in konzentrischer Operation und mit starken Flügeln die vollständige Vernichtung der in der Ukraine stehenden russischen Kräfte noch westlich des Dnjepr anzustreben. Hierzu ist der Schwerpunkt aus dem Raum von Lublin in allgemeiner Richtung Kiew zu bilden, während die in Rumänien befindlichen Kräfte über den unteren Pruth hinweg einen weit abgesetzten Umfassungsarm bilden. Der rumänischen Armee wird die Fesselung der dazwischen befindlichen russischen Kräfte zufallen.

Die beabsichtigten Vorbereitungen aller Wehrmachtteile sind mir, auch in ihrem zeitlichen Ablauf, über das Oberkommando der Wehrmacht zu melden.

Order Nr. 21 – Plan Barbarossa

ployment and later advance of the army group was formed by the Pripet Swamp. Here the land was undeveloped with virgin forest, kilometer-wide swamps, and muddy roads – a natural obstacle that would make itself felt during later operations.

After the enactment of the "Order for Plan Barbarossa", the Army began to deploy from the Eastern Seacoast near Memel to the Black Sea. The staff of the Eastern Front's Army Group South remained in St. Germain near Paris for the summer and winter of 1940. Field Marshal von Rundstedt – the Grandseigneur of German general officers – organized the first considerations for the deployment and the subsequent operation. They considered that 29 infantry and eight panzer divisions would have to attack across the Bug through the Ukraine and up to the Dnepr.

The basis for these first plans did not prove successful during simulated map maneuvers, so a second offensive plan was constructed. This one placed the emphasis on the left flank, to press on to Kiev and, from here, advance down the Dnepr to the Black Sea, in order to encircle the "Red Army" in the Ukraine and destroy it. Accord to this plan, a small combat group would have to advance through Lemberg (Lvov) to fix the enemy; meanwhile, a combined Rumanian – German group would conduct mainly defensive missions on the coast.

The deployment of the armies, corps, and divisions that would be part of Army Group South began in November, 1940. The Army High Command (which we shall abbreviate to OKH) established a large supply center north of the Krakow – Przemysl Highway. This center was divided into four sub-centers, two of which stored ammunition, fuel, and rations.

The deployment of Army Group South – which was assigned the support of Air Fleet 4, under the command of General Loehr – was in full swing by early 1941. At this time, the army group command was in Breslau; the staff sections had already taken up residence in Okocim Palace, 30 kilometers southwest of Tarnow. The armies that were subordinate to the army group deployed in the following order, from north to south:

6th Army (Field Marshal von Reichenau) between Lublin and Przemysl;
17th Army (General of Infantry von Stuelpnagel) between Przemysl and Tomaszow;

Panzer Group 1 (General von Kleist) behind the inner flanks of both armies;
11th Army (General von Schobert) on either side of Jassy in Rumania.

The 11th Army was straddled by the 3rd and 4th Rumanian Armies, while the Hungarian Brigade deployed in the Carpathian area.

While the divisions were being transported to the forward deployment area from Germany, the occupied Western region and, finally, (after the end of the Balkan Campaign) from Southeast Europe, the formations located next to the border received the first attack order.

• • •

Secret, for Commanders Only
Commander, XVII Army Corps,
Abt. Ia Az. Nr. 500/41 g. Kdos.
K. H. QU 12 June, 1941
12 Copies
3rd Copy
For Officers Only

The Corps Order for the Attack

1.
The Enemy. The corps is opposed by a rifle division and units of the Border Guard Corps, in reinforced combat positions, that are determined to offer a stubborn defense.

The enemy line of defense probably runs along the hills and edges of the villages on the eastern bank of the Bug. Expect to encounter well constructed and camouflaged positions in the depth of the main combat sector, especially on either side of the Dorohusk-Luboml railroad line. Two additional divisions (one of which is motorized) are presumed to be in the Kowel area. Details of enemy concentrations are contained in the fortifications map, which has already been distributed.

2.
The 6th Army breaks through enemy border positions in the Krystynopol-Swierze sector and opens the way for Panzer Group 1 to quickly penetrate to the east.

On the right of the XVII Army Corps, the 298th Infantry Division (III Army Corps) attacks through Uscilug to Wlodzzimierz, on the left of the XVII Army Corps, the 255th Infantry Division (XXIV Army Corps) attacks on both sides of Wlodawa to Malorytam Lywin.

The boundary with the III Army Corps (author's note – the locations are not legible in the original order). The boundary with the XXIV Army Corps (also the army boundary): Lubartow (XVII), Sosnowica (XXIV), Kolacze (XXIV), Szack (XXIV), Krymno (XXIV), Wieka Hlusza (XXIV), Dawidgrodek (XVII).

3.
On D-Day at H-Hour, XVII Army Corps crosses the Bug in the Swierze sector, emphasizing the interior flanks of both divisions, breaks through enemy border fortifications, and seizes the high ground on either side of Luboml (Objective of the Day). The next task of the corps is to quickly seize the important Kowel railroad junction and intersection. In the further course of the operation, the main task of the corps is to protect the northern flank of the army from enemy activity coming out of the Pripet region.

For organization and boundaries see the Preparation Order (Gen. Kdo. XVII. AK, Ia Nr. 462/41, g. Kdos. v. 6. 6. 1941), Subparagraph 2).

4.
Tasks: a. the 62nd Infantry Division crosses the Bug east of Husynne, as well as on and south of the railroad line, breaks through the enemy defensive positions on the high ground east of the Bug Valley on their strong left flank, and then seizes the eastern edge of the forest northeast of Rakowiso, as well as the high ground east of Rymacze (hill 186.7) Berezce to complete the encirclement as quickly as possible. From this bridgehead, the attack is to be concentrated against the high

ground south of Luboml, the left flank is to continue on to hill 190.1.

By deep echelon to the right, the division secures the right flank of the corps against enemy activity from the south and southeast. They must avoid being drawn off to the south.

b. The 56th Infantry Division crosses the Bug at the railroad line-Swierze sector, breaks through enemy border positions on either side of Wilozy Przowez with a strong right flank, and then seizes the sector between Jagodzin and Jenkowce maintaining flank cover near Rowno. Wilczy Przewez is quickly captured by encirclement. It is important that the right flank of the division maintains direct contact with the breakthrough of the left flank of the 62nd Division, north of the railroad.

From this bridgehead, the attack is to be concentrated through the high ground north of Jagodzin (hills 192 and 194.0) against the high ground north of Luzboml (hills 205 and 215.3), by deep echelon to the left.

The division secures the attack of the corps on the left flank by echeloning to the left, it must not be drawn off to the north.

• • •

The great German deployment – by the end of February, eight divisions; by the end of March, 16; by the end of April, 30; and by the end of May, a total of 39 divisions – of Army Group South naturally could not be hidden from the Russian command authorities. Since the beginning of March, the command posts of the "Red Army" were alerted. The Commander of the "Kiev Special Military District" (these were the designations of the later named "Fronts"), General Kirponos, prepared his subordinate armies (the 5th, 6th, 9th, 12th, and 26th) and independent motorized corps (IV, V, IX, XV) for action, and his entire complement occupied their prepared rear area positions between Chernovits-the Pripet Swamp-Kiev by the middle of June. At this point in time, he had 20 rifle divisions, three tank, and seven mechanized (motorized) brigades at his disposal.

However, Army Group South's deployment was almost complete.

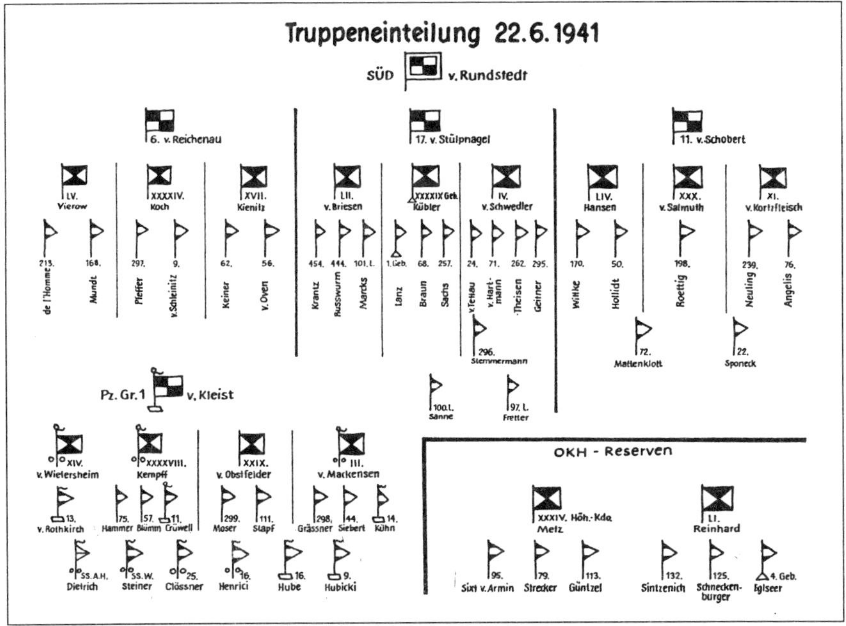

Troop Distribution 6/22/1941

It was a warm summer night, 22 June, 1941. The last preparations for the offensive against the Soviet Union had been made. On this night, the width of Army Group South's front line totaled 1,350 kilometers, of which 250 kilometers were represented by the Carpathian Mountains, in which no German soldiers were located. On this last night, Army group South and Air Fleet 4 numbered three million soldiers, with 600,000 vehicles, 750,000 horses, 3,580 tanks, 7,184 guns, and 1,830 airplanes. In the first hours of the new day, the commanders and officers issued their orders of the day to their troops, which were ready for combat against the "Red Army."

• • •

At the precise minute, the hour of 0315 was marked by the opening of fire by hundreds of guns of all calibers and the launching of thousands of rounds from mortars onto known border fortifications, roads, and communication junctions.

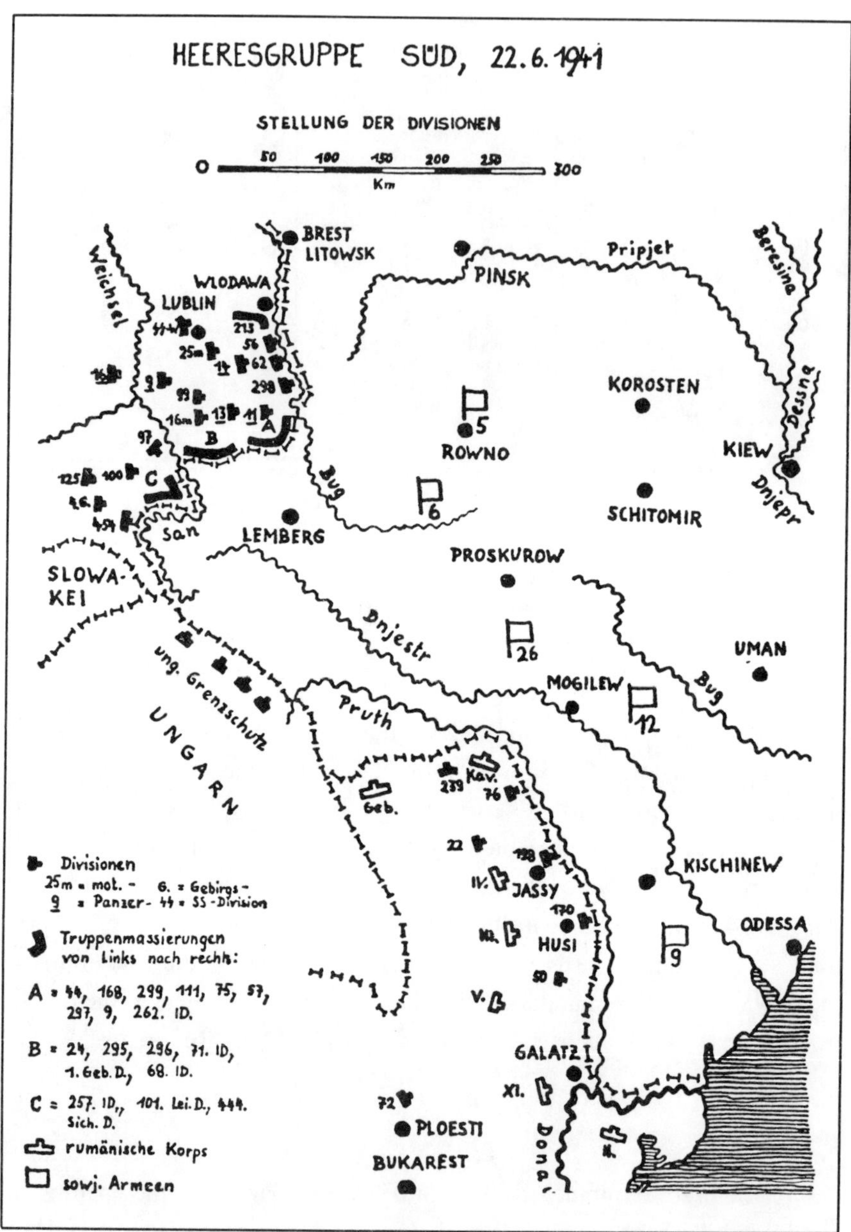

Army Group South 6/22/1941

11. Panzer-Division
Verteiler: C

Div.Stbs.Qu., den 22. Juni 1941

Von den Einheitsführern bekanntzugeben.

D i v i s i o n s - T a g e s b e f e h l

Soldaten der 11. Panzer-Division!

Der Führer ruft zum Kampf gegen den Bolschewismus, dem Urfeind unseres nationalsozialistischen Reiches.
Der Kampf wird an einigen Stellen schwer, Entbehrungen und Strapazen überall sehr groß sein.

Die Gespenster-Division wird sich wie in Serbien auf den Feind stürzen, wo wir ihn treffen – ihn angreifen und vernichten.
Ich weiß, daß ich mich, wie in Südost, auf jeden von Euch, vom ältesten Offizier bis zum jüngsten Mann unbedingt verlassen kann.
Unsere Parole bleibt der Angriff, unser Ziel der D n j e p r. Dort wollen wir, wie vor Belgrad, wieder die Ersten sein.

H e i l d e m F ü h r e r
gez. Crüwell
Generalmajor

11th Panzer Division Order of the Day

The combat and fighter units of the Luftwaffe flew across the border through the smoke of the exploding shells. As the artillery fire shifted to the rear area, the infantrymen and engineers stormed forward. The men in the black collar patches had pulled the rubber boats and rafts into the bushes on the banks in the first hours of the new day and now rowed the first assault troops across the border rivers. At 0315 hours, the start of the attack, the 6th and 17th German Armies were between Wlodawa on the Bug and the Hungarian border.

The army of Field Marshal von Reichenau formed the left flank. The XVII Army Corps was deployed with its 56th and 62nd Infantry Divisions (from now on abbreviated as ID) in the northern sector. The corps had the task of protecting the army's flank to the Pripet Swamp. In spite of strong resistance by two opposing Soviet divisions, both German divisions were able to advance 14 kilometers on the ground!

• • •

During the course of the day, the division advanced 14 kilometers across the Bug in heavy combat. The lead elements of the attack could already see

Luboml. As darkness approached, two battalions from the middle regiment were missing; they had attacked so violently that they became cut off in Russian territory. Luckily, the bravery and circumspection of the Regiment Commander, Colonel von Erdmannsdorf, succeeded in retrieving the two battalions from the enemy encirclement during the night. For a time, the situation of the 192nd Infantry Regiment became unusually critical. The Russian bunker fortifications on the Bug near Wilczy-Przewoz were defending tenaciously and valiantly to the last man. Further advance by the regiment became particularly difficult through the enemy defenses on the Chelm-Luboml-Kowel railroad and road, because the neighbor on the right, the 62nd ID, was having considerable problems on its left flank.

Moreover, during the day the XVII Army Corps had to intervene in the operations of the 56th ID. Since they did not succeed in establishing a bridge near the 62nd ID, a combat bridge was made available in the 192nd Infantry Regiment lane of attack during the morning hours. The commander allowed the units of the 62nd ID to use the bridge without giving priority to the necessary advance of the artillery. The commander, doubtlessly, had valid reasons for doing this. The division worked this order out for itself and it learned a valuable lesson as it attacked across the Bug. The result was that the division was committed on the far eastern side of the Bug without artillery support, because the 1/156 Artillery Regiment, which was already on the eastern bank of the Bug, had already expended its ammunition.

Consequently, the 192nd Infantry Regiment suffered heavy losses and, in several locations, the situation became critical. The circumspect and resolute leadership of the regiment, provided by its distinguished commander, Lieutenant Colonel Ratcliffe, was – next to the bravery of the troops – in a large measure responsible for overcoming the situation. (From the *History of the 56th Infantry Division*, Fulda 1968.)

• • •

The three motorized corps of General von Kleist's Panzer Group 1 were thrust forward on the right of the XVII Army Corps during the first day. The 44th and 298th ID captured the undamaged Bug River bridge near

Hrubaschow, over which the 14th Panzer Division rolled during the afternoon. The XLIV Army Corps, located on the right, also gained ground. As Panzer Group 1 broke through on the first day, the XXIX Army Corps and the XLVIII Motorized Army Corps also crossed the wide border river, so that the 6th Army appeared to have achieved freedom of maneuver on the first day of combat.

On the other hand, the neighboring army of General of Infantry von Stuelpnagel made it through the border fortifications, but not without heavy losses. The IV Army Corps, which was located on the left, came to realize that the Russian soldier fought with a completely different energy and willingness to sacrifice in comparison to the French and British during the Western Campaign. By evening, a 10 kilometer gap in the front line yawned between the 24th and 262nd ID. It was finally closed on the second attempt by the 296th ID, which had to be brought forward.

The neighboring XLIX Mountain Corps was also unable to achieve any immediate initial success. Therefore, the LII Army Corps had to continue to operate as the flank corps, because it had to secure the 80 kilometer wide front to the Hungarian border.

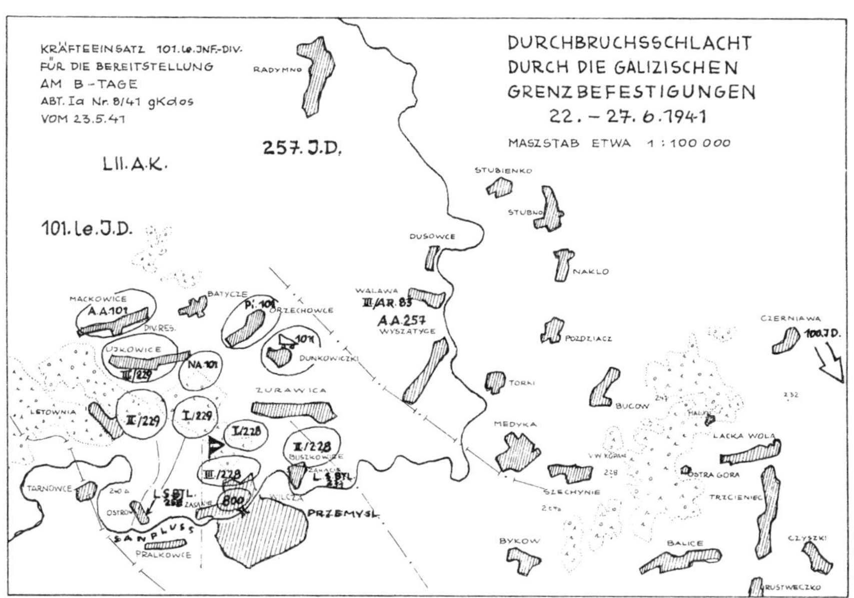

Breakthrough of the Galician border fortifications 6/22-27/1941

The 101st Light Division (Major General Marcks) had the most important mission on this sector, which was to capture heavily fortified Przemysl to provide the XLIX Mountain Corps with a clear route in the direction of Lemberg. The first assault on the fortifications on both sides of the old city failed; therefore, the shock troops and assault companies had to be withdrawn during the evening.

During the first night of combat, the commander of the Russian "Southwest Front" – which is what the southern Russian army group was called on 23 June – ordered the preparation of his tank and motorized brigades for a counterattack to cut off the lead German attacking elements. The "Red Army's" IX and XIX Motorized Corps were prepared northwest of Rowno, the VIII and XV were on either side of Brody and the IV Corps was between Sokal and Radziechow. These corps were led by General Vlassov, who, a year later, was the commander of the German Wehrmacht's Vlassov Army.

The Soviet tank counterattack was unleashed on the morning of the second day of combat and was, in some places, skillfully committed against the German flanks. The type "Kv-I" and "Kv-II" heavy tanks rolled over the forward-most infantry companies and the 3.7 cm anti-tank guns, which were overcome by the steel monsters. On this day, only the heavy 8.8 cm air defense guns were able to destroy some of the enemy's tanks near Radziechow.

After our formations had overcome the first shock from these heavy enemy tanks they no longer allowed them to interrupt their attack momentum. The III and XLVIII Motorized Army Corps tore through the Russian forces near Wladimir Wolynsk and advanced to the east. They captured the city of Luzk on 25 June. The 11th Panzer Division (Major General Cruewell) penetrated the flanks of the 5th and 6th Soviet Armies near Dubno, where a four day tank battle occurred.

The neighboring IV German Army Corps advanced southwest near Rava-Ruska through a gap in the enemy's lines. The 97th Light Division got into a bit of trouble near Magierov, because they were attacked by four Russian rifle divisions and the 8th Mechanized Brigade. However, the infantrymen did not become discouraged, and they advanced into Magierov and shot up 60 enemy tanks!

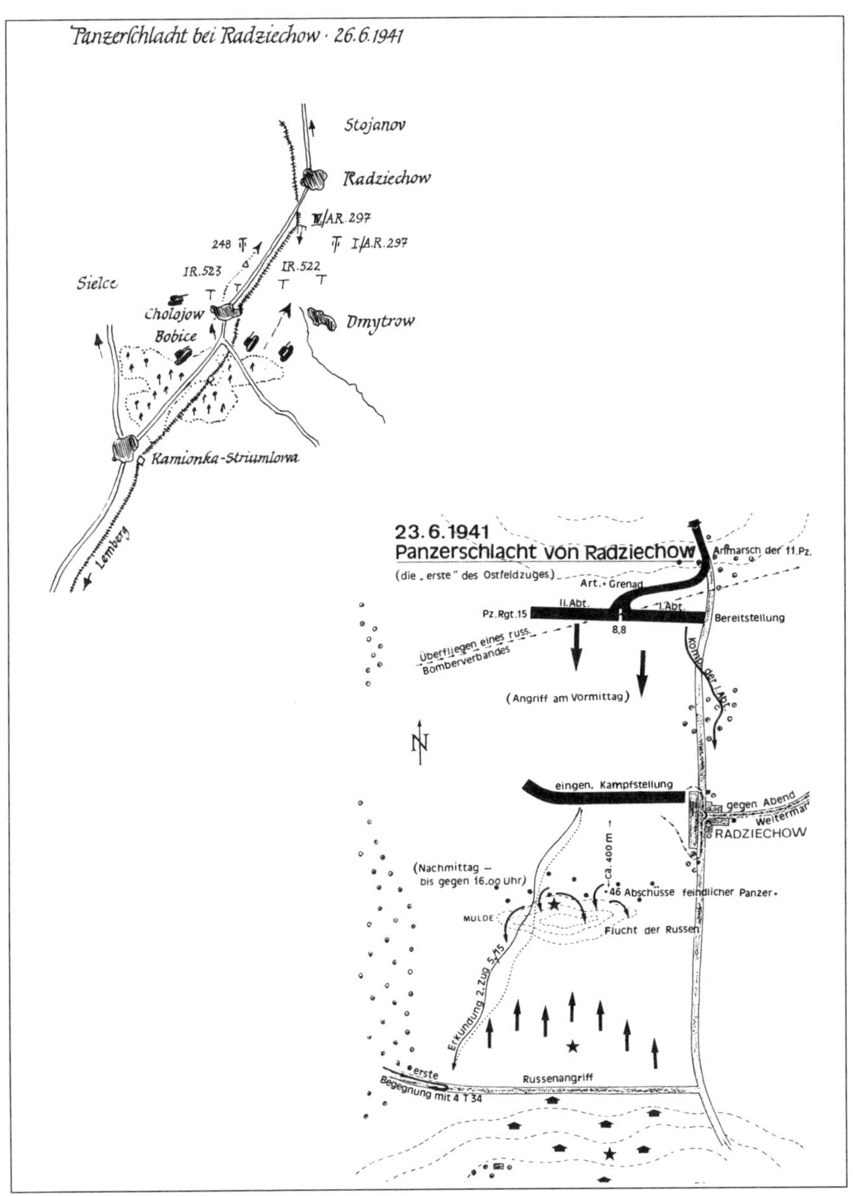

Top: Tank battle near Radziechow 6/26/1941

Bottom: 6/23/1941 Radziechow Tank Battle (The "first" of the Eastern Campaign)

On 26 July, the Soviet command gave up on the border battle. Therefore, both German armies now had freedom to maneuver. Panzer Group 1, which was formerly subordinate to the 6th Army Commander, became independent on this day, in order to allow it to thrust its mobile formations through the gaps in the front line and quickly gain undefended territory.

By the end of the month, strong Russian resistance had deteriorated everywhere. The 5th Soviet Army, which was fighting in the Pripet Swamp and had contained the XVII Army Corps for an entire day, slowly with-

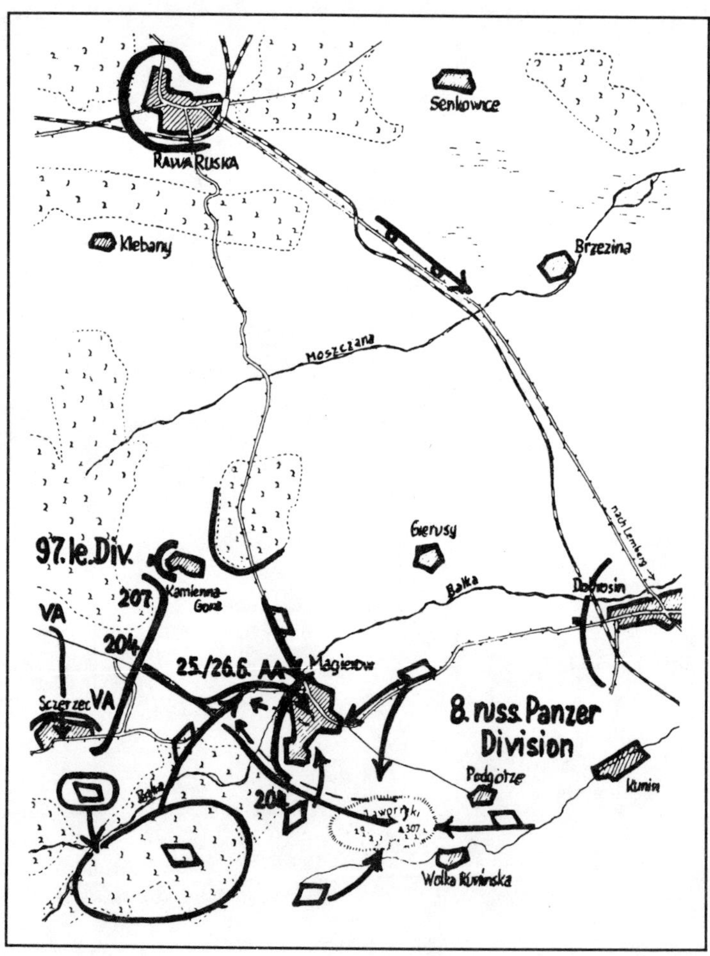

drew to the east. In this manner the corps was able to cross the Turya and, on 28 June, its 62nd ID captured Kovel.

With the general withdrawal of the "Red Army", the southern flank of the 17th Army was able to advance. The army had already gained ground west and north of Lemberg and now concentrated its attack on Lemberg with the 1st Mountain Division (Major General Lanz) and the 71st ID (Major General von Hartmann). Lemberg was taken on 30 June.

Since both flanks of the army group had gained maneuvering room, General von Kleist ordered, "Turn to the east and resume the advance!"

The 11th Army, which had not yet been in combat, received the order to cross the Pruth and participate in the army group's offensive. The fight for the bridgehead was fierce, because of the tenacious defense of the 18th

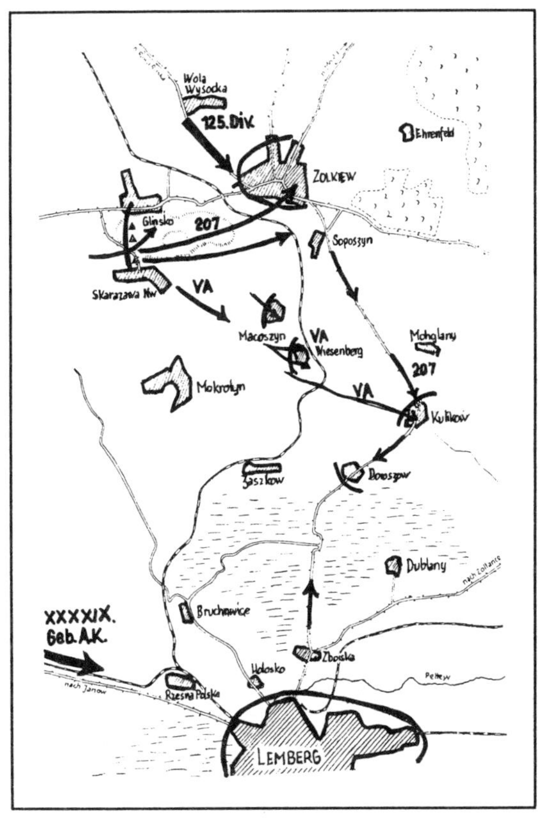

Attack on Lemberg 6/28-30/1941

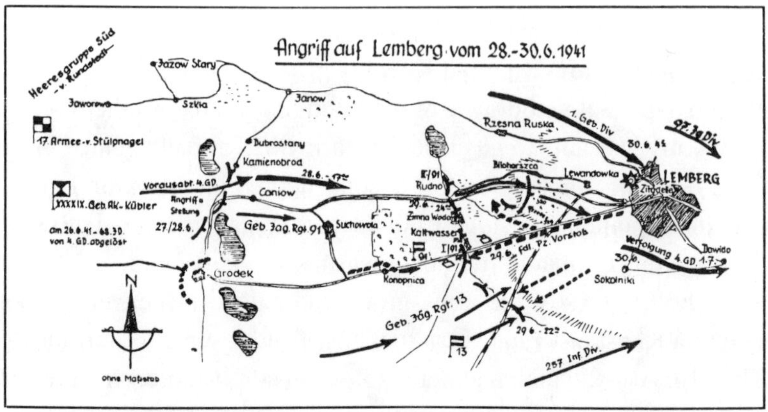

Frankfurter Zeitung

mit dem Stadt-Blatt

Sammel-Nummer für Fernsprecher: Ortsverkehr 20202, Fernverkehr 20301.

I/II 58 **Dienstag, 1. Juli 1941.**

Gebirgsjäger zum zweitenmal in Lemberg.

Berlin, 30. Juni. Die gleichen Truppen, die schon im Herbst 1939 im Kampf um Lemberg Ungewöhnliches geleistet haben, eroberten am Montag nach schweren Kämpfen wieder die Stadt. Bayerische Gebirgsjäger haben am 30. Juni, um 4.20 Uhr morgens, auf der hohen Burg in Lemberg die Reichskriegsflagge gehißt.

Mountain Troops Take Lemberg for the Second Time

Soviet Army. The German and Rumanian forces achieved freedom of maneuver on the third day of combat. After that, the Hungarian government ordered their divisions to cross the Carpathian Mountain passes and participate in the German attack.

The army of General von Schobert pushed across the Pruth on a wide front in the general direction of Mogilev and Kamenets-Podolsk.

The Russian Commander – Marshal Timoshenko had just taken command of the "Red Army" – now ordered the withdrawal of his formations to the so-called "Stalin Line." The Soviet armies, fighting in southern Russia, were now divided into two army groups. Army Group "Southwest Front" received the 400 kilometer wide defensive sector between the Pripet Swamp and Kamenets-Podolsk. The newly formed Army Group "South Front" received the 500 kilometer wide sector between Kamenets-Podolsk and the mouth of the Danube.

In the first week of July, Army Group South stood before the "Stalin Line" along the entire breadth of its front line. The line, potions of which were defended by bunkers, while other portions had field fortifications, extended from about Lakhva in the Pripet Swamp through Zviagel, Berdichev, Prokurov, Kamenets-Podolsk. It was not a continuous fortified line. Strong points were established at river crossings, crossroads, large forests, and villages. The attack against this line developed locally.

• • •

The attempt to take Zviagel in a bold strike failed because the bunkers were constructed on local fortifications and were covered by strong artillery, anti-tank, and air defense fires. Three company commanders of the 108th Rifle Regiment and three officers of the 4th Armored Artillery Regiment fell on 7 July during the planned attack on Zviagel. Since 0430 hours, the battle had been raging around the Zviagel bunker line on either side of the advance road, which came under further enemy air attack. Due to the fierce defensive fire from the bunkers, the attack could not advance, so renewed friendly bombing attacks have been requested.

At 1530 hours, after a stuka attack, our shock troops, suffering heavy losses, worked their way to the bunkers and had to engage each one of them in hand-to-hand combat. In the evening, they finally succeed in busting the first bunker open. Losses were high: about 40 men per company; the 4th Armored Artillery Regiment lost two officers dead and seven wounded. The battle raged undiminished around the bunkers on 8 July. For reinforcement, the 25th Motorized Infantry Division, the 299th ID, and the entire corps artillery were committed.

Meanwhile, the 11th Panzer Division broke through to the south and stood south of Zhitomir, the 13th Panzer Division broke through near Sluszk and attacked Broniki, and the Leibstandarte SS Adolf Hitler advanced south of the 11th Panzer Division and is setting on Kiev.

During the day, the strongly fortified city of Zviagel was finally captured and a bridgehead established on the eastern bank of the Sluczk, and it was widened by elements of the 25th Motorized Infantry Division that worked its way behind the bunkers from the south.

On 9 July, the eastern bank was systematically cleared of enemy forces. While enemy bunkers were still active at the bridging site, the corps engineers began constructing a bridge. By 1900 hours, the bridge was able to transport 16 ton vehicles, and during the night, armored units of the division, including the division staff, reached Zhitomir. Shortly thereafter, a report arrived stating that the enemy had broken through the "Rollbahn" in several places. At this time, the rifle regiment was still in position near Zviagel, where they were awaiting their relief. We were unable to rest during the night of 10-11 July. Buildings in Zhitomir were set on fire by sabotage elements of the Communist Youth. On 11 July, only isolated vehicles, which had started out as convoys, made it to Zhitomir, because the enemy occupied portions of the Rollbahn and fired upon them. On 11 July at 1800 hours, March Group Jesser began the advance on Nebyliza. (From: Grams, R.: *The 14th Panzer Division.* Nauheim 1957.)

On 9 July – to select a particular day – Army Group South was deployed from north to south along the front as follows:

The XVII Army Corps (the 56th, 62nd, 99th, 298th ID) advanced on a broad front toward Horyn south of Sarny. The XXIX Army Corps (the 44th, 299th ID) was advancing to the northeast. The III Motorized

Army Corps, with the 13th, 14th Panzer Divisions and the 25th ID, was assaulting Zhitomir. The XLVIII Motorized Army Corps (the 11th, 16th Panzer Divisions, 16th Motorized Infantry Division) had encircled Berdichev and captured the railroad line south of Zhitomir. The LV Army Corps (the 75th, 111th ID) followed in the Lyubar hills. The XIV Motorized Army Corps (the 9th Panzer Division, 5th SS Panzer Division) advanced south of these units, further to the northwest. The XXXIX Motorized Army Corps (the 9th, 57th, 262nd, 292 ID) advanced to the east through the hills of Proskurov.

At the beginning of July, the 17th Army, under the command of General of Infantry von Stuelpnagel, had the following units assigned to it: IV Army Corps (the 24th, 97th, 125th, 295th ID), XLIX Mountain Corps (the 1st, 4th Mountain Divisions, 257th ID), and the LII Army Corps (the 100th, 101st Rifle Divisions). The 444th and 454th Independent Security Divisions were placed near the boundary with the Slovakian Army Group.

At the beginning of July, the 11th Army, which was attacking in the extreme south, consisted of the Rumanian Cavalry Corps, the LIV Army Corps (the Rumanian 5th ID, German 50th Rifle Division), the Rumanian Mountain Corps, and the IV Rumanian Corps with a total of six Rumanian Brigades, the XI Army Corps (the 22nd, 76th ID and two Rumanian brigades), and the XXX Army Corps (the 170th, 198th ID and three Rumanian divisions), while the 239th ID was maintained in reserve.

The 22nd and 76th ID of the 11th Army were able to reach the approach to Mogilev, while the remaining corps advanced on the Dnestr and the 50th ID captured Orheiu. Here the "Stalin Line" was rent after two weeks of hard combat. Therefore, the army had an open road to the coast.

The main axis of advance was in front of Panzer Group 1. Here, the 11th Panzer Division gained ground south of Zhitomir and the 13th Panzer Division advanced in the area of Broniki. The motorized SS Brigade "Leibstandarte Adolf Hitler" was deployed between the panzer divisions and advanced on Kiev from the west. The tanks of the 14th

Panzer Division fought immediately south of these units. Meanwhile, the 13th Panzer Division was advancing into Zhitomir.

The prospect of capturing the capital of the Ukraine appeared to be good. On 9 July, General von Kleist ordered his divisions: "...to establish a deep bridgehead east of the Dnepr as a base for the continuation of the operation east of the river!" Panzer Group 1 had fought its way to a 200 kilometer advantage over the infantry divisions in the direction of Kiev. And they were advancing further! The III Motorized Army Corps advanced unchecked. On 10 July, the 13th Panzer Division (Major General Duevert) reached the Irpen sector, immediately in front of Kiev. The 14th Panzer Division (Major General Heim) closed ranks the following day – Kiev was next! The soldiers of the reconnaissance detachments were able to make out the silhouettes of the cathedrals in the evening sun – suddenly the OKH was interested!

In view of ever increasing enemy resistance, especially before Army Groups Center and North and the almost unbelievable resistance forces of the "Red Army", Hitler ordered the cessation of any more large scale operations. He would allow only the formation of small pockets. Panzer Group 1 was ordered not to conduct any more unified attacks, but to separate into three corps groupings and operate toward the south. Only the III Motorized Army Corps (General of Cavalry von Mackensen) was left before Kiev. It received the order: "...attend to protecting the flank against enemy activity from the area northeast of Zhitomir-Kiev." Kiev was abandoned!

At the beginning of July, the "Red Army" was reorganized and regrouped. Marshal Budenny, the old veteran of the civil war, was named commander of the entire Southern front. His first order began with the words: "Not one more step back! Halt! Counterattack!"

On 10 July, three Russian tank corps, followed by three rifle corps and supported by four air divisions, attacked, as ordered, into the flank of Panzer Group 1 from the area of Korosten – Malin. Shortly thereafter, there followed a second attack by three additional tank corps in the Berdichev area.

The German divisions, deployed to the east, were in a difficult situation. They had to turn their formations 180 degrees to stop the enemy breakthrough. In Berdichev they were fighting a losing battle; for four days they

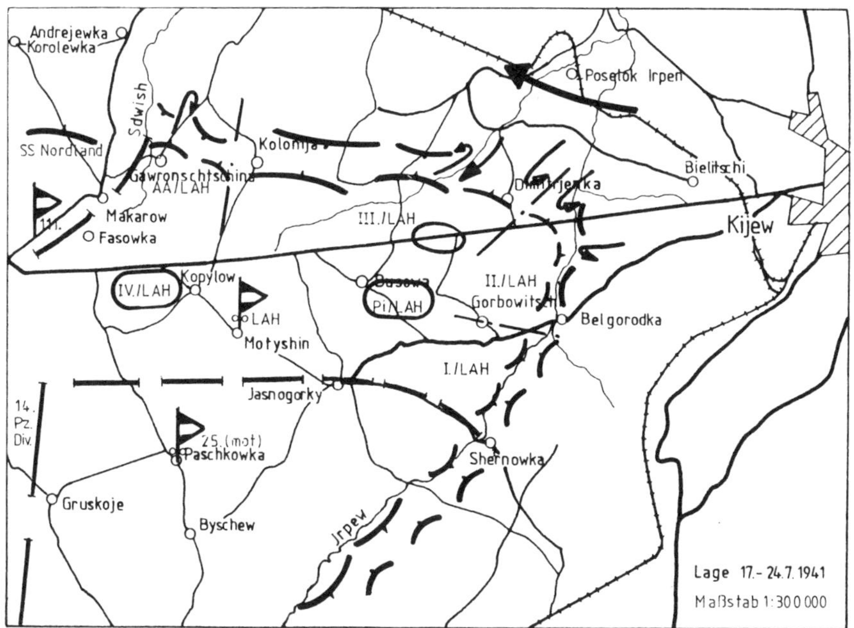

Situation 7/17-24/1941

struggled bitterly over the Teterev sector; the Zhitomir-Korosten and Zhitomir-Novograd-Volynsk roads were cut. After the "Leibstandarte" was committed from Kiev, the persistent enemy attacks diminished.

The army group detached divisions from several frontal sectors and transferred them to the threatened positions. This finally changed the course of the battle. The 5th Soviet Army, which had fought bravely, began to withdraw. While the enemy attack was directed at the forward-most elements of Panzer Group 1 – to the horror of the German soldiers, a new type of tank suddenly appeared, the "T-34", which they had never seen before and for which they had no anti-tank weapon – in the south of the Front, the 11th Army's two left flank corps were able to cross the Dnestr.

Here, after the middle of July, and also after persistent combat in several places, they were able to cross the river on a wide front from Mogilev downstream and slowly gain ground to the east.

On 21 July, the 11th Army had the following units on the eastern bank of the Dnestr, from right to left: The Rumanian Mountain and Cavalry Corps, XI Army Corps, with the 76th, 22nd, and 239th ID; and XXX Army Corps, with the 198th, 170th, and 46th ID. The last two divisions had already gained an open route to the east and were advancing in the direction of Balta. The LIV Army Corps, with the 73rd, 50th, and 72nd ID, was advancing to the west bank of the Dnestr.

In this manner, the 31st of July, 1941, ended in the southern sector... However, the first encirclement battle was already taking place in this large, important area.

• • •

Ukraine, 31 July 1941

A blue sunny sky spread its canopy over us. Only a milky white condensation trail with sharp contours – wide in the west and narrowing to a

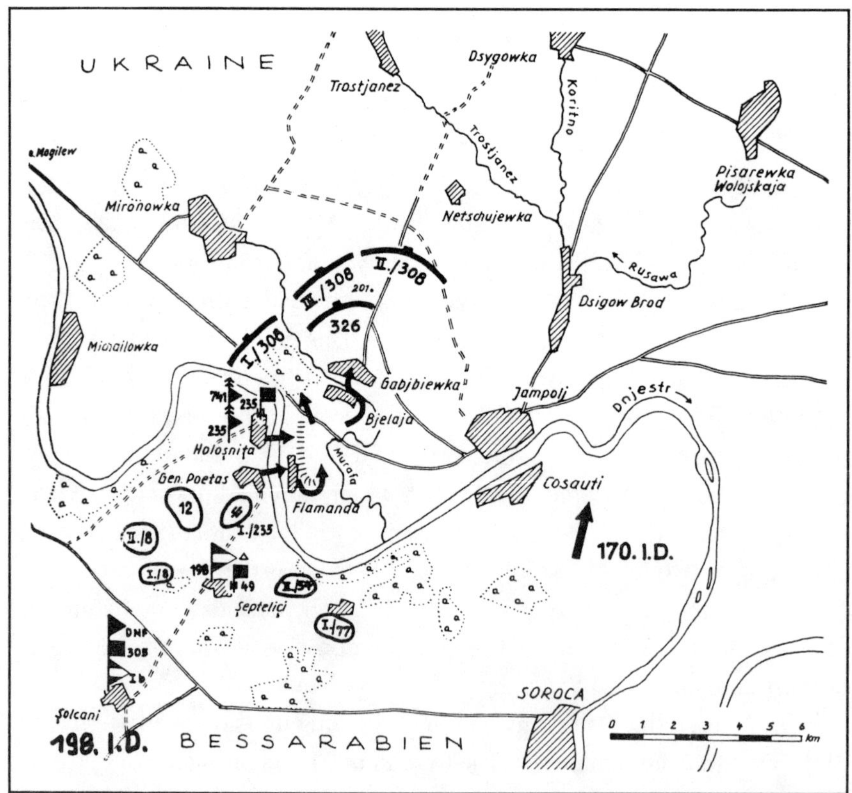

small point to the east – appeared like a gaping wound in the firmament high over our heads. This solitary point is a He-111 long range reconnaissance aircraft. It flies its trace over a world engaged in war.

This earth, steaming in the summer heat, is the Ukraine. Over sandy, wide roads, on a rollbahn made of coarse, cobbled pavement, we enter a land where the horizon never ends. Endless plains, corn, and sunflowers line our routes to the east. The human dwellings are collective villages or one street strip towns with straw covered mud huts and draw wells. In recent days, sedate, wooden windmills complete the pastoral scene. The rest and watering stops on this lonely march through a land that is wide and strange leave an indelible impression on us. (From: Bidermann, G. H.: *Krim-Kurland.* (132nd ID) Hannover 1964.)

• • •

Army Group South

UMAN
(25 July - 8 August 1941)

Since the middle of July, the center of Army Group South had been attacking to the southeast. In order to guarantee centralized command and control in this sector, the army group commander created "Group Schwedler", under the command of General of Infantry von Schwedler. The IV and XLIV Army Corps were subordinated to it. The group was placed on the right flank of Panzer Group 1, in the area between Berdichev (in the north) and Vinnitsa (in the south). The boundary on the left with the neighboring XLVIII Motorized Army Corps was close by. This corps (General of Panzer troops Kempf), with the 11th and 16th Panzer Divisions, was advancing to the south in the direction of Uman and Monastyrishche. The panzer divisions continued to advance in front of the infantry divisions (the right flank was secured by the 16th Motorized Infantry Division) into the rear of the enemy. Portions of the 6th and 12th Soviet Armies were already by-passed.

In order to maintain the momentum of the operation, Army Group South planned a unified strike by the panzer group west of the Dnepr to the southeast to capture the Russian armies that were still in front of the river. Hitler interfered and overruled the OKH. He ordered that the flank of the panzer group was not to advance further to the south, but to stop in the Uman area, in order to await the closing of the lead elements of the 17th Army, which were coming from the west. Therefore, the army group issued the following order:

> "6th Army attacks the enemy near Korosten, occupies the area west and south of Kiev, and later crosses the Dnepr in the direction of Poltava.
>
> Panzer Group 1 advances in the direction of Aleksandriya, later to either the Saporoshe-Dnepropetrovsk area or the Kremenchug-Dnepropetrovsk area.
>
> Group Schwedler advances in the Cherkassy-Kanev direction.

17th Army advances in the general direction of Kirovograd, later to either Krivoy Rog or Dnepropetrovsk.

11th Army advances on the Bug sector of Vossnesenssk-Pervomaisk, later to Krivoy Rog."

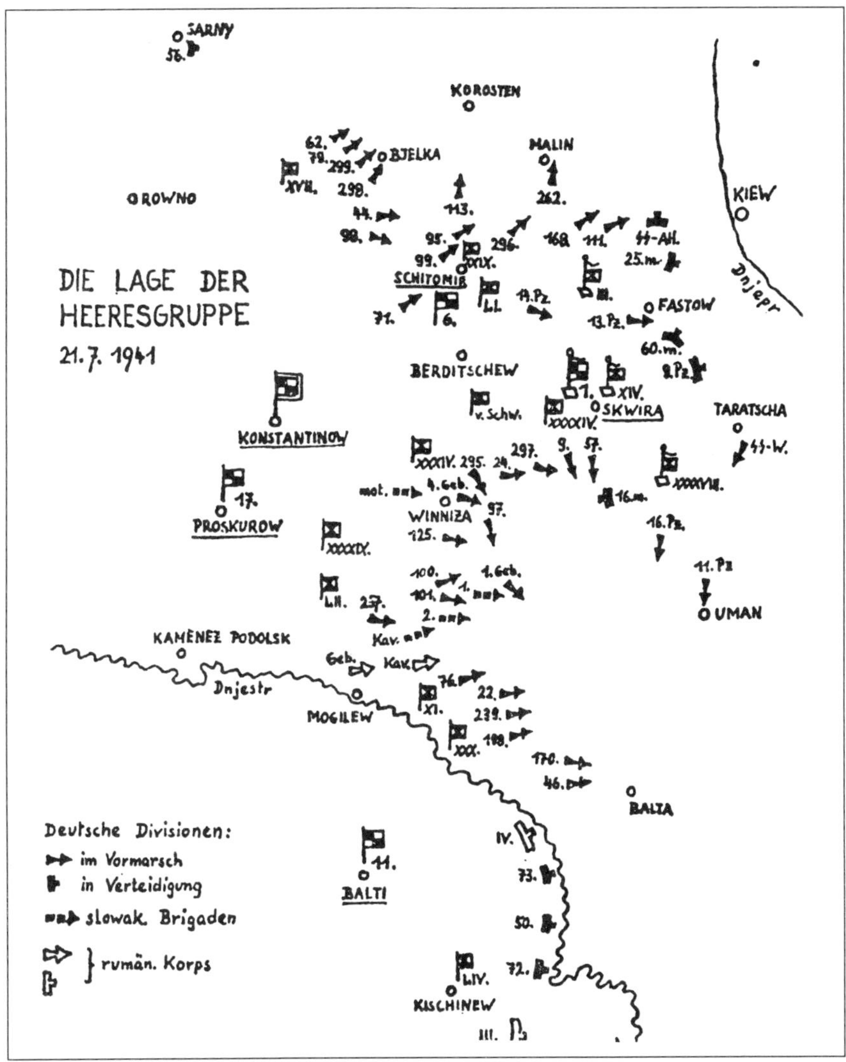

The Situation of the Army Group 7/21/1941

Here, in the Uman area – midway between the Dnestr and the Dnepr – Marshal Budenny retained forces from his 5th and 26th Soviet Armies, along with about 2,400 tanks, in order to attack into the flank of von Kleist's panzer group and stop them at the Dnepr. This is how the battle for Uman developed after 21 July.

The XLVIII Motorized Army Corps was already deep in the rear of the 6th Soviet Army. The 11th Panzer Division (Major General Cruewell) reached the region north of Uman, while the 16th Panzer Division (Major General Hube) forced its way into Monastyrishche. This was where the main headquarters of Marshal Budenny was located no longer than 24 hours ago! On the same day, the advance detachment of the division (Major von

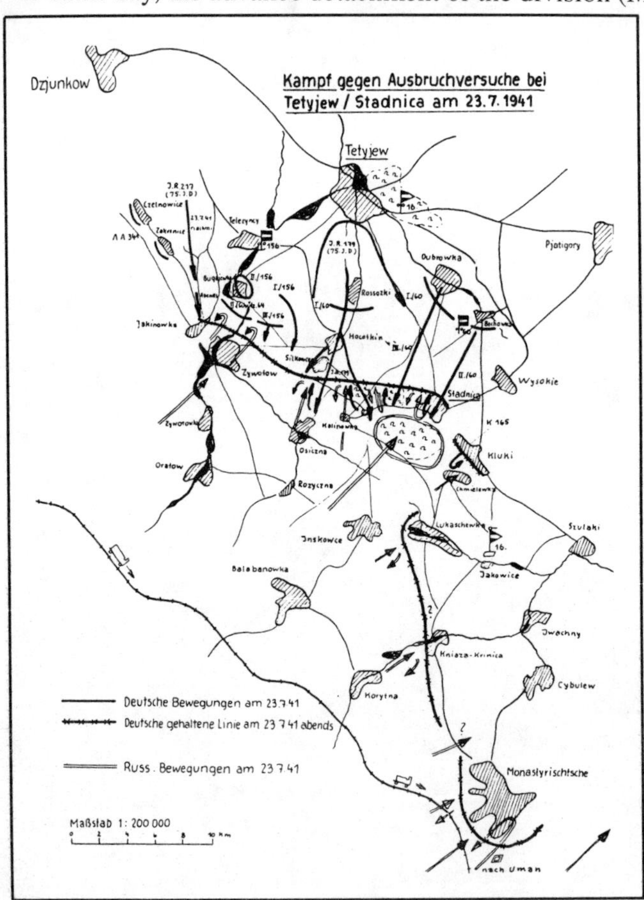

Struggle against the breakout attempts near Tetyev/Stadnitsa on 7/23/1941

Witzleben) cut the railroad line between the two cities. The Soviet commanders understood the danger their troops were in and immediately issued orders to break out to the east. In the meantime, one rifle division stopped the advance of the infantry divisions of "Group Schwedler", while the bulk of the Russian tank brigades tried to break out to the east. The full weight of these huge attacks hit the 16th Panzer Division and 16th Motorized Infantry Division (Major General Henrici), which were deployed near and north of Monastyrishche.

In this sector, the battle seesawed all day long. It developed into a bitter hand-to-hand struggle in which no quarter was given. The situation improved on 25 July when the "Liebstandarte" (SS Obergruppenfuehrer Dietrich), which had arrived from Kiev, was committed between the 11th and 16th Panzer Divisions and strengthened the defensive front line. The Russian formations here were no longer successful in breaking through the front line positions.

Panzer Group 1 (General von Kleist) was now also replaced by the XIV Motorized Army Corps (General of Infantry von Wietersheim), which had previously fought its way to the Dnepr south of Fastov, to the south between the XLVIII Motorized Army Corps and the river. The corps' 9th Panzer Division (Lieutenant General Hubicki) and 25th Motorized Infantry Division (Lieutenant General Cloessner) quickly gained ground to the south, thus strengthening the formation of the German pocket in the east while simultaneously securing the Dnepr.

As before, bitter battles were occurring on the encirclement front. The German soldiers soon discovered that the Russian soldier – the man commonly referred to as "Ivan" – defended not only with self sacrifice, but (at many positions under pressure of the political commissars) with merciless fanatical ferocity against the German soldier.

• • •

30 July 1941. Advance to close the Uman pocket. A short midday pause behind Talnoe. We had pea soup, it was tasteless, rather thin, and without meat, since we are still using first class rations. Barely a half hour passes. The road slopes slightly. To the right and left there is high standing corn.

On the right, behind the cornfield, is the edge of the forest. I believe the 1st and 2nd Battalions of our regiment (156th) are in front of us. Behind us is the 3rd Battalion. To the right, in the cornfield, I see a 2 cm self propelled air defense gun in firing position. It is providing air defense protection. About 300 meters up the road, we suddenly come under artillery fire. The column stops. A band (musicians) unit is in a bus. The order is given to dismount, take cover, and stay near the vehicles. I take cover in a trench near the vehicles. Suddenly, I hear strong gun fire in the direction of the advance.

My mistake was that I hesitated too long. I needed my pistol from the vehicle, where, like most of us, I left it thinking this was only an artillery attack. As I look about, I see my comrade, Franz Hemmer, about 100 meters in front of me. He turns around and fires his pistol into the cornfield. I also turn around, and there is a Russian about 20 meters from me. At the same time, another one is coming from the side out of the cornfield. There was nothing left for me to do but flee. Three Russians were now in front of me, pointing their bayonets at my chest. I am trembling like an aspen leaf. My time was up. They took my wedding ring. The briefcase, which they threw onto the ground, they again picked up and took away. Eight of my comrades were driven onto the road, then I had to join them. We had to advance slowly, step by step, along the entire width of the road, with Russians to our front and rear. We moved about 50 meters, when we were fired on. First Officer Minder from the Music Corps collapsed. As was later discovered, he was shot in the thigh and played dead. We later heard that he died back home.

Approximately one-half hour later, several other comrades collapsed, but they did not die immediately. I heard groaning and many calls for water. I was standing there with three comrades. It was torture to hold my arms in the air. A Russian threatened us with a gun whenever our arms would drop. At the beginning, we had to take off our steel helmets and throw them away. Two meters behind me was a machine-gun on small wheels that was often fired between me and a comrade, who was standing about a meter to my right. To the left, in the cornfield, Russian helmets bobbed up and down. I broke out into a cold sweat from fear. For the entire time, I had intended to fall down and play dead. However, I was afraid that

I would draw the attention of the machine-gun crew behind me and that they would eventually dispose of me with their bayonets. So I remained with the others, waiting to be wounded or shot to death.

After approximately 1 1/2 hours, I heard two shots a short distance behind me, and the three comrades standing next to me collapsed. Then came my shot, but it whistled passed my throat and under my arm. I immediately fell down and played dead with my face in the mud. Another 7 hours passed before the yearned-for evening arrived and it became dark. All this time, the machine-gun was often fired over me.

As dusk finally fell, the shooting stopped. The Russians withdrew. For an anxious moment, two of them stood right next to me and talked. Next to me lay the severely wounded comrade, Armbrust, and his breathing was labored.

The Russians did not touch me and left. Since it was dark, I could take my time and refresh myself. After all, my unit was dead. After some time passed, I attended to comrade Armbrust. Since it was dark, I could only provide cursory aid, but I made him comfortable and told him that I would immediately go for help. While thinking about going for help, I suddenly heard noises in the cornfield. Soon after, I heard a voice call out the name Helmut several times. That was a relief. Several times I had to call: Comrades, there are German wounded here.

Then a comrade came out of the cornfield with a machine-gun under his arm. Soon, a crowd of comrades emerged. A lieutenant was in charge. I gave him my report. He immediately sent for the ambulance, because there were other wounded comrades. He stayed with the trucks as they returned to the march route. I accompanied the wounded to the first aid station and spent a restless night there.(From: Memminger, F.: *Combat History of the Windhund Division*. Bochum 1962.)

• • •

Before the end of July, the thin German front line of panzer and motorized divisions (on the eastern side of the pocket) threatened to break, but the infantry and mountain divisions – including the Slovakian Motorized Brigade – of the 17th Army fought their way there from the west with an unheard-of effort. The XLIX Mountain Corps (on the left) and the LII Army Corps (on the right) threw themselves in the "general direction of the east" without regard for the protection of their flanks.

The XLIX Mountain Corps (General of Mountain Troops Kuebler), with the 1st (Major General Lanz) and the 4th Mountain Divisions (Major General Eglseer), brought up all its remaining divisions, while on the right, the 257th ID (Lieutenant General Sachs) and the 101st Rifle Division (Major General Marcks) tried to hold the corps boundary.

On the same day, Rumanian troops advanced far to the south and won back former Rumanian territory that was given up several years before to the USSR as the result of a political treaty.

With the arrival of the infantry divisions, Panzer Group 1 again had freedom to maneuver and extracted the 16th Panzer Division from the pocket front and sent it in the direction of Pervomaisk. This freed up the rear of the 9th Panzer Division, which was now able to turn around and face the strong Russian forces to the west. The advance detachment of the 1st Mountain Division, under the leadership of the commander of the 44th Mountain Anti-tank Battalion, Lieutenant Colonel Lang, advanced directly to the east through Tarassovka and met a rifle company of the 9th Panzer Division in Sabugskoe on the Sinyucha.

The troops of the 17th Army and Panzer Group 1 shook hands! The pocket around the bulk of the 6th and 12th Soviet Armies (Lieutenant General Musychenko, Major General Ponedelin) and units of the 18th Soviet Army (Lieutenant General Smirnov) was closed!

The 1st Mountain Division immediately shifted the bulk of its troops to the north behind a friendly advance detachment. Colonel Kress (99th Mountain Rifle Regiment) took command of these formations, while Colonel Picker (98th Mountain Rifle Regiment) established the necessary flank protection to the south with two battalions.

On 3 August, the lead elements of the 257th ID arrived from Nowossjolki and, on the evening of the same day, the advance detachment of the 101st Rifle Division passed Josefpol, where the Sinyucha flows near Olschanka – the Germans sealed the southern flank!. Now the situation in the north cleared up, as the 4th Mountain Division advanced through

Peregonovka to Ternovka and relieved the 1st Mountain Division. Indeed, the Soviet formations attempted to break out on all sides – however, the Germans held!

Two days later, the encircled Russian troops were packed into a pocket 20 kilometers wide and 20 kilometers deep, southeast of Uman. The 17th Army and Panzer Group 1 had already extracted the first divisions from outside the pocket and advanced them toward the wide Dnepr. The 9th Panzer Division was also extracted and committed north of the 16th Panzer Division. On 3 August, the 16th Panzer Division captured the city of

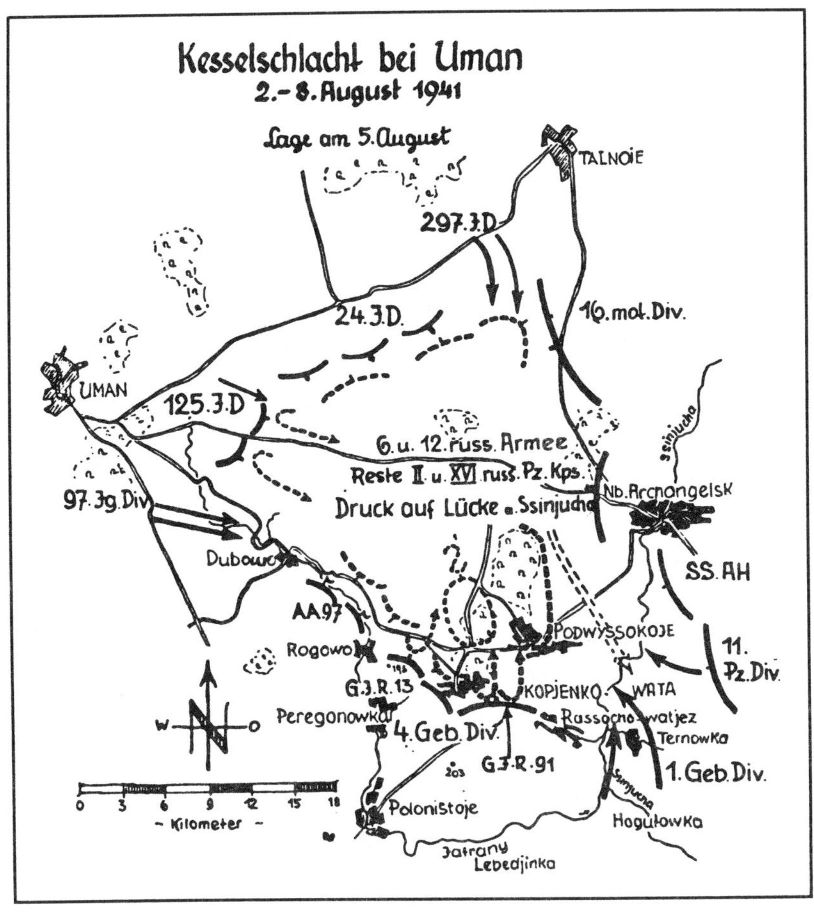

Pocket battle near Uman 2-8 August 1941 - Situation on 5 August

Pervomaisk. A combat group from its advance detachment was able to cross over the Bug on a 100 meter long, undamaged wooden bridge.

The Russian commanders and commissars had been trying for days, without being able to resupply their fighting soldiers, to get their formations to break out of the pocket southeastward to Uman. However, the German defensive front line held fast. On 5 August, the pocket had the shape of an almost perfect isosceles triangle. The eastern portion of the pocket stretched from Talnoe, in the south, to Ternovka on the Sinyucha and was (from right to left) held by the 16th Motorized, the "Leibstandarte", and 11th Panzer Divisions. The 1st Mountain Division formed the southern point of the pocket, while the 4th Mountain Division and the 97th Rifle Division (Major General Fretter-Pico) fought in the southwest from Kopjenco (on the right) to directly southeast of Uman. The northwest line of the front – running directly south of the Uman-Talnoe road – was held, from right to left, by the 125th ID (Lieutenant General Schneckenburger), the 24th ID (Major General von Tettau), and the 297th ID (Lieutenant General Pfeffer). These three infantry divisions, practically "shoulder to shoulder", pushed the encircled Russian divisions – which had already disbanded – further to the southeast. The Russian formations surrendered in droves. There were now only local struggles, where commissars had ordered their formations to hold out, literally, to the "last cartridge." On 7 August, the Wehrmacht High Command released the following special announcement:

> On the southern flank, the army group, under the command of Field Marshal von Rundstedt, has overcome particularly difficult terrain and weather obstacles and a numerically superior enemy. The armies of General of Infantry von Stuelpnagel and General Field Marshal von Reichenau, supported by General von Kleist's panzer group, are advancing along a protracted and difficult front line. They succeeded in attacking into the enemy's flank and drove a wedge beyond Zhitomir to the gates of Kiev. With this penetration into the rear of the Stalin Line it was possible to turn to the south on a broader front, between the Dnestr and the Dnepr, to cut off the retreat routes of the enemy and develop an encirclement battle, which is in full swing at this time.

In this (for the enemy) losing battle, Hungarian and Rumanian formations are standing shoulder to shoulder with the German Wehrmacht in true brotherhood-in-arms. Simultaneous with this operation, the German-Rumanian formations, under the command of General Antonescu, have overcome the strong defense at Pruth and Bessarabia has been liberated from the enemy, in spite of heavy resistance and impassable terrain. Furthermore, the German and Rumanian corps, composing the army of General von Schobert, have crossed the middle sector of the Dnestr to the northeast, in order to make contact with forces advancing from the north.

Current totals for this combat sector exceed 150,000 prisoners, 1,970 tanks, and 2,190 guns. The participation of the air fleet of General Loehr had a prominent effect on the successful development of this operation. They have shot down or destroyed on the ground 980 aircraft of the Soviet Air Force.

And two days later they ran this report:

According to a special announcement, German troops, in cooperation with Hungarian formations, have enjoyed great success in the Ukraine. In the battle for Uman, the 6th and 12th, as well as units of the 18th Soviet Armies – 25 rifle, mountain, and tank divisions in all – have been destroyed. Over 103,000 prisoners, including the commanders of the 6th and 12th Armies, have fallen into our hands. 317 tanks, 858 guns, 242 anti-tank canon and air defense guns, 5,250 trucks, twelve railroad trains, and additional war materials have been captured. Enemy losses total more than 200,000 men.

• • •

Included among the prisoners were the commanders of the Russian 6th and 12th Armies, as well as the commander of the XIII Soviet Rifle Corps. While the battle for Uman still raged, the army group prepared for a new attack to the east.

16. Inf.-Division (mot)
Abt. Ia

Div.-Gef.-St., 9. 8. 1941
22.00 Uhr

Div.-Befehl für den 10. 8. 1941

1. Schwacher **Feind** aus Rakowo — Stscherbany — Wodjano-Loring im Zurückgehen nach Süden und Südosten.
Auf Westufer des Bug westl. Wossnessensk bisher kein Feind festzustellen. Hier geht Feind anscheinend vor den Rumänen, die die Gegegend Mostowoje-Ljachowo erreicht haben, nach Süden in Richtung Odessa zurück.
Gegner wendet neuerdings vermehrt **Verminung von Wegen an.** Daher Pioniere zum Minenräumen nach vorn.
Zur Abwehr der fdl. Jäger und Bomber ist erneut starker Jagdschutz angefordert.

2. **XXXXVIII. A.K.** gewinnt mit 16. I.D. (mot) und SS A.H. zunächst die Linie Nowaja-Odessa — Ssuchoj Jelanez — Nw. Petrowskoje, um von hier auf Nikolajew antreten zu können.
Vorläufige Trennungslinie zwischen 16. I.D. (mot) und SS. A.H.:
Ssolonoje (für 16.) — Dymowka (für SS. A.H.) — Ssuchoj Jelanez (für SS. A.H.).

3. **16. I.D. (mot)** gewinnt hierzu zunächst die Linie Kasnerowka — Nw. Schmidtowka (südwestl. Ssuchoj Jelanez).
Von hier weiteres Vorgehen auf Nikolajew voraussichtlich erst, wenn SS. A.H., die mit vorderen Teilen am 9. 8. abends den Raum südostw. Bratskoje erreicht hat, etwa auf gleicher Höhe steht.

4. **Kampfaufträge:**

a) **Kampfgruppe Becker** stößt im Zuge der Straße ostw. des Bugs auf Nowaja-Odessa vor und gewinnt die Brücke bei Nowaja-Odessa. Hier ist, wenn möglich, ein kleiner Brückenkopf zu schaffen, um Aufklärung auf dem Westufer vortreiben zu können.

Mit Teilen ist am Südrand von Spiridonowa nach Süden und Südosten zu sichern. Während des Vorgehens auf Nowaja-Odessa sind bei allen in Frage kommenden Stellen frühzeitig Übergänge über den Bug (Brücken, Stege, Fähren, im Notfall Einsatz von Floßsäcken), auszunutzen, um Aufklärung auf das Westufer des Bug vorzutreiben mit dem Ziel, Überraschungen von dieser Seite auszuschalten. Ferner sind zur Überwachung einzelne Bttr. auf den Höhen auf dem Ostufer in überschlagendem Einsatz in Stellung zu bringen.
Die 10-cm-Bttr. ist weit vorn einzugliedern, um ihre Feuerwirkung frühzeitig nach Süden ausnutzen zu können. (Vor allem zunächst auf die Brücke von Nowaja-Odessa.)

b) **Kampfgruppe Holm** geht von Stscherbany und Höhe 110 zunächst nach Süden auf Nowaja-Odessa vor und stößt mit Teilen je nach Lage zur Unterstützung der Kampfgruppe **Becker** bis zum Bug und der Brücke von Nowaja-Odessa durch oder nimmt bei Nowaja-Odessa enge Verbindung mit Kampfgruppe **Becker** auf. Mit Teilen ist von der ostw. Straße frühzeitig auf Nw. Schmidtowka abzudrehen (Ausnutzung von Feldwegen, Wegeerkundung), um von hier später nach Süden antreten zu können.
Trennungslinie zwischen Kampfgruppe Becker und Kampfgruppe Holm:
Stscherbanskij — Nordostrand Nowaja-Odessa — Höhe 91.
Wiederantreten 6.00 Uhr.

5. **Krad.Schtz.Btl. 165** erreicht, um 4.00 Uhr antretend, zur Verfügung der Div. Nw. Wladimirowka und nimmt Verbindung mit SS. A.H. auf. (Div.Gef.St. SS. A.H. Iwanowka, südostw. Bratskoje.)

6. **A.A. 341** geht zunächst in Richtung Nowo-Odessa, dann abbiegend auf Nowo-Schmidtowka vor und klärt von hier auf Nikolajew auf.

7. **Artillerie:**
Es bleiben wie bisher angewiesen:
a) **A.R. 146** (ohne II.) auf Kampfgruppe **Becker.**
b) **II./A.R. 64 u. II./146** auf Kampfgruppe **Holm.**
Die **ss.Mrs.Abt. 732** ist mit 2 Bttr. in Gegend Wossnessensk vorzuführen, um sie von hier aus je nach Lage hinter Kampfgruppe **Becker** oder Kampfgruppe **Holm** auf Nowaje-Odessa nachführen zu können.
1 Mrs.-Bttr. wird A.R. 146 unterstellt und ist von diesem heranzuziehen.

16th Motorized Infantry Division Order for 8/10/1941

As a result of the loss of the battle of Uman, the "Red Army" High Command abandoned the western Ukraine and all of Bessarabia. The commanders of the 17th German Army and Panzer Group 1 received the order to regroup and advance to the Dnepr. Meanwhile, the 11th Army had crossed the Dnestr on a wide front, deep to the south, and had captured Balta by the beginning of August.

Ten days later, the 11th Army reached Nikolaev on the Black Sea. Here, on the docks, they found the partially blown up hulls of a battleship, a cruiser, four destroyers, and four auxiliary combat ships.

The important harbor city of Odessa was surrounded by the Rumanian Army on 13 August. The city of Odessa held out until 16 August, when the Russian Fleet evacuated the bulk of the defenders by sea. These great German victories certainly did not obscure the fact that the war in the east had entered a phase reflecting even harder and more bitter combat. On 7 August, Generalissimo Stalin had personally taken command of the "Red Army" and now called on all sectors of the population to come to the defense of "Mother Russia."

The German front line soldier had noticed that, by the end of August, the war had entered a new stage. In addition to the ever increasing difficulty of combat, the doggedness and craftiness of the enemy and the slowly developing resistance in his rear area, he also noticed that the weather was becoming a new, more dangerous enemy. As soon as it began to rain, all of the streets and roads turned to mud and marsh. Tanks, guns, and trucks bogged down, horses sank into the mud, and only the small Russian wooden carts and ponies could master the weather.

When the offensive did advance, it was thanks to the sense of duty and spirit of sacrifice of all the officers and men and also the untiring efforts of the rear area services. Their efforts were not properly appreciated – however, were it not for these men "behind the Front", it would not have advanced at all!

• • •

8. **Flak.**
   IV./Flak Göring scheidet mit dem 10. 8. aus dem Verband der Div. aus. Dafür neu unterstellt II./Flak 43 (3 8,8-Bttr. und zunächst 1 l. Bttr.).
   Einsatz der Abt. am 10. 8. zunächst:
   Je 1 8,8-Bttr. bei den Kampfgruppen.
   1 8,8-Bttr. verbleibt zunächst bei Trikraty.
   1 Zg. der le. Bttr. ist auf Anordnung der Div. von Trikraty auf Pugewitschewa vorzuführen. Masse ist von Wossnessensk frühzeitig, mindestens mit Teilen, auf Nowaja-Odessa vorzuziehen, um hier bald den Luftschutz sicherzustellen.

9. **Pioniere und Pz.-Jäger.**
   a) Einsatz von Teilen der Pioniere bei allen Kampfgruppen weit vorn zur Feststellung und Beseitigung von Minen ist besonders wichtig.
   Die Kampfgruppen sind für die Entminung und gegebenenfalls Bezeichnung der Hauptwege in ihrem Abschnitt verantwortlich. Die entminten Wege sind laufend an den Pi.-Kdr. zu melden.
   Die 2./Pi.Btl. 675 ist zur Verfügung der Div. zunächst nach Bol.-Sserbulowka nachzuführen.
   b) **Pz.-Jäger.**
   Pz.-Jg.-Abt. 670 (ohne 1. Kp.) erreicht, um 6.00 Uhr antretend, zur Verfügung der Div. Scolonoje.
   2./Pz.-Jg.-Abt. 228 ist zur Verfügung der Div. Bol.-Sserbulowka nachzuführen.

10. **Nachrichtenverbindungen:**
   a) **Fernsprech**verbindung bis Pugewitschewa, von da ab zunächst nur Funk.
   b) **Funk** wie bisher. Außerdem: neu wieder zur SS. A.H.
   Funk zwischen Kampfgr. Becker und Holm
   sowie zwischen A.R. 146 und II./A.R. 64
   ist zur Verhinderung gegenseitiger Störung wichtig.

11. **Sanitätswesen.**
   H.V.Pl. (9. Pz.Div.) in Arbusinka aufgelöst.
   H.V.Pl. (San.Kp. 2./66) in Nawossolowka.

12. **Div.-Gef.-St.** zunächst Lenina. 4 km nordwestl. Trikraty, dann Pugewitschewa.

gez. H e n r i c i

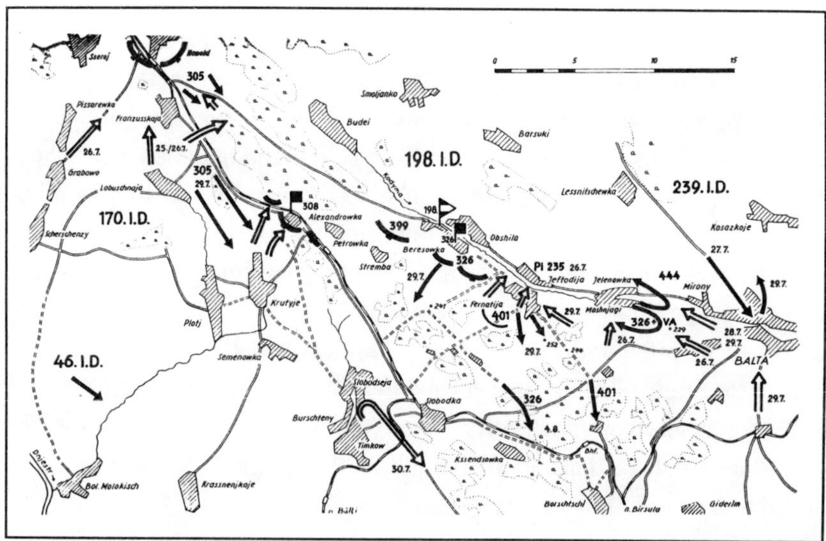

Supply Services

Supply and reinforcement was not a large problem while advancing through Galicia as it was for the other units of the division; having said that, however, they did have to cope with the great distances covered in the successful marches and, here and there, they did have to struggle with obstacles.

The more than two week commitment of the division represented the first great test for the supply troops, particularly regarding ammunition supply. Weapons employment was massive. It was – it is safe to say – fully utilized. Here are some totals for expenditures (note: there is no data for the expenditures of the 15 cm heavy field howitzer shells).

During the sixteen day battle, a total of about 800 tons of ammunition was expended, an average of 50 tons per day! The highest total was recorded on 25 July – on that day, the division fired 121 tons of ammunition of all types.

Examples of expenditures from 22 July to 7 August 1941: 1,155,000 gun and machine-gun shells, 127,000 pistol 08 and machine pistol cartridges, 6,643 3.7 cm anti-tank gun shells, 1,053 5 cm anti-tank gun shells, 1,814 5 cm mortars, 3,606 8 cm mortars, 5,633 7.5 cm infantry gun shells, 989 15 cm infantry gun shells, 20,135 10.5 cm light field howitzer shells (AZ and DZ), as well as 10,290 hand grenades. To transport the ammunition, the divisions had at their disposal the following:

> The combat vehicles of the troop were divided among the 4th to the 6th Field Columns, 7th to the 9th Field Columns, and the 3 small Truck Columns. These transports were not always sufficient, and at times division supply trains and transports had to be utilized.
>
> The division ammunition supply point was always located as far forward as possible, in order to spare the troops long travel distances. Every re-deployment of the supply point required all of the transports, which, however, would also have to continue replenishing the motorized columns from the distant Army installation, almost without interruption. When the division advanced quickly, the ammunition supply point had to redeploy forward repeatedly, so that the division may have had up to four supply points during the same period of time. It proved

beneficial to utilize the field columns as follows: the 4th to the 6th Field Columns were assigned to the 125th Artillery Regiment, and the 7th to the 9th Field Columns to the infantry regiments. A variation from this was when the 2nd Light Truck Field Column would assist in supplying infantry ammunition. Ammunition shortages occurred on only two occasions, on 25 July at the 2/420 and on 28 July at the 421st Infantry Regiment and its supporting artillery battalion. On both occasions, the shortages were the result of the tactical situation and not the fault of the resupply effort.

The Medical Service

The men of both medical companies, of the 125th Field Hospital, of both ambulance platoons and – lest we forget – the troop surgeon and his assistants, the troop medics, and stretcher-bearers, all gave their best to assist the wounded and maintain supplies during operations.

On 16 July, prior to the division's commitment, the 125th Field Hospital had taken over an army hospital in Proskurov, if only for two days. After 20 July, it set up in Vinnitsa to support the divisions of a mountain corps and tended 351 wounded and sick.

During combat operations from 23 July to 7 August, both medical companies established first aid stations by "leap-frog operations" in the following locations (in brackets are the totals of wounded treated): on 23 July at the Karolina main railroad station (29), 24 July in Nizhniy Kropivna (273) (here, the 2nd Medical Company was relieved by the 125th Field Hospital on 26 July), 26 july in Kunka (53), 27 July in Gaissin (309), 30 July in Ivangorod (49), 2 August in Uman (430), on 3 August in Grodsevo (143), 4 August in Babanka (276), and on 7 August in Oksanino (92).

These totals include wounded from other divisions.

The 125th Field Hospital contributed to the operation of the first aid stations in Nizhniy Kropivna and in Uman. The 2nd Medical Company supplied a 19 man surgical team to the division medical detachment, which was formed on 28 July. They treated the 21 wounded, which were at the medical detachment at the time, and improved their conditions so that they could be transported. On 9 August, the 1st Medical Company supplied an operations group to treat 300 wounded Russians at the 419th Infantry

Regiment's prisoner collection point. The capacity of the medical organization (medical vehicles for the transport of medical personnel and equipment) was sufficient, as a rule, to permit the systematic treatment of the wounded, while allowing for sufficient rest and solicitude. Only on the evening of 28 July (the day of Krasnopolka) did the number of wounded exceed the capability of the operations teams at the Gaissin first aid station. By chance, the Corps Surgeon, Professor Doctor Seliger, happened to be visiting the 17th Army, when he heard of this. He immediately went to Gaissin and placed himself and his adjutant at their disposal. Thus, with two additional teams, they were able to control the situation. (From: Breymayer H.: *Das Wiesel*, (125th ID) Ulm 1983.)

The efforts of the soldiers were, of course, recognized and appreciated – however, a difficult year still lay before the German soldiers.

• • •

Commander, Headquarters, 12 August 1941
Panzer Group 1

Soldiers of Panzer Group 1!

After rapidly advancing in spite of flank attacks and after a well-timed turn, the Panzer Group pushed the Russian 6th and 12th Armies out of the way of the Dnepr and, in this manner, created the prerequisite for the great encirclement battle of Uman.

During the ten day encirclement battle, the XLVIII and XIV Army Corps repulsed all enemy breakthrough attempts and destroyed strong enemy units, while the III Army Corps covered the flank and rear of the Panzer Group and, in a spirited attack, advanced to the Dnepr near Krementschug.

25 enemy divisions were destroyed. Both (army) commanders were captured.

The victorious outcome of this great encirclement battle is the climax of a difficult seven week struggle for Army Group South against a numerically superior force. The enemy has suffered a defeat that will contribute much to the final decisive victory.

Army Group South

The Commander-in-Chief of the Army and the Commander of the Army Group have expressed their best wishes and appreciation to the commanders and all participating troop units.

I am happy to pass on my thanks and appreciation to the commanders and troops of my Panzer Group for the enormous efforts of the past weeks.

I also remember, with gratefulness and devotion, our fallen comrades and our wounded in the infirmaries.

Now, on to final victory.

Hail to our Führer
signed, v. Kleist
Distribution:
To each company.

• • •

Commander, Headquarters, 15 August 1941
Army Group South

The campaign that began on 22 June placed extraordinary demands on the leadership and troops.

I know that a great many divisions have been in combat every day since the start of the campaign. I also know that the tasks seem un-fulfillable, and that the difficult combat, inclement weather, and road obstacles require the greatest efforts of the troops.

I am proud to stand at the head of an army group whose troops execute all their tasks with the highest devotion and combat readiness and meet the enemy daily in fierce combat. The units of the Luftwaffe that are attached to the army group have played an essential role with their bold day and night sorties. Communications, supply, and construction troops have made great contributions to the success through their untiring efforts, as have the construction and operations personnel of the railroad units. I repeatedly express my thanks and my unreserved appreciation for all of these outstanding efforts.

It is only Natural that such great effort would result in fatigue, the combat strength of the troops has weakened, and in many places there is a desire for rest. To my joy, I can declare that our combat spirit and combat will remains undiminished. I must demand the same devotion, the same combat readiness, and the same will for victory in the future!

Great success has been achieved and a large portion of red combat strength has been destroyed. However, the campaign has not been won. We must keep pressure on the enemy and allow him no quarter, for he has many more reserves than we. We must not allow the "Red Army" time to fill their gaps and replace their battered personnel and equipment.

Once more, I request all command authorities find the means to create short recuperation breaks for their exhausted formations, during which they can be removed from the Front and, for one day, get the rest they need. The nature of combat operations during the next 14 days, on all fronts of the army group, will make this possible. During these recuperation breaks, don't harass the troops with training. Assign guard duty only to insure security. They should get their fill of sleep, dedicate time for personal hygiene and mending their clothing and equipment and, if possible, further refresh themselves with increased rations.

I request that this order be distributed to the commanders of battalions, etc.

signed von Runstedt

Army Group South

KIEV
(18 August - 26 September 1941)

By the middle of July, the commander of the Soviet forces in the Ukraine, Marshal Budenny, realized the danger his armies were in, after Panzer Group 1 broke through to the Dnepr. With the consent of the High Command in Moscow, he permitted his forces to retreat to a line running from Biala Zerkiev (in the north)-Kamenka-Dnester (in the south) and ordered the 5th and 26th Armies to concentrate their attacks on Panzer Group 1. These attacks failed and resulted in the encirclement battle at Uman.

The commander of the 26th Soviet Army (Lieutenant General Kostenko) was ordered to construct defensive positions along the Dnepr and fortify Kiev. The Secretary of the Communist Party of the Soviet Union in the Ukraine at that time, Khrushchev (the future Premier), mobilized an 89,000 man militia to defend fortress Kiev, and 160,000 civilians who constructed over 750 bunkers, 30 kilometers of anti-tank trenches, and other works in a very short period of time.

The 6th Army (Field Marshal von Reichenau), which was headed for Kiev, was ordered to advance against the Dnepr line alone, because the panzer divisions were diverted to attack to the southeast. Therefore, the 6th Army lost contact on its right; they also had no contact with the neighboring 2nd Army on their left. Here, the almost 250 kilometer wide Pripet Swamp separated the two large German formations.

The 5th Soviet Army, under the command of the talented Major General Potapov, with three rifle and three tank corps, was located in front of and on the left flank of the 6th German Army and inflicted very heavy casualties on them. For a time, the army only had the 56th ID (Major General von Oven) defending an almost 100 kilometer wide front alone.

In the last week of July, the SS Brigade "Leibstandarte" alone secured the Irpen River. They were later relieved by the 168th ID. Meanwhile, the so-called battle for Korosten raged. Units participating in this were (from right to left) the 262nd, 98th, 113th, 298th, 299th, 79th, 62nd, and 56th ID. The losses on the German side were considerably high (the 262nd ID alone lost 634 dead and 1,959 wounded and missing). On 9 August, in view of the stagnating battle, the commander of Army Group South ordered that the combat between Korosten and Kiev be broken off, even though the southern German divisions had come to within 5 kilometers of the fortress.

Army Group South now turned its attention to the Uman-Dnepr area. The 6th Army had to dig in before Kiev.

The advance of the 17th Army to the Dnepr was conducted in the weeks following the battle of Uman. Russian resistance noticeably weakened along the entire width of the Front, because the Commander-in-Chief of the "Red Army" tried to hastily rescue his formations on the eastern bank of the wide river.

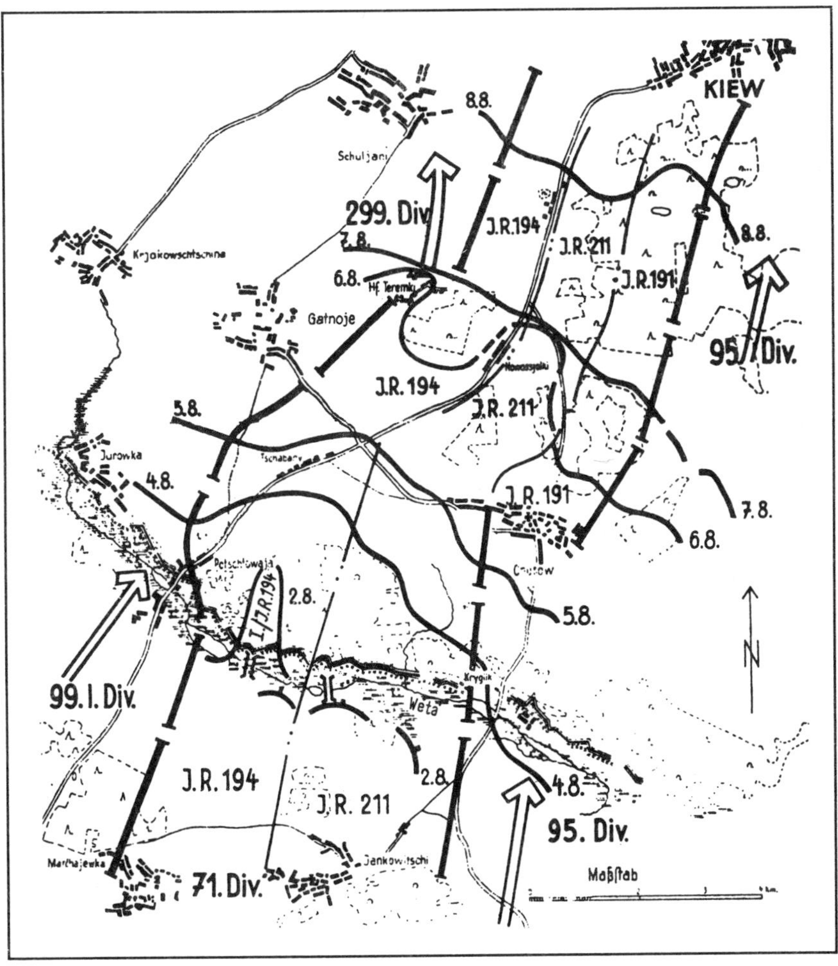

The advance of the infantry and panzer divisions across the dusty roads of the Ukraine, during the hot summer weather, went almost without a hitch. Of course, one would often have to wait for an entire day for resupply and rations because the convoys simply could not keep up with the tempo of the advancing panzer regiments. In all of the cities, and especially in the towns, the Ukrainian civilian population greeted the German troops as "liberators" and welcomed the soldiers with food and drink.

• • •

2nd SS Cavalry Regiment Regiment Headquarters,
Mounted Battalion 8/12/1941

Report
on the course of the Pripet Operation
from 27 July - 11 August 1941.

Combat Impressions: None

Population: Predominantly Ukrainian, 2nd place White Russians, 3rd place Poles and Russians, the latter are completely isolated. Jews are mainly in the large cities, where they make up a large percentage of the population, in some cases from 50-80%, in other cases, of course, only 25%.

The Ukrainian and White Russian population is very accommodating. They point out bands that roam around the region, report them, and in a few cases, will track them down and shoot them.

Additional evidence of their kindness was their bringing milk, eggs, and other rations as soon as the troops marched in. They did this without being asked and free of charge.

Poles and Russians are guarded and refuse to have anything to do with us. They greet German soldiers, however, and give the impression that they are glad that the Bolsheviks were driven away.

In many cases, the Ukrainians accost the soldiers and offer them plates of bread and salt. In one instance, there was even an orchestra to greet the soldiers (Kamien Kuschioski).

Particularly noticeable are the great numbers of children that are found at all locations. It is not rare to find families of 10 to 12.

Racially, the Ukrainian population makes a good impression. Although small, they are proportionate in shape and figure with clear features. The same is true for the White Russians. While they are not so outspoken, they are similar in other ways. Since we only come upon Poles and Russians in small numbers, we cannot characterize them by type.

Ground Obstacles:

The entire region consists of a great marsh with interspersed sandy plains, so the ground is not very productive. For each good section, there is another even worse.

The region is traversed by numerous canals and watercourses, of which a small number are regulated, but the majority are unregulated. Broad forested regions extend between the watercourses, consisting mainly of birch, alder, and pine. (From: *Our Honor Was Called Loyalty* (1st SS Cavalry Brigade) Vienna 1965.)

•••

The Russian High Command strengthened the Dnepr Front, especially the area around Kiev and the sector that includes the cities of Kremenchug, Krivoy Rog, Dnepropetrovsk, and Chersson. The latter sector protected the important industrial region that could not fall into German hands.

Field Marshal von Rundstedt and his staff officers also understood the importance of the Dnepr Line, and so all of the divisions of Panzer Group 1, as well as the 17th and 11th Armies, began to move east to the steep western bank of the third largest river in the Soviet union as quickly as they could. By mid August, they controlled practically the entire river sector from Kiev to Dnepropetrovsk. Here, the great Dnepr noose was drawn by the mighty march of the motorized divisions of Panzer Group 1, while the 11th Army advanced between Odessa and Beresovka on a wide front to the mouth of the Dnepr in the Chersson area.

• • •

The night passed with unexpected quiet.

In the morning of 16 August, loud engine noises triggered the Panzer alarm: Russian trucks were heading for Chersson. The panzers conducted a surprise attack against the column.

At 0900 hours, the lead elements of the 16th Motorized Infantry Division reached the battlefield, and the supply route was once again open. As the 1/64 received the signal to destroy the enemy, the 2/64 advanced to the eastern edge of Nikolaev on the order of Lieutenant Colonel Marcks; stragglers and partisans defended the city. The regiment moved against the narrow passage in close order. Shock troops assaulted the inner city, and the light panzer companies of Senior Lieutenants Kuckein and Mues reached the western end of Nikolaev by midday.

The adjutant and the battalion physician of the 1/64 were lost from a direct hit by artillery. At 1300 hours, Major von der Mark and six men from his staff went to the city hall and hung the Reich's battle flag from the water tower in the center of the city. On the return trip, the Major, his adjutant, and his ordnance officer were all lost to a direct hit by anti-tank gun fire. The Russians were still defending the city. The mopping up of the enemy could not be conducted after the fall of darkness, so all the troops were withdrawn.

The 60th Infantry Regiment was still in contact with enemy forces that had broken through; Combat Group Arenstorff had to launch a diversionary attack to the southwest. This was not expected, because of the reinforcement in front of Nikolaev.

The next morning, the companies, furnished with city maps, combed the city. During an attack on an air defense position, the panzer regiment suffered additional heavy casualties, and 5 tanks of the 1st Company were lost. The division now had 23 of 140 tanks left.

The city was soon cleared of the remaining Russian troops. It was a wretched sight: bullet riddled, burning houses, the corpses of Russian soldiers and civilians plundered in the narrow streets.

In the western part of Nikolaev, the men of the 16th Panzer Division made contact with the bridgehead of the 72nd ID (General Mattenklott), as well as with the Hungarian troops who occupied the city from the north without a fight. The new division command post was set up in the Dynamo clubhouse.

The division took thousands of prisoners and captured rich booty. On the dry-dock they found a 35,000 ton battleship, 10,000 ton cruiser, and two submarines in construction – 65,000 tons of grain were stored in the silo.

The conquest of Nikolaev was a great success. The 64th Regiment ordained the 16th of August as its commemoration day. The men looked proud as they returned to the division: the battles near Verba and Dubno, around the Stalin Line near Lyuban, as well as near Monastyrishche and Pervomaisk were fought to victorious climaxes. In an eight week, uninterrupted commitment, the division stood its ground. Experienced tankers were made out of the infantrymen from Stonne and Mont Damion. They surrendered no line or base, and the enemy ran for their lives when they showed up. The unwritten law of chivalrous combat was still valued in France, but the Russians were not familiar with this tradition. They fought not only bravely and stubbornly, but also with cruelty and treachery, and the men of the 16th Panzer Division had to defend their hides and use combat prudence.

Many comrades had fallen. The 64th Regiment alone, out of a combat strength of 2,394 men, lost 269 dead, 714 wounded, and 19 missing – 992 casualties in all. That was more than a third! (From: Werthen, W.: *History of the 16th Panzer Division*, Bad Nauheim 1958; New Edition 1985)

• • •

During the first week of August, the III Motorized Army Corps (General of Cavalry von Mackensen), with the 13th and 14th Panzer Divisions, and the SS Panzer Division "Wiking", was able to seize the river around Kremenchug and the city itself. Exactly ten days later, Dnepropetrovsk fell into the hands of the SS Panzer Division "Wiking." The remaining two corps of the Panzer Group – the XLVIII Motorized Army Corps (General of Panzer Troops Kempf) and XIV Motorized Army Corps (General of Infantry von Wietersheim) – were tasked with Nikolaev and Krivoy Rog as attack objectives, and they were occupied between 13 and 18 August. The

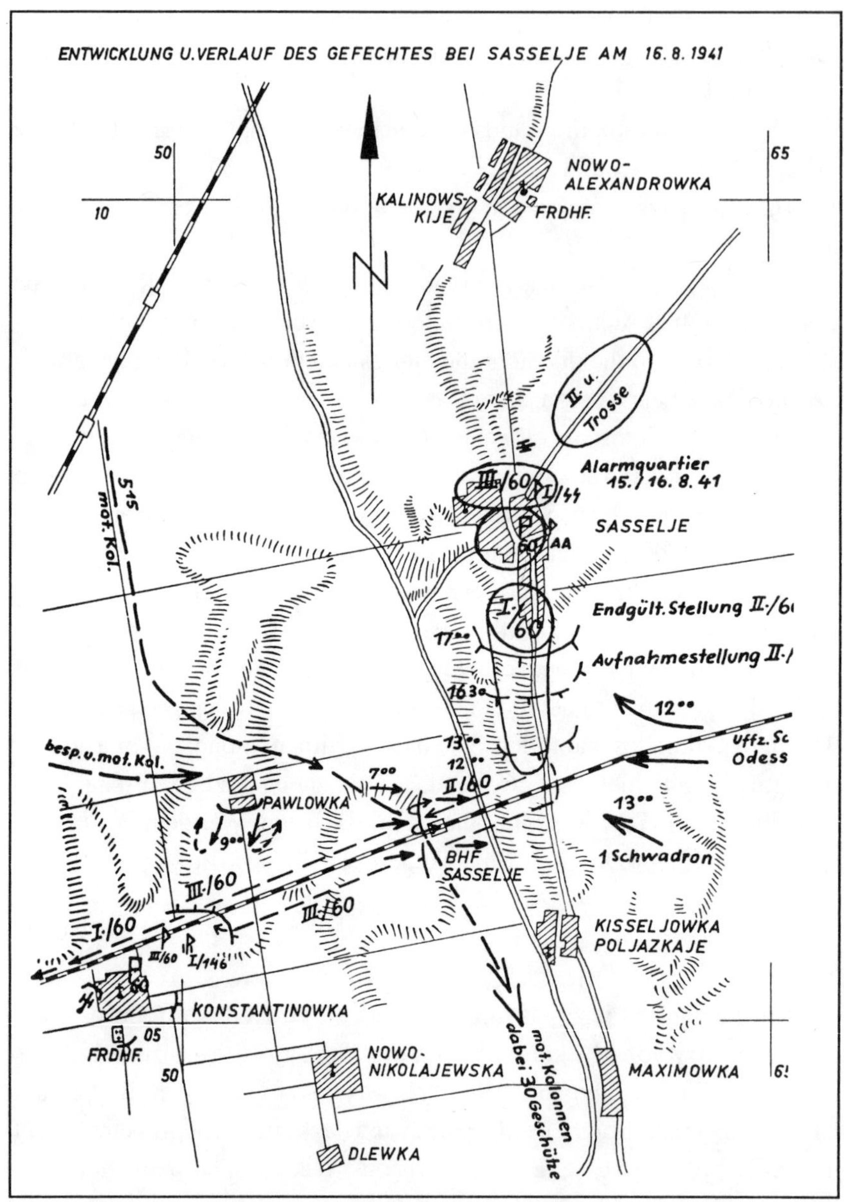

Development and course of the battle near Sassele on 8/16/1941

last objective – Chersson at the mouth of the Dnepr – was captured by the motorized SS Brigade of the "Leibstandarte."

• • •

19 August 1941. The mission for this day read:

"Leibstandarte Adolf Hitler (LAH) captures Chersson in an envelopment attack from the east, north, and northwest, maintains security in front of Singerjowka – and, if possible, establishes a bridgehead near Darevka."

The Standarte ordered the following:

"The 2/LAH – after the completion of the Chersson mission – advances on Darevka, captures it, and establishes a bridgehead across the Ingulets. Beforehand, the villages of Elenovka and Fiodorovka, located to the north, are to be occupied. The attack on Chersson will be conducted by:

The reconnaissance battalion along the Dnepr up to the Harbor railroad;

The 4/LAH by attacking from the north through Seleny to the city center; The 3/LAH crosses the Nikolaev railroad tracks and road, enters Chersson in the Chernobaevy region from the west up to the southern railroad salient on the Chersson harbor."

By 1250 hours, the reconnaissance battalion gained the east bank of the Dnepr and set two large fuel fires east of Chersson. The enemy crossed to the opposite bank in water craft of all types, from the small cargo ships to row boats, and came under fire from two guns of the 2nd Battalion of the artillery regiment and machine-guns that tried to destroy the crossing. Both wheeled rifle companies quickly attacked toward the city center to break strong resistance at a canning factory on the eastern edge of Chersson. The 2nd Company of the reconnaissance battalion, advancing on the left, came under strong artillery fire from

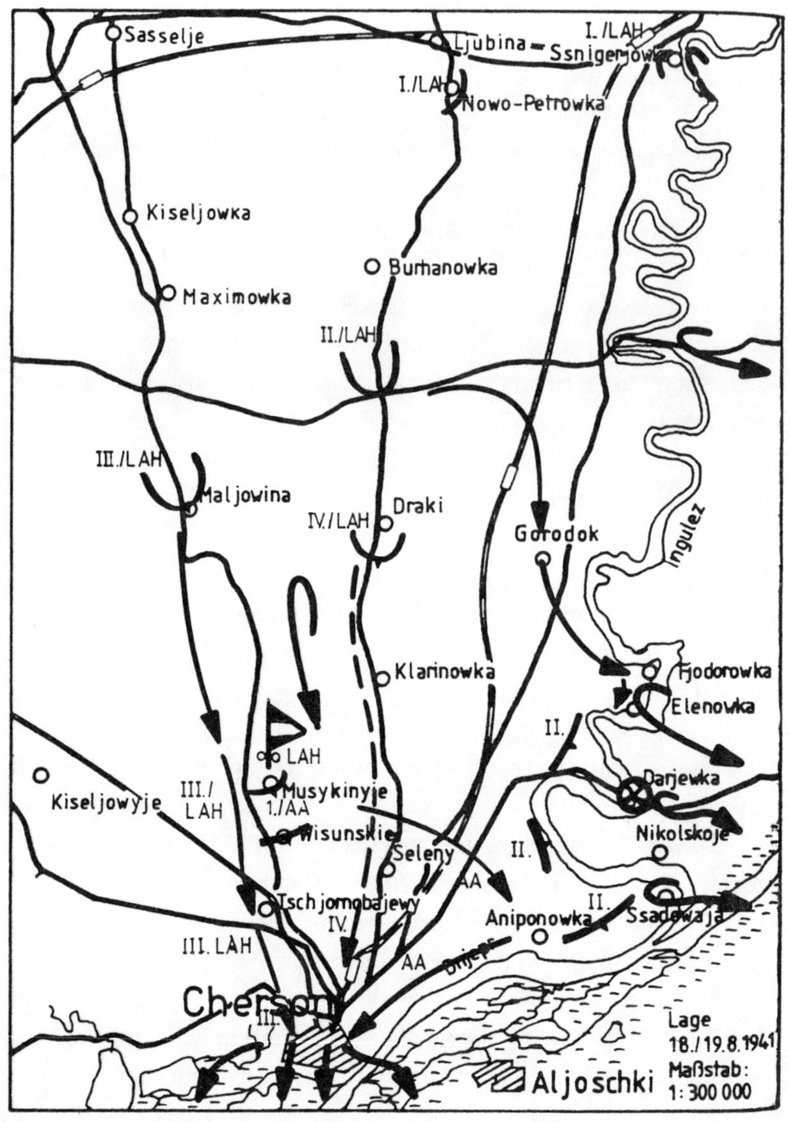

Situation on 8/18-19/1941

the southern bank of the Dnepr shortly before reaching the eastern edge of the city.

Meanwhile, the 4/LAH also entered the city from the fork in the railroad and road on the northern edge of Chersson – supported by well placed fire from our artillery and heavy weapons – and fought its way into the city center until 1530 hours, where it established contact with the 1st company of the reconnaissance battalion. (From: Lehmann, R.: *The Leibstandarte*. Volume 2, Osnabrueck 1980.)

The entire Dnepr bend from Dnepropetrovsk to Chersson was in German hands on 19 August. The infantry divisions that had been arriving on the wide river sector for days now established the defense, while the panzer divisions were already being extracted for further exploitation.

By the last week in August, Army Group South had obtained the entire Dnepr river sector, the goal of all efforts since the beginning of the campaign. It was necessary, of course, to shift the emphasis of the army group from the left (Kiev) to the right flank. Several bridges over the Dnepr were also taken by surprise – as by the 9th Panzer Division near Saporoshe or by the 22nd ID in Berislav – and, therefore, they would provide good departure positions for further attacks into the eastern Ukraine. The advance into the industrial region and the eastern Ukraine was now facilitated.

However, once again Kiev entered the minds of the German General Staff. General Kirponos, the commander of the Soviet Army Group "Southwest Front", had suddenly placed the bulk of his subordinate formations around Kiev and, therefore, could either attack to the south into the flanks of Army Group South or to the north into the flanks of Army Group Center.

In August, the 6th German Army, with its infantry divisions, stood alone in front of Kiev, after all of the panzer units were directed south. The XXIX Army Corps (General of Infantry von Obstfelder) had taken over operations near Kiev. At the beginning of August, the corps had at its disposal, from right to left, the 95th, 71st, 299th, 99th, 75th, and later the 44th ID. On 8 August, as ordered, the corps began its first attack against the fortress of Kiev. The regiments were literally "devoured" by forests, fire, and fanatic Russian soldiers. After four days of bloody combat, they could not force a breakthrough in the fortified positions. The commander of the 6th Army suspended the battle. The 6th Army now stood at order arms.

• • •

8/22/1941: During the nice weather we bathed in the magnificent sun. We played only in bathing suits; then came the day when none of our superiors crossed the bridge to see us and we weren't inspected. However, a flight of Soviet aircraft attacked the bridge again. They flew at great altitude and we were able to clearly see the bombays open and the bombs release. It appeared to me that the timing of the release was early, but, in reality, the bombs were right on us. A short alarm sounded – we were all in the trenches, there wasn't enough time to leave these positions. The bombs were already thundering onto our positions. Luckily we had constructed our trench so well. The ravine was as dark as night, and the noise was deafening. Dirt and dust flew up my nose and into my mouth – but no one was hurt. Only there, where the third gun had stood before, yawned a huge crater. Lucky third gun! It was in its reserve position! – The marvelous construction of the bridge inspired me to use my free hour to take photographs of it.

23 August 1941: During the morning, the Russians suddenly attacked the island. They approached the southern end in large pontoons. We laid down heavy fire and sunk two of the pontoons. They were fully occupied. In spite of this, the Russians were able to get a foothold. During the night, a great number of them must have come through the brush on the bank to the island and were now attempting to overrun our beautiful island from the south. We had to abandon our defensive positions and establish new ones further to the rear. The battery towed the guns to the northern slope and organized a close-in defense. Gun pits and machine-gun positions were quickly cleared. But, luckily, support came in time. With this help we were able to push the Russians back again and re-occupy our old positions.

Our position was a rich paradise: In front of us lay wide melon fields with fragrant yellow fruit. To our left were tomatoes, to our right grapes. In between was an entire plantation of apricot trees. Behind us stretched the marvelous bathing beach. When the bombs don't supply us with fish, we help ourselves with hand grenades. We stand under trees in the shade with a mug of delicious beer, and the mug is always refilled. The snobs, however, are sent forward to the defensive positions, where, to our delight, they miss out on eating chicken. (From: Boehm, E.: *History of the 25th Division*, Stuttgart 1982.)

• • •

This was the time that marked the turning point in Hitler's strategic conception. On 21 August, the Supreme Commander issued "Order Nr. 35", which designated the objectives of the three army groups up to the beginning of winter. Army Group Center had to stop their assault on Moscow. As ordered, it released strong motorized forces to Army Groups North and South, which were to continue their offensives emphasizing Leningrad and the Donets industrial region, respectively. Hitler's order for Army Group South now read:

> "As soon as the operational and supply situations allow, Panzer Groups 1 and 2 are to combine into the 4th Panzer Army east of the Dnepr, and are to advance into the industrial region from Kharkov across the Don to the Caucasus. They will be followed by the infantry and mountain divisions!"

The general front line situation of the German Army on 20 August reflected the following: The forward-most elements of Army Groups Center (in the Bryansk area) and South (in the Dnepropetrovsk area) were located about 550 kilometers in front of the interior flank between the two army groups, which was further back to the west in the Kiev-Pripet Swamp area. Therefore, the front line resembled an equilateral triangle, inside which an entire Russian army group – the "Southwest Front" – was trapped.

This persuaded Hitler and his military advisors to scrap their former strategy. Thus, on 21 August, Army Group South was ordered:

> "... A rare operational opportunity has presented itself. It must be immediately exploited by a concentrated operation by the interior flank-

ing units of Army Groups South and Center to achieve a line Gomel-Pochep. Their objective must be not only to prevent the Soviet 5th Army from breaking through the 6th Army behind the Dnepr, but to destroy this enemy army before it can break through behind the Dessna-Konotop-Sula line. In this manner, Army Group South will be secured, we will establish a firm hold east of the middle Dnepr, and the operation in the direction of Roatov-Kharkov by the middle and left flanks can continue further..."

24 hours after this order was issued, the OKH ordered Army Group Center's Panzer Group 2, under the command of General Guderian, to move all forces out of Gomel in the direction of Chernigov, to fix the 5th Soviet Army and, in this manner, to open the way to Kiev for the 6th Army of Field Marshal von Reichenau.

On the morning of 25 August, at 0500 hours, Guderian's panzer divisions, for all practical purposes, opened the "Battle for Kiev." On the same day, the neighboring 6th German Army was disposed as follows: The 213th ID alone secured the Pripet region behind the Front. The XVII Army Corps (62nd, 79th, 56th ID, and SS Cavalry Brigade) was deployed in the Korosten sector. The LI Army Corps, with the 98th, 113th, and 111th ID was fighting between Korostin and Malin. Behind them, the 262nd, 298th ID, and 11th Panzer Division were pushing toward the Front. The XXXIV Corp, with the 296th and 168th, maintained the western front line before Kiev.

The army attacked as soon as they noticed the Soviet troops begin to move to the rear. The XVII and LI Army Corps advanced on Ovruch after the enemy disengaged. The 11th Panzer Division veered off toward the Teterev River and rolled over an undamaged bridge near Garnostaipol. Kiev was now sealed off from the north.

• • •

At 0400 hours, on 23 August, the advance detachment moved out before everyone else. They moved toward Termachovka, where enemy defenses were quickly overcome. Bridges were destroyed to delay Ivan's withdrawal. Enemy field positions were broken through, columns were destroyed, and Russian guns in their firing positions in front of Priborsk were shot up. Enemy infantry and machine-gun nests were overcome. In some cases, after locating enemy forces retreating in independent columns, the advance detachment would attack into them. During this intermixing of friend and foe a misfortune occurred – the advance guard was bombed by one of their own combat airplanes (Heinkel) from high altitude in Chochevo. This resulted in several dead and wounded. This is where Senior Lieutenant Heinkel, commander of the Air Defense Company, fell. The wooden bridge over the mighty Dnepr rose in the distance. The units of the advance guard pushed ever harder onward to win control of the Dnepr bridge. The approach to the bridge was reached and crossed under the fire of strong enemy resistance from defensive positions and bunkers. The 1st attempt to capture the 3 kilometer long main wooden bridge section across the river, by a daring strike with two assault guns, failed because one of the assault guns slipped off the edge of the bridge when it tried to pass an enemy truck.

The bridge was captured in a second assault under the cover of fire from assault guns and anti-tank canon led by the assault gun of Lieutenant Bingler, and closely followed by wheeled infantry, men towing anti-tank guns, and engineers. The Russians tried to blow the bridge up with prepared explosives, but the ignition cables were severed. Enemy resistance from the bunkers on the eastern bank was overcome, and a small bridgehead was established into which the entire advance guard moved after crossing the bridge.

Details about the successful forced crossing of the Dnepr are clearly expressed in a short extract from a combat report:

> "The assault on the long main bridge section with only two assault guns failed. Now a well planned attack had to be employed. The enemy dominated the bridge with anti-tank guns and machine-guns from 12 bunkers on the opposite eastern bank. The 4 guns of the 3/111 Anti-tank Battalion were able to establish firing positions on either side of the approach to the bridge on the western bank. The enemy bunkers on the eastern bank were engaged with high explosives and machine-guns from all sides, and this blocked the view from their portholes. The assault troops began to attack over the bridge at 1900 hours, supported

by the covering fire of the assault guns. Once again, Lieutenant Bingler took up the lead with an assault gun. Directly behind him was Senior Lieutenant Nacke with a platoon of his 3rd (wheeled) Company of the 50th Infantry Regiment and Senior Lieutenant Hennig, as well as Lieutenant Kroehl with three anti-tank guns from the 3/111 Anti-tank Battalion in tow. Senior Lieutenant Steinmann – who will soon fall on the Dessna – with the engineers of his 3rd Company of the 111th Engineer Battalion, cut the ignition cable and frustrated the attempt of the Russians to blow up the bridge. The assault troops reached the eastern bank with modest losses, enemy fire was erratic, and the Russian bunkers were captured in hand-to-hand combat.

The advance guard of the 11th Panzer Division was also approaching. Their lead element, the 6/110 Motorized Rifle Regiment, arrived in time to participate in the attack across the bridge. A rifle platoon on foot, under Company Commander Senior Lieutenant Sonnenberger, was integrated at the head of the assault troop. Major Hoffmann-Schoenborn took control of the company.

Thus, through the exemplary cooperation of all weapons, the initial part of the task of our advance guard, the crossing of the Dnepr and the establishment of a foothold on the eastern bank, was accomplished." (From: Musculus, F.: *History of the 111th Infantry Division.* Hamburg 1980.)

• • •

The advance of the 11th Panzer Division and 11th ID to the Dessna was, of course, subjected to persistent enemy attacks, which, however, did not influence the influx of the remaining divisions of the 6th Army to the Dnepr. The speedy closing of ranks by the German formations was, at first, not possible because of the serious maneuver obstacles in the Pripet region – there was only one road in the Garnostaipol area that would allow a smooth march.

With the successful development of the new operation on the right flank of the neighboring Army Group Center, the Commander of Army Group South realized it established a suitable departure position for a battle in the grand tradition. On 27 August, Field Marshal von Rundstedt communicated his views for the following weeks to the OKH by telegraph. After that, the 17th Army had to advance out of the Kremenchug area to establish a bridgehead across the Lubny to the northwest, while Panzer Group 1 had to attack between the Vorskla and the Psiol to the north to establish contact with Panzer Group 2. This plan actually resulted in the largest pocket battle of the Second World War.

On 25 August, the 13th Panzer Division (Lieutenant General von Rothkirch) captured the great city of Dnepropetrovsk. In a bold assault, motorized infantry elements of the divisions reached the 1000 meter long bridge across the river, but it had already been damaged by artillery fire. The 60th Motorized Infantry Division (Lieutenant General Eberhardt) set out on the following day and relieved units of the panzer division. A week later, the 198th ID (Major General Roettig) and the SS Panzer Division "Wiking" (SS Brigadefuehrer Steiner) followed. In this manner, the bridgehead at Dnepropetrovsk was secured.

The Soviet leadership believed that the German troops would continue to attack from this bridgehead and, therefore, carted one division after the other from the depths of Russia to the Dnepr Front. However, for the present, the OKH and the commander of the army group did not consider a breakout from Dnepropetrovsk. The divisions located here were merely to provide flank protection for the upcoming encirclement operation at Kiev.

In contrast, the Commander of Army Group South ordered the 17th Army to establish a crossing in the Kremenchug area. On 20 August, the LII Army Corps (General of Infantry von Briesen) was approaching Kremenchug with the (from right to left) 76th ID, 97th Rifle Division, and 100th Rifle Division. To their left, the XI Army Corps (General of Infantry von Kortzfleisch) marched on the river sector with the 257th, 125th, and 239th ID. On 29 August, both corps attacked across the Dnepr with engineers near Derievka and established a 4 kilometer bridgehead during the first night, which was considerably expanded on both sides and to the front during the following days. The rapid developments in the Army Group South area of operations impressed the OKH so much that it quickly issued supplemental orders, because Panzer Group 2 had already reached the area of Gomel and Chernigov from the north. Field Marshal von Rundstedt rec-

Frankfurter Zeitung

mit dem Stadt-Blatt

Sammel-Nummer für Fernsprecher: Ortsverkehr 20202, Fernverkehr 20301.

I/II 59 — Mittwoch, 27. August 1941.

Dnjepropetrowsk im Sturm genommen.

Aus dem Führerhauptquartier, 26. August. Das Oberkommando der Wehr-
gibt bekannt:

Schnelle Verbände der Panzerarmee von Kleist haben gestern nach schwerem Kampf den Brückenkopf von Dnjepropetrowsk und die Stadt selbst im Sturm genommen. Der Feind hat damit seinen letzten Stützpunkt auf dem Westufer des Dnjepr unterhalb Kiew verloren. Bei ihrem Vorstoß in den Dnjeprbogen nach der Schlacht von Uman hat die Panzerarmee von Kleist nunmehr insgesamt 83 596 Gefangene eingebracht, 465 Geschütze und 199 Panzerkampfwagen und zahlloses Kriegsmaterial erbeutet.

Dnepropetrovsk Taken By Storm

ognized the suitability of the situation and, on 4 September, without consulting the OKH, ordered General of Infantry von Stuelpnagel to immediately attack across the Mirgorod-Lubny Line. At the same time, General von Kleist received orders to advance to the Krassnograd-Poltava Line!

The OKH first intervened in the leadership of the operation two days later. After this, the dispositions of Army Group South were so altered that Panzer Group 1 was now to attack Romny, not Poltava, in order to establish contact with Panzer Group 2 attacking from the north. One corps of the 17th Army was instructed to participate in this advance, while its remaining forces were to establish flank security to the east. General Halder, the Chief of the General Staff of the Army, went to the main headquarters of the army group on 7 September to pass on these instructions. The final decision was:

> "... to destroy the enemy forces located on the middle Dnepr and lower Dessna by means of a double envelopment from the Kremenchug, Neshin, and Konotop areas!"

At this point in time there were already three German armies, two panzer groups, and strong elements of Air Fleet 4 deployed for the battle of Kiev. Panzer Group 1, which was deploying out of the Kremenchug bridgehead, had over 331 tanks at its disposal – this was still 53% of the total from 22 June 1941!

General Guderian's Panzer Group 2, which was attacking out of Army Group Center from the north, formed the left flank army of the deployed pincer movement. The panzer group only had at its disposal the XXIV Motorized Army Corps (General of Panzer Troops Baron Geyr von Schweppenburg), which, on the morning of 4 September, in constant rain and on sodden roads, began the encirclement of the Soviet Army Group "Southwest Front"...

... On the same day, the panzer divisions of Panzer Group 1 broke out of the Kremenchug bridgehead. The battle for Kiev entered its decisive phase!

The events of this great battle in the Eastern Campaign were played out during the next three weeks, from north to south, in the following sec-

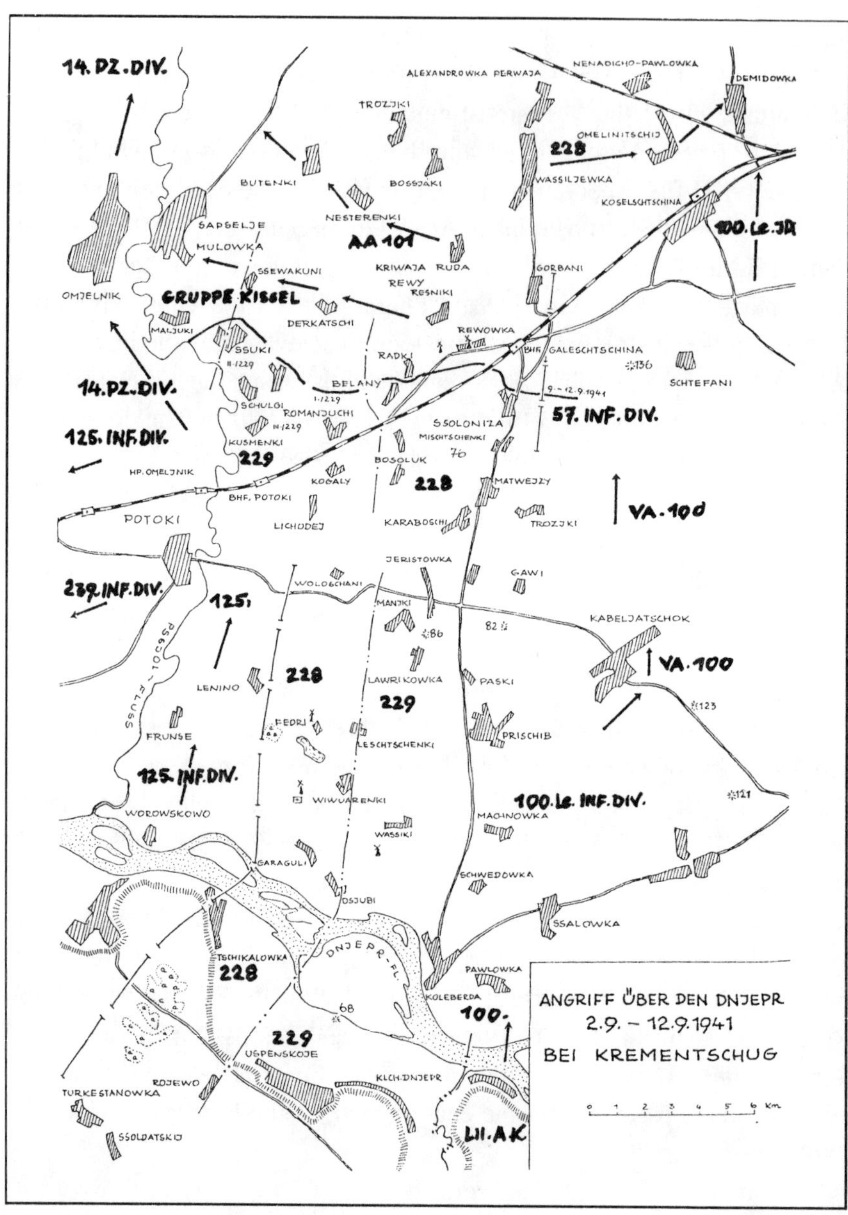

Attack across the Dnepr 9/2-12/1941
Near Kremenchug

tors, ending in the decisive destruction of an entire "Red Army" army group.

Panzer Group 2 (General Guderian) committed the 3rd and 4th Panzer Divisions and the 10th Motorized Infantry Division in an attack to the south. The SS Division "Das Reich" followed closely behind these units. In two days, the divisions reached the Seim, which they crossed after heavy combat on 7 September. On the same day, the corps received the order to advance on Romny.

On 7 September, the XXIV Motorized Army Corps, together with the SS Division "Das Reich" (SS Gruppenfuehrer Hauser) fought on the right flank near Prachi. The 4th Panzer Division (Major General Baron von Langermann) attacked from Mitchenki to Baturin, while the left flank division – the 3rd Panzer Division under Major General Model – reached the Krassnopole-Popovka road. Major General Potapov, Commander of the 5th Soviet Army, recognized the desperate situation of his army, which was already defeated in the east, and requested permission to withdraw. However, Stalin categorically denied this request – and, as a few days later, Marshal Budenny likewise sought permission to withdraw the entire army corps, and the veteran of the "Red Army" was relieved of his command and sent to Siberia.

On 10 September, the XXIV Motorized Army Corps began the pursuit of the battered Russian forces. The 3rd Panzer Division crossed the Romen and reached Romny on the following day despite the pouring rain and muddy roads. Therefore, in just a few days, the first attack objective of Panzer Group 2 was achieved! Panzer Group 2's right neighbor, the 2nd Army (General Baron von Weichs), had to maintain contact with them as well as with the 6th Army, which was located near Kiev. The army slowly fought its way through stubborn enemy resistance and was unexpectedly able to establish a bridgehead near Chernigov. After that, the Russian troops began to break contact and withdraw to the south. On 6 September, the 2nd Army, with its three corps (XIII, XXXV, XLIII) and their divisions (from right to left: the 17th, 134th, 260th, 131st, 293rd, 112th, and 45th ID) were deployed on a wide front, attacking to the south. The resistance of the heroic 5th Soviet Army collapsed.

The Russian 5th Army vacated the southern bank of the Dessna and ordered – without consulting Moscow – a general retreat on 9 September.

Therefore, the last resistance of the 5th Soviet Army collapsed.

The collapse of the 5th Soviet Army gave the 6th German Army (Field Marshal von Reichenau) an open road to Kiev. On 3 September, the LI Army Corps (General of Infantry Reinhard) crossed the Dnepr at Garnostaipol with the 111th (Lieutenant General Stapf), 98th (Lieutenant General Schroek), 113th (Lieutenant General Zickwolff), and 262nd ID (Lieutenant General Theisen).

The opposing Russians defended tenaciously and, after two days, were finally driven out of the thick bushes and forests. The 37th Soviet Army was able to hold its positions between the Dnepr and Dessna at first, and then gave them up only after the 262nd ID succeeded in crossing the Dessna on 7 September.

In the following days the battle seesawed, because the Soviets were always taking new formations out of the east and directing them here, with-

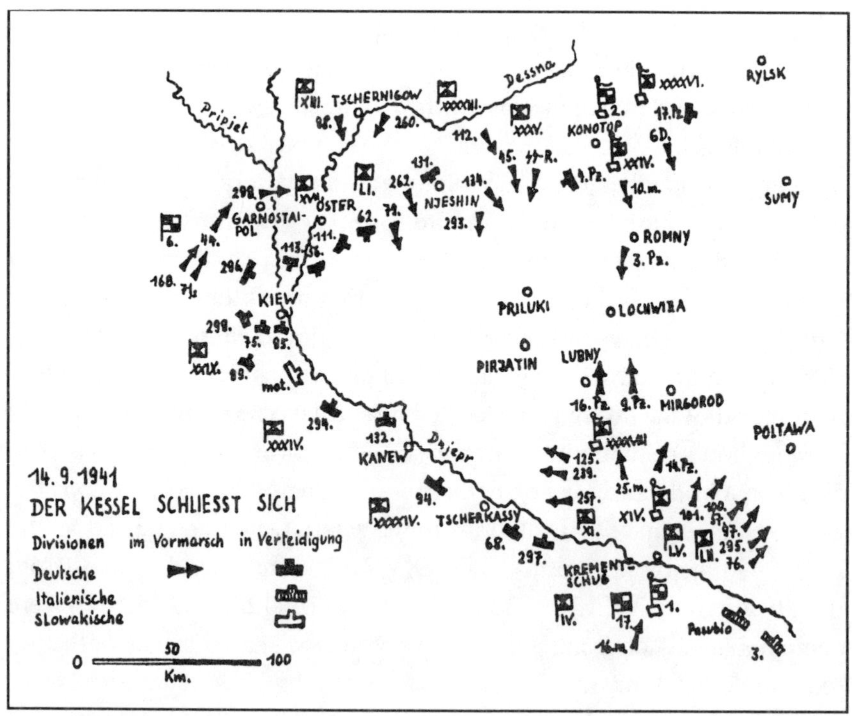

The pocket closes

out realizing that they were opening the road for the advancing divisions of the 2nd German Army.

In spite of this, on the evening of 10 September the LI Army Corps and all of its divisions immediately began to advance in the direction of the Chernigov-Kiev road. The Russian units now lost their cohesiveness and ran off into the bushes on either side of the road. On the same day, the last defense withdrew across the river to the east. Because of this, the XI Soviet Mechanized Corps, which was now compressed into a narrow area, was pulverized by the divisions of the 2nd Army (from the east and north) and the 6th Army (from the west).

Contact was established and maintained between the 2nd Army of Army Group Center and the 6th Army of Army Group South! Field Marshal von Reichenau issued an order of the day:

> "The hour of decision in the southern theater of operations is at hand. From the south and the north, German soldiers are advancing into battles to destroy the enemy.
>
> On the northern flank of our army the LI Army Corps and its valiant divisions are conducting the decisive advance across the Dnepr and Dessna. In a combat accomplishment of the highest order they have overcome the most difficult terrain and an enemy fighting bitterly on the ground and in the air. The Soviets cannot cope with such an attack momentum. Therefore, they have been completely battered here. The road is clear for new exploits!
>
> Soldiers of the 6th Army, let us show the enemy that the heavy combat of the last month has not weakened us, but on the contrary, has tempered us.
>
> The red southern front is ready to be broken through.
>
> The daring will quickly seize victory and reward.
>
> Lets go! Onward to the enemy!"

In the meantime, it was a foregone conclusion that the center of Army Group South would transition to the offensive. On 28 August, Field Marshal von Rundstedt issued an order to these forces. It read as follows:

> "In this situation, we must extract the last efforts from the troops and attack the enemy wherever he establishes himself, regardless of supply and other problems.
>
> Thus, I order the 17th and 6th Armies to immediately transition to the attack on the Panzer Group 1 Front."

On 2 September, the headquarters of the 700th Engineer Regiment was ordered to construct an 8 ton combat bridge near Derevka, across which the bulk of Panzer Group 1 had to attack, with seven engineer battalions, 26 bridge columns, three construction battalions, and one unit of the "Organization of the Dead." The construction of this nearly 1,254 meter bridge was finished two days later.

The bridgehead was defended by the LII Army Corps (General of Infantry von Briesen). The 76th ID (Lieutenant General Angelis) fought at the mouth of the Vorssklyam on the right flank. The 97th Rifle Division (Major General Fretter-Pico) held the center of the 32 kilometer front line, while the 100th Rifle Division (Major General Sanne) contended with the left. In the first ten days, these three divisions withstood the counterthrusts and counterattacks of three rifle, four cavalry divisions, and four tank brigades. The attack began after the 57th (Lieutenant General Bluemm) and 295th ID (Lieutenant General Geitner) reinforced the bridgehead at the beginning of September.

The left neighboring XI Army Corps (General of Infantry von Kortzfleisch) had established a bridgehead near Vorovskovo during the first week of September, and crossed the 101st Rifle Division (Lieutenant General Brunner von Haydringen), 125th ID (Lieutenant General Schneckenburger), and 239th ID (Lieutenant General Neuling) over the Dnepr on an 8 ton combat bridge constructed by the 617th Engineer Regiment. These formations utilized surprise to assault the enemy that was still located at Psiol from all sides and across the Dnepr. Then the rain came. During the night of 9 September, sheets of water fell from the skies continuously, only interrupted by thunderstorms. The ground on the eastern bank of the Dnepr changed into a veritable marsh in just a few minutes. However, combat continued.

On the previous day, the 257th ID (Lieutenant General Sachs) had crossed the Dnepr at Taburishche, not far from Kremenchug, at a point where the river was 4 kilometers wide, in a wild assault that included 68 assault boats and 150 rafts, and, by the evening, had established a 5 kilometer deep and 12 kilometer wide bridgehead. The Russians here surrendered, turning over the city of Kremenchug to the 257th ID without a fight.

These bridgeheads near Kremenchug improved the military position of the 17th Army to the point that the 617th Engineer Regiment (Lieutenant Colonel von Ahlfen) immediately was able to construct a 200 meter, 16 ton combat bridge – the 73rd and 74th Engineer Battalions, 107th RAD Group, and 18 bridge sections supported the effort.

Shortly after this 200 meter long combat bridge was established, the XLVIII Motorized Army Corps received the order to cross the bridge on the following night. In order, the 9th, 13th, and 16th Panzer Divisions, as well as the 16th and 25th Motorized Infantry Divisions crossed to the opposite side of the Dnepr in a pouring rain on a pitch-black night.

At midnight, the commander of Panzer Group 1 received the order to secure the breakout from the bridgehead on 12 September.

A short bombardment from a multitude of guns initiated the attack on the gray morning of 12 September. The panzer battalions and infantry battalions of the 16th Panzer Division (Major General Hube) and the 9th Panzer Division (Lieutenant General Hubici) pressed forward. Their mission was to block the road between Lubny and Kharkov. Close behind, the infantry regiments of the XI Army Corps' divisions attacked into the Russian positions.

The opposing 38th Army (Major General Feklenko) soon collapsed under the weight of the first German attack and vacated their positions in disorder. The headquarters of this Soviet army, which was in the railroad station building in Vesseliy Podol, was occupied in the afternoon by the lead elements of the 1/2 Panzer Regiment, under the command of Major Count von Strachwitz (one of the rashest tank commanders of World War II). Major General Feklenko escaped being taken prisoner only by jumping out of the window.

On the first evening, the German tanks were already 70 kilometers from their original departure positions. The trailing infantry divisions had

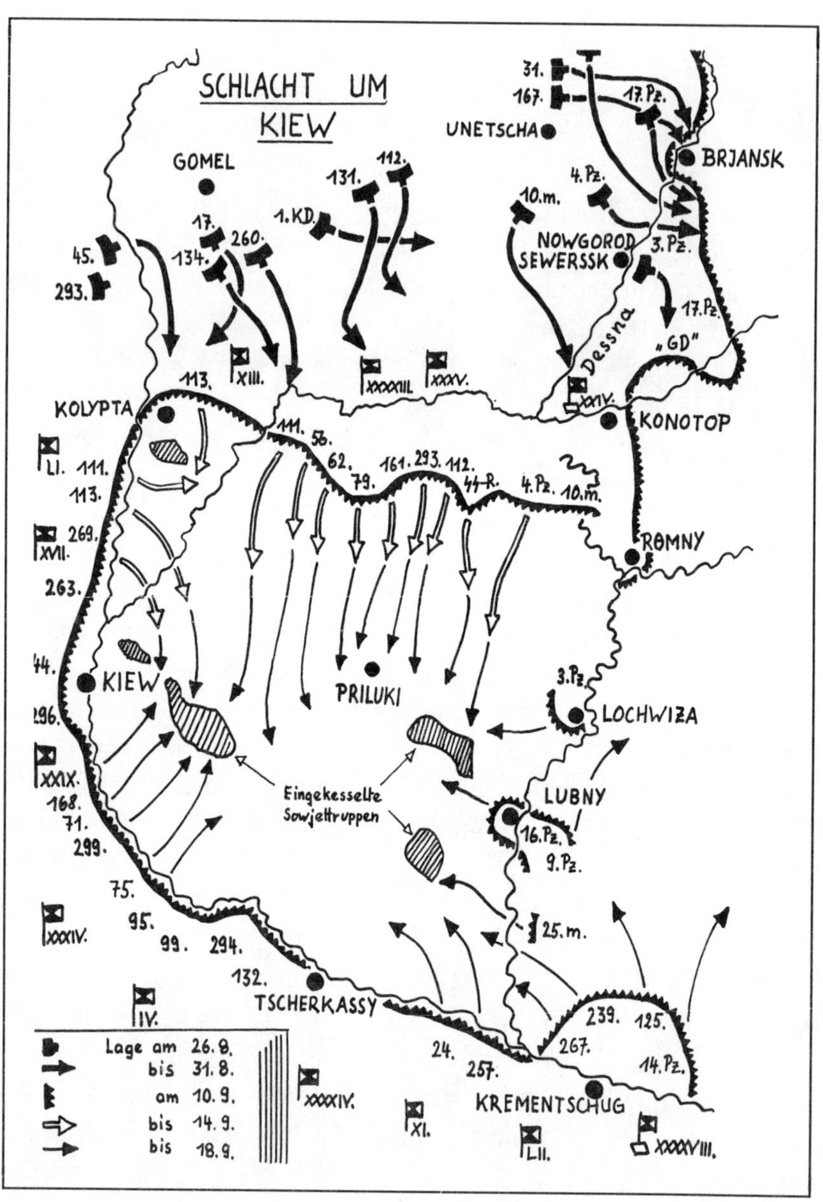

The Battle for Kiev

advanced 20 kilometers into Russian territory. On this first day, 13,000 Russians were taken prisoner, and 75 tanks, 48 guns, and 76 aircraft were destroyed by the troops of Panzer Group 1 and the XI Army Corps. The directness of the breakthrough of the 16th Panzer Division through the Soviet front line caused the panzer group to invert the 9th Panzer Division behind the 16th Panzer Division, thus creating a spot for the trailing XIV Motorized Army Corps, which could now advance to the northeast to secure the flank.

The second day of the attack expanded on the successes of the first. During the early morning, the 16th Panzer Division reached the southern bank of the Sula – a total march of 120 kilometers. The daring strike against Lubny failed, however, because the city was defended by the fanatical NKVD and bands of militia.

The left flank of the forward-most panzer regiments was completely open. This attracted special attention to the follow-on XIV Motorized Army Corps on 13 September. The 14th Panzer Division (Major General Kuehn) broke through the enemy defenses and approached the Khorol sector and the city of Mirgorod. In view of these developments, General Kirponos, the commander of the Russian "Southwest Front", ordered the general retreat of his 5th and 37th Armies to the Dessna. He himself flew to Moscow to obtain a general retreat authorization. Stalin categorically refused and again entrusted Marshal Timoshenko with the leadership of the "Red Army" in the Ukraine. However, the fate of the Soviet "Southwest Front" could not be changed.

Since 12 September, German air reconnaissance predicted an improvement in the weather, especially in the Panzer Group 2 (General Guderian) sector. The General now ordered the advance of his forward-most 3rd Panzer Division (Lieutenant General Model) on Lokhvitsa to make contact with Panzer Group 1. The division's advance guard (Major Frank) set out on this very day and covered 45 kilometers to the south without stopping. They reached Lokhvitsa in 24 hours, but they could not take it. Now a gap of 40 kilometers yawned beyond Panzer Group 1 of Army Group South!

Then the 14th of September arrived – the decisive day of the great pocket battle.

Army Group South

In Panzer Group 1's sector, the 16th Panzer Division of Major General Hube assaulted from the south. At the same time, Lieutenant General (later Field Marshal) Model's soldiers entered the heart of the battle at Lokhvitsa. General Guderian and Lieutenant General Model arrived at midday in the burning city and ordered a combat group of the 3rd Panzer Division to "close the pocket around Kiev"!

• • •

The combat troops began their march at the assigned time. Lieutenant Colonel Mueller-Hauff road at the head of the column. The weather was sunny and clear, the roads were firm, and there were only a few muddy patches. Additionally, it was Sunday – appropriate "riding weather" or "panzer weather." The tanks soon left behind the forward security of the advance guard near Iskovtsy-Senchanskie and had before them the wide and lightly undulating Ukrainian land and, in some places, the enemy, who we knew was still well armed.

After a three hour trip, the first town emerged on the left. A Russian transport column was on the road. As the German vehicles approached, the Soviets abandoned their horse carts and fled into the nearby field of sunflowers. As we moved on, the enemy supply wagons crossed the road. The machine-guns spoke again. We advanced further. It was the Soviets already. This time it was an enormous column of batteries, supply trains, construction battalions, guns, horse carts, and tractors, with cossacks and two combat vehicles riding in between. The machine-guns howled anew, shooting a passage through the Russian column, and the tanks raged with great speed into the middle of the stream.

Senior Lieutenant Warthmann and his men understand only one thing: forward! Thus, the vehicles rolled endlessly through the ravines, swampy lowlands, through the forests and fields and over many brittle wooden bridges. By and by, the column came upon Tichi across the Sula – the halfway point! Suddenly, the division radio spat to life. The friendly vehicles were located in a ravine, however, as they moved further toward an open area, radio contact was made – and we could hear General Model and

Major Pomtow breathe a sigh of relief back in Romny, as they heard: "As of 1602 hours, we were on the hills of Luka."

It had been a while since the red-golden sun set. Finally, the combat group stopped on high ground and hid the vehicles behind scarecrows. The men looked over the silhouettes of the city through binoculars as they moved with the evening sky. Clouds of smoke hung over the houses, and in between the crackle of machine-guns the artillery hits thudded. There was no doubt, the assault troops were standing directly behind the Russian front line, and a few kilometers further on were the lead elements of Army Group South!

Senior Lieutenant Warthmann gave the order: 'Panzers – March!' The combat group rolled forward, traversing a ravine, but Russians emerged and suddenly fired out of the dark, the most frightened of those scattered. A brook blocked further movement. The vehicles searched for a crossing, and there was a bridge. The Senior Lieutenant's vehicle moved to it, but the bridge was destroyed. Gray forms sprang up, mud-encrusted, stubbly-bearded, and they were signaling. It was the men of the 2/16 Engineers of the 16th Panzer Division! It was exactly 1820 hours.

The soldiers pointed out a passable spot through the brook. Senior Lieutenant Warthmann crossed in his vehicle and entered Lubny. A short while later, he reported to Major General Hube. The combat vehicles of the 3rd Panzer Division with the big "G" (Guderian) on their sides stood next to a tank with the letter "K" (Kleist). The lead elements of both army groups had made contact! The pocket around Kiev was closed! (From: Haupt, W.: *History of the 3rd Panzer Division*, Berlin 1967.)

• • •

Again, on the same day, the pocket was closed for a second time, as soldiers of the 394th Infantry Regiment (3rd Panzer Division) met the lead elements of the 33rd Panzer Regiment (9th Panzer Division).

During the first days, the pocket around Kiev had a shape like an isosceles triangle. Each side was about 500 kilometers long, and it had a total area of nearly 135,500 square kilometers. On 15 September 1941, three German armies and two panzer groups had enclosed five Soviet armies!

This developed into the so-called Kiev pocket battle, which was the largest, the most important, and, in its implications, probably the most decisive battle of the Eastern Campaign! Because of the events of the next two weeks, the final decisive German assault on Moscow was neglected. This probably changed the outcome of the Eastern Campaign.

On the evening of 15 September, the German situation reflected the following: Panzer Group 2, with the XLVI Army Corps and the XXIV Motorized Army Corps, was fighting in the extreme north of the pocket. The neighbors on the right, the XXXV Corps, and the XLIII Army Corps of the 2nd Army had already gone out and come back, thanks to the mobility of the motorized formations (The 2nd Army was immediately sent back to Army Group Center). The 6th Army, with the LI and XVII Army Corps, was deployed to the north of Kiev. The XXIX Army Corps secured Kiev from the west and south, while the XXXIV Corps and the IV and XLIV Army Corps secured the Dnepr between Kiev and Kremenchug. The 17th Army, along with the XI Army Corps, was deployed on the Sula, while their LV and LII Army Corps advanced in the direction of Poltava. Panzer Group 1 was located in between, with the XLVIII Motorized Army Corps at Lubny and the XIV Motorized Army Corps south of Mirgorod.

On the morning of the second day of the battle, General Kirponos ordered his armies to break out of the pocket. Units of the 21st Soviet Army advanced against Romny, units of the 5th and 37th Armies advanced against Lokhvitsa, and the 26th and 38th Armies moved against Lubny, where they were shot up en masse. Only the bulk of the 37th Army, under General Vlassov, remained in Kiev (The General himself later flew to Moscow and took command of the 20th Army there).

On the third day, the pocket was systematically compressed and formed into a triangle with the end points in Kiev, Priluki, and Schovnin (approximately the same area as from Wuerzburg-Stuttgart-Muenchen).

The pocket was then split up into smaller individual pockets. The Russian corps and divisions fought without any cohesion. They were separated, broken up, and they surrendered by the hundreds and thousands.

The Russian command recognized the encirclement of their armies on the very first day and tried to break into the pocket from the outside with all

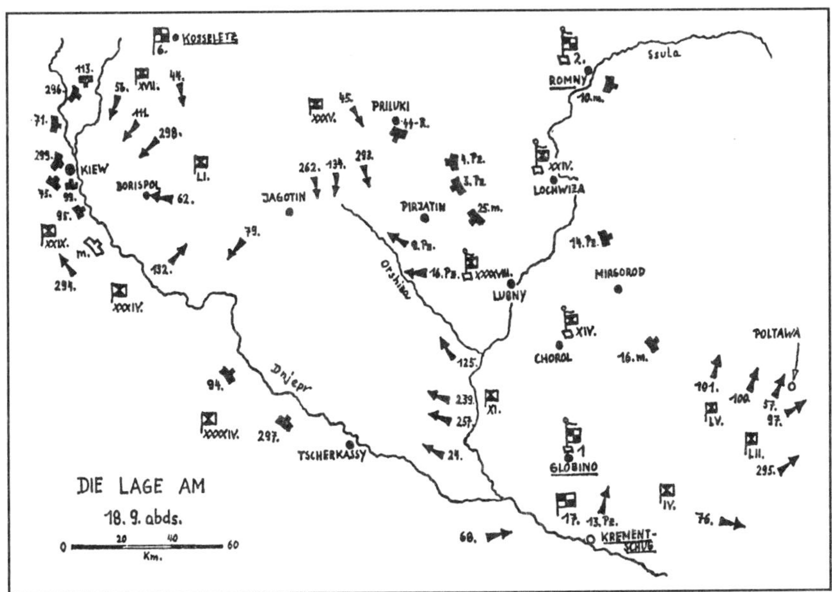

The situation on the evening of 9/18

available means. The "Red Army" directed all available combat troops from the interior to the German Front east of a general line Romny-Kremenchug to tear open the pocket and release the friendly troops.

However, throughout it all, the German pocket held. The 17th Army, which covered the eastern portion of the front line, gave up no ground. In fact, its units transitioned to the offensive and, on 18 September, the LII Army Corps of General of Infantry von Briesen occupied the city of Poltava, including Marshal Timoshenko's headquarters. The main effort of the Soviet breakout attempts was certainly the Romny area. Here, the main formations of the encircled Army Group "Southwest Front" persistently attacked the positions of the XLVI Motorized Army Corps which, in the meantime, had arrived from the north. The 17th Panzer Division and the Motorized Infantry Regiment "Grossdeutschland" fended off the heaviest attacks.

Therefore, the fate of Kiev, the capital of the Ukraine, was sealed. The Commanding General of the XXIX Army Corps (General of Infantry von Obstfelder) published an order of the day on 13 september which closed with the words: "Fly the Reich's battle flag over the citadel of Kiev!"

This noble city, already over 1,000 years old, which sat 100 meters above the banks of the Dnepr was, on 15 September, the objective of attacks by the XXIX Army Corps, with the 75th, 95th, 296th, 299th ID, and 99th Rifle Division. The attack was made possible because both the left and right flanks were secured. Here, north of Kiev, the German Divisions tried to strengthen the encirclement and neutralize the possible threat from enemy formations in the Pripet Swamp.

• • •

Report
of the 62nd Infantry Division
concerning their combat from 19 September to 24 September 1941

19 September

The attack of the 62nd ID on 19 September, on one hand, was based on the telephonic order of the II Army Corps directing them to capture Borispol and to quickly establish contact with the 132nd ID in the Yerkovtsy area with sufficient combat strength. On the other hand, their was the radio communication of the XVII Army Corps at 1205 hours on 18 September ordering the division to organize for the capture of Borispol by committing only a portion of the force directly against the front of the town and by attacking the remainder of the force around the town to the south to occupy it. In addition, the objective of the day was Bornichi. With the capture of Borispol, the division came under the command of the XVII Army Corps. To accomplish the corps' mission, at 0800 hours on 19 September the division began an encirclement attack against Borispol from southwest of Ivankovo and hill 124, with the 190th Infantry Regiment to the front, while the 164th Infantry regiment advanced to the left, by-passing Khrapivshchina. The 164th Infantry Regiment was strictly forbidden from closing in from the north against Borispol; if needed, the 183rd Infantry Regiment was assigned to follow the 164th Infantry Regiment. The 162nd Reconnaissance Battalion was tasked with establishing contact during the day; the mission was renewed on 19 September.

By midnight of 18 September, the 162nd Reconnaissance Battalion had already advanced from Skoptsy to the southwest on the high ground directly north of the Rogostov-Yerkovtsy road. At 0600 hours on 19 September they reported that they were being attacked by superior enemy forces from the west and the south. Since the attack against them was further reinforced, the 162nd Engineer Battalion (minus the 1st Company) was sent to assist them. During the course of the day they were driven back to the high ground north of Skoptsy. From their reports, the enemy picture gradually became clear. It was apparent that strong enemy columns were continuously streaming to the southeast from Rogostov, as well as Lyubortsy and Skoptsy. (From: *The 62nd Infantry Division*. Fulda 1968.)

• • •

On 16 September, the divisions of the XXIX Army Corps attacked the heavily fortified Russian formations, which were mined and equipped with heavy weapons. The battle was as difficult as before and resulted in considerable casualties. However, during the night of the next day, the enemy defenders suddenly left.

We spent the night before the decisive battle in Lesniki, south of Kiev. The front line was directly behind the town. The night came early, and with it the illumination of the flares, the short, sudden concentrations of artillery fire, and the cracking of the machine-gun fire whenever the sentries thought they heard or seen something suspicious. We laid down in the vehicles and tried to get some sleep. It was a futile attempt. The feverish anticipation was too great: will our attack succeed against the latest defenses contrived by the Bolsheviks? What is waiting for us when the infantrymen emerge from their protective covering – death from the artillery fire curtain hanging over the enemy line?

Then the short nap was interrupted by a company, which was assembling to move forward. Finally, it was 0400 hours. The first light of dawn outlined the contours of the hills. The artillery sent its usual morning greetings. It was just the same as every day was before Kiev, however, we knew that soon, very soon, a battle would rage, the objective of which was the third largest city in the Soviet Union on the Dnepr, the outcome of which would effect the future conduct of the Eastern Campaign. We had to be patient for so long. We knew that our leadership wanted to conduct different operations before Kiev, but we felt that this operation made sense, since we had been in these positions for some time. We were longing for the day we could again advance.

Now that day had arrived. It was getting light. The usual time for German offensive operations had long passed. The German soldiers clung to the hill slope. After every new artillery volley, they checked the time. But it was still not time.

To the left of the road to Kiev a steep hill rose, and on the crest a German artillery observation post was established. From here we could view the open territory before us, and to our front ran the Bolshevik positions. In the center of this treeless plain was the town of Pirogovo. Then a new tree-covered ridge rose, and beyond that, we could see what made our hearts beat faster: Kiev's characteristic towers rising clearly in the morning haze! That was our center of interest – there lay our objective! To the right we could make out the large iron bridge over the Dnepr, and behind it two additional bridges leading out of the center of the city.

The front line ran directly below the observation post. Exactly 500 meters behind it was a small factory which was converted into the division command post. The General and his staff worked within range of the enemy's infantry weapons and they waited, exactly like the infantrymen around them, for the signal to begin the struggle for Kiev.

Suddenly – the minute hand leaped to the appointed time – below us broke loose that deafening racket that we had been waiting for. A jolt went through all of us. The time for waiting was over, and now we looked calmly at the towers on the horizon and knew for sure that it would not be long before we would climb those towers of Kiev. What lay in between was combat; a difficult fight to the great defensive wall that ran around the city in a half circle, and the end point lay in the Dnepr.

Friendly shells of all calibers were roaring over us. A formidable concentration of fire for the enemy. It was as if we were under an umbrella. A flowing ribbon of shells arched over us. Then our smoke shells were fired. In front of the Bolshevik positions an enormous smoke screen expanded, as if suddenly a large theater curtain was dropped in front of the enemy. This was the signal for the valiant infantrymen to attack. We could not see from our elevated location, so we dexterously jumped from cover to cover. A few minutes later, a second wall expanded on the edge of the town of Pirogovo, an indication that the first wall was already penetrated. The machine-gun fire pinged lightly as a background for the choir of the artillery bass. The first houses of the town were reached, and from them issued the typical sounds of street combat.

The artillery observers gave new targets to the batteries. Fire rolled along all sides of the town, focused on a brickyard, and then on the edge of the forest on the next hill. The impacts and powder smoke filled the wide depression with a thick cloud, and only the smoke screen could be discerned. Meanwhile, Kiev's towers shimmered as before. The battle emerged from its initial stage. Throughout, the infantry penetrated the desperate, stubborn resistance of the Bolsheviks, and they had to withdraw meter by meter. The concentrated fire of the artillery was enhanced by the precise fire of individual batteries on particularly important targets. But then the enemy composed himself and fired on our high ground, especially the very troublesome artillery observation posts. Thick pieces cracked, and fragments whistled and chirped. However, the artillery officers did not take their eyes off of the infantrymen, for they knew how important their fire support was for the advance. Enemy shrapnel burst over the valley, and shells intended for our assault troops landed on a great sand bank. It was a long time before the Bolshevik commander realized that the situation was lost.

Kiev's defensive wall was the focus of activity, and it had somewhat recovered from the first shocks and was being bitterly defended. The soviet soldiers were, as the first prisoners informed us, forced by the political officers to defend their positions to the last. The infantry was always having to capture newly hidden pockets of resistance. German artillery fired against Bolshevik batteries that they could locate to silence them. Slowly, but with deadly surety, the German ring tightened around Kiev.

• • •

On 17 September, the Russian High Command issued the order to surrender the city.

The XXIX Army Corps – now reinforced by the 71st ID and units of the 294th ID – had already broken through the first line of defense. On 18 September, the 299th ID (Lieutenant General Moser) captured Gatnoe. The 99th Rifle Division (Lieutenant General von der Chevallerie) advanced to the north and occupied Khotov. The assault troops of the 95th ID (Lieutenant General Sixt von Arnim) crossed the Dnepr in assault and motorboats. The first suburbs of Kiev were reached!

During the following days, the 71st ID (Major General von Hartmann) cleared the Irpen sector up to a width of 12 kilometers. On 19 September, the 296th ID (Major General Stemmermann) established an attack to the south between the Dnepr and Guta Meshigorskaya and, within three hours, broke through the fortifications to the north of the city to a depth of 26 kilometers. The first assault troops of the division entered the city! At the same time, combat troops from the 95th ID and 99th Rifle Division had arrived from the south and had entered the southern suburbs together. Between 1000 and 1100 hours on this day, companies from these divisions raised the Reich's battle flag over the citadel. Kiev was in German hands!

The pocket southeast of Kiev burned out! A physician of the 3rd Panzer Division wrote in his diary:

> "Chaos reigns. Hundreds of trucks and cars, interspersed with tanks, are scattered over the land. Often the occupants were overcome by fire when they tried to get out and they hang from the doors, burned into black mummies. Thousands of corpses lay around the vehicles..."

The defensive battle for Kiev died out on 24 September...
While the mopping up of the enormous battlefield was begun, infantry and panzer divisions advanced further to the east.

• • •

A combat report of the 13th Anti-tank Battalion sheds some light on the exploits of individual soldiers. In extract form, this report renders in-

Frankfurter Zeitung

mit dem Stadt-Blatt

Sammel-Nummer für Fernsprecher: Ortsverkehr 20202, Fernverkehr 20301.

IV 100 Samstag, 27. September 1941.

Fünf Sowjetarmeen vernichtet.

Die Schlacht bei Kiew beendet.

Aus dem Führerhauptquartier, 27. September. Das Oberkommando der Wehrmacht gibt bekannt:

Wie bereits durch Sondermeldung bekanntgegeben, ist die große Schlacht bei Kiew beendet. In doppelseitiger Umfassung auf gewaltigem Raum ist es gelungen, die Dnjepr-Verteidigung aus den Angeln zu heben und fünf sowjetische Armeen zu vernichten, ohne daß auch nur schwache Teile sich der Umklammerung entziehen konnten. Im Verlaufe der in engstem Zusammenwirken von Heer und Luftwaffe durchgeführten Operation wurden insgesamt 665 000 Gefangene eingebracht, 884 Panzerkampfwagen, 3178 Geschütze und ungezählte Mengen an sonstigem Kriegsgerät erbeutet oder vernichtet. Die blutigen Verluste des Gegners sind wiederum sehr hoch.

Ein Schlachtensieg ist damit errungen, wie ihn die Geschichte bisher nicht gekannt hat. Die Ausnutzung dieses Erfolges ist in vollem Gange.

Fifth Soviet Army Destroyed
The battle near Kiev is over
(Saturday, 27 September 1941)

formation about the combat activities of the companies and platoons of an anti-tank battalion – a small but important spoke in the overall wheel – of which we knew little before.

> "On 9/30/41 the Commander of 3/13 Anti-tank Battalion (Senior Lieutenant Barth) was ordered to provide protection for the 2/13 Reconnaissance Battalion with his company.... Due to vehicle losses, the anti-tank company had 8 guns at its disposal. Considering that the security sector was several kilometers, 8 guns was not enough!
>
> Senior Lieutenant Barth went to the eastern edge of the town with the company first sergeant, Staff Sergeant Meusgeier, to inspect the terrain. He heard the sound of tracked vehicles from the east. Since friendly tanks might be committed in this direction, he could not close it off to enemy tanks. However, the armored scout troop of the 13th Reconnaissance Battalion (Corporal Simon) confirmed the approach of about 25 enemy tanks.
>
> Staff Sergeant Meusgeier was instructed to remain at the edge of town to observe and reconnoiter the positions. Senior Lieutenant Barth called the guns of Corporals Spengler, Ackmann, Foelsche, Domdex and Oelze in succession to the edge of the town and assigned them their firing positions. Just as the enemy tanks - they communicated by flag signals - began an envelopment attack, the 5 cm anti-tank gun of Corporal Oelze arrived....During the violent enemy attack, under the outstanding guidance of Staff Sergeant Meusgeier, 5 medium and heavy enemy tanks were destroyed within 4 minutes. After the guns had fired, Staff Sergeant Meusgeier jumped onto Corporal Ackmann's unarmored, self-propelled gun, directed it at the enemy tank attack, and destroyed 5 additional enemy tanks in the open and returned with the gun, unharmed.
>
> Of course, the driver, seated directly below the mouth of the gun tube, had both of his eardrums blown out. Returning again to the starting position, Staff Sergeant Meusgeier continued to fight tirelessly against enemy infantry and tanks. Meanwhile, Corporal Spengler's guns destroyed two enemy tanks. A direct hit put him out of combat. Corporal Foelsche's gun was overrun by an enemy tank. In a spirited attack,

Charkow genommen.

Aus dem Führerhauptquartier, 25. Oktober. Das Oberkommando der Wehrmacht gibt bekannt:

Am 24. Oktober wurde Charkow genommen. Eines der wichtigsten Rüstungs- und Wirtschaftszentren der Sowjetunion ist damit in deutscher Hand.

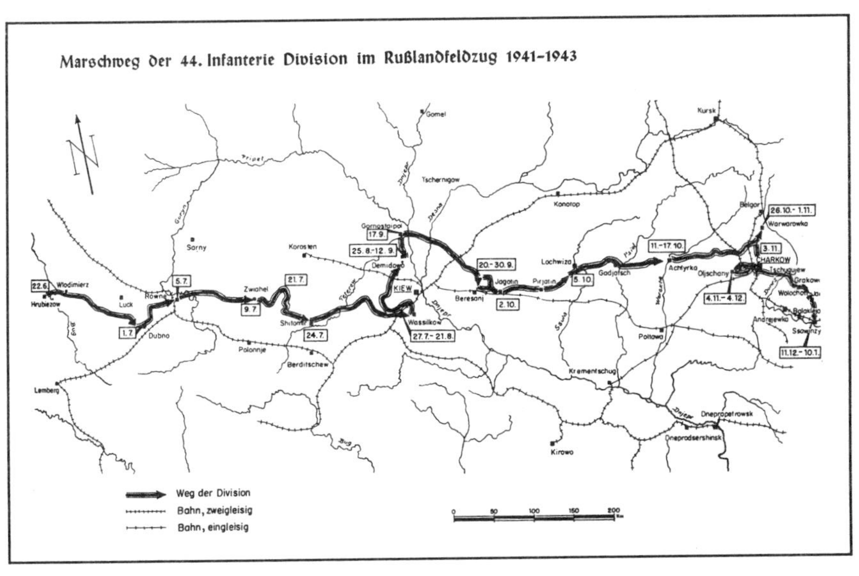

March route of the 44th Infantry Division during the Russian Campaign 1941-1943
Route of the division
Double track railroad
Single track railroad

Corporal Foelsche jumped onto the moving tank with a 3 kilogram explosive charge. Lieutenant Kausch, who had his hands full contending with the enemy infantry attacking into the open flank, in spite of his plight, jumped onto the 2nd unarmored self-propelled gun, which was driven by Private von Holtzendorf, and destroyed two enemy tanks in free fire. And again, through the personal effort of Staff Sergeant Meusgeier, 16 out of 30 tanks were destroyed within 40 minutes. The rest withdrew in disorder.

The spirited opposition of the 1/4 Armored Engineers (Senior Lieutenant Baranek) and the 3/4 Armored Engineers (Senior Lieutenant Klaus) against the enemy infantry attack drove the enemy out of the eastern portion of the town. The tank warning was given by the 2/13 Anti-tank (Senior Lieutenant Ernst), which engaged enemy tanks attacking along the southern edge of the town. The company destroyed 9 tanks in free fire. Lieutenant Herrmann and Staff Sergeant Soldmann, through their spirited efforts, made decisive contributions to this success." (From: The March of Destiny of the 13th Panzer Division. Wulfsfelde 1971.)

The army group's goal, before the beginning of winter, was to occupy the industrial region between the Dnepr and Don and, if possible, reach the area of the Sea of Azov and Crimea. In the course of these further operations, the race to the Sea of Azov developed, and on 21 October, resulted in the occupation of the important industrial city of Stalino and the occupation of Kharkov on 24 October.

Then, the first Russian winter arrived! It allowed for no more terrain seizing operations – and the German divisions were, in some places, more than 1000 kilometers from the German border.

• • •

Chapter 1: 1941

SEA OF AZOV (5 October-31 December 1941)

The III Motorized Army Corps – on 1 October the panzer groups were redesignated as panzer armies and the motorized army corps as panzer corps – did not participate directly in the pocket battle for Kiev. The corps secured the eastern flank of the panzer army and, on 24 September, began a new offensive on the eastern bank of the bridgehead near Dnepropetrovsk. The III Panzer Corps had the 13th and 14th Panzer Divisions at its disposal, which were followed by the 6th Panzer Division, 60th Motorized Infantry Division, and the SS Division "Wiking" of the XIV Panzer Corps.

The two panzer corps of Generals Manteuffel and Weitersheim smashed the enemy forces that were in front of them in the bridgehead, and, in places, advanced into the rear of the Soviet formations. Then they rolled along the eastern bank of the river to the south, drove the five divisions that were located there back, and established a new bridgehead between Dnepropetrovsk and Saporoshe.

General von Kleist assigned the Sea of Azov as the offensive objective for his corps and divisions!

This objective was also given to the 11th Army in the south of the Eastern Front. The army of General von Schobert, to which the 3rd Rumanian Army remained subordinate, did not participate in the pocket battle for Kiev. At the beginning of September, its 22nd ID (Lieutenant General Count von Sponeck) conquered a bridgehead near Berislav from which the army could cross the Dnepr.

On 12 September, the commander of the 11th Army, General von Schobert, landed his "Fieseler Storch" (Nasty Stork), by mistake, in a Russian mine field and perished. His successor as commander came from the Leningrad Front. It was General of Infantry von Manstein, one of the most successful German Army commanders.

By the middle of September, the 11th Army was located on a wide front, advancing on a general line Melitopol-Nikopol. Behind this front, the 3rd and 4th Rumanian Armies continued to surround the coastal fortifications of Odessa and, therefore, were not able to give the German forces their undivided support.

General of Infantry von Manstein sent the LIV Army Corps (General of Cavalry Hansen), along with the 46th (Lieutenant General Himer) and the 73rd ID (Lieutenant General Bieler) against the Crimea. In a bold stroke, with much army artillery and army engineer support, the corps conquered the Crimea, where there were only three Soviet divisions.

The subsequent objective of the 11th Army (which was assigned by the OKH), Rostov, could not be achieved in the first attempt, because, at the end of September, Russian resistance was too strong. Therefore, General of Infantry von Manstein altered the operation plan. He pulled the XXX Army Corps (General of Infantry von Salmuth) and the XLIX Mountain Corps (General of Mountain Troops Kuebler) from their locations on the

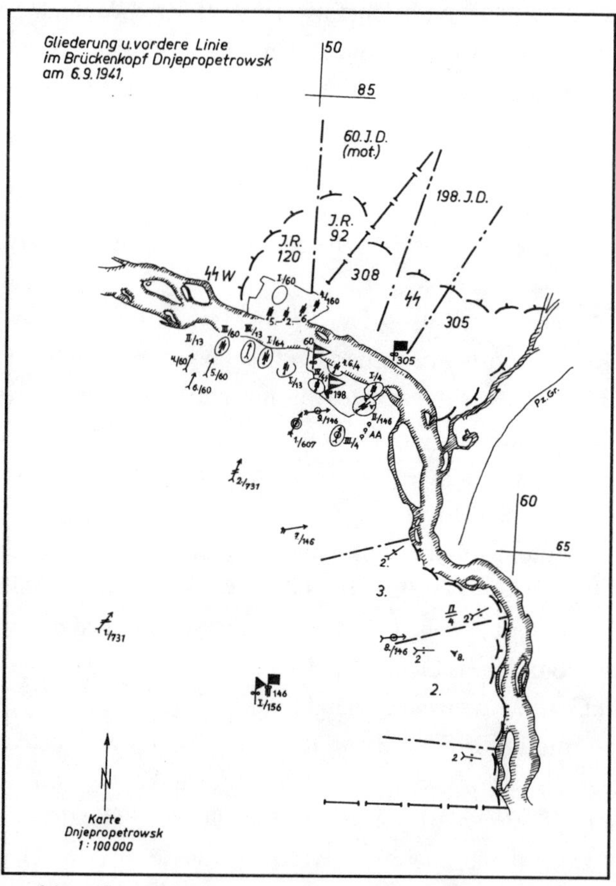

Dispositions and front line of the Dnepropetrovsk Bridgehead on 9/6/1941

eastern front of his army and sent them to the Crimea. The peninsula had priority for capture to prevent the enemy from having a large force in the German rear area.

The LIV Army Corps began to move with the 46th and 73rd ID, in order to assault across the isthmus of Perekop. This isthmus was only 7 kilometers wide and completely without cover, and it was sparsely developed by the Russians. The so-called "Tartar Wall", a 10 to 15 meter deep trench dug in the 18th Century, stretched the entire width of the peninsula from sea to sea. The "Red Army" deployed three rifle divisions (156th,

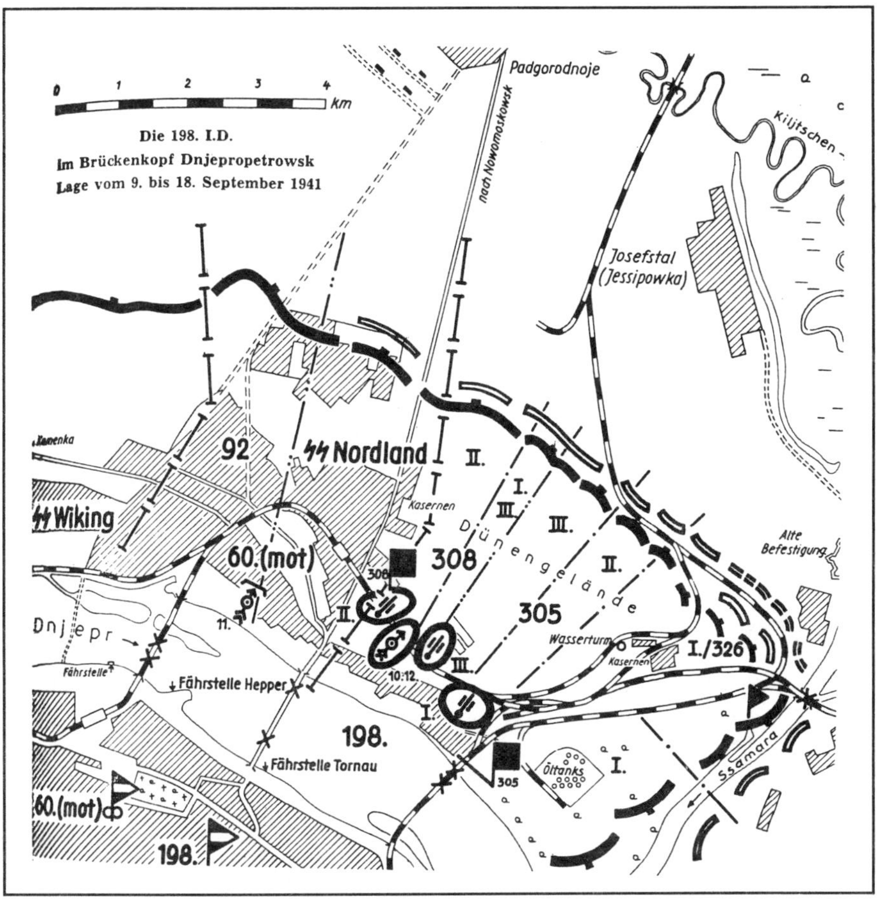

The 198th ID in the Dnepropetrovsk Bridgehead - Situation from 9 to 18 September 1941

271st, 276th) in and behind the wall. These could not be softened up by the assault by the German guns.

An engineer that was there reports:

> "The attack began at 0400 hours on 24 September 1941 with an enormous artillery preparation fire that lasted about 30 minutes. We had the mission of working our way up to the barrier to create lanes for the infantry and assault troops. We had to do this in spite of the heavy enemy artillery fire. The thick infantry fire from the bunkers to our left and right continued for 2 hours until, finally, smoke shells were fired. Then we were able to approach the bunkers and blow them up. We had blown up three bunkers, however, there was still fire coming from them. We realized that the Russians would retreat into the trench system when we set the explosives. We finally destroyed them with hand grenades. The breakthrough battle was supported by about 45 JU 88 and 45 HE 110 that tried to destroy the bunker line, but this was only partially successful. It was not known beforehand that the two towns of Perekop and Preobrashenka were connected by an amazing underground trench system that even connected each house with another. The bottleneck was 8 kilometers wide. The bunkers were manned mostly by disciples of Stalin, who fought fanatically. On 25 September 1941, after we gained about 600-700 meters of ground, almost all of the infantry officers had fallen, and the companies were being led by non-commissioned officers. On the evening of 25 September 1941, a wheeled battalion was brought forward as reinforcement. It immediately fell under heavy artillery fire from all the gun crews in Preobrashenka to the south. On 26 September 1941, we captured another 700-1000 meters of territory and lay in furrows, while the Russians blew up a tank ditch 3 meters wide by 2 meters deep. The explosion was felt throughout the entire width of the isthmus. The blast destroyed our eardrums; if we had been about 300 meters further to the south, we all would have been finished.
>
> Late at night on 26 September, we reached the Tartar trenches, which were now only weakly defended. The Russians were piled high as the result of a stuka attack. However, we could not go directly through the trenches, because we were immediately attacked by heavy tanks

from Armenia. Our savior was a heavy Rumanian mortar battery. Their impacts ripped open enormous holes and the Russian tanks withdrew. We linked up with a forward observer from our artillery regiment – we were then evacuated from the Tartar trenches and had to remove almost 1000 mines from the isthmus. The Russians had buried them all here. There were light anti-personnel mines, engineer mines, artillery shells, and sea mines – enough for a new war."

After three days of hard combat, they succeeded in overcoming the "Tartar Wall" and entering Perekop. However, they could go no further, because the remaining corps from the region east of the Dnepr had not yet arrived.

The Soviet High Command recognized the German attempt to conquer the Crimea in time and detached the infantry formations, which were advancing to the southeast. The Russian leadership took advantage of a the weakness in the German Front – the 3rd Rumanian Army sector.

On 26 September, the 9th and 18th Soviet Armies attacked the Rumanian forces from a line Melitopol-Nikopol and achieved a deep penetration during the first two days.

The 11th Army immediately halted the XLIX Mountain Corps and turned them 180 degrees to the northeast and ordered the only motorized formation available – the SS Brigade "Leibstandarte": "About face (turn)!"

The Army Group South Commander acted quickly and purposefully.

The 1st Panzer Army, whose lead elements had already reached the Melitopol area, were halted and sent south to fix the attacking Russian formations in the rear and encircle them.

The strategy unfolded between 5 and 10 October. They were able to encircle the bulk of the 9th and 18th Soviet Armies in the Chernigovka area. The commander of the 18th Soviet Army, Lieutenant General Smirnov, fell during the second day of the battle; and three days latter, the battle died out.

• • •

From the Führer's Headquarters, 11 October
The Wehrmacht High Command makes it known:

The battle at the Sea of Azov is over. In cooperation with the air fleet of General Loehr, the army of General of Infantry von Manstein, the Rumanian army of General Dumitrescu, and the panzer army of General von Kleist battered and destroyed the bulk of the 9th and 18th Soviet Armies. The heavy losses of the enemy included 64,325 prisoners, 126 tanks, 519 guns, and immense quantities of other war materials. The above named armies and the attached Italian, Hungarian, and Slovakian troops, that is, the army group of Field Marshal von Rundstedt, have now captured a total of 106,365 prisoners, as well as 212 tanks and 672 guns, since 26 September.

• • •

The SS Brigade "Leibstandarte" – which was expanded to a Panzer Division – shared in the battle's successful outcome by capturing Berdyanssk on 7 October. On the same day, the 14th Panzer Division also made a considerable contribution to the victory in this pocket battle by occupying Mariupol.

The XLIX Mountain Corps, which was now subordinate to the army group, and the SS Panzer Division "Leibstandarte" of the 1st Panzer Army received orders to immediately advance on Rostov! Furthermore, the 3rd Rumanian Army (General Dumitrescu), the Italian Alpine Corps, and the Slovakian Motorized Brigade were assigned to the panzer army.

General von Kleist's panzer army began the new attack on 11 October. Both panzer corps (III and XIV) advanced along the coast of the Sea of Azov. The XLIX Mountain Corps entered the industrial area near Stalino, while the attached armies and corps were sent to the still open northern flank of the army.

On 14 October at 2200 hours, the III Panzer Corps (General of Cavalry von Mackensen) issued the following attack order to its divisions:

3. Missions for the Divisions:

a) LSSAH (1st SS Panzer Division Leibstandarte Adolf Hitler) advances to the southeast, seals the peninsula, and clears it. Taganrog is to be occupied.

b) The 13th Panzer Division expands the bridgehead to the east and northeast, surrounds the town of Prokovskoe, to prepare for its advance on Rostov.

c)The 14th Panzer Division secures the northern flank of the corps from the west bank of Prokovskoe to Andreevkoe.

d) LSSAH Reconnoiters Taganrog-Varenovka. Later, the western point of the peninsula.

4. Additional Orders:

a) The 627th Bridge Company (Engineers) will reconnoiter the crossing site by 2400 hours on 13 October, and maintain the 8 ton bridge here.

b) The 13th Panzer Division, during the night of 10/14/41, will cross three battalions to the opposite bank on the bridge or by ferry, relieve the 3/LSSAH, and attack to the northwest beyond hill 49.6 at dawn. The 3rd Battalion, which becomes disengaged by the attack, groups itself in such a manner that it secures both sides of hill 46.1 to the southeast, until a panzer regiment of the 13th Panzer Division crosses the railroad line to the east.

c) The 4th Battalion crosses during the early morning and assumes the boundary on the right flank of the 3rd Battalion where it connects with the boundary of the 1st Battalion.

d) The 1st Battalion mops up the enemy from Nikolaevka during the early morning and then takes over the front line to the south.

e) The 2nd Battalion crosses directly behind the last unit of the 4th Battalion and assembles on the eastern edge of Nikolaevka.

f) The Reconnaissance Battalion remains in their present location, ready to move out before noon, across the bridge or by ferry, in order to be committed in the area of Taganrog-Varenovka and later on in the peninsula.

g) The 13th Panzer Division, during the night of 10/14/41, at the latest the early morning of 10/14, will set up its combat bridging equipment over the Mius, to cross its panzer regiments to the opposite bank at noon on 10/14/41. Detachment Schoenberger and the 2nd Battalion of the artillery regiment is to be ready to cross the bridge after the 13th Panzer Division.

5. Conduct of Combat:

During the course of the day, it is intended to commit the 1st Battalion on the right and the 3rd Battalion on the left across the railroad junction to Taganrog, in order to occupy this town.

The 4th Battalion will, presumably, advance beyond Balka Volovaya to Balka Yagidna, to cover the left flank. The Reconnaissance Battalion clarifies the combat strength opposite the railroad terminal at Novodessergenovka and further along the southern coast and commits another unit on the coast along the Liman and the Lakedemonovka.

After expanding the bridgehead, the battalions will cross to the opposite bank, supported by heavy weapons.

Three days later, the Mius was crossed on a wide front. On the same day, the 14th Panzer Division (Major General Kuehn) captured Taganrog. Three days later, the mountain troops of General Kuebler entered Stalino, after which the newly established 12th Soviet Army (Major General Koroteev) simply "ran for the hills."

The enormous industrial area around Stalino and the entire Donets industrial region lay in ruins. Machine and motor works were demolished, power stations were blown into the air, water and power lines for the cities and towns were severed, and roads and bridges were blown.

Now the winter rains arrived. Cloudbursts turned the entire countryside into a wilderness of mud. Tanks and trucks bogged down in the marshy ground; only heavy tractors could move. Supply vehicles lagged far behind. The 1st Panzer Army continued its advance meter by meter.

On 27 October, far to the north, units of the 17th Army – whose command was taken over by General Hoth on 5 October – occupied Kramatorsk, and the 11th Army of General of Infantry von Manstein broke through the isthmus from Perekop.

After the battle at the Sea of Azov, the 11th Army had, as its single operational objective, the conquest of the Crimea. At this time the army had at its disposal the XXX Army Corps, with the 22nd, 72nd, and 170th ID, and the LIV Army Corps, with the 46th, 50th, and 73rd ID. At the end of October, these six decimated German divisions faced eight Soviet rifle and four cavalry divisions. These strong forces were brought to the Crimea after the evacuation of Odessa (16 October) and occupied defensive positions on the northern edge of the peninsula. At the same time, the Soviet Air Force transferred strong fighter formations to the Crimea.

Aus dem Führerhauptquartier, 30. Oktober. Das Oberkommando der Wehrmacht gibt bekannt:

Auf der Halbinsel Krim stoßen die deutschen Kräfte dem geschlagenen Feinde unaufhaltsam nach. Oertlicher Widerstand seiner Nachhuten wurde gebrochen. Dabei wurden erneut mehrere tausend Gefangene gemacht und weitere Geschütze erbeutet.

Bei der Verfolgung des Gegners im Donezbecken wurde der Oberlauf des Donez von den deutschen und verbündeten Truppen in breiter Front erreicht. Im Verlaufe erfolgreicher Angriffsoperationen zwischen Ilmensee und Ladogasee nahmen Panzergruppen in kühnem Handstreich einen feindlichen Panzerzug und machten zahlreiche Gefangene.

Oberstleutnant Galland, Kommodore eines Jagdgeschwaders, errang seinen 90. und 91. Luftsieg.

30 October OKW press release on the Crimean Campaign

Verfolgung in der Krim.

Aus dem Führerhauptquartier, 31. Oktober. Das Oberkommando der Wehrmacht gibt unter anderem bekannt:

Von deutschen und rumänischen Truppen scharf verfolgt, ist der Feind auf der Krim in voller Flucht. Damit haben die langen und schweren Durchbruchskämpfe ihre Krönung gefunden, mit denen die Infanteriedivisionen der Armee des Generals der Infanterie von Manstein im Verein mit dem Fliegerkorps des Generalleutnants Pflugbeil die schmalen Landengen bezwungen haben, die zu der Halbinsel führen.

Auch im Donezbecken setzten die deutschen und verbündeten Truppen die Verfolgung des geschlagenen Feindes erfolgreich fort.

Pursuit in the Crimea

This was the situation when, on 17 October, the 22nd (Lieutenant General Count von Sponeck), 46th (Lieutenant General Himer), and 73rd ID (Lieutenant General Bieler) attacked to conquer the peninsula. For ten days the Germans fought meter by meter through the Russian positions. The casualties increased from day to day. The companies were already being led by Staff Sergeants, and the battalions by Senior Lieutenants. Finally, the defenders lost their strength and, on 28 October, the Russian defense was penetrated in the northern part of the peninsula. The road through the Crimea was open!

At this time, the XLII Army Corps (which was taken over by Lieutenant General Count von Sponeck) was transferred to the 11th Army. The corps, with the 46th, 73rd, and 170th ID, was immediately set off in the direction of Feodosia-Kerch and toward the east. The XXX Army Corps (General of Infantry von Salmuth), with the 22nd and 72nd ID, attacked to the south in the direction of Simferopol and Yalta, while the LIV Army

Corps (General of Cavalry Hansen), with the 50th and 132nd ID, was committed against the fortress of Sevastopol.

Simferopol, the capital of the Crimea, fell into German hands on 1 November; three days later, Feodosia was occupied. The report from the Wehrmacht High Command on 5 November read:

> From the Führer's Headquarters, 5 November. According to the report of the Wehrmacht High Command, the pursuit continues in the south was well as in all other directions. In spite of difficult terrain obstacles, the Yaila Mountains have been penetrated at one location and the coast of the Black Sea has been reached. The Luftwaffe has bombed the Crimean ports of Sevastopol, Yalta, and Kerch, and has sunk two transports with over 10,000 tons, as well as one escort ship.

A few days later, on 16 November, Kerch fell on the extreme east of the peninsula. A day later, the Commander of the 11th Army issued his order:

• • •

ARMY-ORDER OF THE DAY

Commander Army Headquarters, 17 November 1941
11th Army

Soldiers of the 11th Army

In four weeks, the 11th Army has essentially accomplished its assigned mission, the capture of the Crimea.

The valiant divisions of the army have overcome a numerically superior enemy and difficult combat terrain obstacles, and the enemy has been beaten into the corner of Yushun. It was not the cleverness of the leadership, it was not the superiority of the weapons, it was the will for victory of the soldiers that achieved this victory. Before this will to fight and will for victory, the will of the enemy crumbled.

In a tenacious pursuit, the boldness of the leadership, even with our weakened mobile troops, and the devotion of our infantry, have destroyed the retreating enemy. Neither rivers nor mountains, neither mud nor ice storms can stop you.

The enemy has handed over to you more than 100,000 prisoners, 450 guns, 166 tanks, 300 air defense and anti-tank guns, 2,264 machine guns, and 630 mortars in the bottlenecks of Perekop and Yushun, on the salt plains of northern Crimea, in the mountains and on the coast, and on the Kerch Peninsula.

The Russian 51st and the Coastal Armies have been destroyed, the rest have escaped from Kerch to Sevastopol. With Kerch, the enemy has lost an important armaments center.

Sevastopol still remains as a last fortress and combat port.

We will attack it and your divisions, which will execute this mission, know that they will receive fresh forces to assist them. We will defeat this bastion.

We thank our comrades that have prepared the way with their lives and blood. We pay tribute to them by continuing to fight as they did.

My thanks to you all, from the commander to the man in the rank and file.

My admiration goes out to all the infantrymen and the fighters in the front line.

General of Infantry
von Manstein

• • •

However, the fortress of Sevastopol could not be captured, despite the bloody attacks of the 22nd ID (Major General Wolff) and the 50th ID (Major General Schmidt). Here, they could go no further.

The division could not accomplish anymore. The battalions were so bloodied that they had no more then the strength of companies. The objective Kamary was not reached by the weakened pursuing forces. We had broken through the extreme outside defensive zone of the fortress, which was being reinforced measure for measure with men and equipment. The terrain was becoming more difficult. By and by, both regiments reached a line stretching behind a wide and deep ravine, a range of hills to the southeast, crowned by hills 269 and 287. From hill 449, on which the 3rd Company deployed a machine-gun platoon and two infantry squads, one had a broad view of the countryside. For the first time, the observer could see Sevastopol on the horizon, the prize objective of this struggle, in front of the gray mirror of the sea in the north, laying next to the Severnaya (Northern) Bay, and fading off into the east. There were no more than 16 kilometers to the outskirts of the city! But it was a difficult 16 kilometers, full of fire and iron! A network of combat trenches crisscrossed the hills and plains, partially covered by low shrubbery in their green-gray winter colors. There was a lot of traffic on the road from Kamary to Sevastopol: the battered Coastal Army was entering the city.

One still did not give up hope that the enemy would simply leave. The attack was renewed. Assault troops of the 122nd Infantry Regiment reached the high ground northeast of Kamary and disorganized the enemy columns by fire. Lieutenant Buff of the 4th Company received an adventuresome assignment and marched off in the night with 25 men. Three days later, the assault troop made a great detour to the east with cavalry in pursuit. It was hopeless. The enemy had thoroughly secured his withdrawal route to the north; every town, every hill was occupied. The attack on 8 November was a failure. It is true that the 2/122 succeeded in capturing two bunkers west of Shuli, however, the attack of the 1/122 foundered on hill 287. Also, hill 269 on the northern flank, which was taken by the 121st Infantry Regiment, had to be abandoned after a strong enemy counterattack. The 2/150 Artillery Regiment, which had supported the attack, suffered heavy losses from heavy gun fire from within the fortress. It wasn't as bad for the defenders, who occupied the few terrain points that were suitable for battalion positions. On 11/9 hill 269 still could not be taken, and this eliminated the prerequisite for an attack on hill 287. The Russians felt strong and attacked the positions of the 121st and 122nd. The attack was repulsed with the help of artillery.

11/10 - Heavy rain muddied the road, so the supply bogged down. Further attack had to be postponed. The continuation of the parallel pursuit was also delayed. Indeed, the Russian Coastal Army had plenty to be thankful for, since they had again won their self-reliance in the confines of their fortress and made the 72nd ID pay a high price for every hill and bush with a strong rear guard. The 10 kilometer gap between the two divisions slowly began to decrease. Security measures were taken to temporarily cope with the open flanks. The 50th ID committed its von Bernhardi Reconnaissance Detachment behind the left flank in Ai-Todor. They reconnoitered to the south and east and cleared out a nest of partisans. These malicious phenomenon of the war were also indigenous to the Crimea, but confined to the rugged Yaila Mountains. The Crimean Tartars did not participate in the partisan movement – the numerous stragglers of the Coastal Army formed their main contingents, and they were equipped by the fortress. The 50th ID took their time preparing for the next attack. The weather changed on 11/13, and a light frost stabilized the roads. The 3rd Battalion of the 122nd Infantry regiment, which had previously covered the flank, could now advanced to the front and was committed on the left flank near Uppa. The 72nd ID fought its way forward to the hills 3 kilometers south of Kamary.

11/14 - The thermometer fell to 12 degrees below zero. Our soldiers froze in their thin, worn out uniforms. Sickness took hold. The Russian deserters, which came in small numbers, were already wearing wool coats and fur caps. For some time now, on quiet nights, German deserters would tout the Bolshevik paradise by speaking over loudspeakers. But then why did the Mujiks desert? On the German side, counter propaganda was conducted by means of leaflets, which were taken into no-man's land at night by scout troops. On the morning of 11/14, a single Russian soldier came waving a leaflet – he obviously thought it to be a pass. It was a German warning sign with the words: "Achtung Minen!" (Danger Mine Field!). At this time, the fate of hill 269 was finally settled! The 121st Infantry Regiment advanced after a short bombardment. They ran into a Russian attack and had to return to their departure positions. The Russians were repulsed, and the attack by the 121st was renewed. It succeeded: the hill was taken during the early morning! The 121st dug in as well as the hard ground would allow. The new bulge in the front line extended the division's positions, the boundary was disrupted, and the 122nd Infantry Regiment had to block on the right. The occupied positions were precariously thin. (From: *The 50th Infantry Division. 1939-1945*. Augsburg 1965.)

• • •

The resistance of the Russian troops, which were supported by heavy naval units, increased from week to week. On the order of the 11th Army Commander, the army was again regrouped. The 73rd ID and 170th ID were moved up from Kerch, and they were later followed by the 24th ID and 132nd ID. The new, decisive attack to conquer Sevastopol was set for 28 November.

Since winter began with heavy rainfall, it made all unfortified roads impassable. Deployments and supply columns bogged down in the mud.

While the infantry divisions agonized through the Crimean mud to Sevastopol, the tanks of the 1st Panzer Army advanced through similar conditions along the coast of the Sea of Azov.

By mid November, both panzer corps were on the outskirts of Rostov. The XIV Panzer Corps crossed the Tuslov at the beginning of November and approached the harbor city from the north. On 9 November, the 14th Panzer Division and the SS Panzer Division "Wiking" established a bridgehead across the Kropkaya River. The experience of these times was recorded by an artilleryman:

• • •

Overnight we sank into mud, we could not move forward, and we also lost contact with the enemy. The vehicles were stuck fast, the wheeled guns were pulled out of the mud by our artillerymen with difficulty, and they were covered in mud up to the ammo boxes. A few days later, a cold wave struck overnight, and it chilled everything. With difficulty, we overcame this new inconvenience. We didn't move any faster than before – we crawled. This is the way it went, day in, day out. The front line was wherever the attack ended at dark. Often this was in an open field and in -20 degree weather. And here is where my story begins:

A pitch-dark night, chattering cold, open field. Suddenly there is a blazing fire of great size on the horizon. We are magically drawn to this location, and we sense its warmth – and not only us. From all directions streamed the frozen forms of friend and foe. I must elucidate: When we captured Taganrog, winter clothing from a Russian depot fell into our hands. Blue wool coats, felt boots, and fur caps with Soviet stars on them. These we substituted with the death's head (sometimes not). And so we looked essentially like Russians. The blazing fire was from three huge stacks of baled straw from a collective farm, which someone lit to warm themselves. We are standing around the fire, warming ourselves for half the night, glowing in the front, freezing in the rear, rotating at times. It was a macabre joke from some campfire story. For the rest of the night we crawled into the undisturbed straw bundles. Like bees in a hive, we bored adjacent holes in the bundles. Soon we noticed that there were more fur caps with Soviet stars around the fire. We knew these were genuine Russians. However, we were too weak and too tired to think about it. We had been together for a surprisingly long time. Then we slept together peacefully. On the next morning, we gathered up our sleeping comrades, several dozen, and moved off to the west – homeward.

Not a shot was fired, no hatred was displayed, no anger. The cold made everyone equal. War can also be so human, so peaceful."

• • •

The III Panzer Corps (General of Cavalry von Mackensen), with the 13th, 14th Panzer Divisions, the 60th Motorized Infantry Division, and the SS Panzer Division "Leibstandarte" had to assault Rostov frontally. On 17 November, the corps began the assault, and three days later, at 0600 hours in the morning, the SS Panzer Division "Leibstandarte" (SS Obergruppenfuehrer Dietrich) attacked across Sultan Saly and the Crimea to Rostov. At 1230 hours, the air field was captured and, an hour later, the battalions were engaged in street battles to the center of the city and, during the evening, the 3rd Company (Haupsturmfuehrer Springer) reached the railroad station. Fierce street battles developed throughout. A combatant wrote in his diary:

The city is in an uproar, numerous tracks of fleeing Russians, vehicles, horses, civilians, and a great confusion. All leading in the direction of the Don bridge. Russians on foot with guns are still posted in front of public buildings. The enemy doesn't realize that soon we will be at the bridge."

Then the great Don River bridge lay before the men of the SS:

"It is afternoon and the twilight is descending. We are working our way forward from the end of the bridge and firing at the fleeing Russian tracks. In the middle of all this, a railroad train bursts out of the city. It is full of Russians and equipment. We immediately open fire on the locomotive. It stops and the steam whistles out of all of the holes. This was the luck of war, the enemy's confusion could not have been greater. The men of the 3rd Company and the efficient men of the Fellhauer Engineer Group attacked across the 500 meter steel girder bridge. A thick bundle of fuse at the bridge's foundation led to explosives, and it was skillfully cut by the engineers. On the two large bridge pillars was a large amount of dynamite, but the engineers simply ripped the detonator from the explosives. There was still some fire coming from the south bank, but we surprisingly crossed to the southern bank intact and were able to surprise and disarm the bridge watch (about 30 men) by the evening meal."

The objective, Rostov, was taken – then the "Red Army" struck back! The gap between the 1st Panzer Army and the 17th Army lay open! The flanking corps of the 1st Panzer Army were under full attack, and in the 17th Army area the Russian tank attack surged against the thin front line:

• • •

On 11/17/1941, the deployment to the sovkhoz (state collective farm) began. In extremely cold weather, the 523rd Infantry Regiment and the 2/297 Artillery Regiment came for shelter, in order to keep up the constant enemy pursuit. Near the Grakovo railroad station, the Soviets had covered

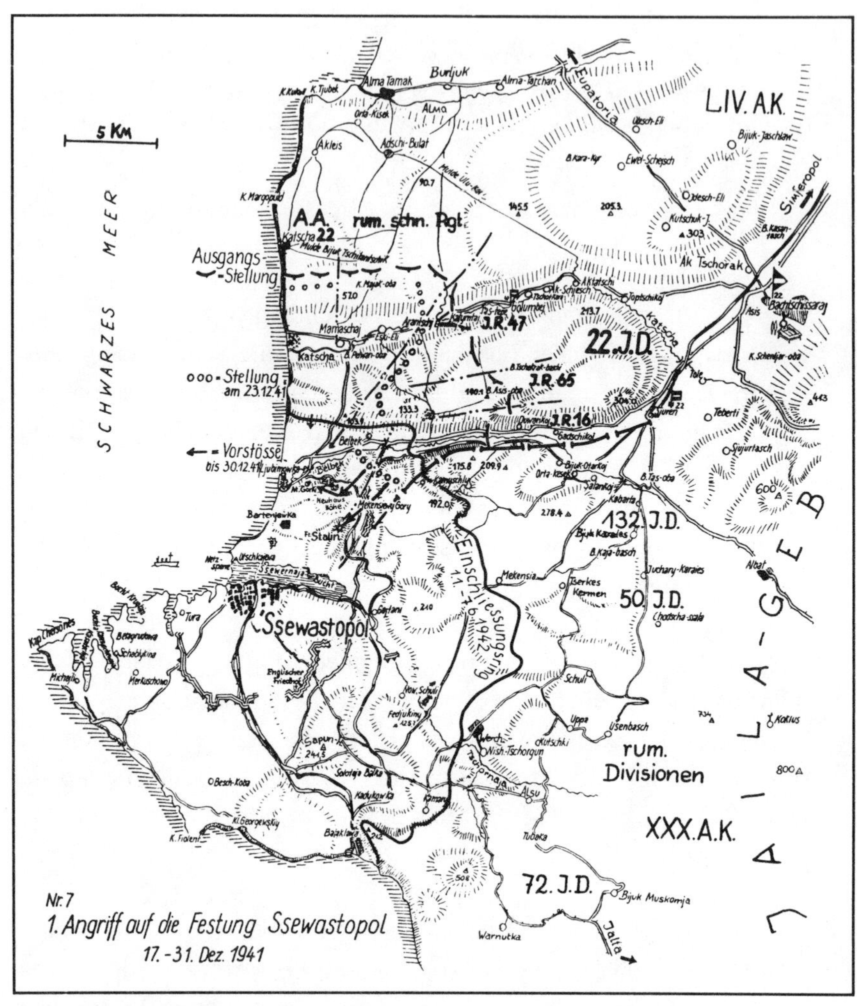

1st attack on the fortress of Sevastopol
17-31 December 1941

stored grain with benzine and set it afire. Although they employed strong artillery fire against us, by evening we reached the sovkhoz and set up the command post, under Major Dorschner.

Meanwhile, the Soviets had attacked our division's unprotected right flank and, by 1530 hours, had penetrated into the firing positions of our 6/297 Artillery Regiment near Novo Gnilitsa. Because our artillerymen were not given sufficient infantry support, they had to abandon their guns and withdraw to the Grakovo railroad station. As the pressure of the enemy on the southern flank increased, the 523rd Infantry Regiment also had to withdraw from the camp during the morning of 11/18/1941; the 300 Soviet prisoners, which were captured the day before, were taken through Grakovo to Chuguyev. On the same day, the firing positions of the 6th Battery were again occupied, however, soon after, strong Soviet elements again attacked, and our artillerymen, who had to defend themselves by firing directly into the attacking Soviets from a distance of 100 meters, had to finally withdraw to Grakovo for a second time, after destroying their field howitzers. A battalion command post was also established in the railroad station there. For two entire days and nights, Grakovo was subjected to heavy enemy artillery fire. As the Soviets attacked again on 11/20, the 523rd Infantry Regiment went into action, and in spite of the opposition of three Soviet divisions, attacked the camp on 11/22 and captured it. The only bridgehead of the German Wehrmacht east of the Donets had to be held, and it was, in spite of 142 Soviet attacks that were conducted against it until we advanced further in June 1942. (From: Beck, A.: *To Stalingrad* (297th ID) Ulm 1983.)

• • •

Both armies now modified their division dispositions where they most needed it – and it appeared that the Russians were becoming stronger week by week. The 17th Army advanced no further between Slavyansk and Belgorod, and established itself with the 9th, 68th, 76th, 97th, 125th, 257th, 295th, and 298th ID along the 80 meter wide Donets to defend in winter positions.

Additionally, the season saw an end to the combat in the Crimea, far to the rear of the Don-Donets positions.

By mid December, the German divisions – the 22nd, 132nd, 50th, and 72nd ID – had closed a solid ring around Sevastopol, but an attack would accomplish no more.

Then Christmas came to the Front. An SS man wrote to his parents back home:

"Sambak, near Taganrog, 12/23/1941

Tomorrow is Christmas Eve already! In earlier years, I would be filled with tension on this day. I had never thought that one day I would be with so many comrades in such a different large family, sharing their friendship in Russia, on this most German of all German holidays.

Will the Russians grant us a couple of quiet hours? – Your loved ones are at home: your Christmas table is also small and poor, we know, you are always in our thoughts. Tomorrow, when the Russians cover our town with all the tubes of their artillery, so that we have to crouch in gloomy cellar bunkers, then we will be with you in our thoughts and thank you for all the love and faith.

12/24/1941 Christmas Eve 2100 hours

"Finally, its here!" That was the wonderful phrase that released all the earlier tension. Then we would discover a world of wonder – in earlier years – and now? A German Christmas deep inside Russia 200 meters from the front line positions of the Soviets! Just a minute ago, Father Christmas came to us. We made him an honorary member of the division. At the exact time that Father Christmas would have appeared, a comrade turned up with our First Sergeant from the division command post and, just like Father Christmas, he carried a huge sack on his back. Now it was truly Christmas. Candles burned and shadows temporarily danced blackly on the painted white wall. German Christmas Eve in far away Russia, with greetings from home! The front line is quiet – we are also silent and at peace."

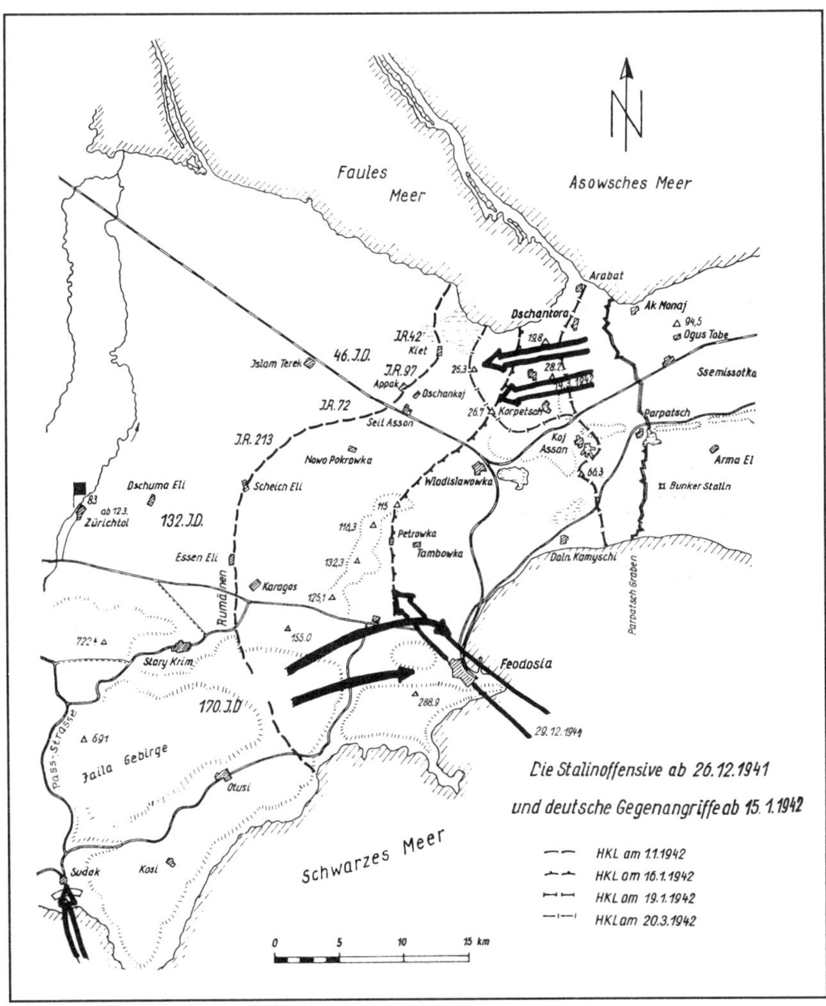

The Stalin Offensive of 12/26/1941
and the German Counterattack of 1/15/1942
Frontline on 1/1/1942
Frontline on 1/16/1942
Frontline on 1/19/1942
Frontline on 3/20/1942

During the night of the second day of Christmas, strong Russian forces surprisingly landed with tanks at two locations in the eastern Crimea. The 44th and 51st Soviet Armies landed with ten divisions. The 46th ID (Lieutenant General Himer), which was all alone here, could not defend against them.

• • •

The tragedy of the division began. After a short period of respite for Christmas, the Russians executed a surprise landing with tanks, during the night of 25 to 26 December, near Kerch-Bulganak and Chelochik/Myssir. With its weakened forces and by committing its reserves, the three regiments blocked the formation of a bridgehead, with difficulty, and slowly countered the attack. The prerequisite for a more thorough clearing was that no further landings follow, especially in the rear area. The battle for this bridgehead took place in -30 degree weather and an icy wind, on frozen ground without winter clothing.

While this battle was taking place, additional strong enemy forces landed 120 kilometers in the rear of the division near Feodosia, on 28/29 December, and threatened to cut them off. After that, the regiment commanders issued numerous, detailed assessments of the situation to the division, whose commander, General Count Sponeck, ordered the immediate break off of contact and retreat of all forces to the isthmus near Parpach-Koy Assan, north of Feodosia. This enormous march of over 120 kilometers was made in cold Russian winter weather and an icy snow storm, without winter clothing, and it will never be forgotten. (From: Bentheim, A.: *The Route of the 46th Infantry Division*, Bayreuth 1952.)

The resistance of the division collapsed. All heavy weapons had to be blown or they would have been lost. Lieutenant General Count von Sponeck ordered the retreat to the Isthmus of Parpach. Directly west of Feodosia, security battalions were able to construct a temporary defensive line, which held up the Russians.

The Kerch Peninsula was lost!

2

1942

CRIMEA
(5 March - 1 July 1942)

German mobility fell victim to the unexpectedly strong, persistent, and cold winter of 1941-42. The Eastern Army was not equipped for a war in such ice and cold. Winter clothing was completely lacking during the first two months, and the bolts of the guns and the engines of the vehicles froze. On the other hand, the "Red Army" had the advantage. In the past weeks and months, the Russian High Command had brought forward troops from Siberia that were winter mobile, and were now assaulting the thin German lines with vehemence, fanaticism, and indifference to death, and were achieving particularly deep penetrations in the front lines of Army Groups Center and North, where, during January 1942, the lines bent and broke.

Army Group South, whose Commander, Field Marshal von Rundstedt, was relieved of his command on 1 December 1941, on the grounds of disagreeing with Hitler, withstood the winter weeks better than the other two army groups. Of course, the divisions averaged a shortage of about 2,000 men each. The 1st Panzer Army had a total shortage of about 20,000 men, 200 tanks, and 100 guns.

Field Marshal von Reichenau, the new Commander of Army Group South, was able to counter the arrogant plans of Hitler and the OKH with the ideas of his commanders, but was not able to carry them out in the few short weeks of his tenure. The Field Marshal died of a heart attack on 17

January 1942 while flying to Germany. The army group received its third commander in six weeks. It was Field Marshal von Bock, who had formerly led Army Group Center.

He began his new assignment as the 11th Army of General of Infantry von Manstein in Crimea prepared to attack the Soviets that landed on the Kerch Peninsula and throw them back.

In January, the "Red Army" had four armies in the Crimea. The 44th, 47th, and 51st Soviet Armies, with 17 divisions, were located on the narrow peninsula between the Azov and Black Seas. The "Coastal Army", transferred from Odessa, defended the fortress of Sevastopol with the active support of the "Black Sea Fleet."

General von Manstein (he was promoted to this rank on 3/7/1942) received an order from the OKH to clear up the situation in the Crimea in the course of executing the planned summer offensive.

Therefore, the 11th Army Commander decided, first of all, to capture the Kerch Peninsula. This was a sore point for the 11th Army, because the Soviet troops could attack from there to the west at any time. Furthermore, with the expulsion of the Soviet armies from the Crimea, Army Group South's flank would be free to advance into the Caucasus, as Hitler had ordered.

General von Manstein prepared the XXX Army Corps, commanded by Lieutenant General Fretter-Pico since December. For the operation on the southern flank of the Crimea, the corps would have at its disposal the 28th Rifle Division, 50th, 132nd and 170th ID, as well as the 22nd Panzer Division. This division was assembled in France in September 1941 and was equipped with captured tanks.

The corps received its instructions: in the first phase, to advance along the southern coast of Crimea and then swing to the north, in order to fix the Russian forces in the rear, while a mixed brigade, under the command of Colonel von Groddeck, protected the eastern flank.

The XLII Army Corps (General of Infantry Mattenklott) had to cover the northern portion of the peninsula, with the battered 46th ID, the newly arrived 4th Mountain Division, and the VII Rumanian Army Corps (two infantry divisions), and tie up the Soviet troops with a frontal attack.

"Operation Trappenjagd" began in the early morning of 8 May 1942. After a short artillery preparation and attacks by fighter-bombers and stukas of the VIII Air Corps, the divisions of the XXX Army Corps began the attack. In the early morning hours, assault engineers with motor-assault boats, in which a mixed battalion (the 5/436 Infantry regiment) was embarked, attacked east from Dalniy Kamyshi into the rear of the Russian line. In this manner, they came upon the confused left flank of the 44th Soviet Army.

In the first assault on the first day of the battle, the regiments of the 28th Rifle Division (Lieutenant General Sinnhuber) and the 132nd ID (Major General Lindemann) were able to penetrate the enemy positions south of the Tartar Hills, but the Russians were pushed back by the bold attack.

On the next morning, the 22nd Panzer Division (Major General von Apell) attacked through a gap in the front line. This practically destroyed the enemy resistance south of the Parpach belt. The 44th Soviet Army (Lieutenant General Chernyak) collapsed south of the city of Arma Eli. Colonel von Groddeck's brigade immediately established flank protection to the east and even gained a kilometer of enemy territory.

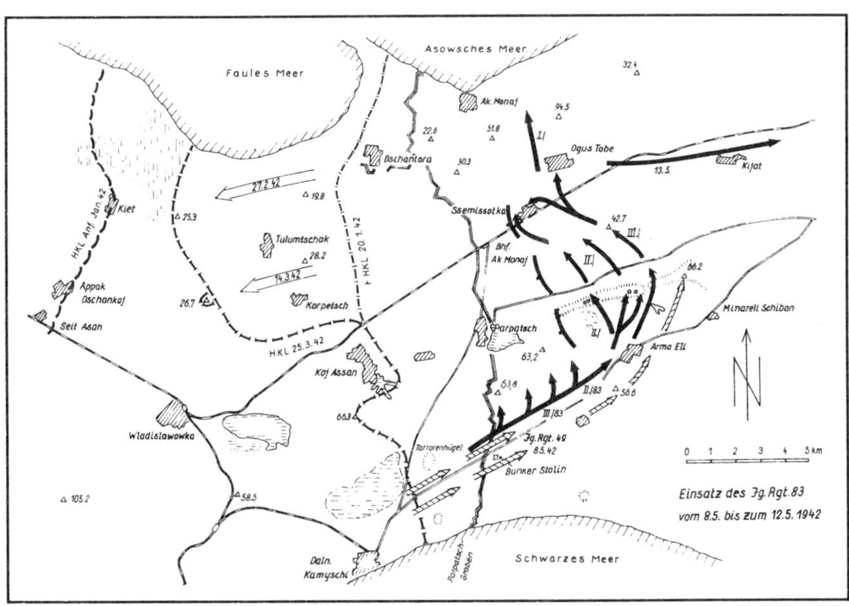

Commitment of the 83rd Rifle regiment from 5/8 to 5/12/1942

The Commander Of the Russian Army Group "Crimean Front" (Lieutenant General Koslov) relieved the 47th Army (Major General Kolganov), which had been located furthest to the north and had just arrived in the Peninsula a few weeks ago, transferring it to the south.

On 9 May, heavy rains came and hindered further attacks. The 22nd Panzer Division was able to mobilize its rear area services, so that their detachments and battalions could be resupplied with ammunition.

As the rain slackened and the first stukas of General Baron von Richthofen attacked the Russian positions, the divisions of the XXX Army Corps advanced further. The 22nd Panzer Division, followed by the 28th Rifle Division, reached the Sea of Azov near Kap Tarchan on the second day and, therefore, stood in the rear of the 47th and 51st Soviet Armies!

This was the hour of the XLII Army Corps, which, with the German and Rumanian divisions, immediately advanced against enemy positions that were still oriented to the west.

On the evening of 12 May, General of Infantry Mattenklot issued the following order:

> 1. Badly battered enemy forces are in retreat, and some units are in downright flight in the direction of Kerch. In front of the XLII Army Corps the enemy still holds, as of this afternoon, the Alibay sector with a rear guard, weak artillery, and a few tanks. The rest of the enemy and supply trains are fleeing to the coast of the Sea of Azov.
>
> 2. On 13 May, the army will continue to pursue on the entire Front. We will overtake the enemy on the road to Kerch with mobile forces before he reaches the harbor. The trailing infantry must, through constant pressure, make it impossible for the enemy to establish himself in positions in Sultanovka and in the bridgehead west of Kerch. Sweat saves blood! Ignore open flanks.
>
> 3. At 0500 hours on 13 May, the XLII Army Corps begins the pursuit, with the 28th Rifle Division on the right and the 46th ID on the left. The first objective is to reach the Sultanovka positions; for the infantry lead elements, the high ground east of there.

4. The 28th Light Division is responsible for securing the preparation for the pursuit.

5. The 197th Assault Gun Battalion (minus the 2nd Battery) will support the 28th Light Division from 1900 hours on 12 May.

6. The corps command post is scheduled to be in Ogus-Tobe on 13 May, and officers of the 28th Light Division and the 46th ID will go there at 1000 hours to receive their orders.

The Russian defensive front line collapsed like a house of cards. The Russian soldiers withdrawing and fleeing to the east were manhandled by the fighters and fighter-bombers of the VIII Air Corps. Russian troops surrendered in battalion strength without further resistance.

Four days later, the battle for Kerch was practically over. The 213th Infantry Regiment of the 170th ID, in one bold assault, gained over 80 kilometers to the eastern edge of Kerch on the 16th of May. The bulk of the

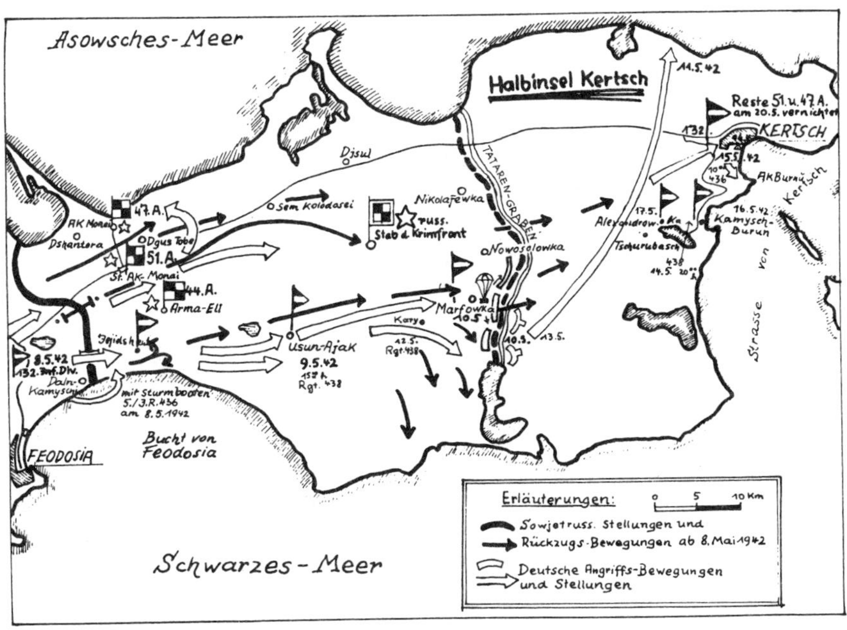

division (Major General Sander) followed close behind and raised the Reich's battle flag over Kerch that evening.

The completely separated and destroyed Russian units tried to reach the east coast between the cottages of Voikov and the 60 meter high hills of Mayakberg, where they hoped to be rescued by ship. However, they would not reach the coast. On 17 and 18 May, German soldiers reached the eastern tip of the Kerch Peninsula. The rest of the Soviet armies could no longer offer any resistance.

169,198 prisoners were left in German hands. In this battle, the "Red Army" lost 284 tanks and 1,397 guns.

The 11th Army's rear area was now cleared and, on 18 May, they regrouped to begin the conquest of Sevastopol. Only the XLII Army Corps (General of Infantry Mattenklott), with the 46th ID (Major General Haccius) and the 4th Mountain Division (Major General Eglseer) and the VII Rumanian Corps (with two divisions) were left in the Kerch Peninsula – all other units were assembled and transferred to the west to Sevastopol.

Since the start of the siege the preceding year, the "Red Army" had considerably built up the fortress, although the rugged terrain alone was

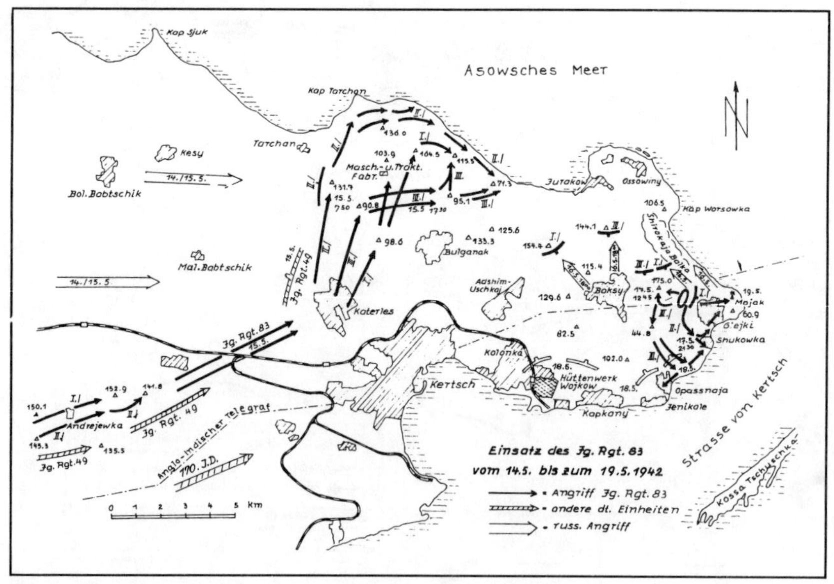

Commitment of the 83rd Rifle regiment from 5/8 to 5/12/1942

equivalent to a ring of forts. Three strong defensive belts surrounded the fortress, and of these, the outermost extended from Balaklava in the south to Belbek in the north.

These defensive belts were filled with anti-tank batteries, guns, and underground shelters, with field fortifications of all types, and among all this, thick mine fields were laid. North of the Severnaya Bay the six great fortification works were located: "Volga", "Siberian", "Lenin", "Stalin", "Molotov", and "Maxim Gorkiy."

In past weeks, the commander of Army Group South provided the 11th Army with those heavy weapons that were available to the eastern German armies. 80 heavy batteries, 65 light batteries of army artillery, 24 mortar batteries, and others were sent to the Crimea on often time-consuming railroad transport. The artillery formations of the 11th Army were subordinate to the 306th Senior Artillery Commander (Harko), Lieutenant General Zuckertort.

A graphic report concerning the massing of this artillery is provided by the history of an infantry division that was committed in front of Sevastopol.

• • •

"The rocket launchers play an important role in the concentration of artillery fire. The 1st Heavy Launcher Regiment, the 70th Launcher Regiment, as well as both the 1st and 4th Launcher Battalions, are concentrated in the special staff of Colonel Niemann in front of the fortress.

21 batteries fire with 576 tubes, the batteries of the 1st Heavy Launcher regiment are especially effective against the fortifications, with their 28 cm and 32 cm high-explosive and incendiary shells, respectively. During each fire salvo, 324 shells leave the tubes of this regiment every second for the targeted sector of the enemy's field fortifications. The effect on the morale of this salvo fire is just as great as the destructive power. When a single battery with six launchers fires 26 huge projectiles into the enemy positions, with their nerve-wracking howls, and the effect is appalling. The fragmentation strength of an individual projectile is not as great as an artillery shell. However, the pressure of the blast of one such fire strike in a narrow area makes the blood vessels burst. Soldiers that are not in the im-

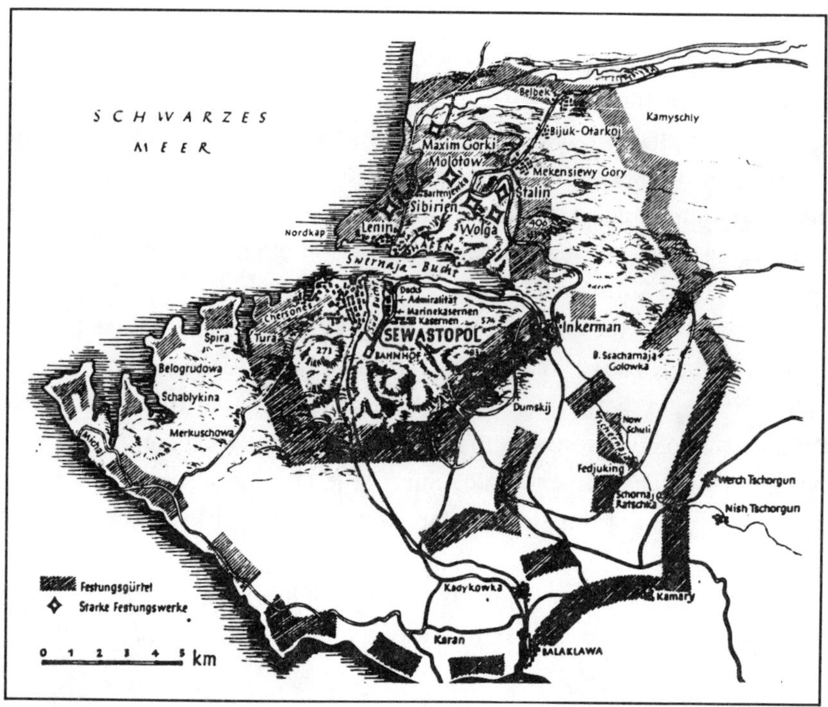

mediate neighborhood of the strike are demoralized by the deafening din of the paralyzing blast of the detonation. Terror and fear lead to panic. Only the stuka attack has a similar effect on the otherwise insensitive Russians. While the Russians have nicknamed our rocket launchers the "Lowing Cow", we call the Russian rocket launchers "Stalin's Organ."

Three special giants are deployed before Sevastopol: the "Gamma Mortar", the "Karl" and "Thor" mortars, and the railroad gun "Dora." All three are wonders of conventional artillery and specially constructed for combating fortifications. The Gamma Mortar is the offspring of the "Big Bertha" from the First World War. The shells are 42.7 caliber, weigh 923 kilograms, and can be fired at targets 14 kilometers away. The length of the barrel is 6.72 meters. 235 artillerymen are needed to service these unusual giants.

However, "Gamma" is a pygmy in comparison to the 61.5 cm mortars "Karl" and "Thor." These are special army weapons used against concrete fortifications. The heavy 2,200 kilogram shells are shot out of a monster that has no similarities with a conventional mortar. The stumpy, 5 meter long barrel and the powerful mechanism of the chassis resemble a factory with an unearthly, stumpy chimney.

However, "Karl" is not the ultimate in artillery. This stands in the "Palace of the Gardens", which is the ancient residence of the Tartar Khans, and is called "Dora." The infantrymen also call it "Heavy Gustav."

This is the heaviest canon of the last war, with a caliber of 80 cm. 60 railroad cars are needed to transport the parts of this monster. Out of a 32.5 meter long barrel, 4,800 kilogram and nearly 5 ton high-explosive shells are fired 47 kilometers, and the even heavier anti-armor shells of 7,000 kilograms are fired by "Dora" to distances of 38 kilometers. Together the projectile and cartridge are 7.8 meters long. Set upright, it is approximately the height of a two story house. "Dora" can fire three times in an hour. The giant gun stands on two double tracks. Two anti-aircraft battalions are assigned to protect its commitment. The servicing, firing, and maintenance of this monster requires over 4,000 men. A major general, a colonel, and 1,500 men control its firing and servicing. (From: Bidermann, G. H.: *Krim - Kurland.* (132nd ID) Hannover 1964.)

• • •

The 11th Army deployed the following forces for the planned attack at the beginning of June:

In the north:

LIV Army Corps (General of Cavalry Hansen)
with 22nd ID (major General Wolff), 24th ID
(Lieutenant General von Tettau), 50th ID
(Major General Schmidt) and 132nd ID
(Major General Lindermann);

In the south:

XXX Army Corps (Lieutenant General Fretter-Pico) with 28th Rifle Division (Lieutenant General Sinnhuber), 72nd ID (Lieutenant General Mueller-Gebhard) and 170th ID (Major General Sander).

The Rumanian Mountain Corps, with its divisions, deployed on the center of the front line to fix the Russian troops here and support the attacking German divisions in the eventuality of a threat to their flanks.

At the beginning of the month of June, heavy German batteries of all calibers fired at the fortifications and the various enemy defensive positions. Combat and reconnaissance aircraft of Air Fleet 4 observed the fire and attacked railroad and harbor installations.

The troops received the first attack order:

•••

132nd Inf. Division Div. Command Post, 5 June 1942
Operations 1500 hours
Nr. 750/42

Division Order
For the Attack on Sevastopol

1). The enemy is stubbornly defending the fortress on Stalin's order. Therefore, it must be assumed that the units committed in the forward-most line will be thinly deployed to allow for sufficient forces in the depth of the fortifications.

The army will begin the attack on D-Day against the fortress in the north and south, containing the enemy in the Mekensia-Verch -Chergun sector.

LIV Army Corps attacks with its main effort by the 22nd ID on Severnaya Bay and strives for favorable conditions to establish, as early as possible, a bridgehead across the eastern part of the bay and the mouth of the Chernaya.

At 0400 hours, the 22nd ID attacks to occupy the high ground west of the Kamyshli Ravine precipice across the railroad embankment opposite the anti-tank trenches to advance with a strong spearhead on either side of the Mekensievy-Gory railroad station to capture Fort Stalin.

2). The 132nd ID crosses the Belbek just east of the town of Belbek with the attack group (the reinforced 438th and 436th Infantry Regiments) and reaches the "Haccius-Ridge"-"Oelberg" (1st attack objective). The enemy is to be fixed between the coast and the right flank of the attack. Attack from the bridgehead south of Belbek across "Neuhaushoehe" (2nd attack objective) to capture Fort Molotov (3rd attack objective), to achieve an advance along the northern shore of the Severnaya Bay to the south and southwest of Bartenevka.

The enemy fortified positions, which lie on the flank of this attack, are to be screened by deep echelonment and then overcome from the flanks and rear by special operations. The deeper the gains on the ground are on the first day of the attack, the better.

3). The lead elements attack out of their assembly areas at 0430 hours:

On the right: the reinforced 437th Infantry Regiment, with the limited objective of the edge of the field fortifications.

In the center: the reinforced 438th Infantry regiment, in the direction of "Haccius-Ridge"-"Oelberg."

On the left: the reinforced 436th Infantry regiment.

The 438th Infantry Regiment executes its order at 0600 hours on 6 June (notified by telephone beforehand).

See the attached map for the boundary lines.

Missions:

a) The reinforced 437th Infantry Regiment attacks with a strong spearhead onto the edges of the field fortifications to destroy the enemy units nestled here and eliminate their flanking possibilities from here into the Belbek Valley. For this purpose, the enemy air defense is suppressed with heavy weapons and, if need be, they are captured by assault troops. The strength and behavior of the enemy in the Belbek Valley and the hills south of here is kept under surveillance by active combat reconnaissance. Maintain contact with the right flank of the 438th Infantry Regiment. When the enemy's resistance diminishes, the regiment can advance within its boundaries across the Belbek in the direction of Shishkova.

b) The reinforced 438th and 436th Infantry Regiments break through the enemy units on the northern slope of the Belbek Valley, at 0430 hours, after an artillery preparation, and cross the valley and stream under the cover of accompanying artillery fire, which will follow in leap-frog fashion, in order to utilize the effect of massed fires and air strikes on the attack targets before the enemy can counter the effects of the fire support.

After reaching the 1st attack objective, a concentrated spearhead (at least one reinforced company) is to attack toward the 22nd ID. Areas of strong resistance are to be by-passed and taken from the rear. Such defenses as "Bastion", Maxim Gorkiy", and "Shishkova Battery", which lie on the flank, are to be screened by rear area units. Their capture and, therefore, the fall of the enemy bridgehead north of Lyubinovka, will be arranged by special operations of the division.

Ignore neighboring units and advance as quickly as possible to Severnaya Bay to force the collapse of the northern part of the fortress.

• • •

German destruction fires were increased on the morning of 7 June to a veritable hurricane.

The objective of the heavy German fire has already been indicated. The 80 cm canon, "Dora", (the heaviest gun in the world) fired on the "Stalin" and "Molotov" forts. The 60 cm mortar, "Karl", sent his fiery greetings to fort "Maxim Gorkiy", while the 42 cm mortar, "Gamma", sent greetings to "Oelberg" and the railroad embankment. The 42 cm howitzer battery placed the Mekensievy-Gory railroad station under fire. The 35.5 cm mortar battery battered the "Forest House" positions, and so on. On the first day of the battle, these heavy guns fired 681 shells.

The sun shone fiery red in the on the eastern horizon and announced the coming of a hot summer day. Then the LIV Army Corps began to attack the fortress from the north. The 132nd ID assaulted it on the right flank and fought its way forward to the fort "Maxim Gorkiy." To the left was the boundary with the 22nd ID. The 50th and 24th ID attacked across the Kamyshly Ravine, advancing on the defenses from the northeast.

An eyewitness describes the first day of battle:

> "This is the moment of the attack, and in a raging tempo it races down the slope, through the valley, and on to the other side, past mine fields, through trip-wires and wire entanglements that were already cut by the engineers. Companies, platoons, and groups one after the other moved forward in the blue-gray powder smoke and thick dust. A magnificent picture of the German spirit of the attack.
>
> Just to the left of the hill is the first attack objective. The going is slow through the thick bushes. There is no chance for the groups and platoons to maintain contact here. The Bolsheviks hide in their numberless holes, and they let us pass and then fall on us from the rear. Several times small and large infantry units are completely cut off. But the connection is always re-established, and then it isn't so good for the sealed off Soviets.
>
> The work of the artillery and stukas is now critical. More and more, the signal pistols guide the fires, shifting them forward or to the rear, and air signals had to be displayed to show combat aircraft and stukas the way.
>
> An enemy machine-gun nest suddenly appears in a small depression. Due to our fire, three men come out of it with their hands up. As we approach slowly, two others, who are still in the shelter, fire on us with the machine-gun. Another takes his life. As we pass, another jumps up and fires at us from the rear. This is the Bolshevik method of combat. On the ground there is mine after mine. Next to me a company commander is flung into the air, he falls back, and almost lands, uninjured, on his feet. However, not everyone has such luck."

• • •

The soldiers of the Russian Coastal Army – these were men of the "Red Army" and the nearby fleet, NKVD units and Komsomol members (Soviet youth organization) – held the strong points literally to "the last man." Even those strong points that were surrounded and out-flanked did not give up. Tenacity, doggedness, and cunning were the order of the day. Officers and commissars blew themselves up with their last hand grenades.

The German commanders recognized the strength of the enemy's resistance and regrouped their units during the night. The 24th ID, which was on the left flank, was little by little transferred to the right. The Rumanian regiments were put in place of the Saxons.

On 10 June, the XXX Army Corps attacked into the ravine, thereby opening the attack against the fortress from the south. On this first day, the 72nd ID succeeded in breaking through the Russian defensive positions and creating a gap. Therefore, the 1st Rumanian Mountain Division, which was located to the right of this, attacked into the gap.

In the next two days, the divisions in the north fought their way, step by step, through the mine and wire obstacles of the enemy positions; and, on 12 June, the 22nd ID stood where they had to suspend their advance on Sevastopol the previous winter, due to the outbreak of the cold weather.

• • •

The most difficult mission was that of the 16th Infantry Regiment, which proudly maintains that no one had one more difficult in this war: the capture of "Stalin." The 1/16, reinforced with Heyer's engineer platoon, was also committed. The first attack on 9 June, from the west, foundered on the northwest hills as it had during the winter. Then, all of the units of the 2nd Battalion were committed from the northeast. The attack began at 0300 hours on the 13th. The "Stalin" fort was fired on by all calibers of heavy and the heaviest artillery (they created shell craters up to 5 meters deep!). The "Andreev Flank" was occupied only by Communist Party members, the most tenacious enemy we had ever experienced. A bunker was fired at with an anti-tank gun and a direct hit into the porthole killed 30, but the remaining Russians still defended! Finally, at 1500 hours, the Russians came out of the ruins.

The friendly officers had all fallen (Captain Schrader). Lieutenant Zwiebler from the command reserve took charge of the units of the 1st and 3rd Battalions. A severely wounded soldier, with his arm in a splint and his head bandaged, pointed out: "That is not so bad – we have the "Stalin" fort!" That was the spirit of the madness, the desire to completely achieve the objective.

The sun burned mercilessly on the steel helmets. Corpses stank on the filthy battlefield. An unbelievable amount of flies spoiled the rations.

While the division operations officer, Colonel Langmann, held our tactical fate in his hands, General Wolff spent most of his time with his infantrymen, urging them on to their highest efforts. After that, the 24th ID advanced on the right, and they went further on the 17th of June. The attack began on the entire northern front at 0230 hours without an artillery preparation. By 0310 hours, the 65th Infantry Regiment captured the "Siberian" fort; the 16th Infantry Regiment, in the course of the morning, captured "Volga", as well as the right neighboring "G. P. U." units. On 18 June, the 65th Infantry Regiment captured "Goldberg" and became the first regiment to reach the Severnaya Bay on the 19th.

On 18 June, the Russians launched a strong counterattack against the 47th Infantry Regiment, which had prepared to attack the tunnel fortifications. A Russian brigade, which had arrived by sea a few days before yelling "Hurrah", assaulted the regiment, which consisted of one battalion under Captain Onnen, with anti-tank guns, infantry guns, engineers, a cavalry platoon, 17 officers, 50 non-commissioned officers, and 372 men.

Under cover of the morning mist, they succeeded in smashing the counterattack by artillery barrage fire, capturing 800 prisoners of the counterattacking force and re-gaining their old positions – in some places, they even surpassed them. Since this battle further weakened the 47th Regiment, the division commander decided to reorganize: on the 19th, the 47th and 65th Infantry Regiments switched combat lanes. The 65th Infantry Regiment (Senior Lieutenant Jabelmann) took over the enemy's tunnel positions and reached the dominant high bank, while the 47th Infantry Regiment was able to reconstitute on the right flank on the Severnaya Bay.

Particularly difficult was the mopping up of the northern shore of Severnaya Bay, where the enemy was entrenched in casements. The entrances to these multi-storied ammunition casements were protected from above by a 2 meter thick concrete wall, and they could not be approached from the sides. As the engineers advanced against the first of these concrete fortifications with explosives, they blew themselves, as well as all of the women and children that were crammed into the casement, into the air. A genuine landslide covered all, even the engineers. After urging those in the casement to surrender, none emerged. Finally, a lieutenant and his assault guns succeeded: 800 meters from the enemy on the other shore of the Severnaya Bay, they fired broadside onto the dock next to the casement and through the portholes of the casement, though both themselves and their assault guns were in danger of being buried by a landslide. This method was finally successful with four of the casements. After the commissars ended their own lives, a miserable, careworn, and scared civilian and a morose soldier emerged. Similar scenes were played out in the battle for the tunnels north of Severnaya Bay and later in the "Horseshoe." In one bunker, 2 kilometers northwest of "Stalin", which had held out for two days behind German lines, the crew had to be killed one at a time. (From: Metzsch, F. A. *The History of the 22nd Infantry Division*. Kiel 1952.)

• • •

The 11th Army Commander learned from previous mistakes in his struggle to capture the world's strongest fortress and did not attack along a single axis. Almost every day, they organized a concentrated attack on some position of the Front in the north. In the early morning hours, the stukas attacked known enemy positions, which was then combined with the fire of heavy army artillery battalions before the engineers and infantrymen jumped out of their trenches to advance against the Russian strong points.

• • •

On 13 June, the staff of the Rumanian 4th Mountain Division arrived and, at 1200 hours on 15 June, after relieving the 102nd, took over responsibility of the 24th ID sector, and the 24th ID was now placed between the right flank division (the 132nd) and the 22nd ID.

During the night of 15 June, a battalion of the 31st Infantry regiment was committed in the new sector. On 16 June, the regrouping of the division, including the artillery, was completed, and the responsibilities in the new attack lane were assumed. On this day, the artillery preparation for the attack against Severnaya Bay began. It was scheduled for the 17th of June. The 32nd Infantry regiment supported the 50th ID. The initial attack objective of the 24th ID was the old fortifications of forts "Molotov", "GPU", and "Cheka." Since the attack went cross country to the left across the "Gabelberg", it seemed appropriate to place the main emphasis there. This assessment was confirmed through the course of the combat. The 102nd Infantry Regiment was deployed on the right, while the 31st Infantry Regiment was on the left. The regiments advanced echeloned narrow and deep, providing for the reserves to follow the left regiment. In the morning of 17 June, the forward-most battalions suddenly began to attack. At the start, the 102nd Infantry Regiment made more headway, reaching the forward slope opposite "Molotov." The 31st fell into hard combat on the "Gabelberg", again pushing the enemy out of his well constructed positions, pursuing him, and occupying "GPU." Now the division ordered that the attack against "Molotov" be conducted on the left regiment's lane to give the 102nd Regiment some room. The 2/31 swung to the west and captured "Molotov." During the night, "Cheka" was also taken after a difficult fight.

In the meantime, the right neighboring 132nd ID assaulted the armored battery, "Maxim Gorkiy", and advanced to the west toward the sea. By dark, the lead elements of the 24th ID were still on a line northeast of Bartenevka – east of the cemetery, advancing on the forward slopes of the Severnaya Bay. On this day, the 32nd Infantry regiment took the "Old Fort" after a difficult fight, and had, therefore, advanced an equal distance.

The following day, an attack was scheduled for the southern direction, which had to take into account the flanking of "North Fort." The fort was also attacked.

The battle that developed in the residential, industrial, and shipyard areas was unpredictable, because the civilian population also participated in the fight.

A breakthrough into the north fort was achieved on the right flank as the artillery was brought to bear. On the left flank "Kurvenberg" was reached,

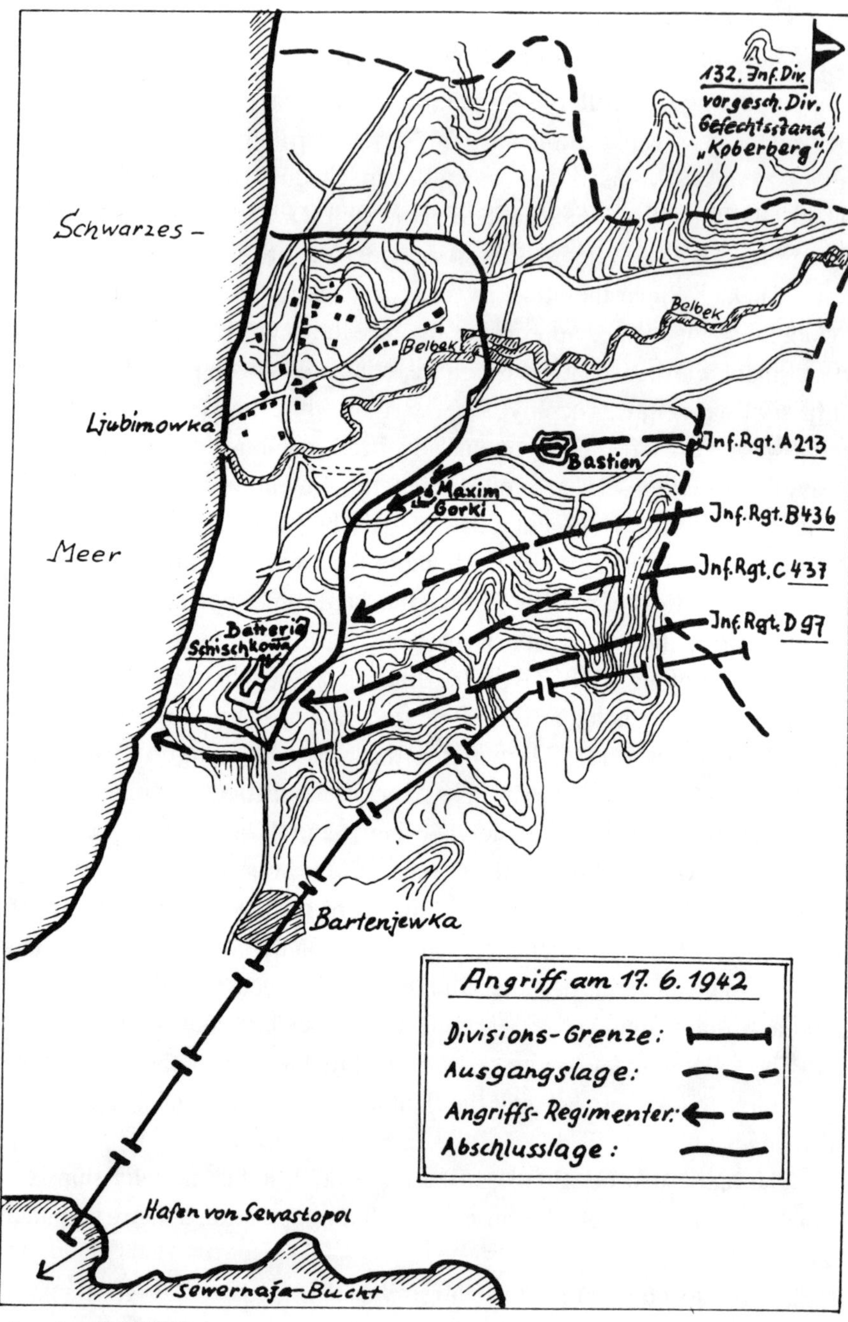

Attack on 6/17/1942

which lay directly over the water of the Bay. (Tettau, H. von and Versock, K.: *History of the 24th Infantry Division.* Stolberg 1956.)

• • •

As in the 24th ID sector, the battle was also played out by the 132nd ID, which advanced against the "Maxim Gorkiy" fortifications.

In spite of a day long bombardment by heavy caliber weapons, the armored battery, "Maxim Gorkiy", still persisted. One of the four 30.5 cm barreled guns that was still operational fired its fatal, gigantic shells at a distance of under one kilometer, with an unprecedented flat trajectory, into the attacking infantry. The installation of this battery on the dominant high ground permitted its fire from the rotating armored domes of the most modern construction to be effective in all directions. It was obvious to the eye and ear that the firing of the gigantic shells rose well over the roar of the battle.

With the capture of the "Bastion" and the no less important high ground south of it, the initial division attack objective on the entire front was achieved, as planned, by 0900 hours. The formation's new order required a break to achieve the objective of the day ("Maxim Gorkiy"-Fort Shishkova-when possible, attack to the sea). For the re-initiation of the attack, the division arranged for a stuka attack on "Maxim Gorkiy." The last bomb fell on it at 1300 hours, and then the infantry began their attack with the assault engineers under the protection of strong artillery fire. At 1230 hours, the first combat group crossed the battlefield. Without interrupting the attack, our stukas hit "Maxim Gorkiy", and the turrets were covered in smoke and dust. However, the Russians, for whom the loss of the "Bastion" already posed a dangerous threat to their entire northern front line had, in the meantime, scheduled a strong counterattack, so that the attack of the right flank regiment, which was directly opposite "Maxim Gorkiy", could not succeed.

On the other hand, the center and left flank of the division gained ground to the west. Again we experienced the 30.5 cm gun from "Maxim Gorkiy", which was firing into our infantry at close range to the southeast. Here only the smoke screen arranged by the division could help.

In the meantime, the division again ordered an attack on "Maxim Gorkiy" which, after coordinating with the air corps, began at 1530 hours. As the "last bomb" of the second large stuka attack fell, the infantry and engineers worked their way forward under the protection of massive artillery fire from all calibers. Again we witnessed the spectacle of a monstrous, almost three-quarter hour stuka attack on the rocky hill. Smoke and dust towered over the site and gradually thickened into an enormous cloud, which slowly withdrew and became the most conspicuous feature on the battlefield.

These birds of prey flew over the battlefield to the "Maxim Gorkiy" and wiped the mountain clean of enemy resistance. Whatever survived this mass bombing attack was then taken care of by our exquisitely laid artillery fire. Thus, the engineers and infantrymen quickly gained ground after 1530 hours. Enthusiastically we made headway. After the artillery put down a smoke screen, "Maxim Gorkiy" fired no more. Without any resistance worth mentioning, our assaulting infantrymen and engineers were able to overcome the last 100 meters in front of the gun tower. At 1640 hours, the lead elements of the attackers surrounded the armored dome of the fortification, whose 30.5 cm gun had caused so much mischief and trouble since the battle for Sevastopol began in November 1941.

The armored battery, "Maxim Gorkiy", which the Soviets had designated the 30th Battery, was constructed in the year 1934, and was, indeed, two stories deep in the rocky ground. Both gun turrets (each 30.5 cm) were 100 meters long and 30 meters wide and had a concrete infrastructure. The thickness of the walls was 2 to 3 meters, while the thickness of the roof was 3-4 meters. The armored gun turrets had walls 30 cm thick, with a roof of 20 cm thickness. The weight of one barrel was 50 tons, and its firing range was 44 kilometers. (From: Bidermann, G. H.: *Krim - Kurland.* (132nd ID) Hannover 1964.)

• • •

Light and heavy tanks of a forward detachment of a panzer division have broken through initial enemy defenses; now the infantry companies advance into the border area.

The regiments of von Kleist's panzer group advance on infantry positions further to the east.

After a stuka attack, Russian positions in and around Luzk are destroyed, and the city fell into German hands after a brief battle.

Lemberg burning. The photograph was taken on 5 July 1941 as the clouds of smoke were still rising.

Field Marshal von Rundstedt, commander of Army Group South. The talented commander was relieved on 12/1/1941 and went to France as Wehrmacht commander in chief.

Units of the XXX Army Corps crossing the Dnestr.

German infantry and panzer troops before Kiev.

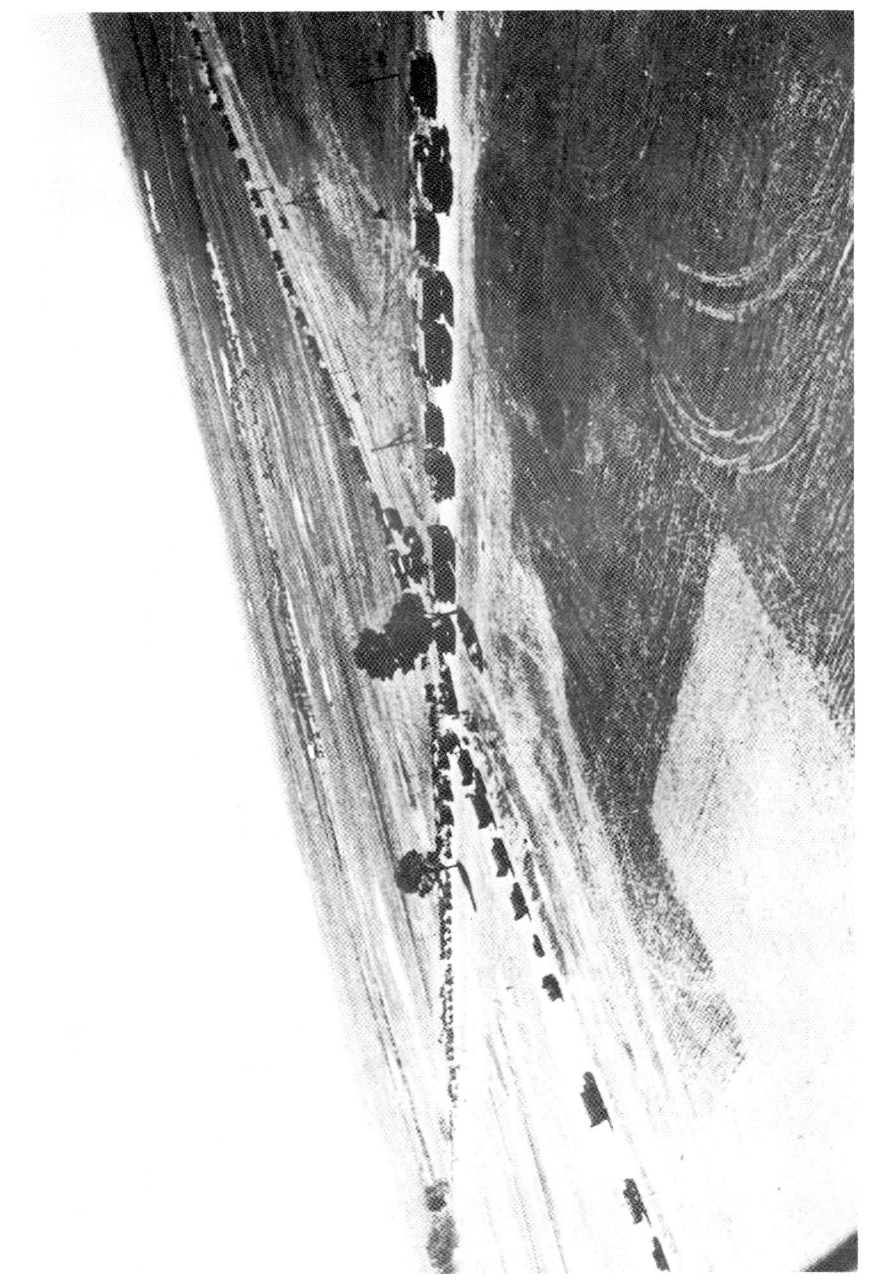

Meanwhile, the direct advance of Panzer Group 1 and the 17th Army crossed several times on their march routes. At the beginning of August, the hot, dry weather arrived.

On 15 August 1941, lead infantry elements come upon a town south of Uman bitterly defended by the Soviets.

The Ukrainian population took no notice of the combat taking place throughout the land; all over, German soldiers were greeted as liberators, as were Austrian soldiers entering Makarov on 7/20/1941 (below).

The first rains fell after the beginning of August, and the tanks, vehicles, and guns – here in the Grushka area – bogged down. The catch-word now was: "heave-ho!"

Where the maps had indicated smooth roads, there were now stretches of mud. At the end of August 1941, nature had become a new, merciless enemy.

The Ukrainian civilian population – especially in the small towns and rural areas – greeted the German soldiers as liberators from the Soviet yoke. (The photograph was taken 9 August 1941.)

At the end of August, German troops were advancing toward the Dnepr on a wide front. The tanks and motorized forces – here a motor-infantry battalion – raced over the few roads to the east, disregarding their flank protection!

An air photograph of the city of Kiev. Taken by a German long range reconnaissance aircraft on 20 September 1941. The numbers indicate: 1. Main cemetery, 2. Freight railroad station, 3. Citadel, 4. Post office, 5. Railroad bridge over the Dnepr, 6. Street bridge over the Dnepr, 7. Pontoon bridge over the Dnepr.

It is 1100 hours on 19 September, as the Reich's battle flag is raised over the citadel of Kiev.

The population of Kiev is completely surprised by the turn of events. In the background is a Soviet propaganda poster, which showed how the men in Moscow were going to invade Germany. Some residents of Kiev look askance as the German troops enter Kiev.

The number of Soviet prisoners reached into the hundreds of thousands after the pocket battle – daily new columns marched to the rear. The Russian Army Group "Southwest Front" had ceased to exist.

The advance of Army Group South was executed on a wider front after the battle of Kiev. In the north, the 6th Army, with a good portion of the 17th Army, attacked in the Poltava-Kharkov area, while in the south, the 1st Panzer Army and the 11th Army reached the Sea of Azov!

Persistent rain in October announced the first Russian winter. The roads became impassable, and heavy vehicles and weapons (the photograph on the left is of a heavy, long barreled gun) became hopelessly stuck in the mud. On 24 October, units of the 6th Army captured the important industrial city of Kharkov. The photograph below shows an assault gun in combat with Russian defensive positions in the city's center.

The operations of Army Group South – at a distance of about 1000 kilometers from the German border – placed a nearly impossible task on the rear area services. The effects of bad weather conditions became more and more noticeable. Here, bread is unloaded at the railroad station in Poltava, which was then transported by horse carts to the front.

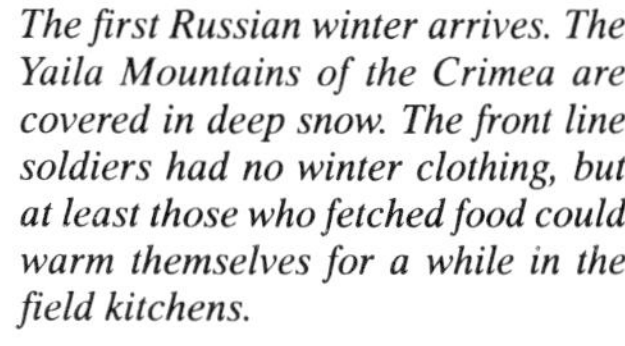

The first Russian winter arrives. The Yaila Mountains of the Crimea are covered in deep snow. The front line soldiers had no winter clothing, but at least those who fetched food could warm themselves for a while in the field kitchens.

A double outpost on the wide, snow-covered steppes of the Don. The advance of the previous summer and autumn has come to a stand still.

As 1941 came to a close, the German front in the eastern Ukraine froze. Meanwhile, since 24 October, the OKH had been working on the initial plans for the continuation of the 1942 offensive in the Caucasus.

Simferopol – the capital of the Crimea – a typical Russian administrative city, with monotonous concrete architecture, fell to the Germans without a fight. The photograph was taken on 11/22/1941 by someone in a propaganda company.

A Sunday in April in the port of Yalta, one of the summer homes of the Tsar's family. German soldiers enjoy the early spring sun.

The German advance to conquer Sevastopol began while the battle for the Kerch Peninsula was still being fought. The 11th Army obtained artillery support like no other army on the eastern front. From the smallest guns – above a 3.7 cm anti-tank gun covering the harbor near Yalta – to the heaviest guns – below a 28 cm railroad gun east of Balaklava – were deployed.

An air photograph of the Sevastopol harbor basin from 14 November 1941. Three Russian ships were in Severnaya Bay. Above it, the entire "Northern front" can be clearly seen.

On 6/30/1942, German soldiers were deployed opposite Sevastopol on the Severnaya Bay. The battle ended after four days.

On 4 July 1942, General von Manstein visited the front line troops and inspected the condition of the soldiers who had just assaulted Sevastopol. After the victory, Manstein was promoted to Field Marshal.

After the 6th Army captured the important industrial city of Kharkov in October 1941, the city became an important Wehrmacht base. For a time, the headquarters of the 6th Army was located here. The photograph above shows a military police guard on "Red Square" on 11/28/1941; below, a lone heavy combat vehicle on the same square on 1/3/1942.

Spring 1942 in Kharkov. Traces of the war and the last winter can be seen all over. The Russian civilian population quickly adjusted to their new life-style.

The 6th Army Post Office, which was stationed in Kharkov and directed the mail for the 6th Army, was responsible for an air post office, an army letter center and field post numbers 540, 541, 542, 543, 767 and 772.

A troop first aid station directly behind the front lines near Merefa. Infantry and the indispensable field kitchen are moving to the north.

Heavy guns of the defeated 6th Soviet Army in the pocket south of Kharkov. German supply columns – in the background – are moving to the front.

After a fitful sleep, a wurst sandwich and rations taste particularly good when the summer sun is also shining.

At 0215 hours on 28 June, the German summer offensive out of the Kursk area began with a total of eleven infantry, three panzer, and three motorized divisions, as well as ten Hungarian divisions. On the first day, German tanks (in the background) penetrated enemy lines to some distance, while infantry (here a mortar crew) secured the flanks. In the background, sunflowers bloomed, distinctive of the Ukraine.

Two days later, the 6th Army, with 16 infantry, two panzer, and one motorized division, attacked out of the Belgorod area. The rear area services – here, a convoy camouflages – followed directly behind as soon as the infantry captured the first Russian strong points.

On 24 July, units of General Baron von Weich's army group reached the Don near Voronezh. On the next day, combat groups of the 24th Panzer Division occupied the burning city.

On 24 July, lead elements of the XXIV Panzer Corps run into a mine field. Engineers were summoned and attempt to dig up the individual mines, neutralizing it, so that the tank columns can continue to advance.

The advance of Army Group South, which was divided into Army Groups A and B in mid July, continued unhindered to the south and southeast until the end of July. The lonely Ukrainian towns faded into the endless expanse of the steppes. The photograph shows a motorized column entering a village, while a motorcycle courier of the lead group is already returning with a message.

On 23 August, motorized units of the 6th Army – here, a combat vehicle of the 16th Panzer Division – reached the Volga near Rynok, north of Stalingrad. Thus began the battle for Stalingrad. The photograph below shows a German security squad, which was guarding an arterial road from Stalingrad with a heavy anti-tank gun, on 13 October.

During the final week of July, the right flank of the German Eastern Army penetrated across the Don Estuary into the foothills of the Caucasus. On 23 July, the 13th and 22nd Panzer Divisions and the 125th ID conquered Rostov. (The photograph shows a rifle battalion moving down the deserted streets of the city.)

The infantry and mountain divisions tried to keep up with the motorized forces in the Caucasus. The photograph shows a company of the 1st Mountain Division on the march in the foothills of the Caucasus on 7 August.

Tanks and guns of the XXIV Panzer Corps roll on to the mountains, while "Red Army" prisoners move to the rear.

A heavy assault gun battalion advancing in the alpine world of the Caucasus.

Since roads were often untrafficable for motorized forces, trucks and tracked vehicles made their way through the shallow mountain streams. The photograph was taken on 4 September by a war correspondent.

On 1 September, the LII Army Corps of the 1st Panzer Army crossed the Terek near Mosdok and, in spite of the heavy resistance of the 9th Soviet Army, established a bridgehead. The Terek Bridge, erected by a construction engineer battalion, near Mosdok.

At the beginning of September, mountain troops stood on the peaks of the Caucasus. View from the summit slope of Elbrus of the mountain post, which was captured by a mixed combat group of the 1st and 4th Mountain divisions.

Mountain infantrymen on a mountain pass 4,800 meters high. Here, the front remained static until the new year.

The following depicts the front line situation on 17 June – a hot and muggy summer day.

On the right was the 132nd ID, fighting south of the Belbek River around the "Maxim Gorkiy" fort. On the left, the 24th ID opposed the "Molotov" fort, with the 102nd Infantry Regiment on the right and the 31st Infantry Regiment on the left. The 22nd ID was advancing from the "Stalin" fort directly to the "Siberian" and "Volga" forts. The 50th ID – supported by the 32nd Infantry Regiment – was on the left flank of the northern attack front and advanced on the "Old Fort" fortification, one of the last strong fortifications before Severnaya Bay.

In the first days, the attack from the south did not give the desired results because the rocky terrain hindered a quick advance. In spite of the bravery of the troops, who suffered heavy losses, they could go no further. Hitler dispatched the Chief of the Wehrmacht Staff, General of Artillery Jodl, to the XXX Army Corps to "set things right." The wise general realized within a few minutes the gravity of the situation and decided - just as the commanders and staff officers of the divisions committed here had – that the attack across the Sapun hills to Sevastopol would no longer be conducted.

• • •

"Tin Pan Hill" extended north of Hill 3 and joined up with it. During the night of 10 to 20 June it was attacked and captured. Hill 4 had received the name "Tin Pan Hill" because throughout the approach trenches thin strips of metal blocked the entrances, which made a lot of noise on contact and told of the enemy's approach.

The approach to the bunker system on the strongly fortified hill had to follow the outer side of the trenches.

At 0230 hours on 20 June, two assault elements, under the command of Lieutenant Kranz, advanced into the depression between Hills 3 and 4, and from there a pincer-type attack ensued. Although additional obstacles had to be overcome and by-passed, they succeeded in entering the bunkered defensive system. The breakthrough failed because the attack occurred in a Russian position where additional reserves were advancing to

"Tin Pan Hill" from the Kadykovka area. Thus, the assault troops fell under fire and they had to withdraw. The ground they had won was again lost. Artillery and heavy infantry weapons placed the enemy assembly under fire. A weak enemy attack occurred on the northern edge of Hill 3, but it was repulsed.

At 1200 hours, the 28th Light Division took on the additional responsibility of the 170th ID sector, which was committed on the right, along with the 105th and 391st Regiments. The 49th Rifle Regiment was brought forward and shifted to the Varnutka area, where it was re-equipped.

The 83rd Rifle Regiment conducted reconnaissance for the entire day in preparation for a new attack on enemy nests that were still on Hills 4 and 5 and in the land in between.

Around midnight, the rest of the 2nd Battalion infiltrated into the reconnoitered assembly area. The operation to capture Hill 5 ("Red Mountain") was led by Senior Lieutenant Wolf, who arranged the three assault groups. The attack on the hill occurred at dawn on 21 June. Shortly before the beginning of the attack, a single Russian plane came from the sea side and bombed the 2nd Battalion assembly area. 8th Company suffered considerable casualties. Since the main assault on the hill was led by 6th and 7th Companies, the operation was not endangered.

In a spirited attack, the assault groups, shouting "Hurrah!", broke into the enemy positions shortly before 0300 hours. The outposts were quickly overcome. While one assault group blocked the sea side, it came upon the main enemy position, where the enemy offered tenacious resistance in fierce trench combat. With anxiety, the increasing sounds of combat and weakening "Hurrah!" on Hills 2.3 and 212.1 was noted. Was the operation successful? There wasn't much support that could be given to the assault groups.

There was a heavy machine-gun group operating against the northwest slope of Hill 5 from Hill 3. They blocked the commitment of enemy reserves. Then the battle appeared to end suddenly. Units with heavy machine-guns were hastily moving down the western slope of the hill. Shortly after that, soldiers from the assault groups reached the summit of the hill. Senior Lieutenant Wolf had captured the long fought over hill with his assault groups after fighting for it meter by meter in the trenches. The difficulty of the fight was shown by the many casualties, which were wounded by bayonet stabs and hand grenade fragments. An enemy counterattack on the hill was broken up by artillery barrage fire. (From: Kranz, B.: *History of the Hirschberger Riflemen 1920 to 1945* (28th Rifle Division) Bad Salzuflen 1975.)

In the middle of June, it was first noted that the Russian defensive forces had diminished. The attackers to the north of the fortress had irresistibly fought their way, step by step, to the Severnaya Bay.

Bartenevka and the "North Fort" fell into German hands on the 21st of June. Two days later, Kossa on the Black Sea – at the end of Severnaya Bay – was reached. At the same time, infantrymen and engineers entered the harbor area north of the Sevastopol suburb. On 29 June, the 31st (24th ID) and 16th (22nd ID) Regiments crossed the bay to Sevastopol in engineer assault boats. On the same day, assault troops on the left flank of the LIV Army Corps crossed the railroad bridge to Inkerman. Therefore, all of the defensive belts before Sevastopol had fallen – and the core of the fortress, with the city of Sevastopol, lay open to the attackers.

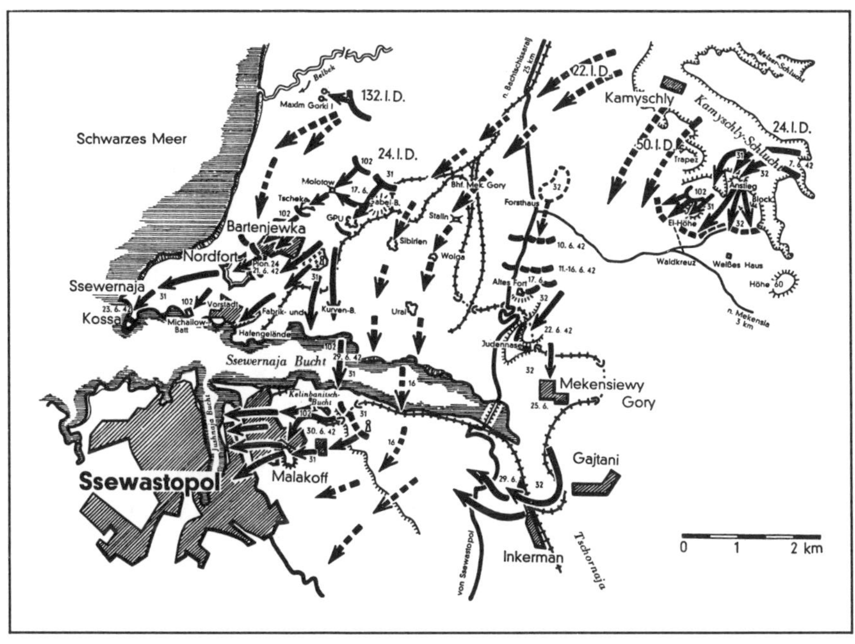

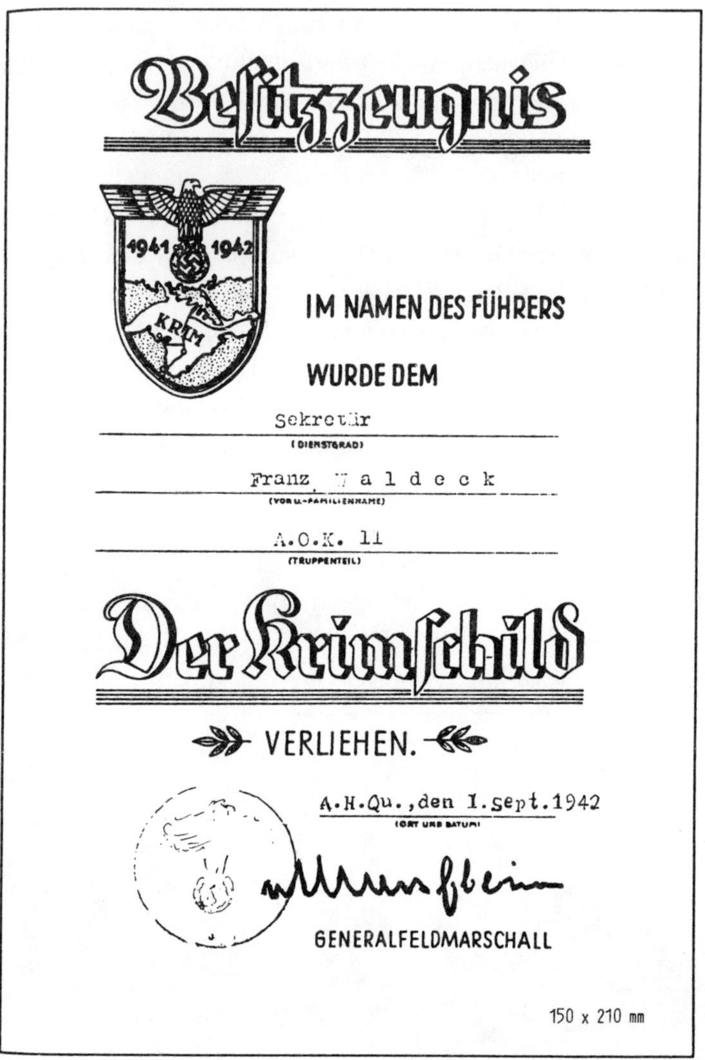

Besitzzeugnis

1941 1942 KRIM

IM NAMEN DES FÜHRERS

WURDE DEM

Sekretär
(DIENSTGRAD)

Franz Waldeck
(VOR U.-FAMILIENNAME)

A.O.K. 11
(TRUPPENTEIL)

Der Krimschild

VERLIEHEN.

A.H.Qu., den 1. Sept. 1942
(ORT UND DATUM)

GENERALFELDMARSCHALL

150 x 210 mm

Crimean Shield Certificate

In these last few days of June, the 11th Army Commander organized for the attack on Sevastopol's inner fortification belt. Heavy batteries occupied their firing positions, and air strikes by the VIII Air Corps hit one bunker line after another. On 1 July, all of the army's batteries opened fire with massive concentrations on the fortifications on the outskirts of the city and on known strong points within the city.

The Coastal Army now evacuated the city and the fortress with lightning speed and withdrew their still intact formations to the coast. Here, the defenders awaited ships from the "Black Sea Fleet", which would bring them to the Caucasus.

The ships did not come. The remnants of the brave "Coastal Army" huddled closely together on the Chersones Peninsula. The German troops continued to track down the last "Red Army" soldiers, which had hidden in the hills of the steep coast until 4 July.

The battle for the Crimea was over. The Soviets lost 97,000 prisoners along with 631 destroyed guns and 26 tanks. The losses of the 11th Army totaled 4,337 dead, 1,591 missing, and 18,183 wounded.

On 25 July 1942, Hitler instituted the "Crimean Shield", which was worn on the left upper arm of the uniform. This honor was bestowed on all soldiers, "that participated honorably in the battle for the Crimea on land, on the water, and in the air, during the time frame 21 September 1941 to 4 July 1942."

Army Group South

KHARKOV
(5 April-28 May 1942)

On 5 April 1942, Hitler issued Order Nr. 41:

> "The winter battle in Russia is coming to an end. The enemy has suffered heavy losses in men and equipment. As soon as weather and terrain conditions allow, the superiority of the German commanders and troops again must force their will on the enemy. The goal is to destroy the remaining active Soviet defensive forces and to deprive him, as far as possible, of the most important sources of his war industry....
>
> The question is whether to adhere to the original precept of the Eastern Campaign, to combine all available forces for the main operation in the south, with the goal of destroying the enemy in front of the Don, to gain the oil regions in the Caucasus and passage through the Caucasus."

• • •

This operation plan corresponded to the given strategic and logistic possibilities of the time. In this manner, the combat groups of the "Red Army", which were opposite Army Group South, were surrounded and encircled by a great attack between the Donets and Don. The attack later continued along the Don in the direction of the Caucasus, with an unprotected flank in the vicinity of Stalingrad.

Hitler's order required a series of offensive operations to produce a more favorable departure base because, during the past winter, Soviet forces succeeded in penetrating deep into the German front line in several places and gaining territory to the west.

Along the entire southern portion of the Front, German troops fell back from the pressure of superior Russian forces from the mouth of the Don in the Rostov area to Mius. By the new year, General von Kleist's 1st Panzer Army, with (from right to left) the III, XIV Panzer Corps, the XLIX Mountain Corps, and the 17th Army (General Hoth), with the LII, IV, and XLIV

Army Corps, were located from the coast of the Sea of Azov directly east from Taganrog along the Mius and Donets to Isyum. The two armies had a total of 10 infantry, including two Mountain infantry, rifle, panzer, and SS divisions, as well as a motorized and an Italian division at their disposal. The XI Army Corps secured the sea coast with a security regiment, while an infantry (the 73rd) and a panzer (16th) division were held in reserve.

The 6th Army (General of Panzer Troops Paulus) was located on the front line from the Donets near Isyum to east of Kharkov and Belgorod, with (from right to left) the XXIX Army Corps (299th, 57th, 168th, 62nd, 75th ID), XVII Army Corps (79th, 294th ID), and LI Army Corps (297th, 44th, 454th ID) as the first heavy Soviet counterattacks broke out between Kharkov and Belgorod in the middle of January.

The combat diary of the 1/132 Infantry Regiment, located with the 44th ID at Taranushin, Grusinovka, and Nikolaevka, contains these words for 24 January 1942:

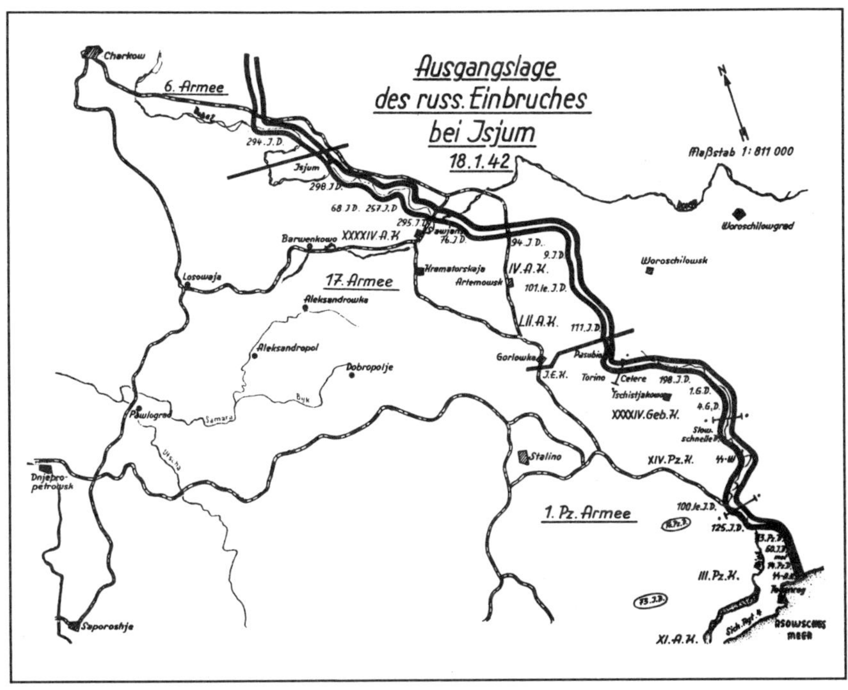

Initial situation of the Russian breakthrough near Isyum 1/18/42

24 January 1942, 0700 hours. Enemy (60-80 men) in burning houses beyond the bridge. As soon as the bridge was constructed we were engaged by heavy mortars, light infantry guns, and artillery.

0800 hours. On a hill west of the burning houses, beyond the bridge, two tanks suddenly appeared. Their number soon increased to seven.

0900 hours. Two tanks advanced from the bridge to the northwest and attacked the left flank with 60-80 men. Strong enemy forces on Hill 164.1 were dispersed by a 21 cm mortar.

0915 hours. The enemy remains. The tanks withdrew to the bridge. The remaining infantrymen were suppressed by well placed defensive fire.

0940 hours. "Weasel Hollow" was attacked. The machine-gun froze in a heavy snowstorm and is out of order. Although the Russians are firing a lot of artillery, they are not succeeding, and they have stopped. Under strong enemy pressure "Weasel Hollow" and "Rabbit Hop" were evacuated. The anti-tank gun was abandoned by the crew. The enemy remains at the wire.

1015 hours. The first Russians have penetrated beyond the wire at "Weasel Hollow." A platoon of the 3/132 (Staff Sergeant Heger) reinforced the left flank.

1030 hours. The Russians expand the breakthrough at "Rabbit Hop" and "Weasel Hollow." The lead elements are penetrating behind the forward defensive positions. The right platoon of the 2nd Company counterattacked into the left flank of the enemy, but they had no success because the enemy forces were already too strong.

Two batteries are firing on the breakthrough location, and the Russians can be stopped without further advance. The 3rd Company is committed to counterattack.

1055 hours. The enemy has turned to the left from the breakthrough location. One tank has burned, one tank withdrew, and two tanks and one armored tracked vehicle are unable to move. They probably rode over mines. The attack has stalled. The Russians are located directly behind the forward defensive positions.

1100 hours. 2/80 Engineer alert.

1135 hours. 1st Platoon of the 3rd Company advances.

1205 hours. Radio message from bunker "Eckstein": Bunker "Fox Roar" has been evacuated. A platoon of the 1/132 is defending opposite "Fox Roar" with a machine-gun. The situation on the left is unchanged. The enemy that had broken through in the center has been effectively shot up by artillery, and the bulk of them have withdrawn behind the wire. The right flank is stable. Two platoons from the 3/132 attacked the strong point occupied by the enemy and recaptured it." (From: Schimack, A.: *The 44th Infantry Division*. Vienna 1969.)

• • •

The situation on the entire front line between Taganrog and Belgorod was ironed out between the end of winter and the beginning of the new year mud so that the army group could begin the initial preparations for the planned summer offensive based on the Führer's Order Nr. 41 of 5 April. The preparatory operations for this large scale attack with the long range goal of the Caucasus began on 18 May with an advance by the 1st Panzer Army and the 17th Army, while the 6th Army advanced against enemy penetrations in the area on either side of Isyum to straighten out the front line there.

Marshal Timoshenko, the Commander-in-Chief of the "Red Armies" in the south of the Eastern Front, realized what the Germans were planning. On 12 May, after an enormous concentration of fire by their artillery formations, the Russian Army Group "Southwest Front", with the 28th Soviet Army – in all, 16 rifle divisions and five motorized brigades – advanced on the front line defensive positions of the XVII and LI German Army Corps. On the same day, the 6th and 57th Soviet Armies, with 30 rifle divisions and 14 tank brigades, tore apart the front line of the VIII German Army Corps and the VI Rumanian Army Corps.

Thus, on the very first day of the Russian attack and for the first time since the beginning of April, the VIII Army Corps (General of Artillery Heitz), in the 6th Army's sector, found itself in big trouble. The forward defensive positions of his three divisions (62nd, 454th ID, and 108th Hungarian ID) were torn apart. As the 113th ID attacked in reserve, it was also defeated.

The 305th Infantry Division at Kharkov 16-26 May 1942

On the third day, the Russian tanks struggled for freedom to maneuver and captured Krasnograd and Taranovka southeast of Poltava and, therefore, gained the railroad line that ran from Kharkov to the southern Ukraine.

The VII Army Corps – as time went on, the 79th (Colonel von Schwerin), the 113th (Lieutenant General Zickwolff), the 305th (Major General Oppenlaender), and the 336th ID (Major General Lucht) were subordinated to it – could not prevent the enemy from advancing to within 40 kilometers of Poltava, but they did not reach Kharkov!

The corps clamped down along the railroad line on either side of Merefa and did not allow the Russian tank formations, which were advancing to the north, to go any further. The attack of the Soviet divisions came to a halt between Smiev on the Donets and Krasnograd. In fact, the German combat groups were even able to gain some ground to the south.

Field Marshal von Bock, the Commander of Army Group South, ordered the 1st Panzer Army to send all available motorized forces to the Dnepropetrovsk-Poltava area to halt the enemy breakthrough to the Dnepr.

However, since they did not want to delay the planned summer offensive, the OKH interfered directly in the command and control. The 1st Panzer Army, which had already started moving, was stopped and – ignoring the Russian breakthrough sector – was directed to attack to the south into the enemy's flank, seeking to make connection with the southern flank of the 6th Army and to encircle the three large Russian formations.

Specific orders included: The 17th Army, on 17 May, set out from the Slavyansk area to Isyum, with the LII Army Corps (257th ID, 101st Rifle Division) and units of the XLIV Army Corps, in order to screen the eastern flank of the friendly panzer forces. On 18 May, the III Panzer Corps, with the 14th and 16th Panzer Divisions, 60th Motorized Infantry Division, 1st Mountain Division, and 100th Rifle Division, had to advance, along with the 6th Army, through Barvenkovo (south of Isyum) to Balakleya to cut off the enemy from his routes across the Donets.

The XI Army Corps (298th, 380th, 384th, and 389th ID), with the subordinate IV Rumanian Corps, had the task of isolating the III Panzer Corps attack from the left. The 6th Army finally set out on its southern flank, along with the LI Army Corps (3rd, 23rd Panzer Divisions, 44th ID) as soon as the advance of the 1st Panzer Army was worked out to its front.

The German attack began in hot summer weather – 90 degrees in some places! – on 17 May. On the second day, the attack formations of the 17th Army were already on the southern outskirts of Isyum. The six bridges, which crossed the Don here, were all taken without any damage, so that the enemy's retreat routes were cut off. On 19 May, the III Panzer Corps (General of Cavalry von Mackensen) reached the area north of Barvenkovo. The Russian command realized the significance of this penetration and tried to split the front line of the VIII Army Corps a little further south of Kharkov, but was unsuccessful.

On 21 May, the enemy attack collapsed!

Army Group South

A member of the 6th Army's Propaganda Company reported on the last days of the bitter fighting:

• • •

Sunday, the sixth day of the battle, began with a wild assault by countless Soviet tank columns on both flanks of the front. The violence of the assault surpassed the vehemence of the previous days. The thermometer climbed to over 90 degrees in the shade, as an enemy tank attack northeast of Kharkov developed into a mighty tank battle on the hilly fields: a battle in which 60 of the 150 participating Soviet tanks were turned into burning torches or shot up and left in the open. In the south the infantry is still being bothered by Soviet tanks streaming into a gap that had been torn between the two division sectors. In the last hours, they cut off a ford here that was very important to us. The enemy tank losses have increased by 300 today.

On the seventh day, the stubbornness of the enemy did not diminish. The Bolsheviks dispatched new tank units on both sectors of the front. Difficult combat followed, with varying degrees of success. For days, the battle was fought in basically one spot. The kilometer that the Soviets were able to advance here and there toward the city was frequently compensated for by their growing enervation brought on by their atrocious losses of men and equipment.

On the eighth day, from the south and east, as well as from the north, new tank attacks were repulsed, but on the other hand, the attacks appeared to lose continuity with those of the past days. To the east combat vehicles were noted that were trying to retreat across the Donets. In the center, the enemy continues to attack, and in the south our troops report that the Bolsheviks are preparing to establish a fortification line. Chalk up 64 additional enemy tanks shot up today.

On 21 May, the army group commander ordered the immediate attack of III Panzer Corps to the north, while the 6th Army, with the VIII and LI Army Corps, were to advance to the south and southeast, respectively, in order to make contact with the panzer forces.

The OKH also relieved some divisions from the middle sector of the Eastern Front and tasked the 6th Army with fortifying the front line north-east of Kharkov with whatever it had available.

The "Red Army" established a bridgehead on these threatened sectors of the Front, at Saltov, and on the west bank of the Donets. It was compressed during the next few days by (from right to left) the 23rd Panzer Division (Major General Baron von Boineburg-Lengsfeld), the 71st ID (Major General von Hartmann), the 294th ID (Colonel Block), and the 3rd Panzer Division (Major General Breith).

Meanwhile, the III Panzer Corps, with both of its panzer divisions – the 14th (Major General Kuehn) and the 16th Panzer divisions (Lieutenant General Hube) – and the 60th Motorized Infantry Division (Colonel Kohlermann) reached the area south of Balakleya where, on 22 May, they made contact with the infantry formations of the 6th Army!

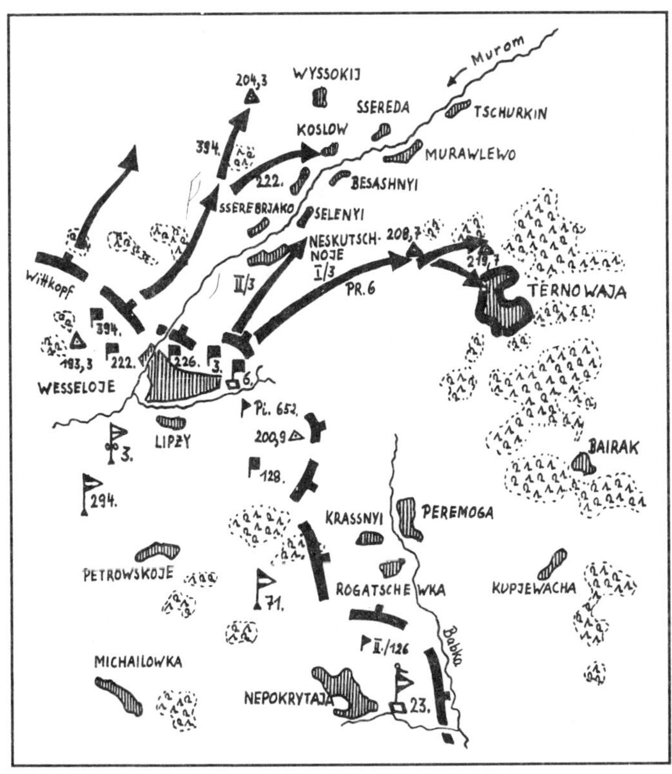

Therefore, the Russian armies were encircled!

The enemy commanders were completely surprised by the German attack. The German occupation of the banks of the Donets cut the Soviet armies off from all supply. The first signs of disintegration were already being noticed, and the breakout attempts against the III Panzer Corps and LII Army Corps front, which was getting stronger every day, between the Donets and the encircled Army Group "Southwest Front" collapsed in the face of the defensive fire.

Up to 24 May the pocket was compressed, as the XI Army Corps closed ranks from the south and the VIII Army Corps held the defensive front in the north.

The first large troop formations surrendered two days later. The Commander of the 6th Soviet Army (Lieutenant General Gorodnyanski) and the 57th Army (Lieutenant General Podlas) fell. Their soldiers – exactly 239,306 men – were taken as prisoners to the POW camp in the Ukraine.

On 30 May 1942, the Wehrmacht High Command reported:

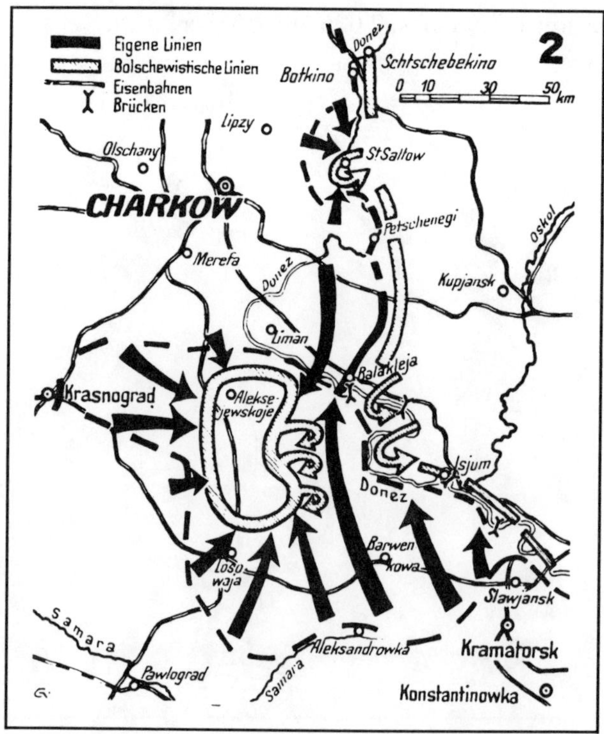

"We have been informed by a special report that the battle for Kharkov has ended.

In Field Marshal von Bock's frontal sector, the armies of General Kleist and General of Panzer Troops Paulus have converted the defense against a very powerful enemy counterattack into a glorious victory. A Rumanian army corps, under the command of General Cornelio Dragalina, as well as Italian, Hungarian, and Slovakian formations, fought side by side with the German troops and brought new glory to their standards.

The air formations of General Loehr and General of Aviation Pflugbeil supported the Army in the defense as in the offense, with relentless sorties, and beat the enemy air force from the battle field.

The Soviet 6th, 9th, and 57th Armies, with about 20 rifle divisions, 7 cavalry divisions, and 14 tank brigades, are destroyed.

The number of prisoners taken exceeds 240,000. The enemy's losses are extremely heavy. The totals of war equipment captured or destroyed in battle are: 1,249 tanks, 2,026 guns, 538 aircraft.

As well as numerous quantities of other weapons and equipment."

VOLGA
(28 June-18 November 1942)

The battle for Kharkov interrupted the army group's preparations for the 1942 summer offensive, but it was not able to stop them. The army group's losses between December 1941 and March 1942 in dead, wounded, and missing totaled 129,500 men. On the other hand, by the 1st of April, almost 112,500 replacements arrived, so there was only a shortage of 17,400 men. Of course, these numbers are based only on the formations that were on the Front in December 1941.

In accordance with Führer Order Nr. 41 of 5 April 1942, the armies of the army group were reinforced with almost 20 additional divisions during this time, so that Field Marshal von Bock now had 68 divisions under his command. To these divisions were added the entire 4th Panzer Army, which was brought in from the central and northern sectors.

Assessment: In comparison with the situation on 22 June 1941, the infantry, rifle, and mountain divisions were almost completely replenished. The mobile units were at least at an equivalent level, and the motorized infantry divisions were even superior. Since the mobile formations were to conduct the decisive attacks and the offensive had been halted in mid flow, they paid particular attention to bringing them to the highest state of combat readiness possible. They had at their disposal for the offensive over 1,495 combat ready tanks, of which 133 were equipped with the longer 7.5 cm canon. On the average, the panzer divisions had 126 tanks, and the motorized infantry divisions had over 50.

The plan for the most important offensive for the eastern armies predicted that the army group would advance in a pincer movement from the Kursk area (in the north) and the Taganrog area (in the south) to encircle the enemy armies that were still located west of the Don. The lead attack elements of the panzer troops were to meet near Kalach. Then – depending on the development of the situation – they were to conduct the advance into the Caucasus.

This operation could no longer be directed from a command post, therefore, in May 1942, a re-distribution of the areas of command of Army Group South was undertaken and implemented on 7 July. Accordingly, Army Group

B (originating from Army Group South), which was responsible for the northern sector, directed the 2nd and 6th Armies, as well as the 4th Panzer Army. Army Group A (the staff was collected in Germany at the beginning of May), which was in the south, took control of the 17th Army and the 1st Panzer Army.

On 5 March, the OKH gave the planned offensive the code name "Siegfried", which was changed to "Blue" on 7 April and ultimately to "Braunschweig" on 30 June.

The allied forces were subordinated to the established armies under German leadership. The Rumanians went to the future Army Group A, while the Italians and Hungarians went to the Commander of Army Group B.

Then, on 19 June, general staff officers of an infantry division had to make a forced landing behind the Russian lines. For some reason the secret papers they were carrying were not destroyed, so the Soviet leadership received the exact German attack plans for the first phase of the summer offensive. The plans now had to be quickly re-worked, because two days

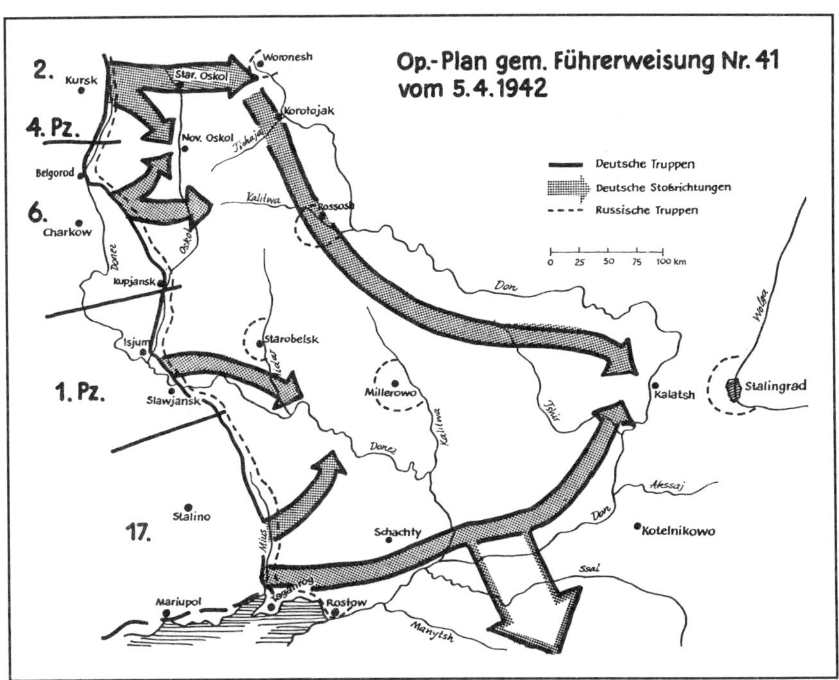

Operations plan based on Führer Order Nr. 41 from 4/5/1942

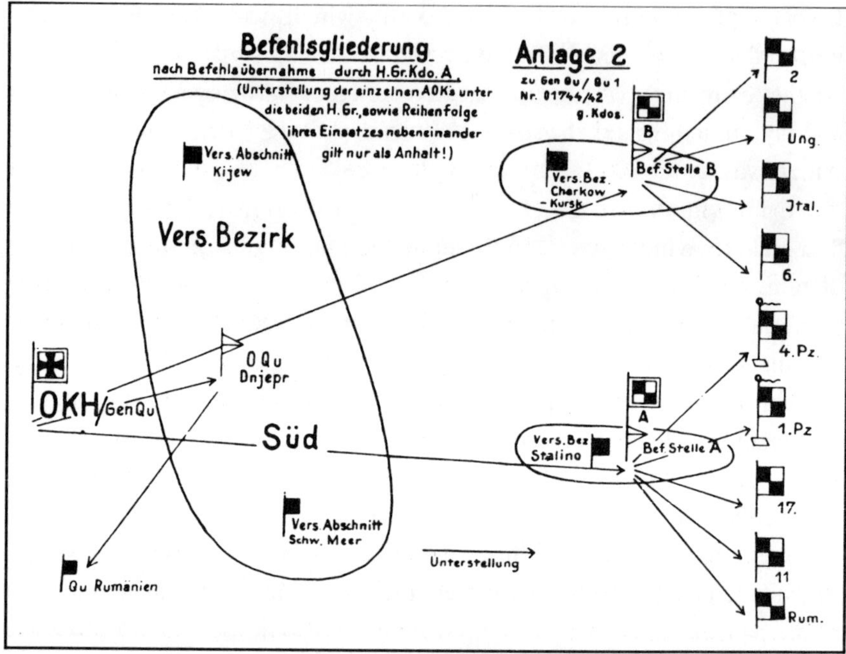

Command Structure upon assumption of command by the commander, Army Group A

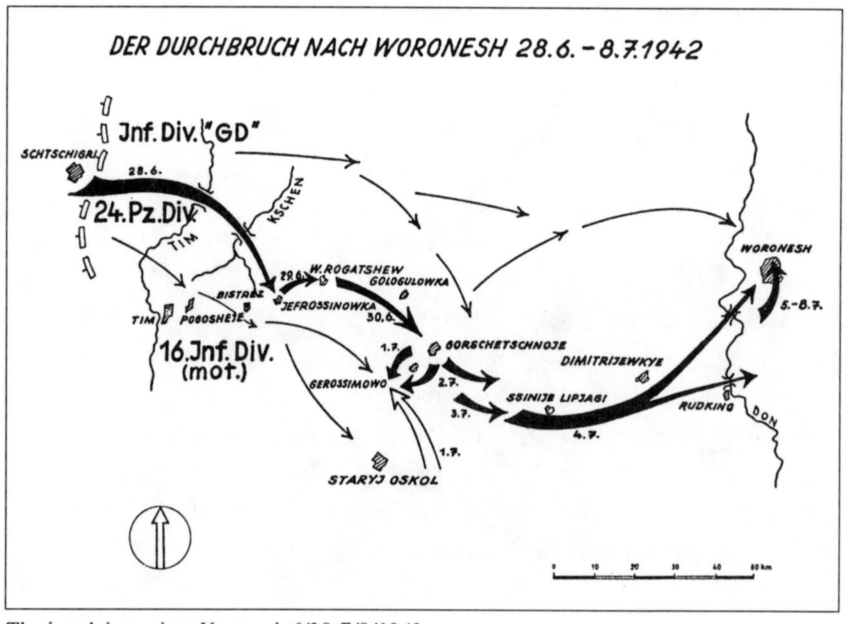

The breakthrough to Voronezh 6/28-7/8/1942

later, the preparatory attack of the III Panzer Corps (14th, 16th, and 22nd Panzer Divisions, 60th ID) was to begin from the area east of Kharkov against Kupyansk. The enemy located here was pushed back to Kupyansk and Isyum in a frontal attack on 24 June, and, thersefore, the Oskol sector, which was about 100 kilometers wide, was gained as a departure area for the upcoming offensive.

The clock indicated 0215 hours on the morning of 28 July, as the soldiers of the 2nd Army (General Baron von Weichs), the 4th Panzer Army (General Hoth), and the 2nd Hungarian Army (General Jany) – supported by units of the VIII Air Corps – began Operation "Blue."

On the first day, the divisions were able to achieve a breakthrough in the positions of the 13th and 40th Soviet Armies, so that the 4th Panzer Army – led by the XLVIII Panzer Corps – gained freedom of maneuver.

General Hoth, who led his army from the front, allowed his divisions to attack further to the east, ignoring flank protection. After three days, the Russian leadership began a counterattack north of Stariy Oskol, with two of the panzer brigades moving up from the east. This developed into a one day tank battle, which was decided in favor of the 24th Panzer Division (Major General von Hauenschild), the 16th Motorized Infantry Division (Lieutenant General Henrici), and the "Grossdeutschland" Motorized Infantry Division (Major General Hoernlein).

However, by this time the 6th Army (General of Panzer Troops Paulus) had already been in attack for 24 hours. The divisions of the army – supported by the IV Air Corps – were able to batter the 21st Soviet Army and push the 28th Soviet Army further to the east in the first two days of their great attack.

Meanwhile, the XLVIII Panzer Corps (General of Panzer Troops Kempf) attacked to the Don, near Voronezh. On 5 July, their advance detachments reached the wide river in the Voronezh area, and exactly 24 hours later the lead elements of the 24th Panzer Division entered the city. In the sector of the neighboring 3rd Motorized Infantry Division (Major General Schloemer) and the "Grossdeutschland" Motorized Infantry Division (Major General Hoernlein), the day proceeded as follows:

On the morning of 6 July, "Grossdeutschland" took the forest east of Podkletnoe and detached a reconnaissance party for the railroad at Voronezh, consisting of a rifle company mounted on assault guns, but the combat group immediately withdrew. The 24th Panzer Division had also crossed the Don further to the south and was entering the city from the south.

At the same time, a panzer corps with the "Grossdeutschland" and the 24th Panzer Division was directed to march to the south. As soon as the "Grossdeutschland" was brought up for the attack, it entered the city without having time for an orderly take over of all of the positions. At that moment, the Russians received the order from Stalin to hold the city. Voronezh is the capital of the central Blacklands region, a large city with well developed industry, and a university that was transferred here from Dorpat. Now, of course, aircraft have destroyed a large portion of the inner city.

On the 6th, our wheeled rifle battalion established a bridgehead on the other side of the Don, north of "Grossdeutschland." In contrast, the neighbor to the right ran into some resistance. The flank was reinforced to the north up to Podkletnoe. Our engineers supported the traffic flow and constructed a 16 ton bridge, which was protected by the 2nd and 3rd Air Defense Battalions.

On the night of 7 July our division received instructions to relieve "Grossdeutschland, and, by doing so, to capture Voronezh, establish a strong flank between the Don and Voronezh, and expand the bridgehead to the northeast. To the right of us, the 16th Motorized Infantry Division took over the 24th Panzer Division's mission. The boundary line is the tracks to the Voronezh railroad station (3rd ID) – projected out to the Voronezh River.

The 8th Regiment received orders to go to the bridgehead and, in the early morning of the 7th, to set the 2nd Battalion in march. The crossing of the Don appeared to have stalled because a unit of "Grossdeutschland" was stuck to the west of the single lane bridge. In the forest east of Podkletnoe, the battalion that would next attack Voronezh prepared. One kilometer beyond this area, the houses of the city can be seen, and among them is a tall building, allowing the enemy good observation. North of the airfield our tanks are firing at the enemy, while the artillery is firing to the north. The arterial roads were placed under fire. The enemy has reinforced the distant slopes with trenches and wire obstacles. Our superiors think these sites are unoccupied, but we had better change their minds soon. The attack is scheduled for 1400 hours; the first two companies were still trying to negotiate the Don at that time; therefore, it was shifted to 1600 hours, and it took this long to bring up the 1st Battalion, the heavy infantry weapons, and the artillery. Now the 2nd Battalion is deployed on the right of the road to Voronezh, the 1st Battalion is on the left, while the machine-guns and air defense guns provide fire protection from raised positions. As soon as the regiment begins to move, the radio broadcast a brief, peculiar message, Voronezh had fallen. An anti-tank platoon, just as this message reached us, took heavy losses from enemy fire. (From:Dieckhoff, G.: *3rd Infantry Division*. Goettingen 1960.)

• • •

The attack organization of the division, which naturally strives to be the first on the Don and to take one of the two bridgeheads before anyone else does, is, by midday, as follows: The 2nd Grossdeutschland (GD) Infantry Regiment is on the right, with the lead battalion, the 1st Battalion, north of Petino – to clear the forested high ground of Russians to the crossing site. Further to the right is the 24th Panzer Division, whose assault troops crossed the Don at 1000 hours in rafts. On the left, with its lead elements slightly forward, is the 2nd Battalion of the 1st GD Infantry Regiment, as well as the bulk of the regiment – almost on the Devitsa sector. In Devitsa itself are the tanks of Major Poessel and the GD Wheeled Infantry Battalion. The GD artillery, with the battalions separated from the regiment, are moving their fire positions in leap-frog fashion and firing at targets north of Devitsa, as well as beyond the Don.

The advanced infantrymen of the 1st Battalion, 2nd Infantry Regiment, which are moving to the north from the forest north of Petino, present a solitary provincial picture: As soon as they reached the advance march route northwest of the hills they turned to the east and traveled on a long road that ran along the northern slope of the wooded hill and emptied into the northeast corner of the forest. The Don could be seen between the peasant huts on the left of the road, which here sharply bends to the east. The railroad bridge is straight ahead! Beyond the banks of the Don are field fortifications, which are reinforced with concrete domes over the firing positions. Directly south of the railroad embankment toward Voronezh is an air defense battery, which was firing on a German reconnaissance plane that was crossing over the bridge at a respectable height. -

On the west bank of the Don, on both sides of the railroad tracks, was a factory with barracks-like buildings. At the factory railroad station a hastily armed armored train was under steam. The guns could be clearly seen sticking out from the sides of the armored train. Two additional transport trains were approaching from the west – unaware of the situation, they stopped about 10 kilometers from the open stretch. Enemy infantrymen poured out of them and disappeared over the hills to the northeast.

It is not apparent to the enemy on the far bank of the Don, in spite of the considerable number of dusty banners on the German vehicles, just what is happening on the western bank. Perhaps he thinks that these are friendly troops moving toward him.

We must figure that the railroad bridge is prepared for demolition and when German troops reach it, it will be blown into the air. For this reason, we must reach the bridge by surprise, or better yet, cross the bridge at the same time as the fleeing Russians do. This task was assigned to the lead company of the 1st Battalion, 2nd Infantry regiment. They ran into the enemy in the village of Yanovishche, so the surprise capture of the bridge is no more a consideration.

Therefore, the 1st Company was committed over the Davitsa, across which the men went in water up to their necks, with the factory railroad station as their objective, and, at the same time, the departure point for the railroad bridge. Unfortunately, the enemy on the far bank noticed this movement and laid heavy mortar, artillery, and air defense fire directly onto the area in front of the railroad bridge. The makeshift armored train in the factory railroad station, with direct hits from a heavy machine-gun, shot up the 17th Company, and the crews fled. In spite of the heavy enemy fires, several men succeeded in getting onto the bridge's approach, which was prepared for demolition, and stepped onto the bridge. However, the infantrymen there came up against extremely heavy infantry fire, which made any movement impossible. Several men were wounded or killed on the bridge. Sharpshooters from the far bank were taking care of the rest; the men had to withdraw, since they had to take cover. A platoon leader, Lieutenant von Kleist, took his severely wounded courier to the rear and rushed back.

Any further attempts to make it onto the bridge were foiled by the heavy sharpshooter fire from the other side. (From: Spaeter, H.: *The History of the "Grossdeutschland" Panzer Corps*. Volume 1. Duisburg 1958.)

• • •

After reaching the Don, Hitler turned down General Hoth's request to cross the river and continue the attack to the east. The panzer armies had to halt and wait for the infantry divisions to catch up. The initial attack objective of the summer offensive was achieved. The OKH now ordered the partition of Army Group South.

Field Marshal von Bock, the former commander, took over Army Group B in the north of the Front, and Field Marshal List was entrusted with the command of Army Group A.

Up to this point, the Soviets had already lost 73,000 prisoners, 1,200 tanks and 1,200 guns.

The "Red Army" High Command, in view of these surprise German successes, rebuilt their forces in southern Russia. Marshal Timoshenko was named to command the new Army Group "Stalingrad Front." Lieutenant General Gordov was relieved after only ten days of command. This new army group was composed of the battered 21st Army, the 62nd and 64th Armies from Central Asia, and the 51st and 57th Armies from the North Caucasus.

However, before the new Russian army group could be formed, the German offensive expanded. The 1st Panzer Army (General von Kleist) began to attack out of the area south of Kharkov to the south on 9 July. Four days later, they were assigned Rostov as an objective, along with the 4th Panzer Army and 17th Army.

As per instructions, the 4th Panzer Army was still located on the Don and could not begin to move. Since the 6th Army had overrun the Oskol sector, only the XL Panzer Corps (General of Panzer Troops Baron Geyr von Schweppenburg) was left here, and it now had to immediately advance to the south, in order to secure the southern flank of the 4th Panzer Army and, at the same time, detach a panzer division (23rd) to the north to support the advance of the remaining infantry divisions.

This splintering of the force and the constant "hither and yon" in the issuance of orders led to Field Marshal von Bock's relief.

General Baron von Weichs was the new Commander of Army Group B. General of Infantry von Salmuth took command of the 2nd Army.

Hitler now actively interfered in the control of the German armies located in the Ukraine and, on 16 July, transferred his main headquarters from Rastenburg (East Prussia) to Vinnitsa. Meanwhile, the German attack continued to roll.

• • •

2/1 GD Inf Rgt Battalion Command Post, 12 July 1942

March Order for 13 July 1942
(on a 1:500,000 map)

1. The enemy is fleeing to and across the Don. While in march order, be prepared to deal with scattered enemy stragglers and air attack.

2. On 13 July 1942, the GD ID continues its advance and reaches the Degtevo-Meshkov road between Setrakovskiy and Lasovskiy, and there blocks the retreat of the enemy to the north.

3. The 2nd Battalion advances as March Group I of the reinforced 1st Infantry Regiment and crosses at 0245 hours upon reaching the Kolkhoz traffic control point on the southeast edge of Babychev in the following march order:

6th Company 8th Company
Headquarters 9th Company
10th Company 7th Company

4. Marchroute: Identified by the 1st GD Infantry Regiment route shield markers: Olychovatka-road fork 9 kilometers east of Yeremenkov-Pyakodonov-Kosinka-road fork east of Kosinka-Mikhailovka-Smagleevka-Kolessnikovka-Annovo Rebrikovoo-Sherebzovskiy-Ahlapilov.

5. Traffic control officer: a staff sergeant from 6th Company.
March Control Officer: Lieutenant von Carlowitz, 8th Company. He is responsible for insuring that no individual vehicles or columns block the march group. Additionally, I task each company commander with the responsibility to insure that, within their march column, no vehicle blocks the march route. Furthermore, assign march control officers for each company. Battalion vehicles that will have to return to the battalion will travel at the end of the battalion column and be re-incorporated with the companies at the first rest stop.

6. On 13 July 1942, the GD ID has priority over all infantry divisions and Hungarian formations. The only vehicles having priority over the units in the division are fuel, as well as solitary vehicles and columns from the XLVIII Panzer Corps and units of the 23rd and 24th Panzer Divisions.

7. Air Defense – expect heavy enemy air activity in the area southeast of the deserted buildings. The companies will take all precautions to guarantee immediate air defense (Machine-guns ready!).

8. Medical Collection Point: is Olykhvatka, while on the march.

9. Captain Peiler is assigned as March Control Officer for the 1st GD Infantry Regiment.

signed in draft
F. d. R. von Mitzlaff LT and Adj von Courbiere

• • •

The 2nd and 6th Armies and the 4th Panzer Army were still located in the north of the huge Front between Oskol and the Don, so only the XL Panzer Corps was available for area attack operations between the Donets and the Don. At this time, the corps of General of Panzer Troops Baron Geyr von Schweppenburg only had available the 3rd panzer Division (Major General Breith), the 23rd Panzer Division (Major General Mack–who fell on the front line on 28 August), the 29th Motorized Infantry Division (Major General Fremery), the 100th Rifle Division (Lieutenant General Sanne), and, for a short time, the 336th ID (Lieutenant General Lucht).

The corps' motorized rifle divisions were already suffering fuel shortages and, in addition to this, were too weak to encircle the enemy formations still located west of the Don. On 12 July, the corps reached Millerovo area and there tried to turn back the Soviet formations struggling get to the Don by barricading the roads. It was not successful.

The Russian High Command had learned from the experience of the summer and autumn of 1941. On 13 July, it ordered all armies, corps, and divisions that were still located west of the Don to evacuate the area as quickly as possible, cross back over the Don, and regroup near Stalingrad.

So, in July there was no great pocket battle as Hitler had expected. The senior German commanders still did not give up on this false estimate and thought that the alleged battered "Red Army" could be destroyed by attacking in two opposing directions. On 23 July, Hitler issued "Order Nr. 45 for the continuation of Operation Braunschweig." The order read:

> "1.) The next mission of Army Group A is to encircle and destroy enemy forces escaping across the Don, south and southeast of Rostov.
>
> To accomplish this, use the strong mobile forces from the bridgeheads... in a generally southwest direction, almost to Tichorezk; commit infantry, rifle, and mountain divisions across the Don in the Rostov area. Next mission is to cut the Tichorezk -Stalingrad railroad line.

> 2.) After the destruction of the enemy force groups south of the Don, the most important mission for Army Group A is to capture the entire east coast of the Black Sea...
>
> 3.) At the same time, by forming force groups out of western mobile formations, secure the flank to the east of the Grossniy area and, as much as possible, block the Osset and Grusin roads at the mountain passes with small units. Related to this is the attack along the Caspian Sea to capture Baku..."

Army Group B received several operational objectives: The defense of the Don, conquest of Stalingrad, blockade of the land bridge between the Don and Volga, and the advance to Astrakhan. To accomplish these almost impossible missions the army group was not reinforced, but actually greatly weakened. The entire 11th Army (Field Marshal von Manstein) had to be left in the Crimea, while five infantry divisions and all of the heavy army artillery went to the Leningrad combat zone. The 22nd and 257th ID, the SS Panzer Division "Leibstandarte", and the "Grossdeutschland" Motorized Infantry Division were also taken from the army group and transferred to Army Group Center or to France. Soon after, the 9th and 11th Panzer Divisions were given to Army Group Center.

According to Order Nr. 45, the 6th Army received the following mission:

> "...to attack against Stalingrad, in order to destroy enemy force groups located there, occupy the city and block the land bridge between the Don and the Volga!"

The operations area assigned to General of Panzer Troops Paulus' army encompassed the entire southern portion of ancient Russia. Part of this territory still belonged to the Ukraine, joining the areas of the Don and the Kalmuk Steppes, which in the region of the Don is a flat treeless and desert-like salt plain.

For the offensive in the direction of Stalingrad, the 6th Army received the 4th Panzer Army (General Hoth), which was already on the far side of

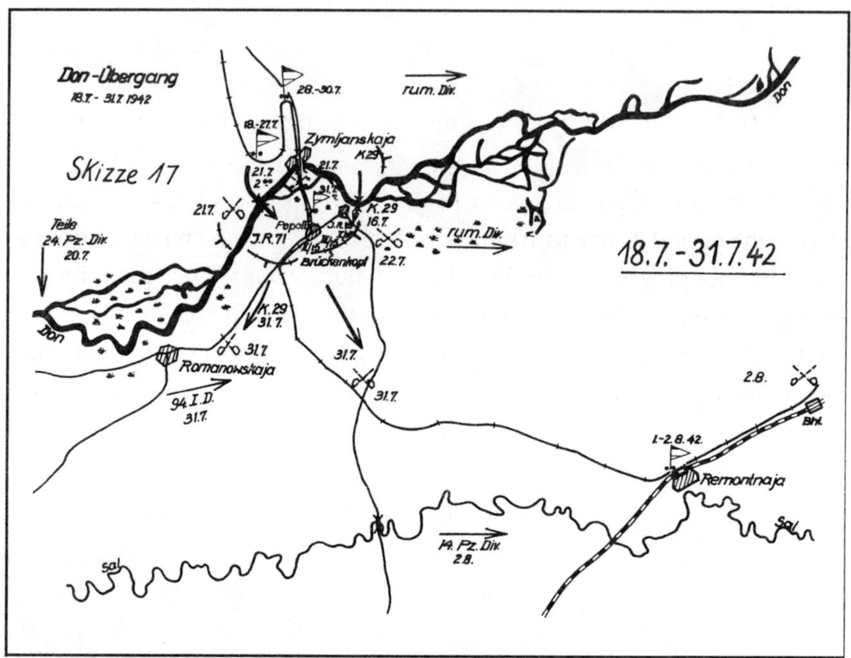

The Don Crossing 7/18-31/1942

the Don estuary. After a short replenishment near Voronezh, this army was transferred to the Don estuary, crossed the Don on 21 July, and attacked into the Caucasus.

They had to stop suddenly and turn to the northeast to make the 6th Army's attack to the Don near Kalach possible. The advance guard of the 6th Army crossed the Chir on 20 July and, three days later, reached the Don bend south of Kremenskaya. The leading XIV Panzer Corps (General of Infantry von Wietersheim) gained the area around Kalach, but could go no further due to a lack of fuel. Behind them, the infantry divisions carried out their deployments.

• • •

Once again, one order rescinded another on the very same day. The division, marching to the north, was to turn to the east, to pursue the enemy, who was avoiding contact with the bulk of his forces on the Don. We crossed the Oskol near Volokonovka. The forward detachment, the anti-tank battalion, passed Olchovatka - Rossosh and reached the Don bend near Novokalitva on 10 July 1942 at 1500 hours.

On 16 July, the division was brought up to the Don in three march groups and, that evening, took over responsibility for the 305th ID sector from the mouth of the Boguchar to the mouth of the Chernaya-Kaltiva. During the period 2 June to 10 July 1942, the division covered 900 kilometers. The mopping up of the Don bend, which was still occupied by the enemy, was successful due to the arrival of the 294th ID on 23 July.

On the evening of 21 July, the division began the advance to the southeast with the 536th Rifle Regiment. During the march to the southeast, the division came upon cossack settlements (Stanitsen) for the first time. The ruins of the farms, destroyed by the Bolsheviks and once occupied by the wealthiest and most respected cossack families, marked their attempt to exterminate the cossacks.

As we advanced further to the east through the great Don basin, quartering and supplying the troops became more difficult. Cultivated fields and cattle herds became more and more scarce. The terrain turned into steppe. On this steppe, which was only broken up by deep, narrow ravines (Balkas), there were no forests to give protection from aircraft, and, above all, no water for the men and horses. After a couple of rainless days, what was called a road was covered by a thick layer of dust that was stirred up by each vehicle and lay over the marching infantry like a heavy impenetrable cloud. The lips chapped and the faces were covered with dust as if the men had painted them gray. Every now and then, a little green would put off our miserable dust-gray existences. Its been a long time since we had shelter from the open. The last ones were, at best, a pair of mud huts.

The advance continued southeastward along the Chir River and turned to the east through Perelasovsk and Kalmikov. A camel trotted past – we are really in Asia.

The bulk of the division became separated from the weather-delayed relief. Between the forward-most and the last march group there was a distance of more than a day's march. From time to time, lack of fuel would delay the motorized units of the division for a day.

During the night of 5 to 6 August 1942, the 534th Rifle Regiment, which was taken command of by Lieutenant Colonel Woelfel (a cavalry officer during the 1st World War) at the end of July 1942, relieved units of the 16th Panzer Division and the 113th ID in the new sector Malo Golubaya to the Oskinskiy hills. On 8 August, the last regiment of the division, the 536th Rifle Regiment, took responsibility for the right sector. Because of the great 25 kilometer width of the sector, a continuous defensive line was not practical. Instead, strong points were established at decisive points.

The lack of anti-tank weapons made it necessary to attach one gun from each battery to the infantry to help combat tanks.

Senior Lieutenant Hennig, the 534th Rifle Regiment's Chief of Anti-tank Guns, reported that almost all of his horses had died when the drivers requisitioned state wheat from a grain silo that was being used to house the divisions maps, and fed it to them. The wheat had rotted. All of the remaining companies of the regiment helped by freely giving horses, so that the anti-tank guns were again combat ready and able to move that same day.

On 11 August 1942, the pocket battle west of Kalach and south of Kalmikov ended, in which units from the division, supporting another division, were participating and in which the division was tasked with providing flank protection for the mobile formations to the northeast. (From: Lang, K.: *History of the 384th Infantry Division*. Rodenkirchen 1965.)

• • •

The commander of the 6th Army partitioned his forces to attack the Don basin into a southern group, with the LI Army Corps (General of Artillery von Seydlitz-Kurzbach) and XIV Panzer Corps (General of Infantry von Wietersheim), and into a northern group, with the VIII Army Corps (General of Artillery Heitz) and XI Army Corps (General of Infantry Strecker).

The advance of both groups was delayed, mainly by supply problems and by a counterattack by Soviet troops, which pushed the LI Army Corps back in places. This developed into the battle between the Chir and the Don, in which twelve Russian rifle divisions and five tank brigades attacked the eastern advancing 6th Army.

As the 4th Panzer Army intervened on 4 August, making itself known as it crossed the Akssaiy against heavy resistance from the 57th and 64th Soviet Armies, the Soviets gave up the battle. The 62nd Soviet Army fled to Kalach and back across the Don, and by 11 August had left 35,000 prisoners in the hands of the 6th Army, which had also destroyed 270 tanks and 560 guns.

Since 1 August, the 4th Panzer Army was south of the Don, advancing to the northeast. The XLVIII Panzer Corps attacked in the center of the army through Kotelnikovo to the Akssaiy River along the railroad line to

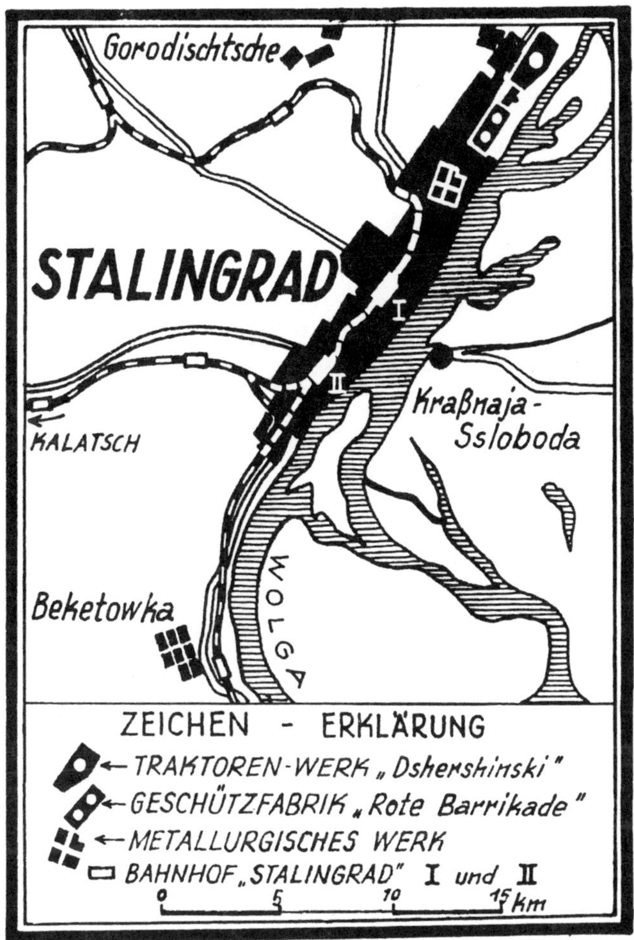

Stalingrad. Here, they had to stop due to a fuel shortage. In the meantime, the IV Army Corps secured the right, while the VI Rumanian Corps secured the left flank.

For the time being, the army was halted. The 24th Panzer Division and 297th ID were dispatched to support the 6th Army. Therefore, on 17 August, the advance in the direction of Krassnoarmeiisk was continued.

On 19 August – immediately after the battle near Kalach – the Commander of the 6th Army issued the order for the assault on Stalingrad:

• • •

6th Army Commander Army Headquarters, 19 August 1942
Ia Az. 3044/42 g.K. 1845 hours
11 copies
9th copy

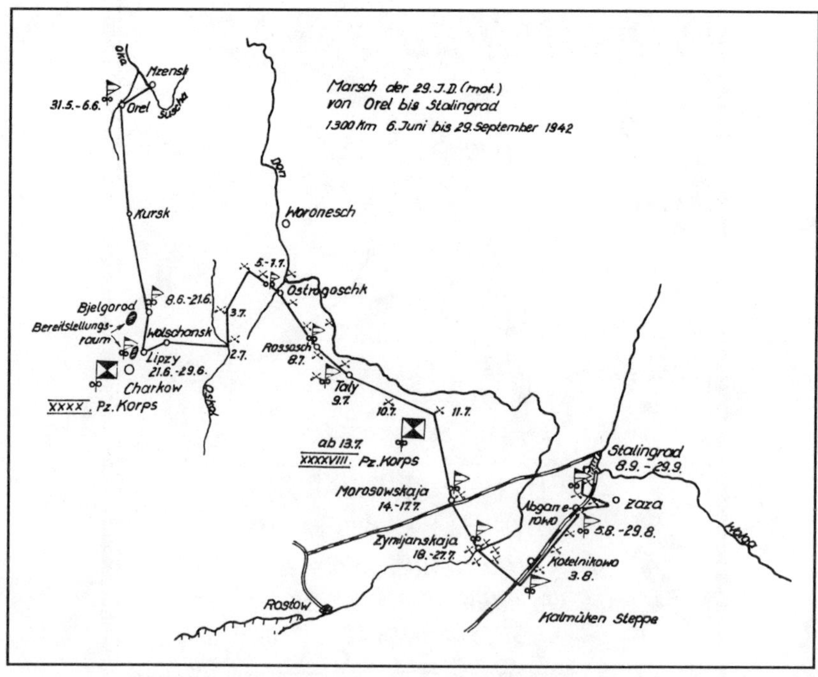

March of the 29th Motorized Infantry Division from Orel to Stalingrad

Chapter 2: 1942

Army Order
for the attack on
Stalingrad

1. The Russians will defend the Stalingrad area stubbornly. They have reinforced and occupied the heights on the east bank of the Don, west of Stalingrad, and in the depth of the defense. We must, therefore, consider that the forces, including the tank brigades around Stalingrad and north of the land bridge between the Don and Volga, are preparing for a counterattack. By advancing across the Don to Stalingrad, the army is counting on resistance to the front and counterattacks of huge dimensions against the northern flank of the friendly advance. It is possible that the Russians may lack the necessary forces for a decisive defense, due to the destructive battles of the past weeks.

2. The 6th Army occupies the land bridge between the Don and Volga north of the Kalach-Stalingrad railroad and secures to the east and north. The army crosses the Don between Pekovatka and Ostrovskiy, with the main effort on either side of Vertyachie. Under continuous cover to the north, they attack with their mobile formations across the hills between Rossochka and Karennaya into the area directly north of Stalingrad to the Volga, while, at the same time, a potion of the force enters the city and captures it. This attack will be conducted on the southern flank and, by the advance of units escorted through the center of the Rossochka, which is southwest of Stalingrad, contact will be established with the mobile units of the neighboring army, which are attacking from the south.

The area between the lower course of the Rossochka and the Kartovka and the Don upstream from Kalach to the northeast will be secured only by a weak force. This area will be taken from the northeast as soon as the forces from the neighboring army advance from the south against the Kartovka.

With a progressive attack on the east bank of the Don, only a weak force is needed to secure the west bank of the river downstream from Mali, which will later participate in the attack across the river on either side of Kalach and the destruction of the forces located there.

3. Missions: The XXIV Panzer Corps secures the Don from the right army boundary to Luchinskoy (excluded) and, after leaving a weak force to secure the Don, prepares to form a bridgehead with the 71st ID on either side of Kalach, with the subsequent attack of this division to the east. The relief of the commands for further employment is being prepared.

LI Army Corps establishes an additional bridgehead across the Don on either side of Vertyachi. For this, artillery, engineer, and traffic control forces, anti-tank, and the necessary communications equipment will be transferred from the XIV Panzer Corps. As soon as the XIV Panzer Corps advances through the bridgehead to the east, the LI Army Corps will cover its flank. From here, it will attack between Nizhne-Alekseevskiy and the Rossoshka, occupy the high ground west of Stalingrad and, by advancing to the southeast, establish contact with the mobile formations of the neighboring army, which are advancing from the south. After that, the corps captures and holds the central and southern portions of Stalingrad. Meanwhile, a weak force will secure between Paskovatka and Nizhne-Alekseevskiy. A special army order will be published, in a timely fashion, concerning the destruction of Russian forces located south of this line and north of the Karbovka.

XIV Panzer Corps advances to the bridgehead established by LI Army Corps. From here, through the hills north of Malrossoshka and Konaya to the east to the Volga north of Stalingrad, blocks the Volga and neutralizes the railroad directly north of Stalingrad. The corps enters the northern portion of Stalingrad from the northwest and occupies it. Tanks will not be employed here. The north, on the hills southwest of Yersovka and south of the Grachevaya sector, is to be screened. Maintain close contact with the VIII Army Corps, which is coming from the west. The VIII Army Corps and XIV Panzer Corps cover the north flank. From here, the VIII Army Corps advances directly to the bridgehead established between Nizhne-Gerassimov and Ostrovskiy to the south and, turning to the north, gains a possible tank line between Kusmichi and Katsakhalinskaya. Close contact with the XIV Panzer Corps is maintained. The XI and XVII Army Corps secure the northern flank of the army, with XI Army Corps in the northern sector: mouth of the Ilovlya-Melov-Kletskaya (inclusive); the XVII Army Corps in the Don sector: Melov-Kletskaya (exclusive) to the left army boundary. As soon as possible, the XI Army Corps prepares the 22nd Panzer

Division for employment by the army in the Daliy-Perekopskoy-Orechovskiy-Selivanov area.

The Commander
signed Paulus

• • •

On 21 August, the Don was crossed by infantry and engineer units. The engineers immediately constructed a 1400 meter long pontoon bridge across the river. The XIV Panzer Corps (General of Infantry von Wietersheim), with the 3rd Motorized Infantry Division (Major General Schloemer) and the 16th Panzer Division (Lieutenant general Hube), prepared to break out of the bridgehead on 23 August.

The 16th Panzer Division reached the bank of the Volga north of Stalingrad. The corps' divisions were now cut off on the bank of the Volga because the Russians immediately closed in behind them. General Eremenko, who was assigned Commander of the "Stalingrad Front" on 13 August, had already published the order for the defense of Stalingrad at the beginning of the German attack on Kalach. On 25 August, General Eremenko announced the state of siege for the city and the surrounding areas.

• • •

After the conclusion of the combat in the great Don basin, the 16th Panzer Division recovered for a day in the Golubaya Valley to prepare itself for new missions. General Hube was informed of the objective of the upcoming commitment: Stalingrad! "This is the decisive commitment of this division in this war." The air reconnaissance reported only weak enemy units between the Don and Volga. The men of the 16th Panzer Division were aware of Stalin's order – the city had to be defended at any price. Up to 21 August, the infantry units of LI Corps succeeded in establishing two bridgeheads northeast of Kalach near Luchinskoy and Vertyachiy. The plan was to drive down a corridor from the Don to the Volga to block

Stalingrad from the north and from the south, thus creating a pocket. During the night before Sunday, 23 August, the 16th Panzer Division crossed the 140 (sic) meter long pontoon bridge across the Don, at the head of the XIV Panzer Corps. At 0430, the tanks of Combat Group Sieckenius broke out of the bridgehead in a wide wedge, just like on the exercise field, and followed close behind Combat Groups Krumpen and von Arenstorff. To the left rolled the 3rd, and to the right the 60th Motorized Infantry Divisions on to the east. The divisions penetrated the strong point-like fortifications and deep defensive positions of the enemy, supported by Henschel 129 armored fighter-bombers.

After the tank attack, an advance march-route across the hills was chosen. Unconcerned about the enemy on the flanks, the 16th Panzer Division rolled to the east through the streams and ravines. The stukas dropped their bombs on Stalingrad in tight formations and, on the return flight directly over the advancing tanks, let their sirens wail in a frolicsome manner. After difficult combat, the 16th Panzer Division overcame the Tartar's trenches and crossed the Frolov-Stalingrad railroad south of Kotluban. Trains were burning. The enemy seemed completely surprised. The advance continued further. In the early afternoon, the tank commanders noticed on the right side of the horizon the imposing silhouette of the city of Stalingrad, which stretched 40 kilometers along the Volga. Winding towers and chimneys, tall buildings, and towers were visible through the clouds of smoke and flame. Far to the north, a cathedral loomed upward from the formless expanse.

We began receiving enemy fire at 1500. Outside of the northern suburbs, Spartakovka, with its tractor plant, as well as Rynok and Latashinka, were Russian air defense positions manned by women. They engaged the attackers with their fire. Gun by gun, the von Strachwitz and the 2/64 Panzer Battalions had to subdue 37 firing positions. And then the first tank stood on the dominant west bank of the Volga. Quietly and majestically, the wide black stream flowed below, barges drifted downstream, the Asiatic steppes extended endlessly, proud and open, and a look of amazement covered the faces of the men. At night, the division set up a circular defense on the northern edge of the city next to the river. The combat groups feverishly prepared for the next day's combat. Already, the Russian tanks and air defense guns were firing on us. The flashes of the gun fire appeared like summer lightening in the clear starry night sky. (From: Werthen, W.: *History of the 16th Panzer Division*. Bad Nauheim 1958.)

• • •

The XIV Panzer Corps (General of Infantry von Wietersheim) remained at Rynok on the bank of the Volga and fought in a circular defense. The corps now could only be supplied from the air and, due to a lack of fuel, could go no further. Suddenly, on 31 August, the Russian attackers surprisingly gave up the attempt to destroy the corps and withdrew to Stalingrad. In the meantime, the situation here had become more critical, so that the first industrial plants were transported across the Volga to the east and the civilians, without regard to sex or age, were mobilized to construct tank obstacles, barricades, tank ditches, bunkers, and so forth.

The 4th Panzer Army (General Hoth) transitioned to the attack here from the south. On 28 August, the army regrouped and attacked into the area west of Stalingrad, along with the XLVIII Panzer Corps!

• • •

Although the XLVIII Panzer Corps had rolled over the outer-most Stalingrad defensive belt east of the railroad tracks, the enemy tenaciously held on in front of the VI Rumanian Army Corps in the Mushkova sector. These outer-most city defensive belts, which continued west of the railroad tracks, opposed the attack with large terrain obstacles. This situation caused the panzer corps to be relieved from its former sector and again prepared for the breakthrough in the area south of Tebektenerovo. In deep, carefully constructed field positions, the enemy established special combat groups here which were led by the commander of the 126th Rifle Division, Colonel Sorokin. They consisted of the 126th Rifle Division, the reconstituting 208th Rifle Division, and the Ordshonikidze and Grozny Military School Regiments, reinforced by two army artillery and multiple rocket launcher regiments. The 29th and 138th Rifle Divisions closed along the railroad tracks to the north.

Without slowing down, the 29th Division, effectively supported by friendly air, was committed in the narrow area between the 14th and 24th Panzer Divisions, and, early on 29 August, broke through the enemy's defenses near Farm Number 1. During the night, the attack tore between two regiments and continued to a short depth into the rear of the enemy Front and up to the division command post, which was cut off from the fighting troops. The enemy broke and ran. During the evening of 29 August, they reached Sety (the 24th Panzer Division) and the high ground southeast of it.

On 29 August 1942, at 1945 hours, the XLVIII Panzer Corps received the following radio message:

To the 29th Division (mot)
"I am pleased with your great success today.
Hurrah for the 29th Division (mot)!"

Kempf

This evening, the Soviet leadership faced the problem of whether to leave those divisions that were not directly involved in the attack in their former positions between the railroad tracks and Tebektenerovo, or to withdraw them in view of the impending encirclement. The withdrawal order was, in fact, given to the combat groups of the 126th Rifle Division by 2200 hours. However, the order did not reach many troop units, because they had already withdrawn before dawn, without waiting for orders, due to the threat of encirclement and heavy loss of leadership.

The nighttime withdrawal of a large number of units degenerated into an unorganized flight toward the divisions that were located east of the railroad tracks, which caused a further mixing of units. A portion of these fleeing columns were either taken prisoner or destroyed east of Sety by units of the division (29th) that were advancing to the north on 30 August. In the shortest amount of time, an entire battalion of over 1,000 prisoners, including 70 officers, was taken. The commander of the 208th Rifle Division, Colonel Kusmin, surrendered with his entire staff. According to their own statements, they had attempted to organize a counterattack behind the penetrated front line, with anticipated reinforcement, but they were cut off from their division. The reinforcements and the staff of the 64th Army, which had been cut off since morning, simply ran into the advancing troops of the division. The way to the Chervlenskaya sector was now open. The lead elements of the division reached it during the evening of 30 August. (From: Lemelsen, A.: *29th Division*. Bad Nauheim 1960.)

• • •

The 64th Soviet Army (Lieutenant General Shumilov) was defeated near Abganerovo and the 62nd Army was pushed aside. The tanks and motorized divisions of General of Panzer Troops Kempf reached the bank of the Volga immediately south of Stalingrad between Yelshanka and Kuperosnoe on 10 September. Therefore, Stalingrad was encircled – the only way free across the Volga was to the east. On the same day, the LI Army Corps (General of Artillery von Seydlitz-Kurzbach) reached the western edge of the city and set up defenses here with the XLVIII Panzer Corps. Now began the hours, days, and weeks of the assault troops, the hand-to-hand combatants, the individual "Landsers" – namely the street-to-street and house-to-house battles for and in this city. The attack order for the 194th Infantry Regiment – which was one of the first German regiments to enter the city – read as follows:

> Ia 194th Infantry Regiment Regiment Command Post 12/9/1942
> Regiment Order Nr. 7 for the Attack on Stalingrad
> (Map 1:25,000 - City Map)
>
> 1. The enemy is stubbornly defending his positions west of Stalingrad. We must estimate that he has fortified field positions and bunkers on the heights of the ravines in front of us, because there are such fortifications on one such height. Friendly formations have reached the Volga on the southern edge of the city.
>
> 2. The reinforced 194th Infantry Regiment attacks, on 13 September at H-hour, the suburban area northwest of the airfield. On the right is the

191st Infantry Regiment, with the mission of clearing the ravines in order to secure the right flank of the regiment. On the left, the 295th Division is to take the airfield.

3. Boundary lines on the right to the 191st Infantry Regiment:

Northern edge of Stalingrad-southwest of the houses of the suburban area west of the airfield-southern edge of the housing blocks (brick houses) southwest of the air school,

on the left of the 295th Division:

The end of the ravine on the present left flank (2 small houses)-bend in the road southwest of the southern edge of the airfield-along the street (inclusive) dividing the Dobberkau Battalion on the right and the Muench Battalion on the left, running parallel to and 300 meters from the rollbahn.

4. Be ready to attack at 0230 hours:
On the right, the Dobberkau Battalion is to be in and behind the left portion of their present positions, while on the left, the Muench Battalion east of the ravine, which has already been reconnoitered.
Security of the assembly area will be provided, especially against tanks, by the reinforced battalion.

5. Organization:
Dobberkau Battalion (a combination of the 1st and 2nd Battalions):

von Hanstein Anti-tank Company, which is assigned the support of one light infantry gun platoon,
one detachment of the 171 Engineers for demolition and mine clearing support.

Muench Battalion (3rd Battalion):

one light and one medium platoon of the 14/194,
one light infantry gun platoon,
one detachment of the 171 Engineers for demolition and mine clearing support.

Regiment Reserve (commanded by Lieutenant Wiehl) in the ravine west of Muench Battalion:

Lantelme Company,
reinforced infantry engineer platoon,
15 cm anti-tank gun from the 14/194,
7.62 cm platoon of the 13/194.

6. Conduct of the Attack

The attack begins at H-hour, with a fire strike by the mortar battalion about 400 meters beyond the present front line.

1/171 Artillery Regiment immediately engages enemy targets on this side of the mortar fire. The 101st Heavy Field Howitzer Battalion engages the fortified bunker in front of Muench Battalion and then supports Dobberkau Battalion by overcoming the enemy positions on the ravine ridge.

The ravine ridges on the right are then engaged by the 4/171 Artillery Regiment, which monitors the large northern branch of the ravine in the direction of the air school during the further course of the battle. Moreover, the 2/171 Artillery Regiment and the 101st Heavy Field Howitzer Battalion support the regiment's attack lanes, while the 101st Heavy Howitzer Battalion will suppress any enemy activity in the area west of the air school.

The battalions will be accompanied to the attack objective and the ravine by a forward observer and heavy artillery from an assault gun battery. The company commanders will maintain contact with the forward observer as long as possible. Muench Battalion is to seize and hold the rollbahn on the western edge of the air school with a small detachment. An engineer detachment will also be dispatched.

Then Lieutenant General von Hartmann's 71st ID assaulted the city of Stalin.

• • •

On 9/14, the 194th Infantry Regiment resumed the attack with spirit and energy. With the help of stukas they were able to advance from their well located departure positions first to the railroad station, and then, after a quick regrouping, to the Volga. The breathtaking report from the commander responsible for the advance (at that time it was Lieutenant Colonel Roske) reads as follows:

> "The attack is now entering the edge of the city, and there is no resistance worth mentioning. The Lutz Assault Gun Battery, which actually belongs to our neighbor, has been brought up to me because, as Lutz told me, the neighboring infantry has not closed yet and does not need the protection. At this time, Lutz is firing at enemy tanks that are blocking the roads west of the edge of the residential area.
>
> Now the critical time was approaching, I had to discover where and how the Russians were defending the town, and how I could get my battalion to the ravine. I also had to advance. At the same time, General von Hartmann was coming to visit me shortly. I had already spoken to the General about the problems with my right flank protection earlier.
>
> I stood on tenterhooks next to my vehicle, because I was called to the division commander's vehicle up ahead. The General, to whom I quickly reported, shouted at me: "You must immediately cover your right flank!" "Herr General, when I reach the Volga today, I will need every man!" I got into my jeep, watched as the General spoke to his assistant, Senior Lieutenant von Plotho, who appeared somewhat astonished and went alone to the head of my left battalion, leaving the General and his concern over my right flank.

My behavior was somewhat stubborn. I had no choice, because all forces were committed and psychologically set in motion and I, with my strong will, impulse, and daring, wanted to reach the Volga and maintain the combat momentum. Soon I was at the lead element, which had just entered the residential area. I was able to establish that enemy resistance was weak, and it seemed the same further on. I tried to set the right battalion in the direction of a neighboring street. The friendly guns were, as I already anticipated, not there.

Down across street to the right I saw an assault gun firing on a parallel road. I slipped behind the houses, the hatch of the assault gun opened, and out popped the head of Senior Lieutenant Lutz. He called to me: "Herr Lieutenant Colonel, that'll cost ya a bottle of champagne; I just shot up two T-34's!" I said: "Excellent, my boy, but I don't have any champagne. How about a little cognac?" I took my small flask from my left shirt pocket, offered him a small cap-full, he took only a sip, I finished the rest, and we extended hands. That was the last time I saw Lutz. He advanced a little further, was awarded the Knight's Cross, and fell a few days later, as did so many great men, that did their duty gladly and naturally.

I walked up the street to the advance party – the left column was still within a sea of houses. My estimation of the enemy turned out to be right, so I was in good spirits, for there was no significant resistance and only occasional artillery fire from the other side of the Volga. Finally we reached the railroad station. It was on the upper edge of a steep slope, from which one could see the wide body of tracks north of the main railroad station, with numerous criss-crossing tracks, and, beyond that, the magnificent 1800 meter wide band of the Volga. This is where the stone house quarter began, and so did the fire from tanks and mortars from beyond the railroad barrier and from individual guns on the east bank of the Volga. It was noon and I thanked God: one could see the camouflaged enemy for a great distance, and then I exhaled, for this line had been designated as the second sector. Then all of a sudden everyone stopped and took cover. Something unexpected happened. There was confusion. Then the sight of T-34's crossing to and fro, the mortars, machine-guns, and enemy artillery observers disembarked, and marked the beginning of the end." (From: *The 71st Infantry Division in the Second World War*, Hildesheim 1973.)

Two days before, General Eremenko, the commander of the Soviet Army Group "Stalingrad Front", had ordered the 62nd Army of Lieutenant General Chuikov to defend Stalingrad by committing all men and equipment available (This was the army that would conquer the capital, Berlin, in April and May 1945!).

The dreadful and bloody battle for Stalingrad began. The combat groups of the 6th Army and the 4th Panzer Army now worked their way meter by meter through the ruined houses and, on 15 September, stood on the Zaryza ridge in the center of the city, where the old city met the new business district. On 22 September, the assault troops of the 24th Panzer Division (General von Hauenschild) and the 94th ID (Lieutenant General Pfeiffer) captured the tall silo, thereby gaining all of the southern district of Stalingrad. And the battle continued.

• • •

15 September 1942. Today I must relieve the squadron, which is to our right. Today, the von Lanken Panzer Battalion attacked the "Kasernenhoehe" through the southern portion of the city, but they couldn't make any headway. The difficult terrain there is strewn with bunkers, defensive positions, and entrenched tanks.

16 September 1942. Again we have been pulled out to attack the city with our tanks and dislocate the enemy's pockets of resistance. We drove in march order along the tracks to the city, where the von Heyden Battalion had just taken the main railroad station and advanced on to the bank of the Volga. Then we turned and drove to the west to the "Kasernenhoehe." Here, the city is completely burned, and the streets are sown with craters within craters.

Supported by fire from the tanks, we dismounted at the outskirts of the city and attacked the nearest strongly defended positions, which ran north to south, horizontal to the hill. We entered the forward-most trenches and overcame them in hand to hand combat. 30 meters in front of us was the second row of trenches and behind them were bushes, with bunkers and tanks. We captured the second row of trenches and cleared them of the enemy. Then we were hit by strong artillery fire; we couldn't tell if it was ours or theirs. After we had a firm hold on the second row of trenches, and the last Russians were extricated from their holes or executed with pistols, we assaulted the bushes like shock troops. There was a small group of houses in front of us, a road went off to the left, and thick bushes were on the right, and in them we could make out several T-34's at a distance of 50

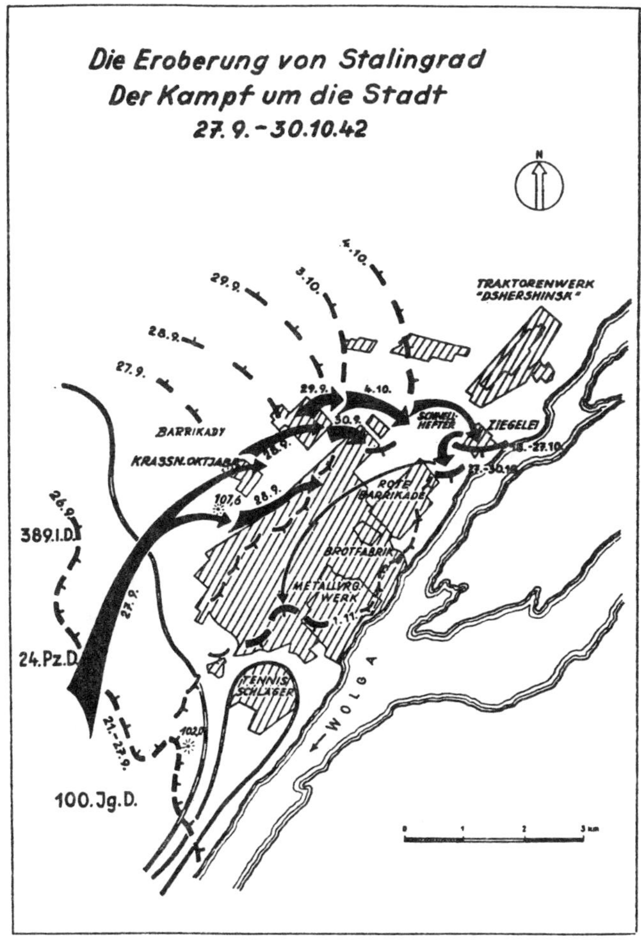

The Conquest of Stalingrad
The Battle for the City 9/27-10/30/42

to 100 meters, which were engaging us at a distance. We cautiously approached the group of houses and cleared them. My platoon was already short three machine-gun crews. Beyond the group of houses lay an open field of some 80 meters width, while to the right, well camouflaged under the trees, were two or three T-34's, and to the left in the bushes beyond the road I could make out the burned tank that I had shot up from the other side yesterday. (From: Senger and Etterlin, F. M. from: *The 24th Panzer Division*. Neckargemuend 1962.)

• • •

Finally, German soldiers stood on a 15 kilometer wide section of the Volga – but through the entire length of the city, the river had a 35 kilometer length. Therefore, the Russian defenders still had a supply route that remained intact, in spite of the bitter combat, whether it was by assault companies or by bombing from combat aircraft. Every foot of ground, every street, every house, and even every floor in the houses had to be wrestled from the enemy.

On 28 September, the Soviet High Command renamed Army Group "Stalingrad Front" to "Don Front" and subordinated it to Lieutenant General Rokossovskiy, while Army Group "Southwest Front" then became "Stalingrad Front." General Eremenko took command of it. Four days later, the commander discussed the first plans for a counteroffensive to envelop the 6th German Army with representatives of the Moscow High Command. Both army groups were mobilized and transported to the counterattack. There were ten armies and the 5th Tank Army – in all, 40 rifle divisions, two each tank and cavalry corps, with a total of 1000 combat vehicles, 12,000 guns, and 1,200 aircraft. The Germans did not have the forces to match this.

• • •

The enemy night bombing attacks were getting stronger. After resting, the 100th's warriors were again ready to attack. Captain Handlos, who had taken command of the 2/54 from Captain Witt in the middle of the month, inspected the defects of the positions that his battalion would be leaving during the day, so that they would learn from their mistakes. Without an escort, he inspected a position on the northern slope of Hill 102 and was shot in the upper thigh by a Russian sharpshooter. And other things happened: One night, a member of the 227th Rifles, carrying a full mess ration for his group in both hands, marched between the picket lines and right into the hands of the Russians. During the next night, after a loud speaker concert, his voice rang out as he called on his comrades to cross over to the "other side."

On 19 October, the divisions to the north of the 100th continued the attack. The 3/54, which was relieved by the 2/227, also began to attack in the muddy, rainy weather on this Monday. With the support of the division artillery and long range artillery, the battalion was able to advance to the steep bank of the Volga near the northern slag heap of the "Red October" plant. The last jump to the river bank itself, however, proved to be impossible. Further to the north, other units made it to the Volga. The command post of the Soviet 62nd Army was still located at a Russian bridgehead near the "Red Barricades." Consequently, General Chuikov, the commander, was located only 400 meters east of the German lines. The Barrikady bridgehead was connected with the "Red October" bridgehead by a narrow strip. Later, this strip was also pinched off after a difficult struggle.

The 2/54, in its positions on the northern slope of Hill 102, were relieved by units of the 369th Infantry Regiment and, after a two day "breather", occupied "Blumentopf", the assembly area for the attack on the 23rd. Together with the 79th ID and the 14th Panzer Division they attacked the unconquered northwest portion of "Red October", as well as Bread Factory Nr. 2 just north of it. The bloody battle lasted until the 26th. The riflemen, reinforced by demolition and flamethrower troops from the 100th Engineer Battalion, had to literally fight for every part of the building. Often, Russians sat ten meters from the riflemen in the destroyed halls, in the cellar, or behind the walls in the next rooms.

Finally, the entire bread factory was occupied and the majority of the "Red October" was cleared. The resistance of the 39th and 193rd Soviet Rifle Divisions was fierce, and, as the struggle for the city continued, the losses on both sides rose accordingly.

In fights for industrial installations, it soon became evident that stuka attacks, which destroyed the work areas, put the defender at an advantage over the attacker. The craters, piles of bricks, and wall remnants gave the defender, who took advantage of the cover to stay out of sight, an ace in the hole over the assaulting attacker.

A Stalin Organ continued to send its rockets against the German positions and strong points from the still unconquered portion of the "Red October." It simply could not be taken, although it was being used in direct fire. It was established that the Russians had mounted the rocket launcher on a crane, so that it was reloaded in the cellar, raised to fire and, after each salvo, it disappeared into the underworld. The attempt of a forward observer of the 83rd Artillery Regiment, who had established himself in a well protected observation post on the upper floor of a house, to put the rocket launcher out of commission failed because of the long flight time of a friendly shell. Although he determined the correct firing data for the guns and the guns fired at the moment they were called on, the Russians had enough time to lower the rocket launcher into the cellar before the rounds hit. (From: Neidhardt, N.: *With Pine and Oak Leaves.* (100th Rifle Division) Graz 1981.)

By the end of October, they could go no further into the ruined city. One fought, starved, and died.

• • •

27 October. Rasgulyaevka Railroad Station. The mission for the division read: Clear the north corner of the metal plant and hold the present line in the remainder of the sector. The night passed with the usual infantry restlessness. The enemy was still very strong with his artillery, heavy mortars, and his rocket launchers.

0600 hours: An enemy attack out of the area of the fuel dump into the 212th Infantry Regiment sector was repulsed by a counterattack against Plant 9. Attack groups of the 212th Infantry regiment advanced against Plant 4. After the attempt to blow up the steel ovens was unsuccessful, the attack could not proceed against the very strong enemy resistance and they remained in the plant. A portion of the attack group had to counterattack near Hall 3. 0800 hours: The northern group advanced against the multi-storied building. They reached the main building by 1400 and took the northern portion. The clearing of the cellar was continued. The assault gun battalion arrived, the attack was continued, and the northwestern portion (in the vicinity of the main building) was taken. The 226th Infantry Regiment reached the vicinity of Rossoshka-Dmitrievka. They took 23 prisoners and deserters and captured weapons. With the fall of darkness, both the 244th and the 245th Assault Gun Battalions were brought forward. They were employed in clearing out the remaining enemy. The enemy continued to offer tenacious resistance.

10/28. Rasgulyaevka Railroad Station. The 208th Infantry Regiment took Plants 1 and 2 from the southwest. On the right flank, the artillery regiment continued its previous mission. The 212th Infantry Regiment held its present line. The corps order for this day was: 0600 hours, the start of the attack of the assault troop, formed from 1/212 Infantry Regiment and the artillery regiment, had to be postponed because of enemy activity (0615 hours the enemy attacked from Hall 4). The 245th Assault Gun Battalion supported the 14th Panzer Division today. At 0900 hours, assault troops and stukas attacked the fuel dump and Hall 4. At 0945 hours forward elements, supported by the 244th Assault Gun Battalion, were engaged in the western end of Hall 4. The western portion of Plant 4 was taken at 1130 hours after overcoming bitter resistance.

The clearing of the multi-storied house continued. 40 prisoners were captured. There were strong enemy fire strikes on the newly captured portions of the building. Again preparations for the attack were resumed. At 1500 hours, the southeast portion of Plant 4 was taken. After the fall of darkness, the attack was initiated, and the assault gun battalions were brought forward. Stuka formations and friendly infantry provided good support.

Through the subsequent assault operation by the 212th Rifle Regiment, the newly attained defensive line at Plant 8, directly southwest of the plant railroad tracks, was further consolidated.

Prisoners: 100; captured equipment: six heavy mortars, eight light mortars, one light infantry gun, four light machine-guns, two anti-tank guns, and ten automatic pistols.

10/29. The division's mission: attack on the left flank to the Volga with the 14th Panzer Division and encircle Plant 4. At 0500 hours, the 1/212 Rifle Regiment and the 208th Rifle Regiment began the attack with the task of attaining the bank of the Volga. An additional battalion was tasked with encircling Plant 5.

0700 hours. The attack is broken off. 0915 hours. The supporting assault guns destroyed three T-34's. Hall 4 is finally enveloped on three sides. The right flank of the 208th Rifle Regiment reached the steep bank of the Volga at 1600 hours. After the fall of darkness, the 226th Rifle Regiment moved to an assembly area between the 79th ID and the 14th Panzer Division to prepare to advance to the bank of the Volga.

30 October. During the night, after a bombardment, the enemy was able to infiltrate between the left flank of the 212th Rifle Regiment and the right flank of the 208th Rifle Regiment and enter the north portion of Hall 10. By 1400, the original positions were regained. (From: Saenger, H.: *The 79th Infantry Division*, Friedberg 1980.)

•••

And that is how it went up to that point.

As the 19th of November dawned, the great Russian offensive to smash the 6th Army began.

Chapter 2: 1942

CAUCASUS (28 June - 31 December 1942)

The partition of Army Group South became an operational reality on 7 July. The new Army Group A, under the command of Field Marshal List, along with its subordinate armies – the 17th Army (General Ruoff), the 1st Panzer Army (General von Kleist), and the 3rd Rumanian Army (General Dumitrescu) – had to advance in an enormous pincer maneuver to the north bank of the Don, in order to make contact with Army Group B.

Just as the 6th Army reached the Millerovo area, they came onto the flanks of the Russian Donets defensive positions. That was the moment, on 9 July, that the 1st Panzer Army began to attack out of the area between Kharkov and Isyum to the Donets on either side of Lissichansk.

The divisions of the 1st Panzer Army quickly overran the Donets sector and, on 14 July, the soldiers of the XL Panzer Corps passed to the southwest of Millerovo.

The 17th Army, which began its attack somewhat later, broke through the Russian positions on the right, along with the V Army Corps (General of Infantry Wetzel), and on the left with the LVII Panzer Corps (General of Panzer Troops Kirchner), and penetrated to the south toward the Don between Rostov and Bataisk.

That was the reason Hitler – contrary to all previous plans – ordered the advance of the 1st and 4th Panzer Armies, as well as the 17th Army, to Rostov, in expectation of a new pocket battle. As a result, the 17th Army had to assault Rostov from the front, while both panzer armies had to advance from the Millerovo area directly to the south.

The 4th Panzer Army (General Hoth) crossed the Don east of Rostov on 21 July in accordance with the new orders from the Führer, but had to be instructed a few days later to retrace its steps and turn to the northeast in the direction of Stalingrad.

A two day rain set in. It did not, however, delay the advance of the German divisions to the Don estuary. The 1st Panzer Army crossed the Donets on 21 July – this was the second time in a few days, but now to the southwest, not to the east – and headed directly for Rostov. The III Panzer Corps (General of Cavalry von Mackensen) attacked to the north against the great city on the Don with the 14th (Major General Heim) and 22nd Panzer Divisions (Major General von Apell), while the LVII Panzer Corps, with the 13th Panzer Division (Major General Herr) and the SS "Wiking" Division (SS Gruppenfuehrer Steiner), approached Rostov from the west.

On 22 July, the divisions reached the outskirts of the city and attacked the city on the next day, along with the 125th ID (Lieutenant General Schneckenburger), which had, in the meantime, arrived from the north.

A difficult street battle ensued. The defenders had erected street barriers, built barricades, laid mines, and stretched barbed wire across the streets. As the men of the 13th Panzer Division approached the Don, the great Don River Bridge was blown into the air. The battle became even more fierce during the ensuing night, but the German combat groups did not lose contact with each other.

On 24 July, the lead elements of the XLIX Mountain Corps – combat groups of the 73rd (Major General von Buenau) and 298th ID (Major General Szelinski) – reached Rostov and joined in the battle. The Soviets now began to flee the Rostov area – and, on the following day, the tanks of the

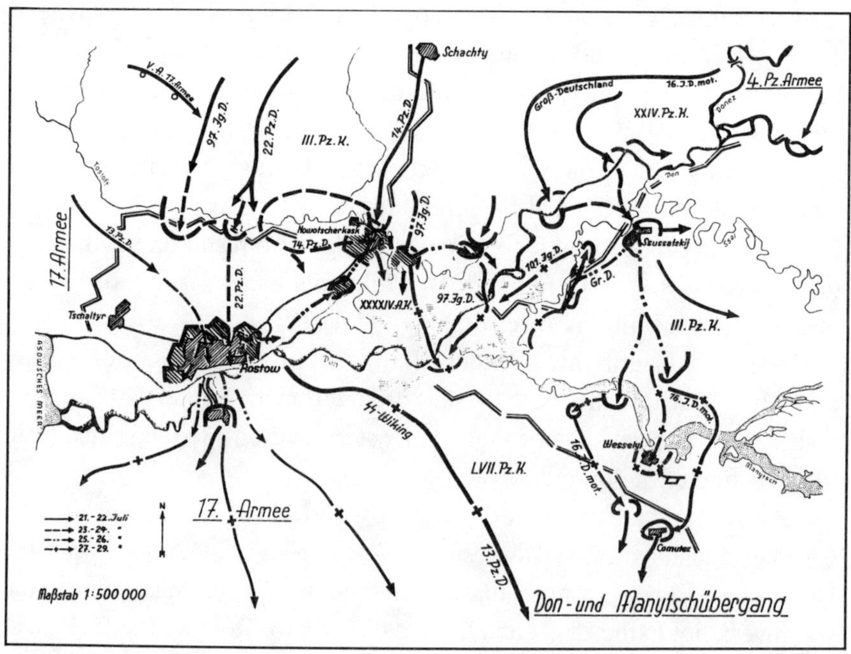

The Don and Manych Crossings

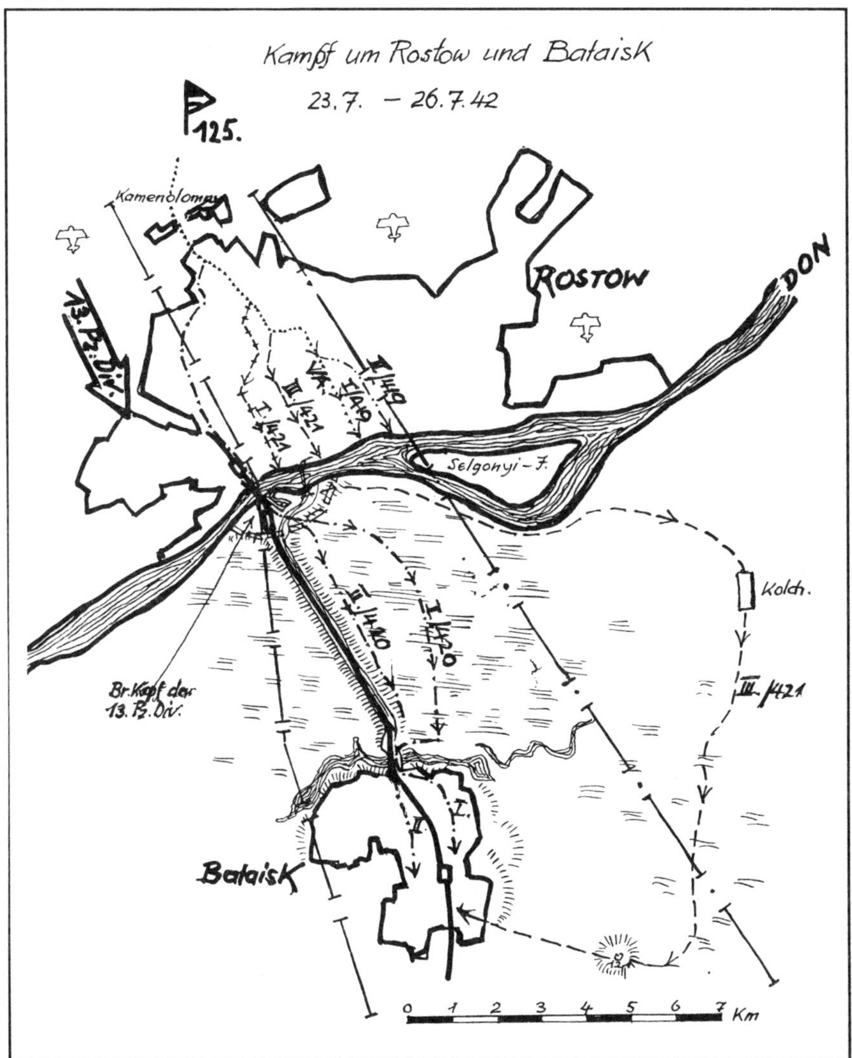

The Battle for Rostov and Bataisk 7/23-26/42

13th Panzer Division and the SS "Wiking" Division rolled over the Don to the south!

Thus began the offensive of Army Group A in the Caucasus! The 17th Army was deployed on the right flank, with four infantry and two mountain divisions. The 3rd Rumanian Army (subordinate to the 17th Army) followed in the center with three cavalry and one mountain division, while the 1st Panzer Army was on the left with three panzer, two motorized, two rifle, and two infantry divisions, as well as one Slovakian division, which had to protect the wide open flank in the direction of the Caspian Sea. Air Fleet 4, under Field Marshal Baron von Richthofen, was assigned for support.

In view of the now critical situation north of the Caucasus, the Soviet High Command formed a new army group, "North Caucasus Front", under the command of Marshal Budenny. Army Group A's mission – which they had, in part, already accomplished – read:

> "1) After making contact with friendly combat groups south of the Don, the most important task of Army Group A is to occupy the entire eastern coast of the Black Sea. The Rumanian Mountain Corps of the 11th Army will be re-subordinated and will cross the Kerch road as soon as the advance of the main forces of Army Group A takes effect.
>
> 2) With an additional combat group, composed of all of the remaining mountain and rifle divisions, the Kuban will be crossed and the high ground near Maikop and Armavir will be captured. These combat groups will then advance over all of the trafficable passes across the western portion of the Caucasus and, together with the Rumanian Mountain Corps, occupy the Black Sea coast.
>
> 3) At the same time, it is essential to form a combat group, composed of mobile formations, to establish flank protection to the east in the Grosny area and to block the Osset and Georgian roads at the mountain passes with a portion of the force. Subsequently, advance along the Caspian Sea to occupy the area around Baku."

On 30 July, after the 4th Panzer Army was again sent back to Stalingrad, Army Group A consisted of the following units, from right to left:

17th Army (General Ruoff)
with the V Army Corps (General of Infantry Wetzel) 125th and 198th ID;

XLIX Mountain Corps (General of Mountain Troops Konrad)
9th ID, 1st Mountain Division, 73rd ID and 4th Mountain Division;
3rd Rumanian Army (General Dumitrescu)
with 1st Rumanian Army Corps 298th ID, 2nd Rumanian Mountain Division;
Cavalry Corps 6th and 5th Rumanian Cavalry Divisions;
1st Panzer Army (General von Kleist)
with the XL Panzer Corps (General of Panzer Troops Baron Geyr von Schweppenburg) 23rd and 3rd Panzer Divisions;
XLIV Army Corps (Lieutenant General de Angelis)
101st and 97th Rifle Divisions;
III Panzer Corps (General of Cavalry von Mackensen)
13th Panzer Division and 16th Motorized Infantry Division;
LII Army Corps (General of Infantry Ott)
370th and 111th ID;
LVII Panzer Corps (General of Panzer Troops Kirchner)
Slovakian Mobile Division, SS "Wiking" Division.

The area, conquered by Army Group A, was classified as being in Asia, with wide steppes and numerous intersecting rivers and brooks, few watering holes, and with scorching temperatures of 40 degrees Celsius. Here we find the extremes of parching sand storms to torrential thunderstorms that cause flooding and mirages. The roads were dusty, but they were wide, so that a number of columns could march side by side. There were only a few settlements, for the land was populated chiefly by nomads. In the west there was luxuriant vegetation, but to the east it changed into pure salt desert. At the end of the steppe between the two seas rose the 1400 kilometer long, 150 kilometer wide Caucasus, a mountainous region difficult to access, the slopes of which are covered by thick primeval forests, with peaks of up to 5600 meters height and only three passes.

The German soldiers entered this unknown, mysterious land with a spirit of adventure. To guarantee security, the troops and lower leadership did not know the overall situation. Only the corps staffs knew of the long-range operations, but even they did not know its destination. They were told to execute the mission, but the divisions didn't know the objective.

The 3rd Panzer Division (Major General Breith) – the farthest advanced division – crossed the Sal on 23 July and reached the Manych, the border between Europe and Asia, six days later! The soldiers of the division crossed the 1.2 kilometer river in assault boats and continued to attack in the direction of Voroshilovsk, the capital of the region south of the Manych. A report from one who experienced this describes the unfamiliar terrain:

• • •

"Pregradnoe is a large, long town, with many branches extending from its center. Towns with several thousand inhabitants are rare here. We have come upon enormous herds of cattle, goats, and sheep, and horses of noble blood lines, always in groups of several hundred. The men are pure nomads. With bag and baggage, in primitive wagons, with mobile cattle watering devices and water barrels, they move with their herds from one pasture land to another. The threshed corn is stored in the fields – like we store potatoes – several tons at a time. In like manner, huge amounts of sunflower seeds are stockpiled. The steppes have become fruitful. An intoxicating sight. The plains undulate.... There are extensive herds of cattle on the slopes of the mountains. One town follows another. The towns give a clean, neat appearance. And each farm is a luxuriant garden....

Our advance took us through the Kalmuk Steppe.... We came upon a town and the scout troop leader reported over the radio that on the eastern edge friendly tanks were approaching. Shortly after that we laughingly realized that the "tanks" were camels. In the following days we often saw camels and dromedaries.... The land became more mountainous and the sun hotter. The armored vehicles were having difficulties climbing up the mountains in the hot temperatures...."

The scenery began to change. Mountains, which climbed to 800 and 1000 meters, appeared. Most of them were barren and yellowish brown in color. Enveloped in dusty clouds, giant herds of cattle roamed... The steppes and pasture-land changed into stretches of grain fields. The villages were kept neat and clean. More and more, the traditional thatched roofs were replaced by red tiles.... Groups of prisoners, without weapons or supervision, would turn themselves in to us. They would often greet us amiably.... With a blasé countenance and a Hapsburg lower lip, the camels would wander leisurely behind. They would again remind us that this land is the border between Europe and Asia...."

• • •

So, now let us move on to the right flank. On 3 August, the V Army Corps crossed the Kuban and continued to attacked all of its divisions in the direction of Krassnodar, the capital of the entire Kuban region.

In front of Krassnodar, the 73rd ID was in the northwest, the 9th ID in the north, and the 125th ID in the northeast. The 198th ID was coming from the east-northeast to take part in the concentrated attack against the city.

In front of Staro Korsunskaya, scouts of the forward detachment were attacking a strongly fortified tank trench. The positions were abandoned by the enemy. Over 100 mines were removed; the route was once again free. The enemy was now in Staro Korsunskaya itself. Therefore, the attack will be like the evening before; house to house combat, lots of prisoners. The rest of the Russians escaped across the Kuban.

That evening, German radio broadcast a special report on the fall of Krassnodar. However, the enemy still maintained a strong bridgehead at Pashkovskaya, an eastern suburb of the city. He tried to save what men and material he could by crossing them over the pontoon bridge that spanned the Kuban in that area. It would, of course, be most advantageous for us to capture this pontoon bridge! Therefore, during the night of 10 August, the 308th Infantry Regiment executed a forced march and received orders to immediately attack the enemy across the anti-tank ditches (which had been fortified on the northern edge of Pashkovskaya), then enter the town and, if possible, capture the pontoon bridge undamaged. At the same time, the forward detachment would try to reach the bridge from the east.

As usual, the division commander was located forward in a command post near the regiment on the main axis. The 2/308 (Major Kromer) began the battle at noon. In spite of two strikes by Soviet multiple rocket launchers and strong defensive fire from heavy infantry weapons of all types, the attack made steady headway. An assault troop of the 7th Company, 308th Infantry Regiment, under the command of Lieutenant Witsch, and secured by the Bachmor Assault Troop, succeeded in entering Pashkovskaya from the east and was able to hold their ground despite a fierce counterattack. Lieutenant Witsch and his men did not allow the Soviet tanks to drive them away. At the same time, units of the 125th ID attacked Pashkovskaya from the north.

At 1745 hours, the 308th Infantry Regiment reported: "Since breaking through the forward-most city defensive positions, the regiment has been engaged in tough hand to hand combat in the houses and vegetable gardens in the difficult environs of the city. Gradually, all units of the 2nd and 1st Battalion of the 308th Infantry Regiment have been shoved through the breakthrough point, in order to be able to fall on the external city defensive positions from behind and continue the attack into the city's center." Colonel Schultz, commander of the 308th Infantry Regiment, was leading the attack himself to maintain its momentum.

During the difficult and critical combat, the improvised regimental heavy infantry gun platoon, as well as the light and heavy air defense guns of the 4th Air Defense Regiment, proved their worth. Colonel Schultz and Lieutenant Witsch later received the Knight's Cross for their personal participation in this battle's success.

The 3/308 Infantry Regiment (Captain Niess), which, in the meantime, had been assigned to the forward detachment, captured the anti-tank trenches directly south of the Korsunskaya-Pashkovskaya road and fought their way through the difficult wooded and shrub land up to Pashkovskaya and the road leading to the pontoon bridge. The bridge was now within reach. The enemy was aware of the immanent threat, collected all available forces, including several tanks, and attacked them into the flank of the 3rd Battalion. The enemy air force also repeatedly entered the battle with low level attacks. The 3/308 did not receive the heavy weapons they were promised, and their anti-tank guns could not follow in the thick underbrush. Thus, their lead attack elements had to be withdrawn by evening. The battalion set up a hedgehog defense under the cover of darkness and in the rough wooded area.

Nevertheless, this day was a great success. Even though the division did not reach its ultimate attack objective. Throughout that entire night, they could hear the noises of vehicles and engines: The Russians were evacuating the bridgehead. (From: Graser, G.: *Between Kattegat and the Caucasus.* (the 198th ID) Tuebingen 1961.)

Just as quickly, the LVII Panzer Corps, which was about 100 kilometers further to the east, crossed the Kuban near Kropotkin and attacked through Armavir to the oil region of Maikop. During their retreat, the Soviet troops thoroughly destroyed all of the drills, conveying equipment, petroleum installations, and refineries, and giant black clouds hung over the entire area. The general front line situation of Army Group A reflected the following on 11 August, from right to left:

The 17th Army had captured Krassnodar and occupied the Yeissk Harbor on the eastern coast of the Sea of Azov. The 1st Panzer Army attacked, with its three panzer corps, into the central Caucasus and their lead elements were located near Maikop, Cherkessk, and Pyatigorsk, south of the Kuma River. On the extreme left flank, the 111th (Major General Recknagel) and the 370th ID (Major General Dr. Klepp), under the command of the LII Army Corps, advanced on a wide front through the almost unpopulated Kalmuk Steppe. The forward detachment of the 111th ID was able to occupy the most important city in the entire area, Elista, on 12 August.

During the middle of August, the 17th Army crossed the Kuban in several waves on either side of Krassnodar and advanced in the general direction of Novorossisk and Tuapse. Russian formations here from the 18th, 47th, and 56th Armies fell back to the coast and into the upper Caucasus. The German infantry, rifle, and mountain divisions were following close on their heels.

• • •

At 0825 hours, the 1/228 was ordered to begin moving from Lyssaya Mountain in the direction of Hill 612.6.

Summary: After a well planned fire preparation, the 1/ and 3/229 had good initial success. After overcoming strong enemy resistance in a ravine northeast of Hill 374.2, the hill was captured by assault. The 3/229 attacked Sattel between Hills 374.2 and 519.6.

At 0900 hours, the 2/228 succeeded in capturing Hill 350.3 further to the south with little enemy resistance. The 3/228 advanced southwest of the Shchish bend directly into strong enemy resistance. The battalion had no success. The 1/228 was able to reach Hill 612 from Lyssaya Mountain without encountering enemy resistance.

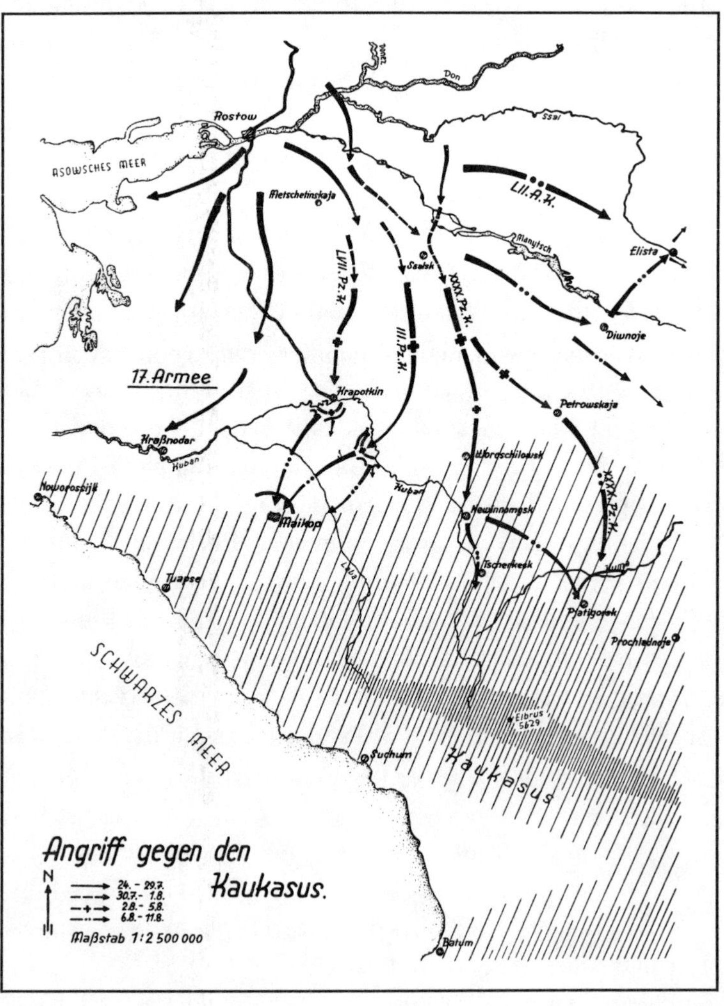

Attack against the Caucasus

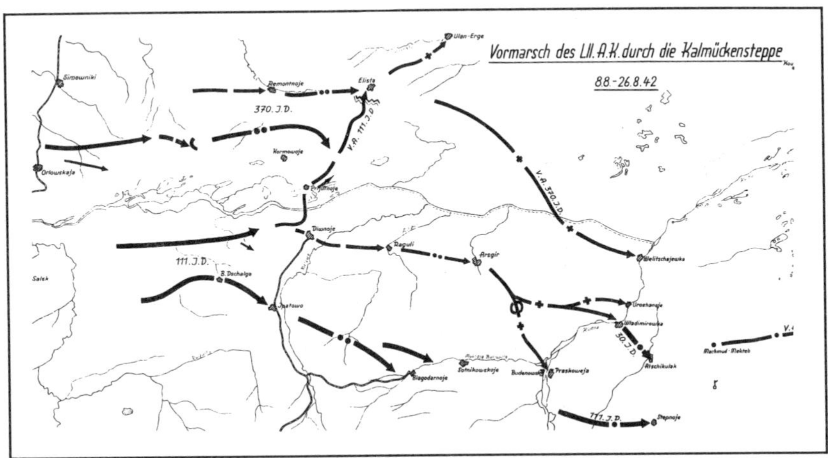

Advance of the LII Army Corps through the Kalmuk Steppe 8/8-26/42

All of the battalions were hampered by low combat strength and low fire power (except for the 1/228, all of the rifle companies had about 40-60 men), as well as the considerable difficulties in the wooded regions, which were overgrown in thick underbrush or Rhododendrons. Numerous steep ravines, many of which were not designated on their maps, made much of the terrain impassable for vehicles, and at times even for draft animals.

The 500th Battalion, which had deployed at 0900 hours, had reached the tunnels against strong enemy resistance by 1000 hours and had to hold their ground in a ravine south of the tunnels while being engaged by strong defensive fire. At 1030, the 1/500 attacked Paporotniy with the support of the assault gun battery. The assault guns advanced to the west until 1100 hours. The 1/500 came under enemy fire on the eastern edge, especially from Shchish bend.

At 0845, the 229th Rifle Regiment reported that their regimental command post was transferred to Hill 374.2, together with their 2nd Battalion.

At 0905 hours, the operations officer of the IV Air Corps called and told us that there were concentrations noted in Mirnaya Ravine and near Hill 501.1. The artillery commander and the 229th Rifle regiment were informed.

At 1045 hours, discussion with Colonel Eisenstuck (228) of the report, that the 3rd Battalion established extensive enemy deployments from Paporotniy

The Commander called at 1145 hours – Hill 519.6 must be quickly captured.

1150 hours, the 500th Battalion reports that there is strong enemy resistance west of the northern tunnel entrances.

1205 hours, the 228th Rifle Regiment reports that, in the northern sector of Paporotniy, the 1/500 is receiving heavy fire from the Hill 114/4 region.

1300 hours, the 85th Artillery Regiment is with the 3/229 about one kilometer east of Hill 519.6.

1400 hours, the wheeled battalion, minus one squadron, and with the support of an assault gun battalion, was tasked with supporting the 228th Rifle Regiment in clearing out the Shchish bend.

1525 hours, 1/228 reports that they reached the area of Hill 612.7 at 1515 hours.

1610 hours, the 1/228 is ordered to rest and conduct a reconnaissance. Further orders will follow.

Summary: Hill 519.6, which is crucial for the continuation of the attack, was captured by 1700 hours, in spite of considerable enemy resistance and terrain problems. A good reconnaissance, especially to the west, is being conducted. Senior Lieutenant Auffermann, with two companies, was deployed to the south from Hill 374.2, with the mission of attacking the road and railroad station. By 1600 hours, they reached the ravine south of Hill 374.2, which runs into the road. From here, they can effectively disturb the traffic on the road to the Chadyshenskaya railroad station. The 1/228 remains on Hill 612.6. They are conducting a good reconnaissance to the west. The 2/228 on Hill 350.3 is reconnoitering in the direction of 134.4 to the north.

The clearing of the Shchish bend is now taking place. The 3/228, the wheeled battalion, and the assault gun battalion are not making any headway.

1655 hours, the 500th Battalion reports that the enemy is very strong. A heavy infantry gun platoon of the 229th will support the battalion.

1745 hours, Major Busche reports that Hill 519.6 was captured at 1700 hours.

1905 hours, the 229th Rifle Regiment reports that Senior Lieutenant Auffermann, with the 3/101 Engineers and a reinforced company of the 1st Battalion, was located south of Hill 374.2, 100 meters north of the road.

1800-2000 hours, detailed situation review with the chief and the Commanding General. Approval of the order for the continuation of the attack. (From: Weinmann, W.: *The 101st Rifle Division.* Offenburg 1966.)

• • •

The 3rd Rumanian Army conquered the Black Sea port of Anapa and encircled the forces of the 47th Soviet Army on the Taman Peninsula during the last week of August. Units of the XLII Army Corps (General of Infantry Mattenklott), which were left in the Crimea, crossed the Kerch road and entered the battle on the Taman Peninsula on 1 September. They were able to completely occupy it within a few days.

The XLIX Mountain Corps (General of Mountain Troops Konrad), which was fighting on the left flank of the 17th Army, attacked with the 1st (Major General Lanz) and the 4th Mountain Divisions (Major General Eglseer) into the upper Caucasus through the fierce resistance of the 46th Soviet Army (Major General Sergazkov). The mountain infantrymen experienced the mountain world of the Caucasus with its snow-covered peaks, the high rocky passes, and deep valleys during splendid summer weather.

On 17 August, a combat group of the 1st Mountain Division climbed to the "Elbrushaus", at an altitude of 4200 meters, and captured the Russian garrison on the 5633 meter high Mount Elbrus – the highest mountain in the Caucasus, known locally as the "Throne of the Gods." Four days later, a mixed combat group of the 1st and 4th Mountain Divisions, mostly composed of elements of the 39th Mountain Rifle regiment, raised the Reich's battle flag on this highest of peaks.

Before the German soldiers stretched the incomparable beauty of the Caucasian Mountains. It was impossible to conduct war here on the snow covered peaks and between the mountain stone walls. Combat centered solely on seizing the few passes leading to the south towards the coast.

However, on 22 August – 28 kilometers before the harbor city of Suchum – the XLIX Mountain Corps had to give up hope of reaching the Black Sea coast because of combat losses and serious supply problems. Henceforth, the front line in the upper Caucasus remained constant.

At the end of August, the V Army Corps on the right flank, with the 73rd (Major General von Buenau) and the 125th ID (Lieutenant General Schneckenburger), reached the important harbor of Novorossisk, which later became a solid supply base for formations of the Black Sea Fleet.

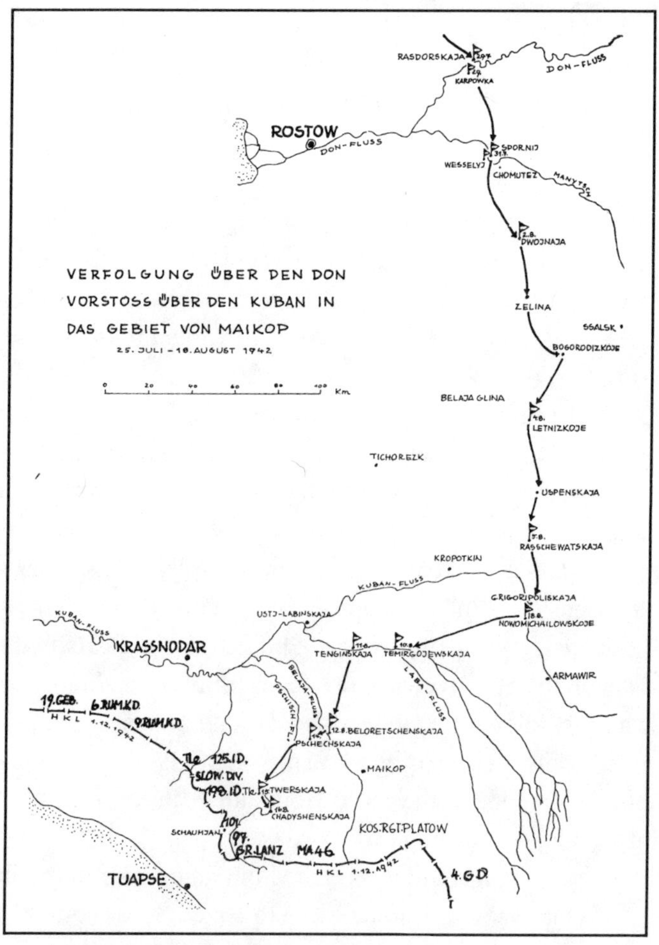

Pursuit Across the Don
Advance Across the Kuban in the vicinity of Maikop

The attack of the LVII Panzer Corps, with the 198th ID, SS "Wiking" Division, and the Slovakian Mobile Division on the right flank, and the XLIV Army Corps, with the 97th 101st Rifle Divisions against Tuapse, seesawed between the mountains and villages for about a week. A breakthrough to the coast could not be forced at this point either.

The attack of the 1st Panzer Army on the left flank could not sort itself out at this time. Here the motorized combat groups rolled forward into unknown territory.

• • •

In the gray morning of 21 August 1942, the 2/201 Panzer Regiment began to pass through Novo Ivanovskiy and cross the Urvany. At 0515 hours, the enemy deployed combat outposts from the Kolkhoz south of Pravurganski, and some of them were captured. At 0800 hours, the panzer battalion reached the Nalchik-Maisiy railroad line and fired on the double locomotive freight train that was approaching Nalchik.

The accompanying engineers blew the railroad tracks at several locations, and then the 2/201 Panzer Regiment returned to the Kolkhoz, as directed, where they were assembled as the Burmeister Combat Group to attack the bridge near Maiskiy. At 1000 hours, the combat group began the attack, supported by the 1st and 3rd battalions of the 128th Armored Artillery Regiment. The tanks fought their way to within 600 meters of the bridge in the face of heavy defensive fire from Soviet Artillery. Four anti-tank guns were firing from two anti-tank defensive belts. In front of the bridge, the enemy artillery was laying down a barrage fire. At 1600 hours the enemy blew the bridge up. The attack was broken off.

At 1745 hours, the 2/201 Panzer regiment again deployed. The objective this time was the railroad bridge across the Terek, located to the south. The 23rd Wheeled Infantry Battalion followed. The attack advanced to within 500 meters of the bridge with artillery and rocket launcher support. The attackers advanced to within 100 meters of the bridge against tenacious enemy resistance, as well as massive anti-tank and artillery fire, and then this one was also blown into the air. The attack was suspended. The Burmeister Group returned to their departure positions.

On the morning of 22 August 1942, the 8th Company of the 201st Panzer Regiment, together with elements of the 23rd Wheeled Infantry Battalion, in spite of Russian barrage fire, succeeded in approaching the Maiskiy bridge from the Pravurganski bridgehead, which was being pressured by the Soviets, especially from the west. The 12 ton bridge was destroyed, and a crossing over the deep flowing Terek is impossible. Repeated enemy attacks on the Kolkhoz west of Pravurganski was exerting pressure on the half company of the 800th Regiment (Brandenburg) that was deployed there. The commitment of the 5th Company of the 201st Panzer regiment, as well as support from a rocket launcher battery and the 1/128 Armored Artillery regiment, brought some relief to the beleaguered infantry. A tank platoon, which was brought from Nalchik to support the Soviet combat here, was set afire at noon by the 3/128 Armored Artillery Regiment, so that the Russians had to dismount.

On 23 August, the 5th Company of the 201st Panzer Regiment, with infantry and engineers, attacked to the south, pushed the enemy back from the railroad tracks, and broke through at two points. The enemy increased their fire on friendly bases and positions. The Russians continued their attempts to break through the bridgehead at Pravurganski. After his recovery, Colonel von Buch resumed command of the 128th Armored Artillery Regiment.

A barricade was formed on the left flank of the division under Colonel Brueckner, which was guarded to the south and east by the von Unger Combat Group (1/128 Rifle regiment) and the von Eisenhardt-Rothe Combat Group (128th Anti-tank Battalion). The 2 cm air defense and anti-tank guns of the 128th Anti-tank Battalion were deployed in the forward defensive positions with weak infantry elements.

On 24 August, the enemy launched several counterattacks against the division's defenses. The enemy did not gain any ground at any location.

Because of the terrain problems, there was no chance of succeeding in an attack from the present line to the south. Realizing this, the 3rd Panzer Division has already withdrawn from the Pyatigorsk-Nalchik road and advanced to the east behind the 23rd Panzer Division sector. Their attack succeeded to the east, bypassing Prokhladny. The XL Panzer Corps instructed the 23rd Panzer Division to withdraw the main combat line to the northern bank of the Baksan and detach the 201st Panzer regiment (minus the 3rd Battalion) and the 126th Rifle Regiment to the 3rd Panzer Division. (From: Rebentisch, E.: *To the Caucasus and to the Tauern.* (23rd Panzer Division) Esslingen 1963.)

The 3rd Panzer Division (Major General Breith), with the support of the 3rd Company of the "Brandenburg" Regiment, was able to establish a bridgehead across the Terek on 30 August. It would become the Wehrmacht's eastern-most, forward-deployed position on the German Front! No German soldier would go any further to the east!

• • •

The enemy had quickly recovered from their first shock. Russian artillery and especially mortars fired on the crossing sites without pause. The enemy shells constantly fell on the banks. Hundreds of fragments flew through the air and tore the first gaps in the scurrying ranks of the armored infantry. They also fell on the water and tested the courage of the engineers of the 52nd Engineer Battalion and the 96th Assault Boat Detachment. Friendly artillery was already firing on Mundar-Yurt, the first objective on the southern bank of the Terek.

The brave commander of the 1/394 Armored Infantry Regiment, Captain Baron von der Heyden-Rynsch, was mortally wounded while still on the near bank.

With him fell his adjutant, Lieutenant Ziegler, and Lieutenant Wurm. Then the first German soldiers made it to the opposite bank! Courageous officers and non-commissioned officers spurred their men forward, jumping onto the muddy bank, dashing forward for a few meters, stopping to fire ahead, and then attacking further. Senior Lieutenant Eggert was now leading the battalion.

The empty assaults would quickly return to pick up new soldiers. Many boats were blown up by shells and sank into the rapids of this mountain stream. However, the second wave occupied the boats and floated to the southern bank. By 0530 hours, the 1/394 Armored Infantry Regiment, with the 1st and 2nd Companies of the 39th Engineers, had crossed and were able to establish a small bridgehead!

Then the men of the 2/394 Armored Infantry regiment worked their way to the river. The Russian shells continued to fall. Captain Stein, the battalion commander, was severely wounded in the upper lerft thigh by a shell fragment as he was boarding a boat, and he had to be quickly evacuated. Senior Lieutenant Pollman, the commander of 6th Company, took over command without a moment's hesitation and led the second German battalion to the opposite bank.

The 1/394 Armored Infantry regiment had, in the meantime, fought another 100 meters to the south, and they slipped under the enemy's artillery fire and reached the southern edge of the forest. The 5th and 7th Companies established contact with this battalion and the river. From the 36 assault boats available in the morning, 6 were still intact by 0720 hours. The German soldiers could not re-cross the river!

From the brigade command post one could make out a trail of smoke on the southern bank that was moving in the direction of the bridgehead and was caused by enemy columns rushing to the scene. At 0700 hours, General Westhoven ordered: "Entrench and hold the bridgehead in the river bend!" Any further attack by these weakened forces against the strong enemy formations near Mundar Yurt was senseless sacrifice. Since the assault boats were out of commission, the engineers set to work. They were still being torn up by enemy shelling. All of the artillery forward observers that were brought over had been killed or wounded. Among them was Senior Lieutenant Liebke from the 5th Battery of the 75th Armored Artillery regiment. Any crossing of reinforcements would only lead to further losses. General Geyr von Schweppenburg, who arrived at the brigade command post, approved this decision.

The 1/394 Armored Infantry Regiment registered 120 casualties on this morning! The 2nd Company of the 39th Engineers was completely routed. The 52nd Engineer Battalion suffered 30% losses. In spite of all this, the men who crossed from the 394th Armored Infantry Regiment, the 1st and 2nd Companies of the 39th Engineers, the 52nd Engineer Battalion, the 906th Assault Boat Detachment, and the 3rd and 7th Companies of the 3rd Armored Infantry Regiment held their small bridgehead. (From: Haupt, W.: *The History of the 3rd Panzer Division*. Berlin 1967.)

When this attempt did not succeed, a second crossing of the swift flowing Terek was executed on 2 September by the LII Army Corps (General of Infantry Ott), which had arrived from the Kalmuk Steppe. The 111th ID (Major General Recknagel) launched a surprise crossing of the Terek near Mosdok with five battalions. Therefore, a bridgehead was established that was widened by follow-on German combat groups during the next few days.

• • •

The 8th Company is essentially engaged in the effort to widen the bridgehead as part of the combat group of the Armored Infantry Brigade of the 13th Panzer Division.

On the evening of 13 September 1942, this panzer division had a front of about 13 kilometers.

During the day long attack, the Soviet 151st and 275th Rifle Divisions and the 57th, 59th and 60th Rifle Brigades, which were committed to the battle as the day wore on, were badly battered.

On 19 September 1942, the objective of the 13th Panzer Division was the breakthrough of the Soviet mountain defenses near Elkhotovo in the valley of the "Terek" and the establishment of conditions for the continuation of the attack to the east in the direction of Grozny.

During this movement, the 5th Company accompanied a combat group of the 13th Panzer Division, which set out along the "Terek" to attack the city of Arik. Thereby, Lieutenant Lau of this company received the task of occupying the road and railroad bridge west of the city. The following is a short report concerning this:

> "Under the leadership of Lieutenant Lau, we began the daring operation against the double bridge (road and railroad bridge) across the Terek west of Arik and successfully accomplished the task.

The approximately 1200 meter long railroad bridge of the Baku-Grozny-Rostov oil transport line provided a crossing over the river. This was the objective of the operation. While there was also a street bridge that was recently constructed by the Soviets further to the south, it was less well known and not included in the attack. So the planning for the operation, which had to be conducted in just a few hours before the advance of the 13th Panzer Division, was confined to the railroad bridge. In the misty morning hours, 35 men succeeded in penetrating into the bridge defensive positions, bypassing the dirt bunkers and trenches and cutting the fuses. The enemy was so bewildered and surprised that, during the attack, which immediately followed from the defensive positions to the opposite bank, they forgot all about the fuses for the street bridge. During the operation, the Soviet demolition plan for the railroad bridge was captured, which showed that there were about 4 1/2 tons of explosives attached to three of the bridge's columns. In addition, under the first bridge span there was another charge of 32 aerial bombs.

The men that participated in this raid were awarded the Iron Cross First Class and Iron Cross Second Class, and the detachment leader, Lieutenant Lau, was presented the Knight's Cross.

Lau was first committed to provide security in Osselinskaya, and shortly after that, this operation: The assault on the great Terek bridge near Arik. The combat spokesman later released some details. Lieutenant Lau spent the night before the strike amongst the enemy's scout troops. He attacked several bunkers by himself. Lau received the Knight's Cross. We are mighty proud to have such a person in our company." (From: Spaeter, H.: *The Brandenburgers*. (The 800th ID) Munich 1982.)

• • •

Hitler, who did not fully agree with the development of the operations of Army Group A, relieved Field Marshal List as commander on 9 September and personally took command of the army group. He now commanded the army group from his headquarters in Vinnitsa. Only the chief of staff,

Lieutenant General von Greiffenberg, remained in the former headquarters in Stalino – which now became an intermediate headquarters.

Hitler demanded the breakthrough to Tuapse. By mid September, all non-essential forces before Novorossisk from the V Army Corps and units of the XLIX Mountain Corps were brought forward. The systematically prepared attack did not achieve initial success along the passes to Tuapse. The resistance of the 56th Soviet Army (Major General Ryschov) was too strong here and the 17th Army was compelled to give up any further breakthrough attempts on the fourth day of combat.

Combat continued on the eastern portion of the Caucasus Front. Units of the 13th Panzer Division (Major General Herr) and the SS "Wiking"

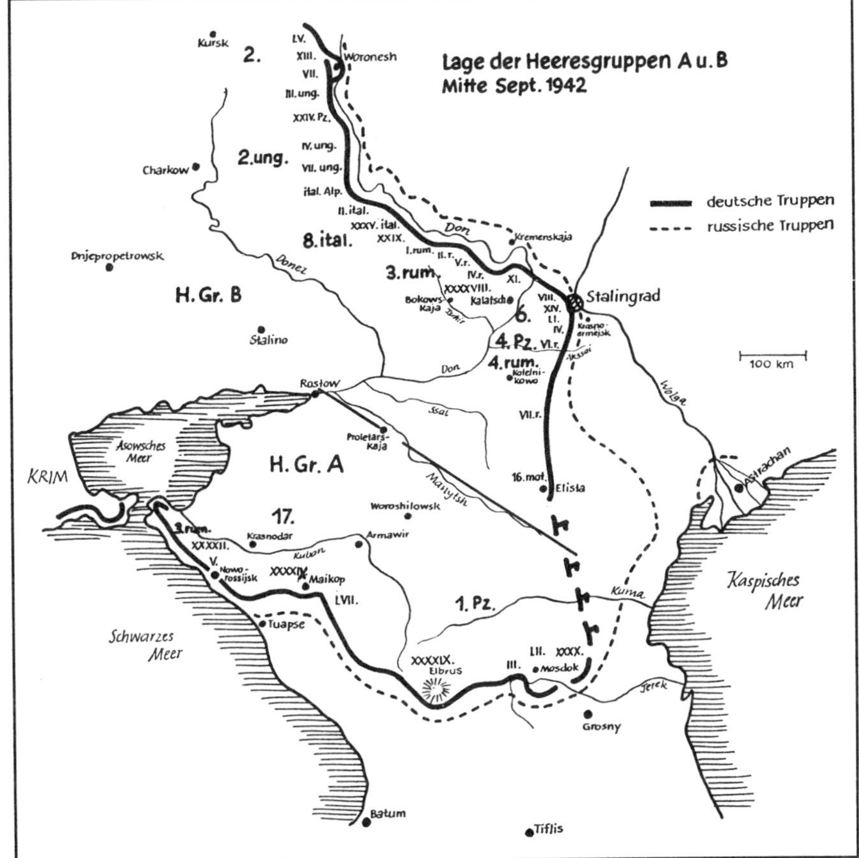

Dispositions of Army Groups A and B

Division (SS Gruppenfuehrer Steiner) began the attack on Grozny and were able to capture Malgobek on 6 October.

As the "Wiking" Division reached the Terek, the situation was already becoming serious. They had to break through obstacle belts, constructed by the Soviets south of Mosdok, and through Malgobek and Sagopshin to reach the "Georgian Road", over which the Soviets were receiving American war materials from Iran. This was the strategic route through Armenia and Georgia to the interior of Soviet Russia where, at this very moment, the battle of Stalingrad had begun.

For Army Group South this meant fighting simultaneously in the Caucasus and on the Volga – a strain, especially since the Luftwaffe shifted its emphasis to Stalingrad.

The SS Gruppenfuehrer knew, on the other hand, that the Soviet barriers which blocked the roads from Grozny to the Caspian Sea had to be removed. Therefore, he divided the division into four columns. The "Northland" had to attack on either side of the Kurp River to Malgobek. The panzer battalion was ordered to establish a bridgehead within the enemy's defense. Together with them, the "Westland" had to eliminate the enemy in Sagopshin. The engineers also had to advance along the Kurp. However, the plan's execution ran into unexpected obstacles.

The attack began during the night of 25-26 September. It was already cold and the valley was covered in fog. At 0500 hours, the German artillery began its fire strikes. The men of "Northland" soon discovered that, not only was the enemy in front of them numerically superior, but they were also established in well constructed defensive positions. A half hour after the attack began, half of the men had fallen. Several of the commanders and their deputies fell or were wounded. Nevertheless, they succeeded in capturing a hill, from which the buildings of Malgobek and the refineries of the city were visible. Now the Soviets began to use their artillery. (From: Mabire, J.: *SS Panzer Division "Wiking"*, Oldendorf 1983.)

• • •

A last major attack was attempted in the 1st Panzer Army sector on 25 October. This time, the objective was Ordshonikidze, halfway between Terek and the capital of Georgia, Tiflis. The III Panzer Corps (General of Cavalry Mackensen) deployed the 23rd Panzer Division (Major General Baron von Boineburg-Lengsfeld had again taken command) on the right, and the 13th Panzer Division (Major General von der Chevallerie) on the left, while the SS "Wiking" Division (SS Gruppenfuehrer Steiner) maintained contact with the LII Army Corps near Mosdok.

The attack went contrary to expectations. The 37th Soviet Army fell back and surrendered Nalchik. Three of its divisions were smashed, and 7,000 prisoners were taken. By 1 November, German combat groups were in Alagir and, the next day, they reached the northern edge of Ordshonikidze – the city itself could not be taken.

• • •

The objective of our attack was visible in front of us: Ordshonikidze.

The only thing separating us was a bare plain.

According to the statements of prisoners, the city was completely fortified, surrounded by concrete bunkers, anti-tank defenses covered by steel bunkers, and the usual mine fields and such.

After overcoming enemy resistance in the Gisel area, the lead battalions came upon some of the anti-tank trenches near the airfield. Our armored infantry advanced further and further and approached to within 1800 meters of the eastern edge of the city.

Ordshonikidze was an important ordnance site for the Soviet armies in the Caucasus. Beyond the city ran the Georgian Road, one of the important routes over which the Soviets transported supplies from Tiflis in the Transcaucasus. The 2/93 was deployed to the right, to the left was the 2/66, and the 1/66 was in the rear. Combat Group 43, reinforced by the 3/4 Panzer regiment, covered the left flank, while the 1st and 2nd Battalions of the 4th Panzer regiment were held in reserve.

To protect the right flank adjacent to the mountains, the 1/99 Mountain Rifle Regiment, which was subordinated to us, was deployed with a battery of the 203rd Assault Gun Battalion and a company of the 627th Engineers. These units were to try to advance to the Georgian Road.

Combat Group Barth, reinforced with a panzer company, protected the flank in the north of our sector, advancing against enemy tanks moving in from the north. They destroyed 9 enemy tanks here.

Nevertheless, this did not stop enemy units from attacking our march routes, vehicles, and supply convoys.

Now all units, including the supply troops, had to take up the defense.

The Russians hit us not only with reinforced artillery, rocket, and antitank fire, but also with waves of air strikes. He also sprayed us with Phosphorous. Friendly aircraft did not show up. Allegedly, they were urgently needed in the Stalingrad area. General von Mackensen tried to get through to us, but the route (there were no roads) was occupied by the enemy.

In this difficult situation, our new division commander, Major General von der Chevallerie, took command. He had to push his way through in one of our tanks that was being used for supply convoy escort. Following in a second tank, the deputy operations officer, Captain Soldan, was wounded.

The repeated enemy attacks in our rear, which were inflicting great casualties on us, made it clear that the enemy was aware of our weaknesses and wanted to separate us from our rear support area, in order to encircle us. Under these circumstances, we had to establish alert companies from the rear area units and even arm the field hospital to protect the rear area services. (From: *The Fate of the 13th Panzer Division*, Wulfsfelde 1971.)

• • •

Thus, the last German offensive operation in the Caucasus Mountains fizzled out. On 1 November, Hitler left his headquarters in Vinnitsa and went back to Rastenburg (East Prussia) and the "Wolf's Lair." A few days later, he relinquished command of Army Group A to General von Kleist. The command of the 1st Panzer Army was given to General of Cavalry von Mackensen. The Caucasus was relegated to a secondary theater of operations after the 6th Army was encircled at Stalingrad. The army group was placed at "order arms." During the night of 17 December, the 17th Army evacuated the bridgehead over the Pshikh and established solid defensive positions in the mountains. All further offensive engagements were terminated. The losses of the divisions were enormous, as the example of a division in front of Tuapse shows:

Losses of the 101st Rifle Division

	During the attack of 1941-1942	*KIA*	*WIA*	*MIA*
6/22-6/27	Breakthrough the Galician border fortifications			
6/28-6/30	Battle for Lemberg			
7/1-7/14	Pursuit battle to the Stalin Line			
7/15-7/16	Breakthrough to the Stalin Line			
7/17/7/24	Pursuit to the Sod			
7/25-8/8	Battle near Uman			
8/9-8/30	Advance to the Dnepr			
9/2-9/12	Attack across the Dnepr			
9/13-10/6	Pursuit battle through Poltava			
10/7-10/30	Pursuit to the Donets	777	2,852	92
11/1-11/30	Combat on the upper Donets	14	61	7
12/1-1/5	March from Kharlov to Gorlovka	4	6	
1/6-1/17	Defensive battle in the Donets Basin	180	700	60
1/18-4/7	Defensive battle in the Donets Basin (the Puechler Group is an estimation)	124	390	11
4/8-5/16	Spring defensive battle in Donets Basin	4	20	
5/17-5/27	Extermination battle of Barvenkovo	163	710	62
5/28-6/2	Defense in the Donets Basin	4	23	
6/3-6/21	Defensive battle around Isyum	11	52	
6/22-6/26	Battle of Isyum and Kupyansk	100	420	40
6/27-7/8	Preparation and regrouping in the Slavyansk area for the breakthrough in the Donets Basin	11	45	
7/9-7/24	Breakthrough and pursuit in the Donets Basin to the lower Don	23	61	5
7/25-8/6	Pursuit across the lower Don	6	13	
8/7-8/18	Attack across the Kuban in the Maikop region	70	310	37
8/18-1/15	Combat in the upper and west Caucasus	1239	5750	149
		+ (1508 illnesses)		

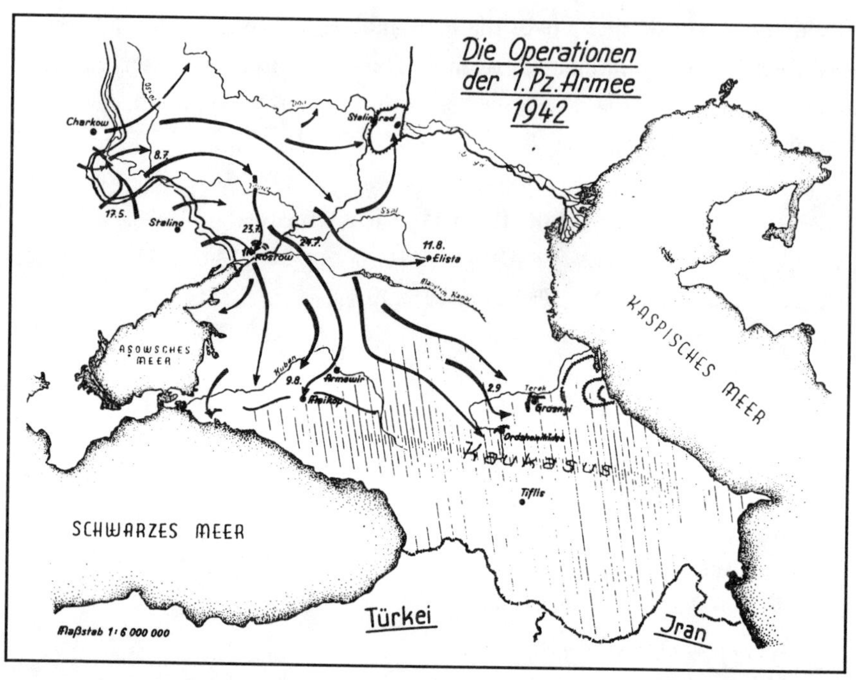

Die Operationen der 1. Pz. Armee 1942
Charkow
Stalingrad
Stalino
Rostow
Elista
Armawir
Maikop
Grosnyj
Ordshonikidse
Tiflis
ASOWSCHES MEER
KASPISCHES MEER
SCHWARZES MEER
KAUKASUS
Türkei
Iran
Maßstab 1:6 000 000

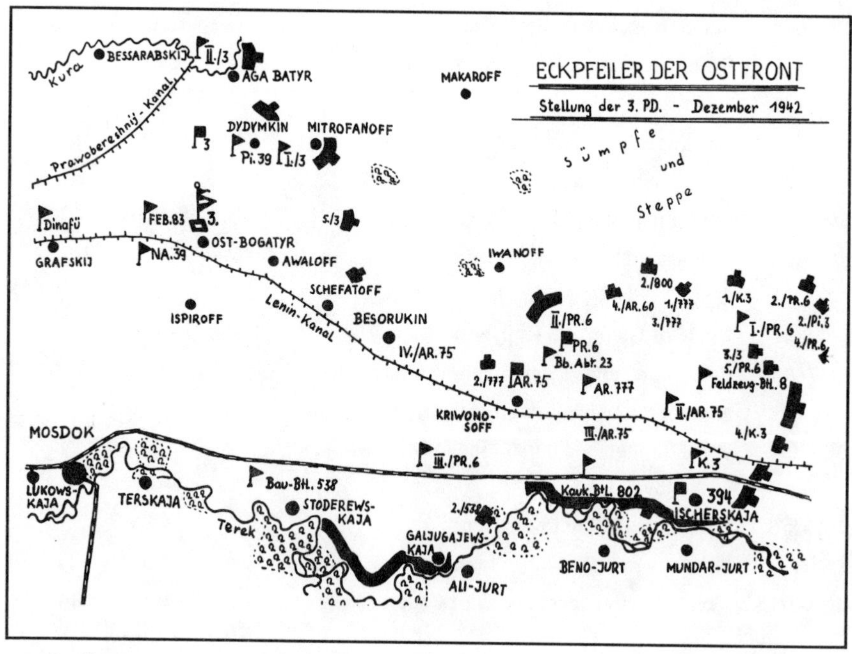

ECKPFEILER DER OSTFRONT
Stellung der 3. PD. - Dezember 1942
Kura
Prawobereshnij-Kanal
BESSARABSKIJ
AGA BATYR
MAKAROFF
DYDYMKIN
MITROFANOFF
Sümpfe und Steppe
Dinafü
FEB.83
OST-BOGATYR
GRAFSKIJ
NA.39
AWALOFF
IWANOFF
SCHEFATOFF
ISPIROFF
Lenin-Kanal
BESORUKIN
IV./AR.75
KRIWONOSOFF
MOSDOK
LUKOWSKAJA
TERSKAJA
Terek
Bau-Btl. 538
STODEREWSKAJA
GALJUGAJEWSKAJA
ALI-JURT
BENO-JURT
MUNDAR-JURT
ISCHERSKAJA
Kauk. Btl. 802
394
III./PR.6
III./AR.75
II./AR.75
K.3
4./K.3
Feldzeug-Btl. 8
AR.777
AR.75
2./777
Bb. Abt. 23
PR.6
II./PR.6
I./PR.6

In the second half of December, the divisions of Army Group A reported an average personnel shortage of about 4,000 men per division. Especially heavy were the losses of the infantry divisions, which had lost many of their commanders, officers, and non-commissioned officers. The battle for the Caucasus was practically over.

On 28 December, the OKH Ordered the withdrawal of Army Group A from the Caucasus. Hitler finally gave up the region beyond the Don and withdrew Army Group A to the Crimea and the southern Ukraine to the Mius line. The retreat began during the night of 1 January 1943.

3

1943

STALINGRAD
(19 November 1942 - 2 February 1943

Combat in Stalingrad practically came to a standstill in the middle of September, as the great march of the "Red Army" to destroy the 6th German Army neared completion. At 0500 hours on 19 November, more than 10,000 guns of all calibers fired their shells onto the positions of the German, Italian, and Rumanian troops on the Don Front.

Two Russian army groups set out from the Kletskaya and Serafimovich bridgeheads north of Stalingrad against the 3rd Rumanian Army (General Dumitrescu). These were Army Group "Southwest Front" (Lieutenant General Vatutin), with the 5th Tank Army, the 1st Guards Army, and the 21st Army, supported by the VIII Cavalry Corps and the 2nd and 17th Air Armies, as well as Army Group "Don Front" (Lieutenant General Rokossovskiy), with the 24th and 65th Armies, and supported by the 16th Air Army.

At the same time, three cavalry and three tank corps, as well as 40 rifle divisions, attacked in the first hours of this winter's day, scattering the five Rumanian army corps and threatening the XI Army Corps on the left flank of the 6th Army. However, on the next day, the situation came to a head as units of Army Group "Stalingrad Front" (General Yeremenko), with the 51st and 57th Armies, as well as the 8th Air Army, overran the 4th Rumanian Army near Krasnoarmeisk, directly south of Stalingrad.

The Russian attack was launched on a wide front and had the objective of encircling the 3rd Rumanian Army by the second day. The 1st Guards Army (Lieutenant General Lelyushenko) penetrated to the east to the upper Chir, while the bulk of the two other armies – including almost all of the tank forces – wheeled to the south and southeast behind the 6th Army.

The army commander (General Paulus) still had not realized the strength of the Russian offensive by the evening of the second day of the battle. Only the officers at the front and their men in the trenches perceived it.

• • •

On 18 November, a sunny autumn morning, a terrain briefing was conducted with the commanders. Before dawn, one could hear heavy artillery fire far to the north and had the vague feeling that something was amiss. I had arrived at the command post of the 4th Panzer Army with the briefing

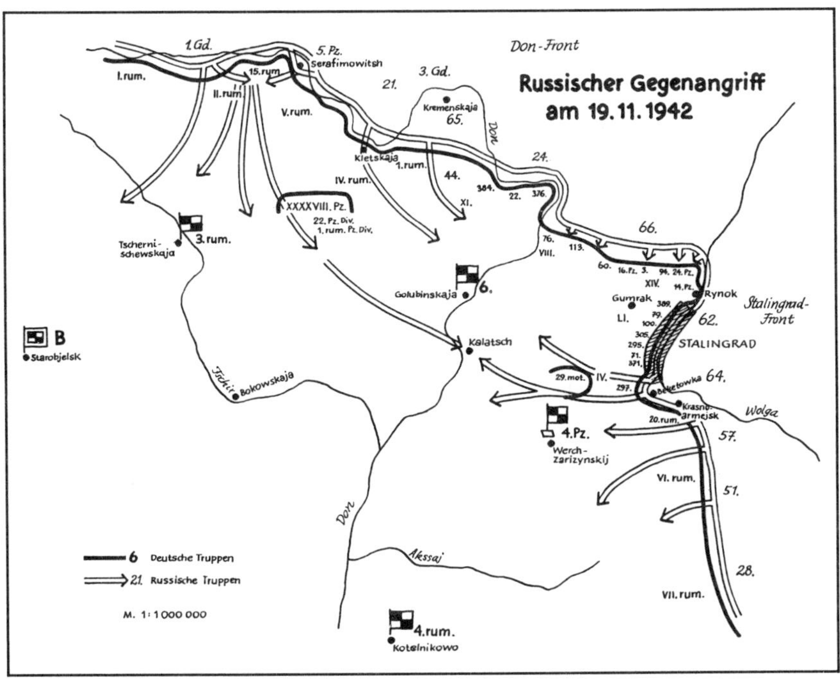

The Russian Counterattack on 11/9/1942

participants, just as a courier vehicle arrived with instructions to report to General Hoth. The General quickly briefed me on the following situation:

This morning, after heavy artillery preparation, the Russians broke through the area west of the 6th Army's northern front, near the Rumanians and Italians, on a wide front with tank forces and a probable strike direction to the south and southwest. The situation there was still very unclear. The XLVIII Panzer Corps northwest of Kalach, which was also in the threatened area, was tasked with restoring the situation with several of its panzer and motorized formations. The 29th Motorized Infantry Division was to be prepared to march immediately, and during the course of the day they would probably be subordinated to the XLVIII Panzer Corps. They were to conduct a route reconnaissance immediately. The General told me that he estimated the situation to be serious, because reports on the enemy in the area south of Stalingrad were also alarming. Then I was dismissed.

I then went back to where my commanders were waiting and issued a corresponding order.

The noise of the battle in the northwest increased at times. My route reconnaissance reported that at the Don crossing near Kalach there were no attempts to cross and alleged that the Russians were already in the city with tanks. Then we awaited orders; the division was, so to speak, mounted and ready to go, but we didn't.

We then were informed by the panzer army that the Russians had penetrated deep, but the situation was still unclear. On the morning of 19 November, the sound of combat directly east and south of our assembly area alerted us that the fun had begun to the south of Stalingrad.

The morning of 19 November still brought no clarification of the situation. From high ground in the vicinity of our location, one could see heavy movement in the south on the Stalingrad-Kotelnikovo-Rostov railway, but we did not know if it was friend or foe. My reconnaissance soon revealed that the Rumanians had completely disintegrated.

During the late afternoon, the commitment order for the division arrived: the enemy had broken through at all locations. The commitment of the division in the north was impossible. During the night, the 29th Motorized Infantry Division prepared to attack to the south on the morning of 20

November and to push the enemy back that had broken through in the south, by attacking to the south in the direction of Ellista, and destroy them.

The mission was not difficult for a well rested, fully refreshed, mobile motorized division, but under these conditions – the Russians from the north were already near Kalach – it was not encouraging.

The reconnaissance was conducted, and the area was sufficiently covered.

After the preparation, the division set off in the instructed direction with the tank battalion in the lead. (From: Lemelsen, A.: *29th Division*. Bad Nauheim 1960.)

• • •

Army Group B (headquartered in Starobelsk) realized the danger of the Russian breakthrough early on the first day and mobilized its only available reserve. It was the XLVIII Panzer Corps (Lieutenant General Heim), with the 1st Rumanian Panzer Division and the 22nd German Panzer Division (Colonel Rodt), that was immediately alerted and sent forward in the direction of Kletskaya. Both divisions slowly advanced, becoming separated from each other as they moved to the northeast due to road obstacles, and were frittered away by the concentrated forces of the advancing 5th Soviet Tank Army (Lieutenant General Romanenko).

The XLVIII Panzer Corps, after running into the superior Soviet tank troops, were split apart, encircled, and lost half of their vehicles in the first two days of combat.

In the meantime, the front to the south of Stalingrad was also broken through. Indeed, the 29th Motorized Infantry Division (Major General Leyser) – the sole reserve of the 4th Panzer Army – was committed to counterattack. In the first attack, the division was able to advance almost to Betekovka – on the southern edge of Stalingrad, but then they were compelled to withdraw.

The commander of the 4th Panzer Army (General Hoth) in Werch-Tsaritsynski was driven out of his headquarters and, therefore, lost contact with his division. The 4th Panzer Army was temporarily subordinated to the commander of the 6th Army in Stalingrad.

However, the situation deteriorated further. On 22 November, the opposing pincers of the Soviet offensive made contact on the Don! Therefore, the entire 6th Army, the IV Army Corps of the 4th Panzer Army, and the 1st Rumanian Cavalry Division were encircled! In all, 250,000 soldiers, with about 100 tanks, 1,800 guns, and 10,000 vehicles of all types were caught in the Stalingrad pocket.

Hitler, the Supreme Commander of the Wehrmacht, stayed in the Berghof near Berchtesgaden during the first two days of the battle. On 22 November, he immediately returned to his headquarters, the "Wolf's Lair", in Rastenburg. His first decisions regarded the leadership of Army Group A, which was still fighting in the Caucasus. He appointed General von Kleist as commander of Army Group A and General von Mackensen as commander of the 1st Panzer Army. On 22 November, he ordered General Paulus:

"The 6th Army is to dig in and await relief!"

A few days later, General Paulus sent a reply and asked for permission to break out. However, Hitler turned him down after Reichsmarshall Goering, the commander in chief of the Luftwaffe, told him, during the first situation briefing in the Führer's headquarters, that he could fly in 300 tons of supplies to Stalingrad daily.

The air supply of Stalingrad began on 25 November, as the transport squadrons of the Luftwaffe, which were gathered from the remaining fronts, under the command of the VIII Air Corps (Lieutenant General Fiebig), tried to sustain the encircled 6th Army.

The situation on the 6th Army front worsened. General Paulus established a bridgehead northwest of the Don, in which the three divisions of the XIV Panzer Corps (General of Panzer Troops Hube), along with the 14th (Major General Baessler), 16th (Lieutenant General Angern), and 24th (Major General von Lenski) remained. However, these three divisions were encircled by two Russian tank corps and driven across the Don to the east, north of Kalach.

The 6th Army was now firmly encircled, since a breakout was forbidden by the highest authority. Luckily, the Russian formations also remained in and around Kalach, so the 6th Army was able to stabilize its front.

The encirclement was quickly strengthened. Supplies were exhausted, the daily ration was cut dramatically, ammunition was rationed, and the first aid stations overflowed. However, the hardest thing for the soldiers to endure was the loss of the mail from home.

Caught in the Stalingrad pocket, the front line of which extended close to 200 kilometers, were:

The 6th Army Commander,
The IV, VIII, XI, LI Army Corps and the XIV Panzer Corps;
The 14th, 16th, 24th Panzer Divisions;
The 3rd, 29th, 60th Motorized Infantry Divisions;
The 44th, 71st, 76th, 79th, 94th, 100th, 113th, 295th, 297th, 305th, 371st, 376th, 384th, 389th Infantry Divisions and the 20th Rumanian Infantry Division;
The 1st Rumanian Cavalry Division;
The 648th Army Signal Regiment;

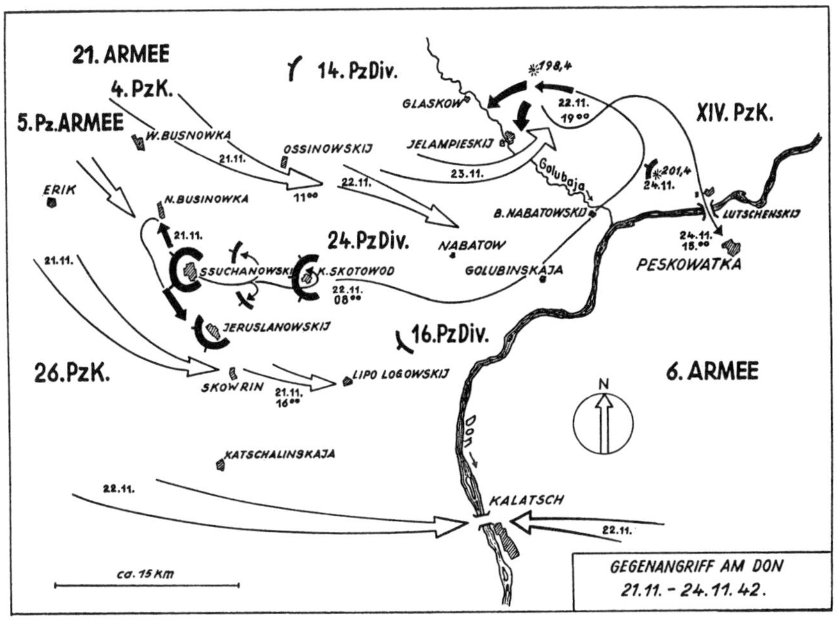

Counterattack on the Don 11/21-24/42

The 2nd and 51st Mortar Regiments;
The 91st Air Defense Regiment;
The 243rd and 245th Assault Gun Battalions;
The 45th, 225th, 294th, 336th, 501st, 605th, 652nd, 672nd, 685th, 912th, 921st, 925th Army Engineer Battalions;
In addition, 150 independent army artillery units, construction battalions, military police battalions, and others.

On 23 November, General Baron von Weichs sent a message to the OKH. The commander of Army Group B stressed that he supported rescuing the encircled 6th Army. Unfortunately, the army group commander was not given the corresponding order, and the OKH reacted otherwise.

Field Marshal von Manstein, the former commander before Leningrad, was recalled to the southern front and had to take command of the newly formed Army Group "Don" that was responsible for the German formations in the greater Stalingrad area. Therefore, Field Marshal von Manstein commanded the 6th Army, 4th Panzer Army, and 3rd and 4th Rumanian Armies. These units – with the exception of those divisions located in Stalingrad – were tasked with stopping the Russian offensive and freeing the 6th Army.

The battle for Stalingrad entered its second phase at the beginning of December. Russian assault troops attempted to break through the German defensive positions on the outskirts of the city and capture the area west of the city. However, because the OKH did not allow the troop commanders freedom of operation, the Germans could not take any countermeasures. Only the commander of the LI Army Corps, General of Artillery von Seydlitz-Kurzbach, ordered the troops in his sector to withdraw to better defensive positions.

• • •

On the 5th of December, the enemy broke through near Novo Aleksandrovskiy. 17 tanks of the 16th Panzer Division, together with 30 guns, attempted a counterattack. They had to retreat twice – nine tanks survived. They put all of their eggs in one basket. They started up their engines and advanced against the enemy, ignoring the enemy fire, but there were so many Russians. They took flight. Five friendly tanks reached the old defensive line. Here, there were many mortars and anti-tank guns – the Russians abandoned them. But the price for this success was too high.

Each panzer battalion of the 16th Panzer Division now had only about ten operational tanks. The maintenance companies fixed the damaged tanks by taking replacement parts from other destroyed tanks. However, the men were not replaced.

On the 6th of December, Combat Group Strack advanced to cut off a 6 kilometer deep penetration near Barbukin. They recaptured the high ground in a surprise attack. Suddenly, heavy Russian tanks and infantry attacked. Neither the anti-tank guns nor the artillery were set up, so there was nothing left to do but flee. The men ran for their lives. Half of Combat Group Strack was wiped out. Among the dead were Senior Lieutenant von Mutius and Lieutenant Wupper. Lieutenant Kirchner then took command of the remainder of the company.

The men were kept together and were placed in the combat reserve with some tanks from the 24th Panzer Division, but the groups quickly melted away. They last fought as the 24th Panzer Division reserve in the southwest of the pocket, west of Karpov.

The groups in the northern sector of the front had to endure constant combat. The Russians constantly attacked Hill 147.6 with assault groups in company strength and tanks. Twice they succeeded in breaking through the defensive positions, and twice they were thrown back by counterattacks with cold steel. Again, the old demon of combat reigned, and more and more shortages of necessities paralyzed the conduct of combat. Friendly artillery had its hands tied. Heavy caliber artillery was not flown in; the daily ration for light batteries had to be set at 16 rounds, and for heavy infantry guns, only two rounds. Only infantry ammunition avoided rationing. This was because, instead of the required and promised 500 tons, during the beginning of December no more than 100 tons were flown into the pocket daily. In December, 246 transports were lost over Stalingrad. The artillerymen blew up their canons and attacked with carbines and machine-guns. The men of the 1/16 Artillery Regiment began to transform themselves into infantrymen. Also, all non-essential drivers were sent to the front lines. However, they still did not have enough forces to cover the wide division sector. Above all, there was a shortage of fuel. Fuel was authorized only for the transport of the wounded. The other men needed material to construct positions and firewood for the bunker ovens. Each authorized trip into the ruins of Stalingrad was a special event.

Positions were slowly constructed. Captain Immig's engineer battalion, which was retained as the division reserve, moved forward night after night and, in spite of the biting cold of minus 20 to 30 degrees, laid mines and stretched wire obstacles. But the Russians were alert, and on moonlit nights, the engineers suffered many casualties.

On the 6th and 7th of December, the enemy artillery fire increased; assault troops put out feelers into the German trenches, and during the night the engines of the tanks droned.

On the morning of the 8th of December, two Russians deserted to the 16th Panzer Division and gave away the plan and time of the attack. Radio warnings were passed to all combat groups. Staff reports were hastily sent forward. Already the artillery, including eight Stalin Organs, began the artillery preparation. On the right, in front of Combat Group Reinisch, the attack collapsed, for its main effort was located in the center.

Tanks equipped with guns broke through the defenses of the wheeled infantry and destroyed foxhole after foxhole, though crews fought to the last cartridge. Then the Russian infantry followed in several waves. They captured the majority of Hill 145, but then came under defensive fire. The 5/65 and 2/16 Artillery regiments, committed as infantrymen, suffered heavy losses. The few remaining friendly artillery pieces and rocket launchers were silent – they had no ammunition..

A small band of men, armed with only rifles and bayonets, were nearly exterminated by the atrocious superiority of the enemy in equipment and men. (From: Werthen, W.: *History of the 16th Panzer Division*, Bad Nauheim 1958, reprinted 1985.)

• • •

The commander of Army Group Don (Field Marshal von Manstein) immediately set out to relive Stalingrad. On 12 December the 4th Panzer

Army (General Hoth) left for the Kotelnikovo area, along with the LVII Panzer Corps (General of Panzer Troops Kirchner) with the 6th (Major General Raus) and 23rd Panzer Divisions (Lieutenant General Baron von Boineburg-Lengsfeld), to attack to the northeast, with the objective of making contact with Stalingrad. Five days later, the 17th Panzer Division (Major General von Senger und Etterlin) participated in this attack in the central sector of the Shisdra Front.

General Raus intended to commit the tanks at night to reach the Aksai crossing, but Colonel von Huenersdorff refused, "because it was very difficult to orient at night and the chance of tanks slipping into icy ravines was very high." This is according to the combat diary of the 11th Panzer Regiment.

The losses of the division on the first day of the attack were low: 2 officers, and 13 non-commissioned officers and men wounded.

"In the early morning, Combat Group Quentin (the 6th Armored Reconnaissance Battalion) and Panzer Group Huenersdorff started out to a crossing over the Aksai," noted the combat diary on 13 December. "Combat Group Quentin quickly ran into enemy tanks at point 90.7. There were also Stalin Organs and other strong artillery there."

The combat diary of the 11th Panzer Regiment states: "The advance was delayed by two icy ravines. A short fire fight occurred with enemy tanks east of the bend in the railroad tracks. East of the tracks, Group Quentin requested assistance against these tanks. The commander decided not to allow them to break contact with these tanks, but ordered them to continue forward to the northwest to Salivskiy."

The crossing over the Aksai near Salivskiy was conducted by the tanks at 0800 hours.

The combat diary of the 11th Panzer Regiment:

> "The 1st Battalion moved to the north and prepared to attack Verchne-Kumskiy. While the 1st Battalion was crossing, the regiment commander's tank broke down on the bridge while crossing, and blocked the crossing for the following vehicles. The 1st Battalion could not redirect the remaining forces. The 114th Armored Personnel Carrier Battalion and artillery were assigned to support the regiment in the

attack. After a stuka attack on Verchne-Kumskiy, the commander decided to attack with only the 1st Battalion. Verchne-Kumskiy was captured at 1200 hours with weak enemy resistance. Bridging over the Aksai was then initiated, because the broken down tank could not be removed from the bridge."

Group Quentin (6th Armored Reconnaissance Battalion), after reporting on enemy tanks, was tasked with security near Biryukovski, because the 23rd Panzer Division still had not advanced as far as the 6th Panzer Division.

During the morning, panzer forces, which were gathered near Verchne-Kumskiy before the beginning of the attack, arrived. They secured the northwest of Verchne-Yablochniy, which was captured the day before, and then they moved to the northeast. As they turned from Verchne-Yablochniy, infantry also suddenly appeared. Therefore, the division requested the 4th Air Corps to commit stukas, which were sent to protect the Aksai crossing. The combat diary of the operations officer:

> "The effect of the stuka bombing was devastating. The tanks wildly drove into each other and tried to seek cover in the Yablochnaya Ravine. The stukas renewed their attack in the afternoon, and continued until darkness fell.
>
> Scout troops from the 2nd Battalion of the 4th Armored Infantry Regiment were able to establish that half of the tanks were destroyed or damaged and that the Russian equipment and dead had to be abandoned. On the whole, it appeared that the Russians were interrupted in their construction of a continuous defensive line on the Aksai and that the division could now continue its preparations. At any rate, it appeared that the Russian forces were not part of a systematic resistance effort, but were quickly thrown together to hold our advance." (From: Paul, W.: *Fire Point.* (6th Panzer Division) Krefield 1977.)

At the same time, the army group commander established a new defensive front along the Chir. General of Infantry Hollidt, the former commander of the XVII Army Corps, took command of both the XVII Army Corps (Major General Cholitz) and the XLVIII Panzer Corps (General of Panzer Troops von Knobelsdorff) defensive fronts to halt the complete collapse of Army Group B (The former commander of the XLVIII Panzer Corps was relieved of his post by Hitler, due to the failure of the first counterattack against the 5th Soviet Tank Army).

The attack of the 4th Panzer Army – supported by combat air formations taken from the IV Air Corps in the Caucasus – initially went well. In a four day battle, three Russian corps were thrown back and the Aksai was crossed at several locations. On 19 December, the lead elements of the panzer corps approached to within 48 kilometers of the southern Stalingrad front. However, on the Myshkova, the advance was stopped by defensive fire from the 51st Soviet Army and the sudden arrival of the 2nd Guards Army.

The 6th Panzer Division fought for three days against three Soviet tank brigades, losing the bulk of its vehicles and officers. The division took up the defense and then had to withdraw. The same was true of the 23rd Panzer Division, which was practically at the end of its strength and could advance no further.

And they would go no further! On 16 December, the Russian Army Group "Voronezh Front" (Lieutenant General Golikov), with the 1st and 3rd Guards and the 6th Armies, attacked the defensive positions of the 8th Italian Army in the direction of Chir and Rostov. The front line of the Italian formations was penetrated on the very first day. Soviet tank forces continuously attacked the Millerovo-Tartsinskaya-Morozovsk line. The 124 "JU-52" air transports, located in Tartsinskaya, which were prepared to fly supplies to Stalingrad, were just able to take off under enemy fire – so quickly was the new phase of the Russian offensive executed.

Meanwhile, the winter battle now raged around Stalingrad. The 6th Army described the difficulty of the battle – to quote only a few – in two messages as follows:

"10 December, 1950 hours:
Heavy losses during the defensive battles of recent days, together with physical exhaustion due to the lack of supplies, necessitates our taking

immediate measures to relieve the defending formations after the opening of the fortress."

"11 December, 2115 hours:
The amount of supplies flown in is far below expectations. Since 23 November, 70 tons have arrived daily. The necessary 600 ton ammunition supply has been precariously reduced. There have been a lot of supply shortages since 19 February."

• • •

The new Soviet offensive against the 8th Italian Army (General Gariboldi) was threatening the collapse of the entire front from Chir to the Sea of Azov. Field Marshal von Manstein, with a heavy heart, called off the friendly attack in the direction of Stalingrad to avoid further catastrophe. The encirclement of Army Groups A and Don had to be prevented! He ordered the halt of all further advance of the 4th Panzer Division and the immediate withdrawal of the panzer divisions.

The 6th Army remained alone in Stalingrad – and its soldiers continued to perform their duties with obedience and discipline. An order of the day of one of the encircled divisions follows:

24th Panzer Division Div Command Post, 12/18/1943
Directorate IIa

Order of the Day!

The following members of the division have distinguished themselves by special accomplishments and bravery in recent combat around Stalingrad and in the greater Don Basin. I thank them, in the name of the division. Their deeds will be recorded in the history of the division.

1. Senior Lieutenant von Borcke, 24th Panzer Regiment
On 1/21/42, Senior Lieutenant von Borcke was tasked with deploying

his panzer squadron parallel to the division, from Yeruslanovski to Skotovod. It turned out that the bridge over the Liska, which was indicated on the map, was not actually there. Since the villages to the north and south were already occupied by the Russians and a detour to the west was out of the question, the squadron was cut off from its supply vehicles. An attempt to reach the division's march route failed, because of the difficult terrain. Nevertheless, Senior Lieutenant von Borcke, completely encircled and under enemy attack, succeeded in breaking out with his entire squadron and, on 11/23/42, was able to rejoin the division.

2. Lieutenant Melville, 3/4 Motorized Battalion
On 11/26/42, after a long preparation by artillery, Stalin Organs and mortars, and supported by 5 heavy tanks, the Russians succeeded in penetrating both flanks of the 3/4 Motorized Battalion. Lieutenant Melville, as squadron commander, gathered his squadron and organized a counterattack against the enemy, which had already overrun the left flank. In spite of friendly losses, he succeeded in winning back positions occupied by the enemy, with his few people, and halted the infantry which were following behind the tanks and, in this manner, stopped a Russian breakthrough in his sector. Lieutenant Melville died heroically in subsequent defensive combat.

3. Lieutenant Koehler, 5/26 Armored Infantry Regiment
While defending against enemy attacks in Karpova and Marinovka on 12/3/42, in which the Russians launched a strong attack against Hill 135.4, Lieutenant Koehler held an important position by displaying exceptional courage, and conducting energetic and resolute operations.

4. Lieutenant Keiler, 6/26 Armored Infantry Regiment
After distinguishing himself in defensive combat in Karpova and Marinovka, Lieutenant Keiler played an important part in the defense against a strong Russian attack on Hill 135.4 on 12/3/42. At this time, he led a counterattack that resulted in the destruction of 130 Russians.

5. Sergeant Major Zimmerman, 8/26 Armored Infantry Regiment
On 11/26-11/27/42, Sergeant Major Zimmerman, with a group composed mainly of supply troops, repulsed a Russian attack by his personal example and exemplary bravery and captured several prisoners and a quantity of equipment during a counterattack.

On 12/3/42, Sergeant Major Zimmerman, with the same group of people, repulsed a large Russian attack and threw back the enemy, who had broken through the defensive positions in some places, and destroyed them, in cooperation with 4 tanks.

6. Corporal Prahl, 8/26 Armored Infantry Regiment
Corporal Prahl, as a squad leader during a counterattack on 11/26-11/27/42, played a great part in its success by his courage as a leader and soldier.

During a breakthrough by the Russians on 12/13/42, he held his position against superior forces and inflicted heavy losses on the enemy during a counterattack.

7. Lance Corporal Gillmeister, 6/26 Armored Infantry Regiment
During a Russian breakthrough on 12/3/42, near Orlovka, after all of the men in his group had fallen, Lance Corporal Gillmeister held his position with a machine-gun by himself and, without contact with his superiors, inflicted heavy losses on the enemy until he was relieved by a counterattack.

8. Staff Sergeant Wuttke, 1/40 Armored Infantry Battalion
Staff Sergeant Wuttke, through circumspect, intrepid, and exemplary leadership of his platoon and, after the fall of his company commander, distinguished himself in all engagements and, without consideration for his own safety, contributed to the success during combat around Stalingrad.

9. Sergeant Waschk, 3/40 Armored Infantry Battalion
Sergeant Waschk had, on numerous occasions, especially during the laying of mines, distinguished himself through exemplary commitment,

> reliable and accurate work, often under strong enemy influence. On 12/7 and 12/8/42, he laid 290 mines in front of friendly lines, at times under strong infantry and artillery fire.

The last chance to rescue the 6th Army – a breakout by this army code named "Thunder" – was categorically forbidden by Hitler on 23 December.

The army's misfortunes had not yet ended, as the "Red Army" began another major offensive on Christmas Eve. Army Group "Stalingrad Front" (General Yeremenko) attacked with the 2nd Guards, 5th Shock, and 51st Armies in the direction of Kotelnikovo to the southwest, during which the fragmentary front of the 4th Rumanian Army completely collapsed.

A new, large gap was broken into the German front and it could no longer be closed.

It was Christmas.

An Austrian communications soldier wrote in his diary:

> We will never forget the sad Christmas of 1942 we spent in the Stalingrad pocket. The men celebrated this holiday modestly, or when it was possible, in small groups. We made a Christmas Tree out of prairie grass. It put us in the Christmas spirit, deep in Russia, far from our loved ones. Our battalion commander, Major Yarbelow, went from trench to trench and had a consoling word for everyone. Most of the soldiers in the pocket knew that this was probably their last Christmas. The Russians did not attack on Christmas Eve, but set up a Christmas Tree in the front line, they also set up loudspeakers and played German Christmas songs and marches. Occasionally, they would bid us surrender, and promised that we would be treated well and be fed, clothed, and sheltered. Additionally, they assured us that we would be safely returned to our homeland, after the war. Also, they promised to treat the wounded.

The Army Chief of Staff, General of Infantry Zeitzler, urged the establishment of a front further west of the Don and Kuban, to guarantee the unity of the German eastern armies. On 29 December, Hitler issued the

1942
WEIHNACHTEN IM KESSEL
LICHT
LEBEN
LIEBE
FESTUNG STALINGRAD

order for the general withdrawal of Army Group Don from the Volga and Don fronts and the accelerated withdrawal of Army Group A from the Caucasus.

At the end of December, the pocket around the 6th Army ran from the northern edge of Stalingrad in a large bow of about 50 kilometers west of the city and, from here, to the northern edge of Betekovka, directly south back to Stalingrad. The following Russian armies were located in the northern portion of the pocket, from left to right: the 66th, 24th, and 65th. The 21st Soviet Army held the western front, while the 57th and 64th Armies fought in the south and the 62nd Army maintained their positions in the ruins of the city itself.

The Soviet Army Group "Don Front", under General Rokossovskiy, attacked on 10 January 1943 with all of these armies concentrated on the pocket front.

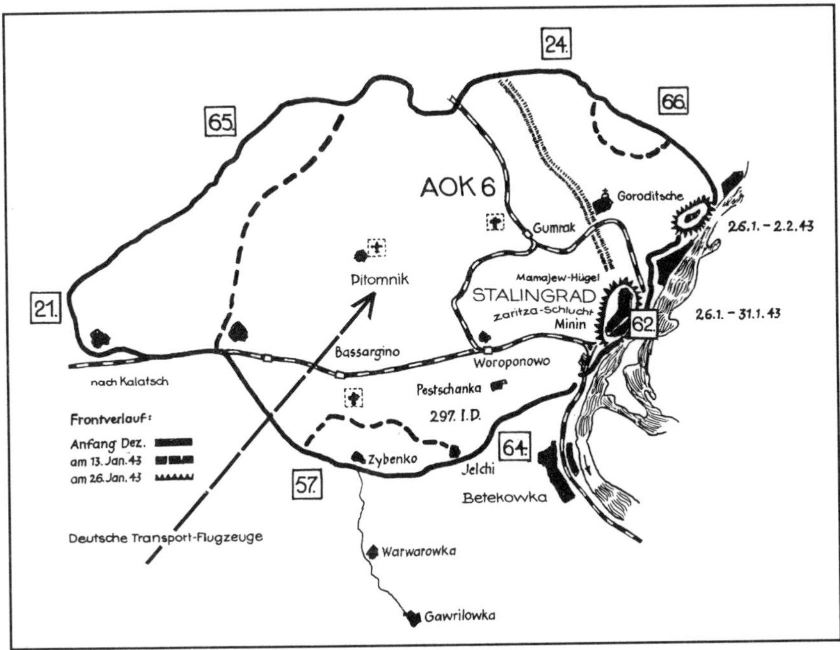

Development of the front line beginning of December
on 13 January 43
on 26 January 43

• • •

On 1/10/1943, all hell broke loose. The major Russian attack began. An hour long barrage fire – in the course of the 2nd World War, there was only one other of this magnitude and, according to perceptions of participants, the battle for Verdun in the 1st World War surpassed it – suppressed the German defensive positions. The earth rumbled under the torrent of iron, and the thunder of the guns condensed into a horrible, dull rumble. It bordered on wonder, that in spite of this deadly fire and the flimsy German cover, there were not more substantial losses. And then the enemy attack began. Strong tank formations supported the infantry. Clusters of the Russian companies could be vaguely seen approaching. The friendly defensive line was in deep silence. Had the men broken down or were they no longer emotionally capable to resist? No, at the decisive moment, the men were there – the men of the 44th ID.

Because there was an ammunition shortage, only five guns of the division's artillery were permitted to fire, and only the light infantry weapons were available for the defensive battle. Shortly before the lead attackers approached the defensive positions, the machine-guns began to hammer and the enemy assault began to stagger. Heavy losses caused the first wave of the attack to collapse. But just like an ocean, wave after wave followed – the Russian attack was so vast that one could not conceive from where they came. The second and third waves were also destroyed. However, the attack was constantly renewed, and ever closer approached the Russian infantrymen, and loud cries of "Hurrah" were heard. All of the heroic and superhuman resistance efforts could no longer be coordinated against their superior force of men and equipment. The 131st Rifle Regiment had to withdraw to the northern edge of Sovkhoz Nr. 1, where they were able to stop the assault. A breakthrough of the regiment sector was prevented by heavy losses of men and equipment.

On Kasachi Hill, near the 29th Motorized Infantry Division, the defense collapsed. The 132nd Rifle Regiment held its positions. The enemy was able to break through the 1st Battalion of the 134th Rifle Regiment and roll over the positions on the right. Senior Lieutenant Eimannsberger dragged a gun into an open fire position and operated it in direct fire. The firing masses raced forward endlessly, and fell as the result of direct hits by their own artillery fire. Captain Weniger (commander of the 3/96 Artillery Regiment) lost his life while fighting like an infantryman. On the southern edge of the Pereesdra Ravine, at the armored infantry command post, a 2 cm anti-aircraft gun laid down a devastating fire and stopped the attack. Lieutenant Niedermayer, who was both the battalion adjutant and communications officer, worked untiringly to maintain communications.

The attack was stopped, but the enemy had achieved an almost 3 kilometer wide penetration. He stood on the upper edge between points 124 and 127, which dropped off behind the Rossochka Ravine and gave him a direct shot into our rear area. In view of the enormous enemy superiority, it was no longer possible to hold any longer. The division sent the 3rd Construction Company of the 7th Observation Battalion, under Senior Lieutenant Held, to the 131st Rifle Regiment. They were established in Sovkhoz Nr. 1, where Senior Lieutenant Woelfel (commander of the 534th Rifle Regiment) took over the defensive sector. With great anxiety, they awaited the coming day. (From: Schimack, A.: *The 44th Infantry Division*, Vienna 1969.)

The breakthrough of the "Red Army" troops occurred in the west and east; then the southern front collapsed. The Luftwaffe could no longer fly into the Pitomnik airfield. For a few days, daring pilots of the "JU-52's" succeeded in flying out the wounded; then there was no longer any contact with Stalingrad!

Due to the cutting off of supply, the physical and emotional strength of the defenders came to an end. The guns had no more shells to shoot, the machine-guns grew silent, the trucks were burned, and the medical units were almost out of bandages and operated without anesthetics.

• • •

From the beginning of September, all we had left was horse meat. At first it tasted repulsive and was hard and tough. Then it was prepared in dumplings and something equivalent to sausage and was halfway palatable. The daily ration was 200 grams of bread, and 1/2 mess tin with one dumpling and coffee. Now and then we received an additional allowance of sausage. The non-combatant troops, for example, those farther in the rear area as in the regimental command post, received only 100 grams of bread daily. During the Christmas holidays, we received a small additional allowance. Christmas packages did not arrive. Our strength weakened.

We couldn't even consider basic body hygiene. The constant combat left no time for that. The beards sprouted. In the cellars the round iron stoves, with the oil soaked wood-block paving, heated the remnants of the factories. They gave off horrible fumes, and a black soot coated everything. Everyone was covered in it. More and more we became disfigured by hunger. Our eyes became sunken and our faces took on strange expressions. The vermin took over and allowed our fatigued bodies no rest. One could only obtain relief by seeking a quiet place in the open, taking off your shirt, in spite of the cold, and punish the tormentors with a flat hand. That would suffice for about an hour. Our ammunition supply situation was very serious. Much was left in the buildings and factories during the days of combat in October. It was eagerly collected, and each unit rejoiced when they found a mortar or a hand grenade or some infantry ammunition. On 1 January 1943, the order arrived: "From now on, heavy infantry guns can be fired no more than once every other day, light infantry guns once daily." The Russians, however, were lavish with their grenades: their artillery and Stalin Organs almost buried us in fire. Daily, more and more, the ring tightened. We had to endure everything patiently.

And how were the first aid stations? On 28 January, a man from the command post reported to a first aid station. He was shot through the upper thigh. After two hours he returned. With a tearful voice he reported on the situation there. The wounded were lying in the open, intermixed with the many dead. No one was available to take care of the wounded, and no one had the strength to remove the dead. The surgeons no longer had any medical supplies. "I asked to return to my comrades, I did not want to be a burden. I had to see the supervisor to get permission to return to my unit." When the commander heard this, he said with tears in his eyes: "Find a place here and stay with us."

The 305th Infantry Division held out until the last grenade, to the last bite of horse meat, and to the last bandage.

From the middle of January, the dead piled high due to exhaustion and starvation. The approach routes were blocked by the dead. They lay peacefully sleeping in the snow banks. Their exhausted bodies finally found a little rest, and they slept forever, in spite of the cold. Spotted fever raged. Death reaped a harvest at Stalingrad: Starvation, freezing, combat, epidemic, and, worst of all, despair. (From: Hauck, F. W.: *A German Division in the Russian Campaign*, (305th ID) Dorheim 1965.)

• • •

By the 16th of January, the Russian troops had squeezed the front of the 6th Army to one-third of the size it had been at the beginning of December. From this time on, even the common soldier knew that there would be no salvation.

On 22 January, after the capture of the Gumrak airfield, the Russians succeeded in approaching the last remaining airfield, Stalingradskiy. The very last men available, those with light frost bite and wounds, were tasked with defending it. During the withdrawal, all heavy equipment had to be abandoned because of fuel and ammunition shortages, and therefore the defense had to be conducted only with rifles, hand grenades, and machine-guns. It soon became clear that the end of the battle of Stalingrad was near. A few people who were not needed for the continuation of the battle were permitted to be flown out of the pocket. On 19 January, those receiving permission from the division, with the exception of the wounded – who were flown out on the aircraft that were still operational – included the commander of the 36th Panzer Regiment, Senior Lieutenant Langkeit, along with Captain Wagemann, who, in spite of his artificial leg, spent the last month with his combat troops; also, Major Seide from the division staff, who only had one arm, and the staff physician, Dr. Kindermann, who had a serious kidney disease.

On 23 January, the last aircraft took off from the Stalingradskiy Airfield and out of the pocket. It carried a few of the division's recent battle casualties. On the evening of the 23rd, the rest of the division's units were ordered to return to downtown Stalingrad. This return trip, due to the lack of available vehicles, was executed on foot during the night of 23-24 January. For the same reasons, it was not possible to take the wounded with them from the Stalingradskiy Medical Collection Point. Assistant Medical Director Rentzsch, of the 2/4 Armored Artillery Regiment, who led a detachment of several hundred men at this medical collection point, remained with the wounded, along with all of his medical personnel. As best as possible, the division supplied them. Bandages and medications were still available in sufficient quantities. Although the medical collection point, as per regulation, displayed the red cross flag, neither assistant medical advisor Rentzsch nor any of the wounded were ever heard from again.

At dawn of 24 January, the division assembled in the vicinity of the so-called "Red Square" and took cover in cellars and destroyed buildings. Here again, out of the very last of the force, two groups were created, one of which was deployed on the southern front – which, in these final days, was located on the Tsaritsa Ravine – and the other on the western front on the railroad tracks between Stalingrad Railroad Station Number 1 to the south. Here, in the final pocket, which was only a few hundred square meters, the Russian attack could no longer be withstood, in spite of reinforcement. Of course, the forces that were now on the front consisted of the battered remnants of the division.

In general, there were no more experienced infantrymen. Equipment consisted solely of rifles and machine-guns; several positions did have an anti-tank gun, but these did not have sufficient ammunition.

In these final days, morale and discipline were still high. Everyone performed his duty at his position – even after troop units became intermixed during the retreat and because of the disintegration of entire divisions, organizational shortcomings were common in other units. Here, our operations officer, Colonel Scholz, was able to keep the division intact, as well as was possible under the circumstances. (From: Grams, R.: *The 14th Panzer Division*, Bad Nauheim 1957.)

However, the combat groups still held out in the cellars of the ruined houses, in foul bunkers of stone and wood, and in demolished factory buildings or on open snow-covered fields.

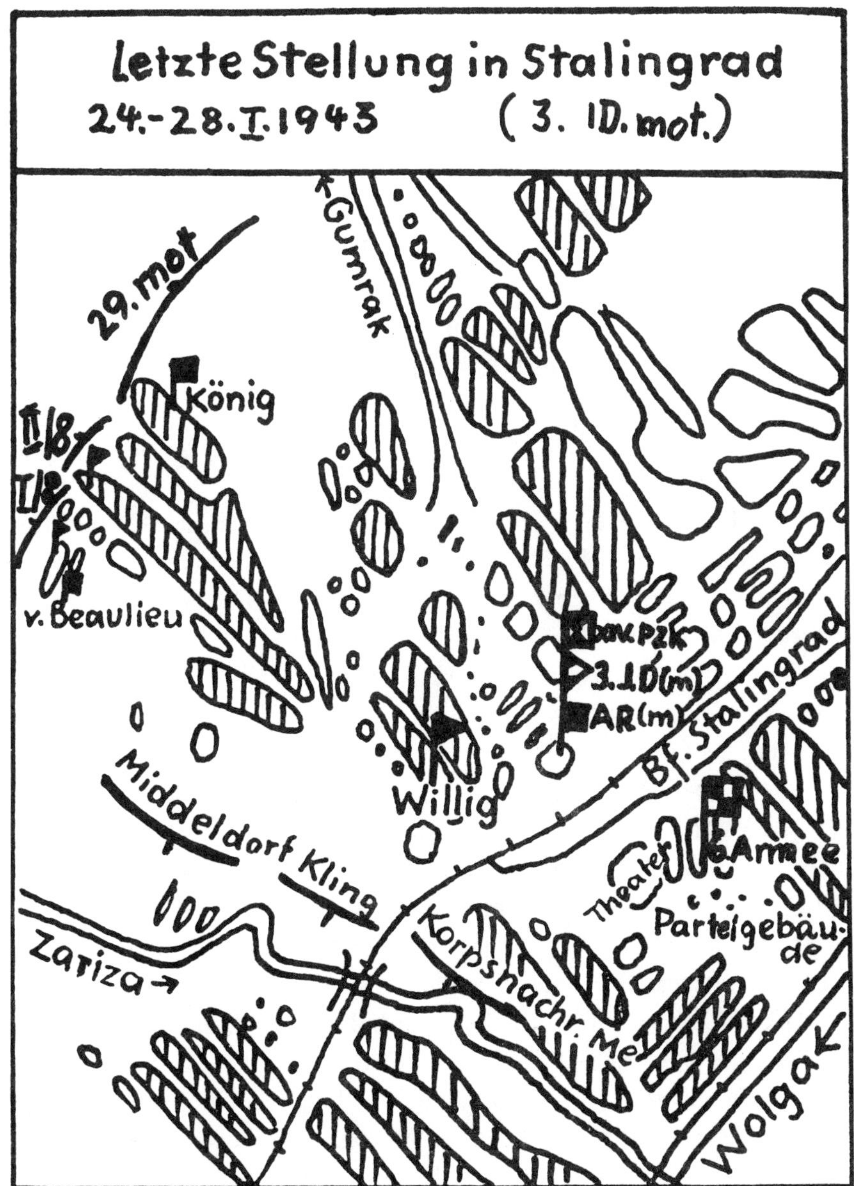

The last positions in Stalingrad 24-28 Jan 1943 (3rd Motorized ID)

The last German aircraft left the pocket on 23 January. 488 Luftwaffe aircraft were shot down by the enemy while flying supplies to Stalingrad and returning with wounded. 1000 Luftwaffe pilots, radiomen, and observers died in the last four weeks and were left in the snowy wasteland between the Volga and Don forever.

On 25 January, the Russian assault troops broke through the front of the last combat groups of the 6th Army and split them into a northern and a southern pocket.

On 30 January, Hitler promoted General Paulus to Field Marshal – however, he surrendered one day later. His headquarters was in an office building on "Red Square" – today it is a warehouse, on the outer wall of which is a bronze plate recalling the surrender. During these last days of January 1943, Field Marshal Paulus had no troops to command.

Two days later, General Strecker surrendered with the last German formations still remaining in Stalingrad. The 91,000 soldiers of the 6th Army marched to the prison camps far to the east of the Soviet Union – for most, the march was a one-way trip.

On the next day, 3 February 1943, the OKW reported:

From the Führer's Headquarters, 3 February

The Wehrmacht High Command reports:

The battle for Stalingrad is over. True to their oath of allegiance to their last breath, the 6th Army, under the exemplary leadership of Field Marshal Paulus, fell to the superiority of the enemy and unfavorable circumstances. Their fate was shared by an air defense division of the German Luftwaffe, two Rumanian divisions, and one Croatian regiment, who, in the true spirit of brotherhood-in-arms, performed their duty to the utmost with their comrades of the German Army.

This is not the time to describe the course of the operations that led to this. However, one can say: The sacrifice of the army was not for naught. Like a bastion of our historic European mission, they had withstood the assaults of six Soviet armies for many weeks. They were completely surrounded by the enemy, and they tied up strong enemy forces for weeks. Therefore, they gave the German leadership the time and the ability to take countermeasures, upon which depended the fate of the entire eastern front.

To accomplish this mission, the 6th Army had the support of the operations of the Luftwaffe for the duration of the encirclement, which, in spite of extreme exhaustion and heavy losses, established a sufficient air supply, as the possibility of relief slowly dwindled. Twice they proudly rejected the enemy's demands for surrender. Under the Swastika, which was raised on the highest ruins of Stalingrad, they fought their last battle. Generals, officers, non-commissioned officers, and soldiers fought shoulder to shoulder to the last cartridge. They died, therefore, Germany lives. Their example will be remembered for all time, in spite of all of the false Bolshevik propaganda. The divisions of the 6th Army are already being formed anew.

• • •

The collapse of the front of the 6th German Army, the neighboring 3rd and 4th Rumanian, and later the 8th Italian Armies resulted in a dreadful debacle for the entire south of the German eastern army.

The divisions were battered, exhausted, and consisted almost solely of small combat groups, which fought exceptionally well in spite of the number of positions between Belgorod and Rostov which were under attack.

As the offensive of the Russian Army Group "Voronezh Front" began on 12 January, resulting in the destruction of the 8th Italian and later the 2nd Hungarian Armies, the tanks with the "Red Stars" poured out on a wide front to the west.

German combat groups resisted the surging masses with the courage of the desperate and went down fighting. Thus, on 17 January, the XXIV Panzer Corps (General of Infantry Wandel, who died here) was encircled. His successor, Lieutenant General Eibl (who fell on 21 January) was able to hold the formations together, along with the Italian Alpine Corps, and break out on 18 January. Only a few combat groups reached the vicinity of the Valuiki ten days later.

The 2nd German Army (General von Salmuth) had to evacuate its positions near Voronezh due to these events. Of course, the army was not able to fend off the superior 13th and 38th Soviet Armies. As these armies finally made contact with the 40th Army (advancing from the south) near Kastornoe on 28 January, the bulk of the VII Army Corps (General of Infantry Straube) was encircled. The rest of the seven encircled German divisions (57th, 68th, 75th, 88th, 323rd, 340th, and 377th ID) broke through to the west.

Shortly after Christmas, in the vicinity of Voronezh, the 245th Infantry Regiment took up positions near Burarevo, and the 248th Infantry Regiment took up positions near Podkletnoe. The 188th Artillery Regiment also deployed in this area. The 246th Infantry regiment then occupied the former positions of the 245th Infantry Regiment at Olym and, on 12 January 1943, as the Russian attack on the Hungarian positions near Ostrogoshk (100 kilometers south of Voronezh) began, was transported there by railroad. The 3rd Battalion reached the city on 13 and 14 January, and just as the Hungarian front could no longer hold, the 168th ID was attached and immediately committed to those positions that were particularly threatened.

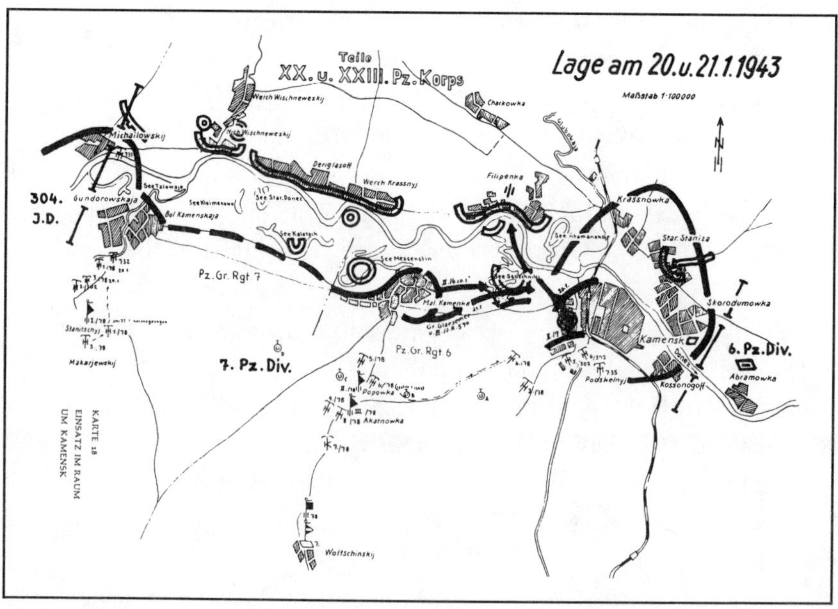

Situation on 20 and 21 Jan 1943

While being transported, the regimental units were battered by Russian tanks that had already broken through. On 16 January, the 2/246 was out-flanked by 60 Russian tanks and beaten down into a small group composed of the troop physician, 12 wounded, and 28 other men that were later taken up by the 1/246. On 20 January, after a bitter defensive battle, the 1/246 and 3/246, together with the commander of the 168th ID, several German units and a number of Hungarian units were encircled in the city. During the night of 23 January, the 1/246 slipped through the old river bed and out of the encirclement, established a gap, and kept the hole open for the other encircled units with the help of heavy weapons. They then took up with the remainder of the 3/246 and, as "Combat Group Wensaur", formed a rear guard for the troops that were attempting to fight their way to the west. Behind and between the advancing enemy formations they fought their way to Budenny (1/27), Novi Oskol (2/2), the Oskol River south of Stary Oskol (2/6), and then to Klinoe (2/8), where they were encircled and defended against a strong attack (the Russians lost 400 dead), broke out, and captured 32 anti-tank guns, 50 mortars, and 80 machine guns. On 2/11, Belgorod was held against a strong attack until the remainder of the 168th ID was taken up, which had, in the meantime, executed their breakout, and then fought their way between Russian formations, reaching Noviborisovka on 2/12 and Akhtyrka on 2/22. Meanwhile, on 2/27 a further encirclement was broken out of by making radio contact with a friendly commander who sent combat aircraft to their assistance, and so the regiment was able to fight its way to the "Grossdeutschland" Panzer Division and establish a new defensive front. In torn felt boots, almost 200 members of the 246th Infantry Regiment, after a punishing march of over 600 kilometers in constant combat in an almost hopeless situation, after six break outs from encirclement, after difficult privations, partly wounded, or with frost bite, finally made contact with friendly units. (From: Pfister, J.: *History of the 88th Infantry Division*, Bayreuth, 1956.)

Now, the Germans were in retreat everywhere, and after 9 February, the important city of Belgorod fell. For a long time, the Donets was the front line, where similar fierce combat occurred.

• • •

Lieutenant General Baron von Gablenz appeared at the front and was briefed by the commanders on the situation.

80 new enemy tanks were detected, and the majority of the remaining anti-tank weapons were out of order. There were no available reserves. With a heavy heart, General von Gablenz decided, "the troops would break contact with the enemy tonight and occupy new positions west of the Chir River."

It was only a few kilometers to the other side of the Chir, but it was at that obstacle that the enemy could oppose us. For more than three weeks we held these positions from daily attacks by the numerically superior enemy. We suffered heavy losses.

The bridgehead, which was held by "Combat Group Sauerbruch" on the east bank of the Don near Verchne Chirskaya against constant enemy attack and whose defense was at great cost, had to be evacuated. This bridgehead was bitterly defended to allow the 4th Panzer Army to commit strong forces in an attempt to liberate the 6th Army from the pocket. The wooden bridge over the Don fell into enemy hands after the removal of "Combat Group Sauerbruch", because the demolition group, striving to the last man, who was either killed or wounded, could not succeed in preventing the enemy from cutting the fuses on the explosives.

The withdrawal was executed as planned; the new positions were occupied during the morning of 12/15.

The "Division Combat Group 384" held the positions on the Chir near Nizhne Chirskaya against all enemy attacks until Christmas. The Christmas holiday was relatively quiet, but a new enemy attack, which threatened Army Group Hollidt between Christmas and the New Year, forced them to execute a delaying action to new positions in the rear.

On 12/30 came the order to occupy new positions 30 kilometers to the southwest. The attack of General Hoth's panzer army was coming to a halt. Therefore, the hope of relieving Stalingrad faded.

The withdrawal began at 1600 hours. Ice hindered the move. The vehicles often became stuck in the snow. We saw endless Russian columns two kilometers on the other side of the Don, and they were marching south in the same direction as we.

On the morning of 31 December we occupied the new area. During the afternoon, new orders came to withdraw further. The new positions were 40 kilometers to the west. The enemy was close on our heels, always trying to make contact with us, or to outflank our combat groups. Finally, on 9 January, the German tanks arrived and stopped the Russian advance. (From: Lang, K.: *History of the 384th Infantry Division*, Rodenkirchen 1965.)

• • •

On 18 January, the combat groups, before marching through Forshchadt, were on the south bank of the Donets at the large bend between Forshchadt and Olkhovskiy (360 kilometers from Kharkov). They were attached to the 6th Panzer Division. At the end of the day, one could read the following about their versatile missions: "On order of the division, they [the combat groups] are not to be committed in the front line in direct defense, but as a mobile reserve in the offensive when the enemy tries to cross the Donets. They are to provide security in the form of bridge watches, observe the enemy sector, and observe enemy movements. Their immediate mission is:

1.) Constant reconnaissance by scout troops between the left and right neighbors and the connecting boundaries, and reconnaissance, especially during the night, of the opposite bank of the Donets to establish the enemy's approach.

2.) Establishment of an all-round defense in case of a breakthrough. Combat Group Dietrich has the sector to the west and southwest up to ravine 5 and the local coke oven. The embankments between the Donets and the railroad tracks. Combat Group Dietrich is the left flank of the Zollenkopf Regiment. Their neighbor to the right: Senior Lieutenant Franke's group (rocket launcher battalion and a mish-mash of insufficiently equipped remnants). The neighbor to the left of the Zollenkopf Regiment is the Huenersdorff Regiment."

As at Forshchadt, during the first half of January the enemy shifted strong forces to the west near the recent failure in the vicinity of Kamens-

Kamenskaya. Obviously, this was to force a crossing over the Donets at another location.

On 22 January – Forshchadt itself was given up on the 20th – Combat Group Dietrich was located in prepared positions 10 kilometers northwest of Forshchadt on the Donets near Olkhovskiy-Ravine 5 and the local coke oven. The combat group still belonged to the 6th Panzer Division and was attached to the regiment of Colonel Zollenkopf. On 23 January, Huebner noted with surprise and annoyance that the enemy near Forshchadt was not impeded by the Donets bridge defensive positions. No one did anything, although there was sufficient artillery in the area! "No wonder Colonel Zollenkampf sweated blood; because the Russians were then able to penetrate into our rear area."

On 22 January, the 7th Panzer Division again had to turn over a strong combat group. It was directed to an area about 40 kilometers northwest of Kamensk. The Soviets were advancing across the ice of the Donets near Lichaya to the west. The combat group was to defeat the enemy between Davydo Nikolskiy and Marakov.

By the evening, Ilevka and Krushilovka were recaptured from the enemy. On the following day, 23 January, Marakov was also reconquered. The combat group – which was led by Colonel von Steinkeller – had fulfilled its mission. (From: Husemann, F.: *In Good Faith. The History of the SS Polizei Division*, (4th SS Division) Osnabrueck 1973.)

• • •

Hitler decided on 14 February to concentrate all of the German combat formations from Kursk to the Sea of Azov under one, new Army Group South commander. Army Group B was removed from the front and Field Marshal von Manstein became responsible for the entire southern sector of the Eastern front. He established his headquarters in Saporoshe, where it had been previously.

In the middle of February, the II SS Panzer Corps (SS Obergruppenfuehrer Hausser) was ordered to hold the entire Kharkov front as the last and most important line of defense. However, on 16 February, SS

Obergruppenfuehrer Hausser had already issued the order to evacuate the city. He wanted to spare his troops a second Stalingrad.

Then, on 6 March 1943, the battle between Kharkov and Belgorod occurred. On this date, the reconstituted 4th Panzer Army (General Hoth) and the newly established army of General of Panzer Troops Kempf began to attack the 3rd Soviet Tank and the 69th Armies of Army Group "Voronezh Front." The SS Panzer Corps (SS Obergruppenfuehrer Hausser) formed the spearhead of the German troops and entered Kharkov on 16 March, with his three divisions – from left to right: SS Division "Totenkopf" (SS Gruppenfuehrer Eicke), SS Panzer Division "Leibstandarte" (SS Obergruppenfuehrer Dietrich), and SS Division "Das Reich" (SS Gruppenfuehrer Steiner) – and regained their old positions!

During the following days, the XLVIII Panzer Corps (General of Panzer Troops von Knobelsdorff) smashed additional enemy forces south of Kharkov. Therefore, they stabilized the German front here in the south!

• • •

Leibstandarte SS Adolf Hitler Div Command Post, 3/10/1943
Operations

Division order Nr. 8

1.) The enemy has been completely surprised and pushed back by the mobile attack of the Leibstandarte.

2.) On 3/11/43, the SS Panzer Corps captured Kharkov, while units of the SS Division "Das Reich" screened the east flank on the Merefa, and the SS Division "Totenkopf" shielded the north and northwestern flanks on a line Russkoe-Dergachi-Festki-Olshany.

3.) The attack:
SS Division "Das Reich" will attack with strong regimental groups from the west, while the Leibstandarte attacks with two regimental groups from the north.

For boundary lines and axes of advance refer to a 1:100,000 map and a city map.

4.) Missions:
a.) The reinforced 2nd Armored Infantry Regiment (1/55 Mortar Regiment, the assault gun battalion minus one battery, one 8.8 cm air defense battery, and the 1st and 3rd battalions of the 5th Artillery Regiment) attacks along the road west of the northern edge of Kharkov, advances to the boundary line with SS "Das Reich", and clears the enemy from this part of the city.

b.) The reinforced 1st Armored Infantry Regiment (Combat Group Meyer, a corps rocket launcher battalion, otherwise the same as earlier) attacks along the road east into the northeast portion of Kharkov with a combat group immediately to the southeast of the approach to Rogan, clears the enemy from the center of the city, and drives to the east and northeast.

For security lines see the 1:100,000 map. A reinforced assault gun battalion follows the combat groups to the Stepanov bend in the road. Their commitment requires division approval.

During the night of the 10th to the 11th, the combat groups will approach as close as possible to the outskirts of the city. The attack begins at 0400 hours.

5.) After penetrating into Kharkov, reports will be issued according to the mapped-out/allocation areas. (1:100,000 map)

6.) Combat reconnaissance will be conducted on both sides of the routes of advance, to the east and the west.

7.) The main first aid station is in Lyubotin. The medical collection points are Dergachi and Cherkaskoe.

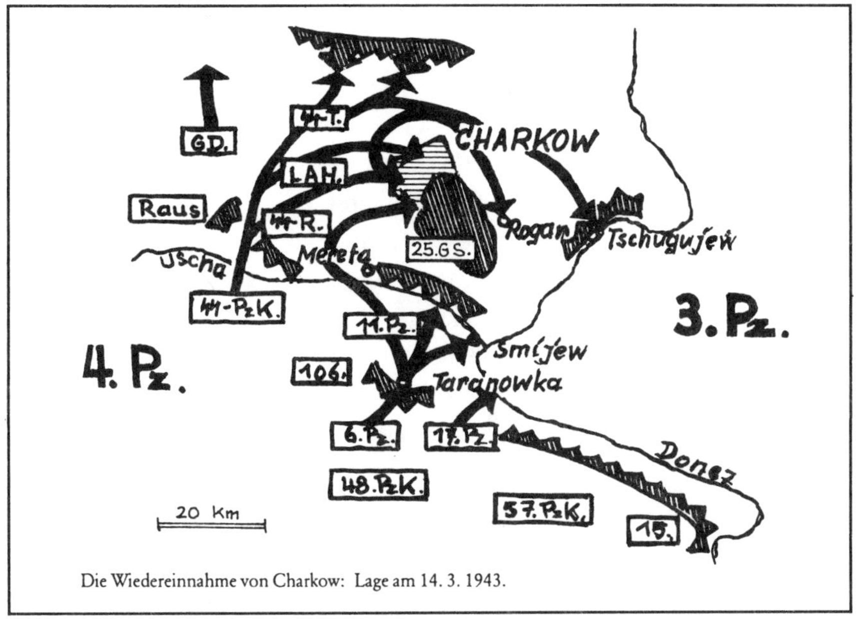

Die Wiedereinnahme von Charkow: Lage am 14. 3. 1943.

The recapture of Kharkov: situation on 3/14/1943

8.) The fuel and ammunition issue point is 3 kilometers west of Kovalenkov on the march route (Kolkhoz).

9.) At the start of the attack, the division command post is at Dergachi, and, after the capture of Kharkov, the northeast sector of Kharkov.

signed Dietrich
SS Obergruppenfuehrer and General of the Waffen SS

(From: Lehmann, R.: *The Leibstandarte.* vol 3. Osnabrueck 1982.)

After this operation kicked off, the city of Belgorod was conquered by the 4th Panzer Army. Then, the offensive of Army Group South faded away – and the spring mud period set in.

KUBAN
(2 January-9 October 1943)

As the morning of the first day of the new year dawned, troop units of the 1st Panzer Army of General of Cavalry von Mackensen were detached from the Kalmuk steppe sector, to the Terek and eastern Caucasus. For three days, the army executed the assigned order to withdraw. Already in the last two days of the old year, rear area service units were taken from their former quartering sites and lead back to the Manych, so that in the forward sectors, only the experienced front line combat groups remained, which – under the protection of a rear guard – began to withdraw from the forward defensive positions on 1 January 1943.

The following units (from right to left) of the 1st Panzer Army, gave up their positions:

LII Army Corps (General of Infantry Ott)
with the 50th and 111th ID;
III Panzer Corps (Lieutenant General Breith by proxy)
with the 13th Panzer Division, 370th ID, 2nd Rumanian Mountain Division;
XL Panzer Corps (General of Panzer Troops Henrici)
with the 3rd Panzer Division, Combat Group von Jungschulz.

Colonel von Jungschulz's combat group consisted of squadrons of Germans and Cossacks, which secured the wide Kalmuk steppes. Therefore, a mounted troop of regimental strength was located on a battlefield of several hundred meters width. On 1 January, the combat groups gave up Elista and linked up with the withdrawing 3rd Panzer Division (Major General Westhoven). General of Cavalry von Mackensen issued an order, which briefly and precisely read:

> "It is important that we not be broken through. Defending to the last man is not necessary."

Thus, the 1st Panzer Army conducted an orderly withdrawal to the intermediate line on the Kuma River. Of course, such a withdrawal was not conducted completely without problems. For instance, while the 111th ID (Major General Recknagel), which was shifted to the northern flank, came upon several obstacles on the flat steppes, the 50th ID (Lieutenant General Schmidt – he later fell in the battle at the Kuban Bridgehead) and the 370th ID (Major General Klepp) had to put up with the foothills of the Caucasus and the tributaries of the Terek. The division columns moved off to the northwest. During the withdrawal, they came upon fleeing Kalmuks, Cossacks, and other inhabitants of the Caucasus.

On 4 January, the 17th Army (General Ruoff) was directed to join the withdrawal that began on the left flank and in the mountains, while the center and right flank stayed put for the time being. At this time, the army was organized as follows, from right to left:

Rumanian Cavalry Corps
    with 9th, 6th Rumanian Cavalry Divisions, 19th Rumanian ID;
V Army Corps (General of Infantry Wetzel)
    with 9th, 73rd ID, 3rd and 10th Rumanian ID;
XLIV Army Corps (General of Artillery de Angelis)
    with 101st Rifle Division, 125th, 198th ID, Slovak Mobile Division;
XLIX Mountain Corps (General of Mountain Troops Konrad)
    with 46th ID, 1st and 4th Mountain Divisions;
Reserve: 97th Rifle Division.

The "Red Army" slowly followed the withdrawal. The main emphasis of their armored attack was directed, as previously, against the 4th Panzer Army (General Hoth), which was in the north. Therefore, the 28th Soviet Army attacked along the Manych to the west and the neighboring III Guards Tank Corps reached Konstantinovka on the Don. Here, the Russian tanks turned to the south to advance in the direction of Proletarskaya. There stood the 23rd Panzer Division – which was just taken over by Colonel von Vormann – and was able to prevent a collapse of the friendly front.

Meanwhile, the 1st Panzer Army reached the Kuma sector on a broad front and crossed to the northwest. Contact with the neighboring 17th Army on the right was not lost in spite of all the enemy attacks. Just the same, this army had a hard time, because they had to fight their way back across swamps and frozen plains almost without winter shelter.

On 10 January, the regiment commanders were summoned to the 235th Artillery Regiment at Triduba. The division commander informed them that the overall situation in the west Caucasus also made a withdrawal necessary. The "Cable Car Movement", which was the code name assigned to this, was to begin in about 14 days. The evacuation of heavy equipment, as well as the heavy guns, was started immediately.

Unfortunately, a thaw set in at this time, and the roads became bottomless. In spite of this, the salvage of equipment got under way, with much exertion, of course.

For the first time, the division began to execute a large scale withdrawal. For the officers and men, this was a great emotional disappointment, because they were evacuating terrain that had been fought for at great cost. The division commander issued a special order to the regiment, independent battalion, and battalion commanders, in which he instructed the officers to examine the published order from their superiors and to conscientiously monitor its execution.

Since 19 January, the enemy showed great interest in the left flank and the center of the division. During the morning, an attack by 300 men was launched against the left flank, where the 326th Rifle Regiment was located. The attack was repulsed. The enemy obviously assumed that, since we withdrew the left flank of our corps, the 198th ID also withdrew. The enemy now carried out attacks, one after the other, in an attempt to destroy our troops.

As the morning of 23 January dawned, our troops again anticipated the enemy, but he did not come. The resolute defense of the riflemen exhausted the enemy.

At the proper time, the order to leave the forward defensive positions arrived. Again they traveled through the Psekups Valley to the blood-soaked hills south of Sosnovaya Ravine, and to the left of the high peaks of the

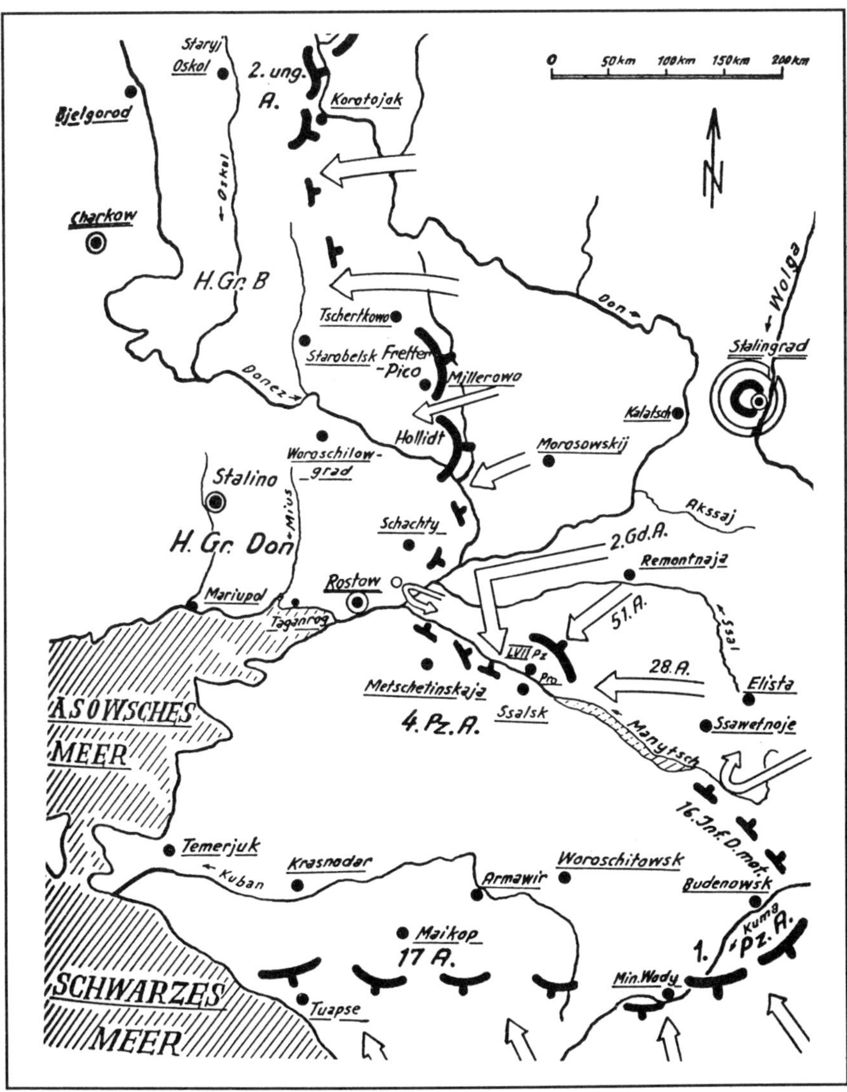

Sarai Mountains and across the edge of the forested mountains, behind which lay the Black Sea and Tuapse, the objective that was now unattainable. Each man packed his few personal belongings. The last mail parcels were emptied, and the pictures of home and fallen comrades were taken down from the bunker walls. Pack animals were loaded, and at the very last, the ammunition cases were shut and the machine-guns were taken from the parapets. Then the groups, platoons, and companies prepared to march. A warm, light rain fell. Unnoticed by the enemy, the left flank broke contact in the twilight of the evening; the center and the right flank of the division followed later. Soon the communications troops also left their positions. The Kochkanova front was empty.

The night fell quickly. Not a sound was made. Each man had to deal with himself, to advance over the muddy routes, which just yesterday were somewhat frozen but had since thawed and mired under the hooves of the horses and boots of the riflemen. The supply trains, field kitchen, and, most of all, the guns sank deep into the mud. Small brooks, which yesterday were frozen and easily crossed, were obstacles today. The night was pitch dark. On difficult sections of the route, the guns were towed by the division tractors. We continued the march on the following day. Only through superhuman effort could the troops continue the withdrawal and, after over 24 hours, completely exhausted, they reached their objective. (From: Graser, G.: *Between Kattegat and the Caucasus.* (198th ID) Tuebingen 1961.)

• • •

Several crises occurred in the 17th Army sector near the Rumanian formations, which could no longer take the stress. Here, the army had already committed its only reserve – the 97th Rifle Division (Lieutenant General Rupp, who fell in combat later in the Kuban Bridgehead) – as their "corset rod."

On 13 January, the 1st Panzer Army reached the Nagutskoe-Aleksandrovskoe line and vacated Shuravskoe. A week later, its divisions were located on a line Ernanskoe-Bogoslovskoe-Voroshilovsk-Sandata. Here, they finally established a solid contact with the 4th Panzer Army on the Manych. Four days later, the 1st Panzer Army gave up the important city of Armavir. Then they received the order to transfer to Army Group Don and had to withdraw across the wide river mouth to the Rostov area as quickly as possible. The 17th Army received a "Führer directive" to occupy the so-called Kuban Bridgehead and stop.

At the end of the month, the 1st Panzer Army left the steppes, pastures, fields, and rivers of the Caucasus foothills and took up the defense of the most important city of Rostov, against which, in the first week of February alone, three Soviet armies began to assault.

The LVII Panzer Corps (General of Panzer Troops Kirchner), which belonged to the 4th Panzer Army, was charged with the defense of Rostov.

At 0900 hours, the LVII Panzer Corps received a preliminary order to transfer to the Mius positions on the evening of 13 February. Accordingly, the 23rd Panzer Division and the 16th Motorized Infantry Division had to cover the withdrawal of the 111th ID and the 15th Airfield Division. Later, the 23rd Panzer Division formed the army reserve in the area 20 kilometers north of Taganrog.

On the morning of 13 February, the enemy concentrated strong forces at Semernikovo. At noon, two tanks with infantry attacked the 2/126 Armored Infantry Regiment; the attack broke down. The 51st Armored Engineer Battalion repulsed repeated attacks by Soviet assault troops in house to house battle. The bridges near Sultan-Saly (15 kilometers northwest of Rostov) were prepared for demolition.

The withdrawal began at 2000 hours. The bridges in the city were blown. The 128th Armored Infantry Regiment had to withdraw from the city amongst the attacking Russians. Little by little, the regiment was put in order. By midnight, the division's combat groups were at the new defen-

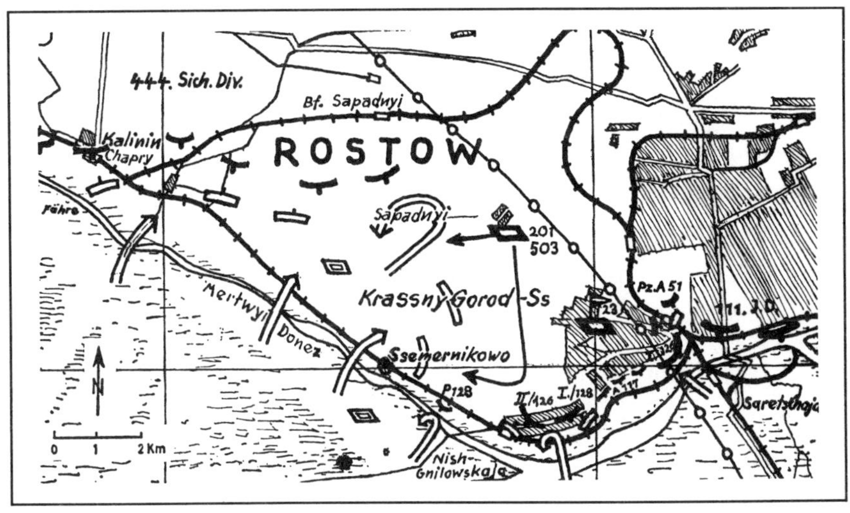

sive line: the 128th Armored Infantry Regiment 2 kilometers northwest of Zapadniy; the 126th Armored Infantry Regiment at Leninavan-Trud; and Combat Group Sander at Krasniy Chaltyr and the 51st Armored Engineer Battalion in Krym.

At the end of the battle of Rostov, Major General von Vormann issued the following order of the day:

> "We have held Rostov as ordered by the higher leadership to allow them to execute their plans.
>
> The enemy's planned breakthrough west of the city, which threatened the entire greater Don Basin, was prevented by us. This placed high demands on the defensive strength of the infantrymen. They have accomplished their mission. I pay tribute to you.
>
> During the attack, the tank assembly areas and the penetrating enemy were destroyed. My special thanks to the 503rd Heavy Panzer Battalion for their enthusiastic commitment and helpfulness.
>
> To force the breakthrough, the enemy committed:
>
> from 2/8: The 271st Rifle Division, 34th Guards Rifle Division, 52nd, 79th, 159th Rifle Brigades, rifle battalions of the 6th Guards Tank Brigade, and 15th Tank Brigade;
>
> from 2/11: Units of the IV Guards Cavalry Corps with the 9th, 12th, 30th Guards Cavalry Divisions, and the 248th Rifle Division.
>
> In five days, the division destroyed 31 tanks, including two T-34's, and four armored scout cars. 13 guns, 21 anti-tank guns, 58 bazookas, two infantry guns, 31 machine-guns, and numerous hand guns and other equipment were destroyed. The enemy lost 350 prisoners, and their losses in blood were very high.
>
> Onward to new feats!
>
> signed von Vormann"
>
> (From: Rebentisch, E.: *To the Caucasus and to the Towers*, (23rd Panzer Division) Esslingen 1963.)

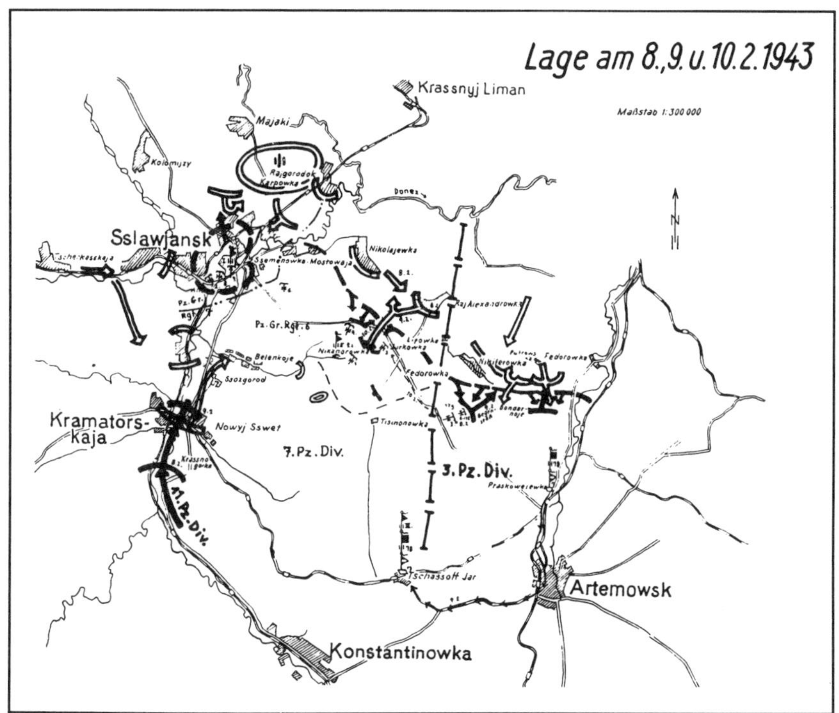

Situation on 8, 9, and 10 February 1943

While the battle for the Mius positions developed north of the Don Estuary – where the 1st Panzer Army (General von Mackensen) succeeded in conquering Slavyansk and Bogorodichno and the 4th Panzer Army (General Hoth) was able to establish a bridgehead across the Donets near Balakleya – the month-long battle of the Kuban Bridgehead began.

The XLIX Mountain Corps (General of Mountain Troops Konrad) entered the so-called "Gotenkopf" [Gothic Head] positions at the end of January, which formed the front line of the Kuban Bridgehead until practically the autumn of 1943.

However, the lines of the Kuban Bridgehead, specified by the command posts, were not reached because the "Red Army" fought its way into the sector first.

A strong Russian naval unit, consisting of two cruisers, three battleships, two torpedo boats, three gun boats, and several landing craft entered the two inlets south of Novorossisk on the morning of 2 February. Before the Germans could deploy a defense, soldiers of the 165th Rifle and sailors of the 83rd and 255th Marine Infantry Brigades were landed. They established a bridgehead near the old fortifications and were able to expand it before the first German counterattack was launched.

This triggered a ten day battle south of the important port city, during which neither side gave any quarter. Thanks to the support of ships from the Soviet Black Sea Fleet, the landed sailors were able to be supplied with rations and weapons – always at night – with landing craft and even with rafts.

The Russian brigades finally succeeded in establishing a bridgehead south of Novorossisk, which ran from the eastern part of Stanichka in a wide half-circle across Feodorovka to the Myshako Estuary. It had a frontal length of about 15 kilometers and a depth of 8 kilometers.

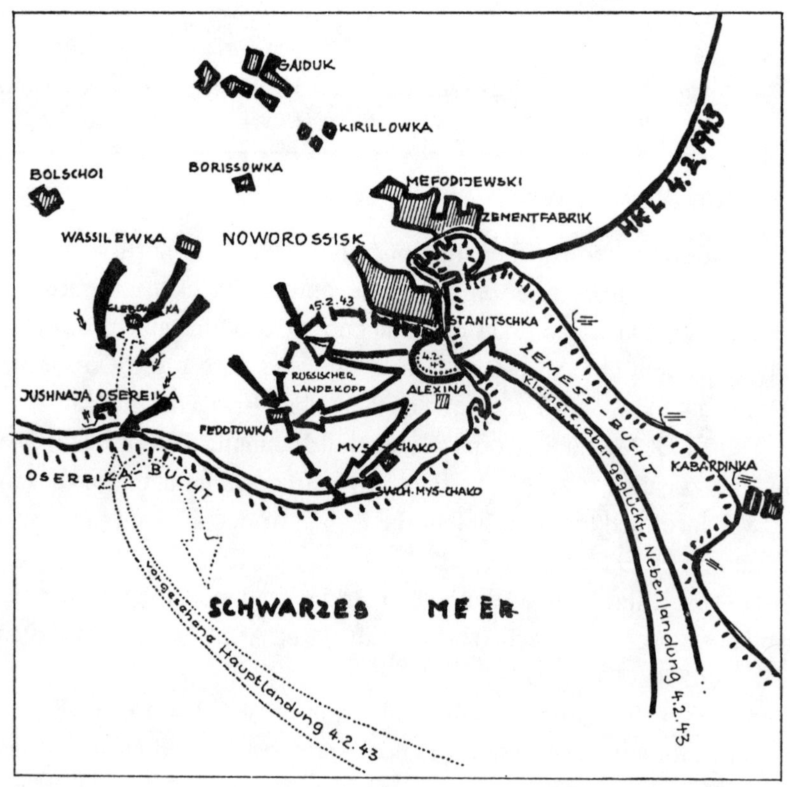

Only by harnessing their last ounce of strength were the German defenders able to prevent a wide penetration so that, finally, by the end of February, the Russian attack here was suspended. However, the Kuban Bridgehead could not be compressed.

In view of this development, the 17th Army became anxious and transported all non-essential equipment and personnel from the Crimea to Army Group Don. Up to 8 March, 10,084 Russian POWs, 10,290 Russian civilians, and 101,384 soldiers of the relieved divisions of the Kuban Bridgehead were left behind, while 62,647 soldiers were flown out by air transports.

By 5 April, the 17th Army occupied their final defensive positions and were disposed in the bridgehead as follows (from right to left): the Rumanian Cavalry Corps, with the 6th and 9th Rumanian Cavalry Divisions, took up positions on the Taman Peninsula opposite the Crimea. To the left closed the V Army Corps (General of Infantry Wetzel), with the 10th Rumanian ID and 73rd and 125th ID. Later, the 4th Mountain Division was additionally transferred to this sector. The XLIV Army Corps (General of Artillery de Angelis), with the 9th ID and 97th and 101st Rifle Divisions, made contact with the 3rd and 19th Rumanian IDs in the central sector of the front around Krymskaya. The XLIX Mountain Corps (General of Mountain Troops Konrad) was on the left flank with the 50th and 370th IDs.

From mid-April, the forward line of defense ran along the following line:

The right flank began near Novorossisk on the Black Sea, ran from the eastern edge of the bay through a 12 kilometer impenetrable forest to the northeast up to the village of Neberdkhaevskaya. From here, the front line ran through the heavily fought over village of Krymskaya to the north to Adakum near Kievskoe. The front then turned to the northwest back to the wide Kuban River. Between Varenikovskaya and Krasniy Oktyabr the line crossed the river, extending through the reeds, bogs, and lagoons to the Sea of Azov directly east of the Kuban Estuary.

At the beginning of April 1943, the V Army Corps planned "Operation Neptune", which included the clearing of the front to the coast south of Novorossisk. The corps formed three strong division combat groups, from the 73rd ID (Lieutenant General von Buenau), the 125th ID (Major General Friebe), and the 4th Mountain Division (Major General Kress). The mission of these groups was to capture the dominant Myshako Mountains southwest of the bridgehead.

The battle on the steep mountain slopes, in the deep ravines, in the thick forests, and the matted vineyards was, in spite of the bravery of the attackers, so difficult that it couldn't succeed in driving the fanatically fighting Russian soldiers and sailors out of their strong points. They literally had to destroy the enemy in their defensive positions; otherwise, he would not give up one meter.

On 21 April, the corps suspended the battle to prevent further bloodshed. The front stabilized and stayed that way for almost six months!

The battle in the Kuban Bridgehead was distinguished by the type of terrain, which differed from that of the rest of the Army Group South sector. Particularly difficult was life in the lagoons of the Kuban Estuary. Here, combat could only be conducted on the ground adjacent to the lagoons. If one dug to a depth of 30 cm into the ground, brackish, muddy water gushed forth.

In the month of May, the "Red Army" began concentrated attacks against the entire German defensive sector, and, in some places, found some soft spots. The Russian High Command had decided to remove the German "Plague" for all time.

On 13 May, the OKW issued a routine report on the combat in May:

•••

Berlin, 13 May

On Thursday, local combat flared up on the Kuban Bridgehead. The Bolsheviks attempted, through several attacks by rifle regiments, to improve their positions. The attacks were directed against the sector of a German division on the eastern flank, and collapsed in bloody failure. Through these attacks, the enemy wanted to offset the success of the previous day's German offensive operation, which had cost them 400 dead and the loss of many weapons. In spite of suffering new serious losses, he could not achieve his combat objective.

It remained quiet on the remainder of the Kuban Bridgehead. Friendly air activity was lively. Tactical aircraft, dive-bombers, and fighter-bombers continued to bombard Soviet positions, reserves, and troop concentrations. They again attacked the landing craft concentrated by the Bolsheviks in the lagoons. They destroyed 45 new vehicles, vehicle positions, and field positions, and battered bunkers and supply stockpiles with direct hits.

• • •

Heavy combat occurred during the end of the month in the area of the XLIV Army Corps. Strong Soviet attack formations pressed against the Kievskoe-Moldavanskoe line. However, the Germans held; only locally was any ground given up. On the other hand, at other locations, they succeeded in pushing the Russian infantry back through counterattacks. On the German side, the lack of air support was noticeable, while the Russian

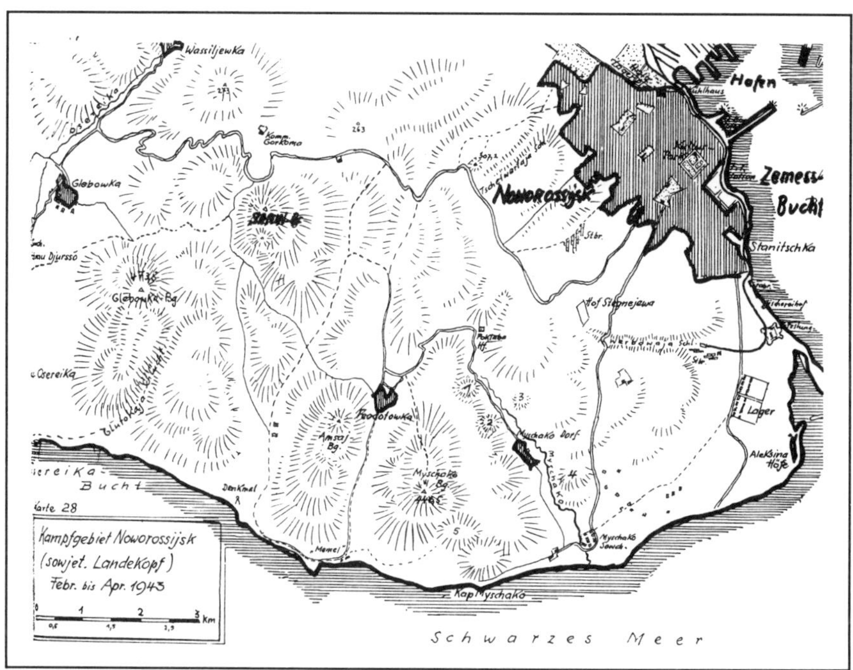

The Novorossiisk combat region (Soviet beachhead) Feb to Apr 1943

fighter-bombers energetically hit the German defenders. The 9th German Air defense Division, which was deployed in the Kuban Bridgehead, had at its disposal 16 heavy (8.8 cm) and 15 light (3.7 and 2 cm) batteries. Nevertheless, the fighter defense it provided was almost perfect. One could truly count on one hand the number of fighters that were able to get through.

The right flank of the 1/204 Rifle Regiment could not advance, because of being outflanked on the right and, above all, the strong anti-tank gun fire. Soon all five available assault guns received direct hits and were put out of action.

Because the attack of the left neighbor from Podgorniy to Tambulovskiy gained no ground, Hill 71.0 remained in enemy hands, and Attack Group Dietz, which fell under heavy enemy defensive fire from the east, north, and northwest had to withdraw, suffering heavy losses from enemy fire on the flank from the northern edge of Samsonovskiy. Because the attack of the left neighboring 208th Rifle Regiment and the von der Chevallerie Group gained no ground and obviously collapsed due to heavy losses of men and equipment, the transition to the defense along the line of the Mekerstuk Trench (500 meters north of Hill 114.1) – a hill northeast of Svoboda – was ordered north of Samsonovskiy and approved by corps.

Additional heavy losses due to the unsuitability of the terrain were suffered on the northern edge of Samsonovskiy in the afternoon, forcing the forward defensive line to be shifted back to the southern portion of the city. Because of the hasty and independent operations of the division, this fourth large attack against the Kuban Bridgehead, which did almost result in a breakthrough, was repulsed. With great sacrifice, the division assisted the threatened left neighbor in typical infantrymen fashion. They achieved a victory that was decisive for the entire bridgehead. Soviet losses were enormous. Alone, our division encircled 32 tanks. (From: Ott, E.: *Infantry Against the Enemy*. (97th Rifle Division) Munich 1966.)

• • •

In June, the "Red Army" gave up their breakout attempts. The battle in the Kursk sector required all of their forces. In spite of this, it never quieted down in the Kuban Bridgehead. Local scout and assault troop operations were conducted daily and isolated mountain peaks, hillocks, forests, and lagoons were fought over with unequaled vehemence.

The report of a man in the 4th Mountain Division about the battles in the second half of July read:

> A Bavarian rifle battalion occupied the trenches on the high ground, when all of a sudden, at sunrise, a thunderous barrage fire was begun by Soviet artillery that hammered the German main defensive line and the positions stretching behind it with monstrous impact for more than an hour. A continuous gray cloud of smoke covered the hilly terrain, over which a hundred enemy aircraft dropped their bombs and fired their aircraft weapons. While the disastrous fire strike was in full swing, the Bolshevik infantry rose up from their trenches after leveling their defensive wire entanglements and blowing a path through their mine fields, and attacked the German positions on the entire sector, supported by numerous tanks.
>
> The enemy's main strike was directed on the bald mountain, whose summit literally trembled under the impact of the shells that fell as thick as hail. The enemy swarmed from three sides, far outnumbering the defenders despite the undiminished hammering of the fire from the guns of the friendly infantry, and three heavy Soviet tanks rolled onto the half-destroyed German trenches, which no longer offered any protection. The Bolsheviks were able to count on the hail of shells to break down the resistance of the Germans and be able to capture the hill in a bold strike. As the enemy emerged from the powder smoke and tried to enter the German positions, they were engaged at close range with rifle and machine-gun fire; in many positions, the infantrymen fought for their lives with shovels and hand grenades, until, finally, the crushing superiority of the enemy forced them to fall back. They immediately regrouped to counterattack and threw themselves at the Bolsheviks, who had just won the ground, and recaptured their battered trenches.
>
> While the infantrymen fought on the hill so desperately, a wild battle was occurring in the remainder of the division sector, in which the enemy committed new reserves. While under heavy fire themselves,

> the German batteries fired barrages without pause against the approaching enemy reinforcements and destruction fire against targets acquired further in the enemy's rear area. Throughout the sector, where the enemy succeeded in penetrating the German main defensive line with massed assaults the infantrymen immediately launched vigorous counterattacks that destroyed the penetrating enemy or threw them back, where they fell under the barrage fire of the German guns.

After the ten day battle, the main defensive line was again in German hands. Only the struggle for the hill continued with undiminished vehemence.

• • •

The great offensive of the "Red Army" against Army Group South began in August and resulted in the withdrawal of all of the armies. During a discussion on 3 September in the Führer's main headquarters, "Wolf's Lair", Field Marshal von Manstein, as commander of Army Group South, insisted that the Kuban Bridgehead must be evacuated.

Hitler finally gave in to the pressure and authorized Army Group A (Field Marshal von Kleist) to initiate the evacuation of the Kuban Bridgehead.

The 17th Army – which was taken over by General of Engineers Jaenecke on 17 June – immediately drew up an evacuation plan with the navy. The navy established four convoy routes, all terminating in Kerch. The harbor cities of Anapa, Senaya, Taman, and Temryuk were designated as embarkation ports.

The evacuation of the Kuban Bridgehead continued until 7 September 1943. In total, 12 barges, 12 naval transports, 11 tugs, seven engineer ferries, and numerous smaller vessels were employed. The transport was controlled by the navy, and only the engineer landing craft from the 770th Engineer Assault Regiment were employed.

Naturally, the "Red Army" tried to interfere with the evacuation. They energetically attacked the divisions that were slowly withdrawing to the west. In the course of this operation, troops of the 18th Soviet Army landed north of and directly in the vicinity of the harbor of Novorossisk. The 4th

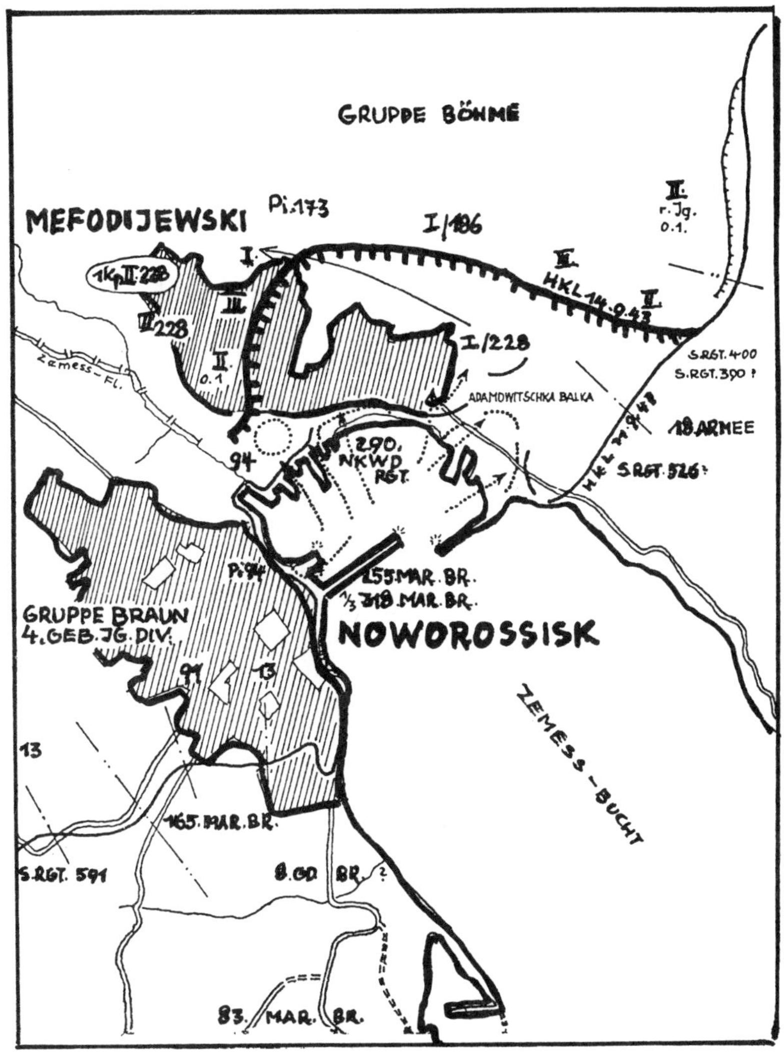

Mountain Division (Major General Braun) – the previous division commander, Lieutenant General Kress, had fallen recently – and the left neighboring 73rd ID (Colonel Boehme) could not deal with the superior Russian formations and had to evacuate the city.

Weeks before, the 17th Army established prepared positions on the Taman Peninsula, behind which the withdrawing divisions could be removed sector by sector. The first of these defensive lines, the so-called

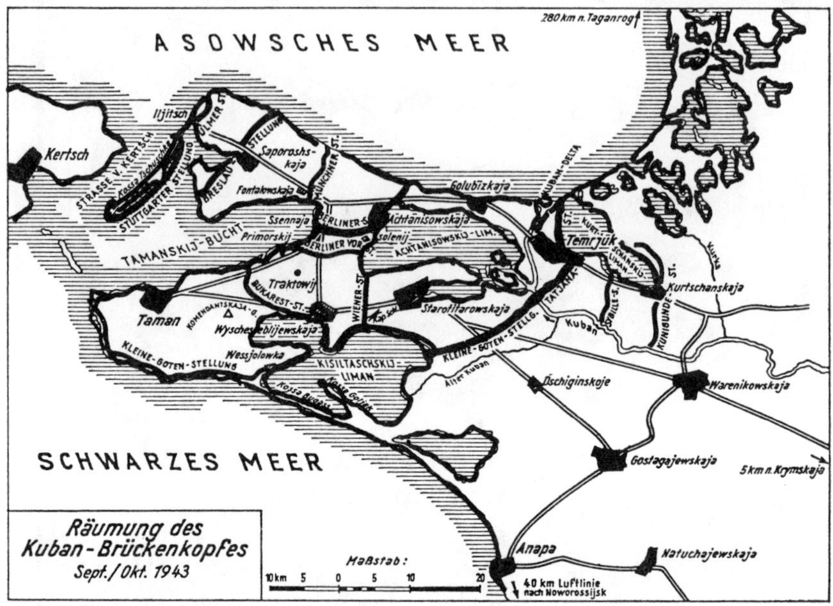

Evacuation of the Kuban Bridgehead Sep-Oct 1943

"Little Gothic Line", ran from Temryuk in the north to Kisiltashskiy-Liman and then along the coast to Taman.

Little by little, the divisions left from the front and were transported to Kerch and then from there to the Crimea. Several formations were transported to Army Group South, and some even went to Army Group Center.

The XLIV Army Corps was transferred to Sivash, and later to the Nikopol area. At the beginning of October, the 17th Army consisted of the V Army Corps and XLIX Mountain Corps, with the 4th Mountain Division, 50th, 98th, 370th ID, and 97th Rifle Division. The Rumanian Mountain Corps had two divisions to protect the Taman Peninsula.

After the beginning of October, the last rifle and infantry battalions withdrew across the "Berlin Line", "Munich Line", "Breslau Line", and "Stuttgart Line", and were on the way to Kerch.

On 9 October, the last soldiers left the Kuban Bridgehead.

During the four weeks, 239,660 soldiers, 16,311 wounded, 27,456 civilians, 21,230 vehicles, 1,815 guns, 74,657 horses, and 94,937 tons of equipment were transported to the Crimea.

Chapter 3: 1943

On 20 September 1943, Hitler instituted the "Kuban Shield", which was awarded to soldiers of all branches of arms that participated on and behind the Kuban front sector between 1 February and 9 October.

Army Group South

BELGOROD (5 July-14 July 1943)

The great Russian winter offensive of 1942-43 coincided with the onset of the mud period. The greatest Russian penetration to the west was in front of Kursk. This situation required the Germans to launch a two-pronged attack to cut off the salient.

In February, the commander of Army Group South (Field Marshal von Manstein) proposed – just as the winter battles were reaching their climax – to forestall the attack of the "Red Army" and, when necessary, to withdraw the friendly main line of resistance to the Dnepr.

Hitler did not agree and, on 13 March, issued the first operation order for "Operation Citadel." This operation included an attack on the Soviet armies on the Kursk front. A month later, on 15 April, the senior leadership ordered Army Groups South and Center to prepare for "Operation Citadel."

At this time, Army Group South was located on a line (see map) from Belgorod, where they were in contact with Army Group Center, to and along the west bank of the Donets and Mius Rivers, and on to the Sea of Azov near Taganrog.

From left to right, the army group deployed:

The 4th Panzer Army (General Hoth), with two panzer and one army corps, the 1st Panzer Army (General von Mackensen), with three army and one panzer corps, and the 6th Army (General of Infantry Hollidt), which was re-formed in March 1943, with three army and one panzer corps.

Army Group A (Field Marshal von Kleist), which was still deployed in the south of the Eastern Front, consisted only of the 17th Army in the Crimea and the Kuban Bridgehead.

From the beginning, during the first phase of preparation for "Operation Citadel", the OKH and both army group commanders did not agree on the details, so that the date of the attack had to be shifted several times. During the middle of June, formations conducted the deployment to the assembly areas to prepare for the attack. Then, on 25 June, Hitler declared 5 July 1943 to be the day of the start of the attack.

Army Group South's mission read:

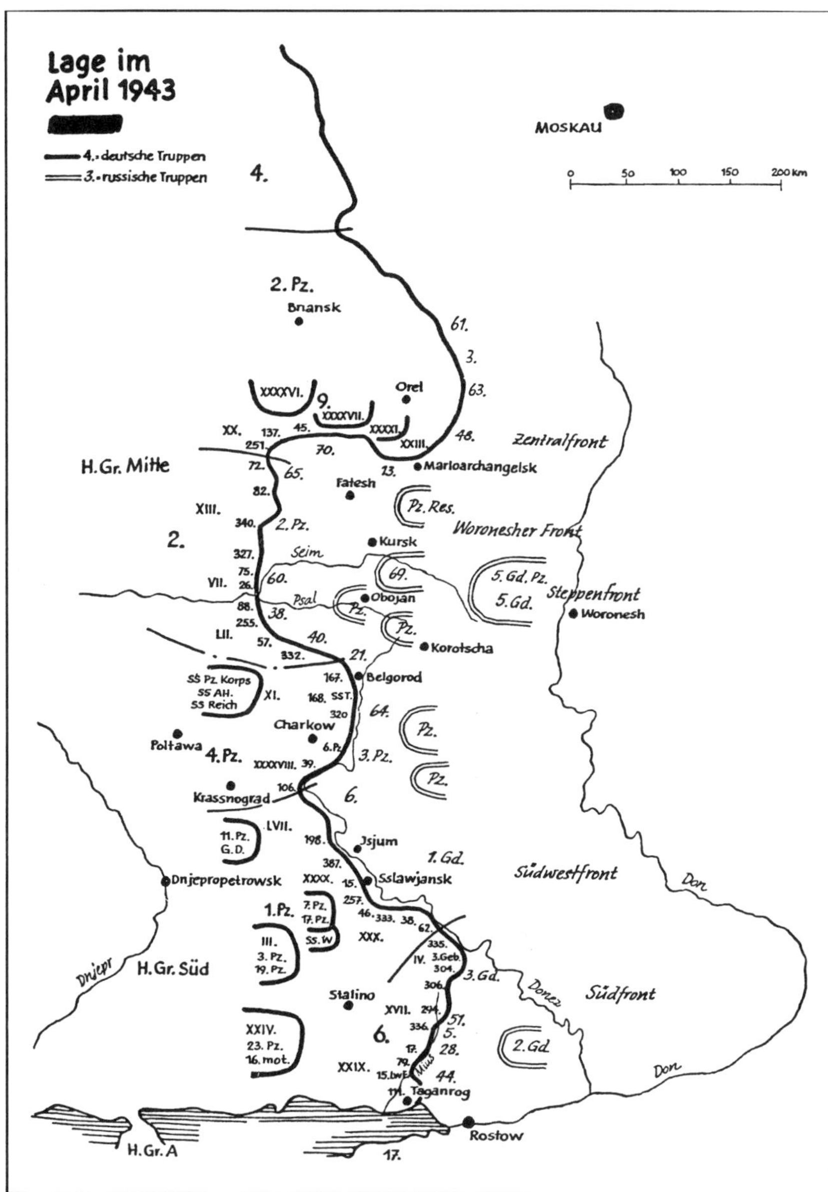

Situation in Apr 1943

> "With concentrated forces, Army Group South breaks out to the west of the Belgorod area, advances on a line Prilepy-Oboyan to the east and makes contact with Army Group Center near Kursk. The attack is screened to the east and west."

At the beginning of April, in preparation for this operation, the army group pulled the 4th Panzer Army from the front and authorized them to refresh the seven panzer and six motorized infantry divisions in Dnepropetrovsk. General of Panzer troops Kempf led the newly formed Army Detachment Kempf, which now took responsibility for the old front. Later, while the 4th Panzer Army had to break through the Russian positions west of Belgorod, Army Detachment Kempf had to secure the eastern flank of the panzer army.

During the preparation for deployment, special attention was, of course, given to re-equipping the panzer divisions. It had become noticeable throughout that the Russian tank troops were superior to the German combat vehicles, not only in number, but in strength. Thus, the 4th Panzer Army

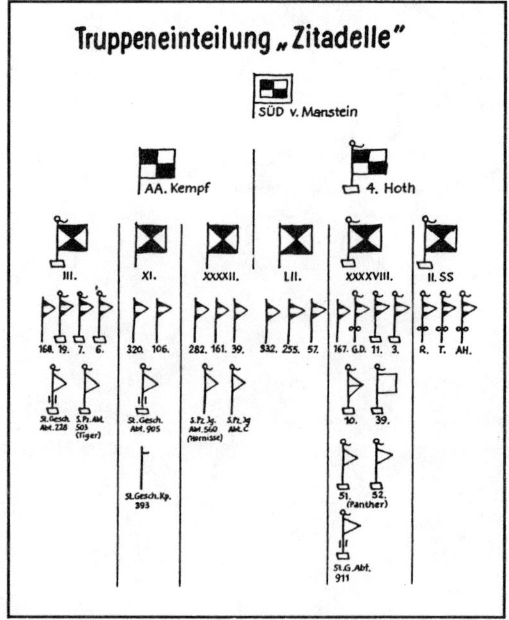

"Citadel" Troop Distribution

received the 10th Panzer Brigade. This brigade was directly assigned for "Operation Citadel" and was composed of the 51st, 52nd, and 503rd Panzer battalions, which were equipped with over 204 of the newest "Tiger" tanks, committed for the first time during "Operation Citadel."

The total number of tanks can be derived from the following table:

Allocation of armored combat vehicles (ACV) and assault guns (AG) to troops participating in Citadel (Derived from a report on 30/6/1943)

1. Army Group South

Formation	Combat Ready		In Repair		In Supply		Total	
	ACV	AG	ACV	AG	ACV	AG	ACV	AG
Arm. Inf. Div:								
GD	113 (11)	34	16 (1)	1	34 (0)	0	163 (12)	35
SS-LAH	100 (7)	34	8 (0)	1	16 (0)	0	126 (7)	35
SS-R	113 (0)	34	15 (1)	0	0 (0)	0	128 (1)	34
SS-T	104 (5)	27	27 (3)	8	9 (0)	0	140 (8)	35
SS-W	31 (15)	6	0 (0)	0	0 (0)	0	31 (15)	6
Panzer Div:								
3	56 (32)	2	2 (2)	0	5 (5)	0	63 (39)	2
6	78 (29)	0	8 (2)	0	0 (0)	0	86 (31)	0
7	81 (22)	0	6 (3)	0	0 (0)	0	87 (25)	0
11	74 (15)	0	23 (5)	0	1 (0)	0	98 (20)	0
19	62 (19)	0	3 (1)	0	5 (1)	0	70 (21)	0
23	55 (11)	0	2 (0)	0	4 (0)	0	61 (11)	0
Panzer Bde:								
10	244 (0)	0	5 (0)	0	3 (0)	0	252 (0)	0
AG Bns		94		3		9		106
Total:	1111 (166)	231	115 (18)	13	77 (6)	9	1303 (190)	253

Strong air formations under Air Fleet 4 (General of Aviation Dessloch) – in all, 1100 fighter, pursuit interceptor, tactical, dive-bomber, and reconnaissance aircraft – and the I Air Defense Corps supported Army Group South in their attempt to breach the front of the opposing Russian Army Group "Voronezh Front" and cause a breakthrough.

In the beginning of July, the 4th Panzer Army and the Army Detachment Kempf completed their initial deployment.

From left to right, the 4th Panzer Army (General Hoth) committed: the LII Army Corps (General of Infantry Ott), with three infantry divisions as flank cover for both of the neighboring panzer corps; the XLVIII Panzer Corps (General of Panzer Troops von Knobelsdorf), with two panzer and one each motorized infantry and infantry division, was located in the center; and the II SS Panzer Corps (SS Obergruppenfuehrer Hausser), with three panzer divisions, was on the main axis.

Army Detachment Kempf, which was deployed for flank protection to the east, had at its disposal (from left to right) the III Panzer Corps (Gen-

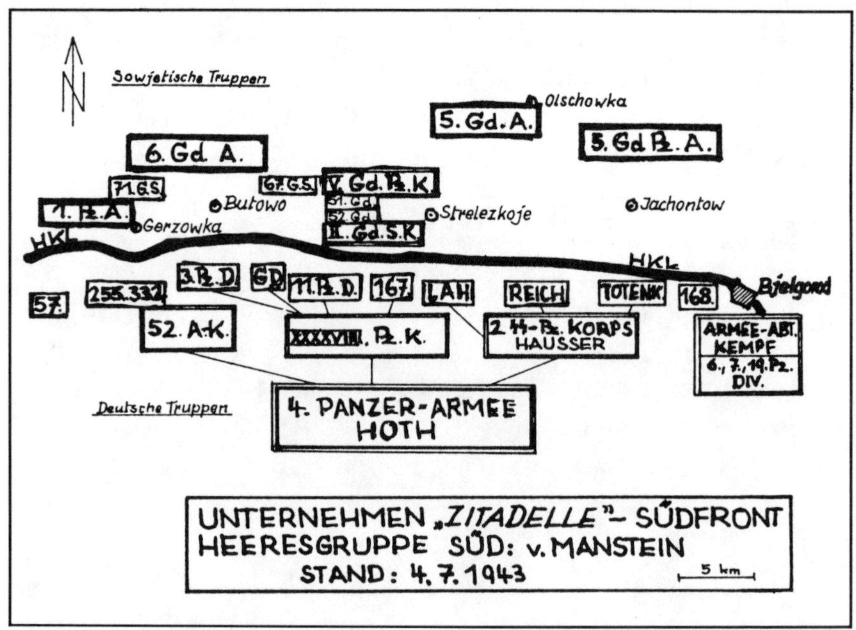

Operation "Citadel" – Southern front
Army Group South: von Manstein
Positions: 7/4/1943

eral of Panzer Troops Breith), with three panzer and one infantry division, and the XI Army Corps (General of Panzer Troops Raus), with two infantry divisions. Both of these corps were to secure the flanks near and southeast of Belgorod, while the right corps of the army detachment – XLII Army Corps (General of Infantry Mattenklott), with three infantry divisions – had to maintain contact with the Donets and the remainder of the main line of resistance.

The day before the start of the attack, Hitler issued two orders to the two army groups. The appeal to the commanders ran:

> My Commanders!
>
> I have published the order for the first offensive of this year.
>
> You and your soldiers are designated to successfully execute this mission no matter the circumstances. The importance of this first offensive of the year is extraordinary.
>
> The initiation of this new German operation will not only strengthen the German people in relation to the rest of the world, but also infuse new confidence in the German soldier himself. Our allies will be reaffirmed in their belief in our final victory, while the neutral countries will become more cautious and reserved. We must wrest the initiative from the Soviet leadership and create the prerequisite for Russian defeat during this offensive. It can have far reaching effects on the morale and composure of the Soviet soldier.
>
> The armies scheduled to participate in the attack have been provided with all the weapons that German ingenuity and technology can produce. Personnel strengths have been raised to the highest levels possible. The supply of ammunition and fuel have been secured in sufficient quantities for this and future operations. The Luftwaffe has concentrated all of its strength to destroy the enemy's air capability, to bombard his firing positions, and support the infantrymen with continuous sorties.
>
> I, therefore, turn over this battle to you, my commanders. More than ever, the decisive battles in the fourth year of the war depend on the commanders, on their leadership, on their vitality and progress, on

their ruthlessness, their unbending desire for victory and, when necessary, their personal heroic commitment.

I know, that you have already given much in the preparation for this battle, I thank you for this. You must also realize that much depends on the successful execution of this first great battle of 1943, such as final victory.

I don't doubt that, under these circumstances, I can count on you, my commanders.

Adolf Hitler

• • •

On the afternoon of 4 July, the XLVIII Panzer Corps tried to obtain more favorable departure positions through several assault operations, but did not fully succeed due to the sudden arrival of torrential rains and the alerting of the Russian divisions by their command authorities. Enemy artillery immediately engaged the attacking combat groups with heavy fire, which caused unexpected casualties.

Then the 5th of July dawned. Before the troops of the 4th Panzer Army stretched a plain, rising gently to the north, west of Belgorod. Brooks, valleys, and small hills, with difficult-to-survey corn fields pervaded this terrain, and its sandy roads were long soaked by the persistent rain.

Then it was 0300 hours – the first salvos roared forth from the German batteries – and "Operation Citadel" began.

• • •

At 0300 hours, the SS Panzer Corps began the attack with heavy artillery and air support. 88 Stukas attacked Beresov. After the last bombs fell, the breakthrough into the main line of resistance failed. The attack bogged down under heavy enemy artillery fire from the west bank of the Vorskla and the Shuravliny Forest, as well as before the deep mine fields.

The SS war correspondent, Martin Schwaebe, described this attack:

"The morning of 5 July 1943 dawned pale. For two hours, the engineer assault troops cleared the front line trenches.

They took the Soviet outposts by surprise while it was still dark. Now it was our turn, the time of the armored infantry. The Soviets established bunkers, field defensive positions, and anti-tank ditches thirty kilometers deep. This had to be overcome! By evening, the bunkers of the last line of defense had to be captured.

The 3rd Battalion of Deutschland was on the main axis. Its mission: to overcome the positions in front of the tank ditches, conquer the town, and break into the large anti-tank ditches!

The ammunition trains were to be quickly moved forward.

All hell broke loose: suddenly, Soviet barrage fire fell all around! The attack bogged down 400 meters in front of the anti-tank ditches. The "Tigers" and assault guns did not arrive as planned. The thunderstorms of the previous night made the heavy caissons impossible to move."

The commander, General Hausser, observed the attack from the command post of the Deutschland Regiment. "It's underway, Obergruppenfuehrer!" reported the regiment commander, Heinz Harmel. The 3rd Battalion, Deutschland, formed the spearhead. The battalion commander, Wisliceny, juggled his companies hither and yon, but always to the front.

The forward-most 10th Company, under Hauptsturmfuehrer Helmut Schreiber, fell under heavy fire at the first line of anti-tank ditches, dug in and, in spite of furious Russian counterattacks, did not retreat. The attack had to be conducted without the help of tanks and assault guns. After a horrible night, during which many had become stuck in the mud and had to pull each other out, the assault guns were finally able to reach the battlefield, as the men of the 10th Company Deutschland, along with the engineers of the 16th Company Deutschland, entered the anti-tank ditches.

At 0620 hours, the attack was still under the influence of heavy artillery fire from the west bank of the Vorskla. The breakthrough finally succeeded after a renewed artillery fire was concentrated on Hill 220.5 and Beresov, as well as stuka sorties on the hills west of the Vorskla and in the Shuravliny Forest.

At 0815 hours, units of the 3rd Company Deutschland advanced to the west of Beresov and attacked the village to its north. At 0837 hours, the bulk of the Deutschland Regiment had overcome the anti-tank ditches. Another stuka squadron was committed in front of the LAH sector, as well as in front of the Deutschland Regiment.

At 1000 hours, the flame-thrower troops, with the assault troops of the 10th Company (Schreiber) Deutschland, overran the trench system up to the southern edge of Beresov and deployed into the southern outskirts of the town. (From: Weidinger, O.: *Division Das Reich*, vol 4. Osnabrueck 1977.)

0300 hours Friendly artillery preparation.

0430 hours Regiment commanders move forward in their armored reconnaissance vehicles.

0450 hours Artillery fire strike.

0500 hours Friendly infantry and tanks leave the departure line: Butovo - Gerzovka, with assault guns and the 4th Company of the Grossdeutschand Armored Assault Engineer Battalion near the 3rd Battalion under Captain Senger.

0900 hours Point 237.8, west of Cherkaskoe is reached! - The 12th Company penetrates to the west. - Friendly tanks have difficulties in front of the anti-tank ditches at the Gerzovka Valley. - The neighbor on the right - the 11th Panzer Division - is located near Hill 237.8. The neighbor on the left - armored infantry - has advanced the same distance as we. Strong enemy air activity.

0915 hours A direct hit on the regimental command post casualties: The regiment adjutant Captain Beckendorf, Lieutenant Hofstetter the 4th Battalion adjutant, Lieutenant Stein of the anti-tank battalion, Grossdeutschland are all dead.

1000 hours Instructions from the division operations officer to the panther brigade: advance on point 210.7. - The 1st and 2nd battalions are to link up. - The execution was delayed by the halt at the anti-tank ditches. - The 2nd Battalion had problems making the connection, because the anti-tank battalion blocked the way. -

1100 hours A bridge is constructed across the Gerzovka Valley - near the center of the division attack lane.

1350 hours The Soviets attack with 7 tanks in the direction of Korovino, in the vicinity of our 3rd Battalion.

1353 hours All 7 attacking Russian tanks are destroyed by friendly tanks. From time to time, the enemy renews its air activity.

1430 hours The 1st Battalion and the panther brigade are at the beginning of the anti-tank ditches. The 2nd and 4th Battalion lead elements are south of point 229.8 and in the depression.

1530 hours The temporary bridge over the Beresoviy Valley is destroyed by the crossing of the panthers.

1750 hours The regimental command post is redeployed to the western edge of Yamnoe.

1900 hours Bethke's Battalion (2nd) is ordered to attack Cherkaskoe from the direction of Butovo, through point 237.8. The 11 Panzer Division is northeast of Cherkaskoe. In the early afternoon, elements of the 1st Battalion attacked the northern portion of Cherkaskoe with tanks. The 1st battalion assaulted enemy batteries and entered the northwestern portion of Cherkaskoe.

1955 hours The 2nd Battalion began its attack on Cherkaskoe - to the southwest. - Freedom of movement in the southwestern portion of Cherkaskoe was soon established by the attack of the 2nd Battalion. - Flame thrower tanks from the 11 Panzer Division had already worked over the area. - At night, there was heavy enemy air activity.

(From: Spaeter, H.: *History of the "Grossdeutschland" Panzer Corps.* vol 2. Duisburg 1958.)

The attack of the XLVIII Panzer Corps quickly got under way. By 0700 hours, the three panzer divisions – the 3rd (Lieutenant General Westhoven), 11th (Major General Mickl), and "Grossdeutschland" (Lieutenant General Hoernlein) – were able to break through the initial enemy defensive positions. Then the tanks could move no further, because the rain had soaked the ground so much that the wide tank treads stuck fast in the mud. The corps couldn't move for almost twelve hours.

Likewise, the neighboring II SS Panzer Corps, with its three panzer divisions – the "Leibstandarte" (SS Brigadefuehrer Wisch), "Das Reich" (SS Gruppenfuehrer Krueger), and "Totenkopf" (SS Gruppenfuehrer Eicke) – were also able to overcome the initial enemy defensive positions, but then they bogged down in front of the second defensive belt of the 5th Soviet Guards Army under the strong defensive fire of Russian heavy artillery batteries.

In the early morning, the left and center corps of Army Detachment Kempf, which was charged with flank security, crossed the Donets and fought its way across the rolling terrain that was heavily mined by the enemy and studded with tank traps. They succeeded in entering several enemy trenches, but could not effect a breakthrough.

The divisions of the army detachment had the following missions for the first two days of combat:

The 6th Panzer Division (Major General von Huenersdorf – a few days later, he was mortally wounded) had to advance to the north, with the 168th ID (major General Beaulieu), was to maintain contact with the II SS Panzer Corps. The 19th Panzer Division (Lieutenant General Schmidt) attacked to the southeast, while the 7th Panzer Division (Lieutenant General Baron von Funck), the 106th (Lieutenant General Forst), and the 320th ID (Major General Postel) advanced to the east. The XLII Army Corps, deployed on the right flank of the army detachment, crossed the Donets with only the 282nd ID (Major General Kohler). The other divisions remained in their main lines of resistance.

The second day of the attack was characterized by a decrease in the Russian resistance. The SS panzer divisions were able to quickly and surely penetrate into the enemy's second defensive belt, while the neighboring corps were not able to keep up. Here, broad mine fields, entrenched "T-34's", permanently emplaced Russian anti-tank guns, and the fanatical combat of the defenders hindered the proportionate advance of the formations. The first heavy losses were suffered.

• • •

On the 6th of July, the division panzer combat group was subordinated to the 7th Panzer Division as per instructions of Colonel von Oppeln, in order to exploit the success of the right flanking combat groups of the 7th Panzer Division (Schultz) on the southern bank of the Rasumnaya, through Generalovka, one kilometer southeast of Yastrebovo.

At 1200 hours, they marched to the 60 ton bridge in order: Tiger Company/11th Panzer Regiment, 2 (armored personnel carrier)/114 Armored infantry Regiment. After crossing at 1430, they echeloned themselves for the attack on Generalovka. The Tiger Company took the lead, and then the regimental staff followed with Colonel von Oppeln. The armored personnel carrier battalion followed the tanks at a distance. The combat diary of the 11th Panzer Regiment states: "Under severe enemy artillery fire and tank fire, the combat group reached point 216.1 and Hill 207.9. The 6th and 8th Companies, supported by the tigers, established themselves at the Soloev Kolkhoz, but they came upon strong enemy resistance. Both companies suffered losses. At 2000 hours, contact was established with the advancing right flank regiment of the 7th Panzer Division. During the night, Combat Group von Oppeln occupied a hedgehog position on hill 207.9. They achieved the day's objective. Achievements: 7 enemy tanks, 10 anti-tank guns, 1 infantry gun, three 17.2 cm guns, 1 air defense battery (four 7.62 cm), and 120 enemy dead. Losses: 8 tanks by fire, 3 by mines.

During the night, the 6th Panzer Division closed ranks in the Generalovka area. During the evening, they reported the events of 7 July 1943 to the panzer corps:

> "After a preparatory stuka attack on enemy targets in and around Yastrebovo, Panzer Group Oppeln began to attack out of the 207.9 area and Combat Group Unrein out of the Belinska area to the north on the enemy located at Sevryukovo-Yastrebovo. The panzer group, with the 2/114 Armored Infantry Regiment, and Combat Group Unrein, with the 1/4 Armored Infantry Regiment, quickly crossed the Rasumnaya, pushed the enemy out of the city, and captured the high ground directly west of the northern edge of Sevryukovo. All of the bridges leading to the roads on the eastern bank were destroyed. While the bridges on the southern edge of Yastrebovo were repaired in three hours' time, tank

attacks were launched from the north, but they were all repulsed. Combat equipment was not installed on the bridge to allow the tanks to cross the Rasumnaya. Combat Groups Bieberstein and Unrein did cross over the bridge.

During the occupation of Generalovka and Belinska on 6 July and of Yastrebovo and Sevryukovo on 7 July, the enemy offered tenacious resistance, supported by tanks. The withdrawal, which was also observed from the air, and which was expected to become a retreat, was contrary to the continuous resistance and the contents of an intercepted radio signal, in which they were ordered to hold on. The enemy air force made its presence felt by bombs and aircraft weapons."

The combat diary of the 3rd Panzer Corps relates the following about this day: "Friendly losses reflected the severity of the combat. Thousands of mines had to be removed. The approach of the enemy's operational reserve toward the front and flanks of the corps was not discovered by air reconnaissance. Only in the 7th Panzer Division area were two new divisions discovered in addition to tank and anti-tank regiments. For the continuation of the attack on 8 July, the 7th Panzer Division is to protect their deep right flank. The 6th and 19th Panzer Divisions are to break through the rib of hills northeast of Blizhnaya Yumenka, concentrating with tanks in the lead on Melikhevo and Dalnaya Yumenka respectively. (From: Paul, W.: *Focal Point*. (6th Panzer Division) Krefeld 1977.)

The German panzer troops became confused by the natural terrain obstacles, the mine fields, and the numerous anti-tank obstacles. The engineers had a difficult time clearing the mine fields under fire and establishing tank crossings on the muddy ground. Additionally, the first superior enemy tanks made their appearance, and they quickly and agilely advanced against the flanks of the attacking German panzer battalions. They would vanish as quickly as they would appear. The new heavy tanks of the "Panther", "Ferdinand", and "Tiger" varieties could not maintain the speed of the mobile "T-34" and "T-70" and suffered more transmission and engine damage. Of the 200 combat vehicles of the type "Panther", which were committed on the second day of the battle, only 40 were still running by that evening.

Only the three divisions of SS Obergruppenfuehrer Hausser had penetrated to a depth of 18 kilometers by the evening of the second day of the battle.

Thus, all of the other corps of the army group were left behind. The army group commander determined that both of the attacking armies had come apart. During the night, Field Marshal Manstein ordered the regrouping of Army Detachment Kempf and the integration of the III Panzer Corps into the II SS Panzer Corps. The SS panzer divisions were to cease movement until the XLVIII Panzer Corps fought its way to the same point.

• • •

The continuation of the attack appeared to become critical, because the enemy was obviously concentrating new forces. An armored group, under the leadership of Colonel Schulz, was assembled from his own regiment, the armored personnel carrier company of the 6th Armored Infantry Regiment, a battalion of the 78th Armored Artillery Regiment under Major Schmueckle, elements of the 42nd Anti-tank Battalion, and the 58th Armored Engineer Battalion. The mission of this group was to attack through a gap in the forested area near Batrazhaya Dacha, utilizing the ridgeline east of Yastrebovo for cover, then penetrate to the north and, advancing east of the forest, attack the high ground south of Scheino (7 kilometers northeast of Myasoedovo). The weak armored infantry battalion from the flank security (to the east), under Colonel von Steinkeller, had to be dispatched posthaste to the northern tip of this forest. The mission of flank security was taken over by units of the 7th Armored Artillery Battalion and the 7th Company. The division's left combat group, the 6th Armored Infantry regiment, was tasked with absorbing the attack of the armored Group Schulz in a wider and looser form on either side of Myasoedovo, in order to draw the enemy's attention. Additionally, the division commander ordered the shifting of all available reserves to the north. The division artillery and artillery attached in support had to be supplied with sufficient ammunition.

Thanks to the careful planning of the regrouping of the division during the hours of darkness on 8 to 9 July, the plan had been worked out in detail.

Led by our many proven commanders, the armored groups would cross to the edge of the forest under the cover of the ridgeline and utilizing their high speed. Here, they had to then move diagonally to the enemy, firing ample amounts of smoke shells from the tanks and artillery to hinder their observation. Having succeeded in penetrating into the gaps in the forest, the groups continued to attack further to the east. Without delay, the attack of the groups, which penetrated the gaps in the forest without incident, continued to the north along the eastern edge of the forest with the result that, on 11 July, the high ground south of Scheino, which had paralyzed the attack in the past, was occupied by the division. The armored infantry battalion, committed on the northern edge of the forest under the personal leadership of Colonel von Steinkeller, immediately closed ranks with the violent advance of the armored group and the 6th Armored Infantry Regiment committed its last reserves; this regiment energetically drove its attack on Myasoedovo, as planned, making immediate use of the enemy's paralysis and the smoke rounds. With strikes on three sides, we completely broke the enemy's resistance on the high ground. From here, the artillery could now observe the approach of the enemy in a timely manner and effectively combat him. (From: Manteuffel, H. E. von: *The 7th Panzer Division in the Second World War*, Krefeld 1965.)

• • •

The Russian 5th Guards Tank Army approached the battlefield on 7 July. Its tank battalions fearlessly attacked the reorganized German formations, which could advance no further on this day. Unfortunately, air support was also lacking, because in accordance with the highest orders, half of all stuka and tactical aircraft were shifted to support the 9th Army of Army Group Center, because this army could not advance at all.

On 8 July, Field Marshal von Manstein decided to continue the attack on the entire front before the superior Russian tank forces deployed their shock forces. However, it was already too late. The divisions of the 4th Panzer Army were hit in the rear and flanks and had to give up some conquered territory. The II SS Panzer Corps was likewise being attacked from all sides and could not close the gap with the neighboring Army detachment Kempf. Here, strong forces of the 69th Soviet Army were able to break through.

On 9 July, torrential rains completely weakened the momentum of the German attack. The combat groups of the German corps – partially wedged into one another – had to restrain the Russian tank attacks from all sides. Losses increased practically hour by hour. The relief attack from the west by the LII Army Corps was not successful. On the other hand, the XI Army Corps was the only major formation that was able to stabilize its front.

The Russian leadership understood the diminished combat strength of the 4th Panzer Army. Army General Vatutin, commander of the "Voronezh Front", issued, on the evening of the following day, the order to attack Army Group South. During the night, the 5th Guards, 6th Guards, 7th Guards, 1st Guards, and 5th Guards Tank Armies prepared for the major attack against the severely battered and remnant forces of the 4th German Panzer Army and Army Detachment Kempf.

This was the largest tank battle of World War Two.

Two Russian tank armies, with a total of ten tank corps – almost 10,000 combat vehicles – rolled on 11 July against the II SS Panzer Corps and the III Panzer Corps. Around Prokhochovka developed a battle of such a scale not seen in the Second World War. The tank regiments attacked each other frontally; the individual crews tried to destroy the enemy combat vehicles by daring, agility, and fearlessness. One who was there wrote home:

> "Then the hellish defensive battle began. It was a free for all battle on all sides, and some went all day without supplies. The Russians tried to cut off our panzer wedge with massed tank attacks. Tanks all day and all night. Four battles in one day. Then we withdrew. With half of my tanks, a portion in tow, I returned in a pouring rain to the attack departure area. Never have I experienced a ten-fold superiority in enemy tanks such as this. It was a raging turmoil. On this day, our regiment destroyed 62 enemy tanks. My company led the rest with 20 kills. Until today, my company had destroyed 43 enemy tanks and I had only one of the total. Now the company has become a blood brotherhood. It dominates the spirit and morale and can motivate us to uproot trees. One of my tanks was shot up, though I got there in time and only the

radioman was wounded. I am writing this letter to you just before the start of another battle. We are at the halt behind a hill. In front of us the infantry and artillery battle is simmering. All around us are wide plains with the treacherous Balkas. A wind blows between the rain showers, exposing the sun for a few seconds. The battle is developing. Soon we must rattle across the infantry lines and attack into the enemy's depth."

• • •

The battle continued. By evening, 220 destroyed Russian tanks and 150 burning German tanks lay on the battlefield before Prokhochovka.

Then came the decisive day of 12 July 1943.

12 July 1943: On this day, the enemy attacked the lead elements of the II SS Panzer Corps with two new Tank Corps (XVIII and XXIV) in an attempt to destroy it. Since the three divisions of the II SS Panzer Corps were committed almost simultaneously, a tank battle developed that had no precedent in size.

Details:

0400 hours, the 1/2 reports the advance of enemy reconnaissance with tanks, but they were driven off.

0600 hours, a regimental strength attack across the Prokhochovka-Petrovka line with about 50 tanks against a Panzer Group of the LAH. This battle lasted about two hours. A platoon leader from a platoon in the 3(armored)/2 reported:

"They attacked in the morning. They went around us, over us, and between us. We fought man against man, jumped out of our trenches, fetched the magnetic anti-tank hollow charges from our armored personnel carriers, jumped out of our vehicles, and attached them to the enemy's. It was like hell! At 0900 hours, we held firm on the battlefield. We helped our tanks out quite a bit. My company alone destroyed 15 Russian tanks."

0915 hours, a tank attack ensued with 40 tanks from Yamki against the reinforced 1st Armored Infantry Regiment. Hubert Neunzert, from a platoon of the 3rd Company of the LAH Anti-tank Battalion, graphically reports the events of this day:

> "It was approximately 0400 hours as a new order was received by motorcycle courier: Secure the Stalinsk Kolkhoz. We were to secure generally to the right of the woods and in the direction of the railroad embankment. Soon, we saw about 25-30 T-34's off to our right at about 6-7 kilometers distance, and they were marching toward the main line of resistance of the Das Reich Division. Too far for us, however, but the artillery had already taken aim and insured that they would not reach our right flank unmolested. Then all became quiet. With a slap, the spell was broken at 0800 hours. Salvo after salvo from the Stalin Organs laid suppressive fire on our positions. Mortars were intermixed with the artillery fire. All in all, it looked like an artillery preparation, and it lasted for 1 1/2 hours. A German scout, who had just returned from deep in Russian territory, threw down a message case and then two violet smoke signals were already rising to the left of the railroad embankment. At the same time, the fire slackened, and there – coming over the hill to the left of the railroad embankment – 3, 5, 10, too many to count. At full speed, T-34 after T-34 roared over the hill, and one after the other into the infantry defensive positions. As soon as the first tank appeared we opened fire with our 5 guns, and perhaps a second later, the first T-34 was covered in a black cloud. At times we had to let a target go, as the infantrymen jumped onto the tanks loaded with Russian infantrymen and engaged them in hand to hand combat. However, another 40 to 50 were coming toward us on our side of the embankment. Now we had to swivel around and place these under fire.
>
> At one time, three very saucy giants – they were stalking through the depression toward the kolkhoz, taking to the road that lead to the kolkhoz. I didn't have time to fire. The gun on the right jammed and apparently it could not be cleared. Also, the tanks moved between the buildings of the kolkhoz. I couldn't see, but I fired at the first T-34. I missed. It quickly moved between the buildings – and as I stood in

front of one of the cabins, the blockage was removed. Again, the first one emerged, and my loader shouted into my ear: "The last shell is in the barrel." I cranked the gun toward a T-34 about 150 meters distant, and it was the next monster to pass by: The rear of the gun lurched and the barrel of the 7.5 cm canon raised into the air. I tried with all my might to crank the barrel. I succeeded in getting the turret of the T-34 into the cross-hairs and fired. Its a hit! The hatch opened and two men jumped out – one remained, and the other skipped between the buildings.

After several gunfights with the Russian infantrymen and dismounted tank crews, during which our infantrymen were magnificent, we were able to race through a gap between burning T-34's to the woods. Here, there was another Russian tank attack, supported by 3-4 waves of infantry, that pushed our brave infantrymen back, breaking through.

Burning tank carcasses were strewn about the sector at about 1500 meters distance, destroyed in close combat and some, perhaps, by the 10-12 guns. 120 attacked, perhaps more. Who could count them? Sammetreiter was awarded the Knight's Cross for the conduct of his platoon during this engagement."

0920 hours, another tank attack out of Prokhorovka with 35 tanks against the LAH panzer group, with 40 tanks out of Petrovka on the crossroads one kilometer southeast of Oktyabrskiy. The tank attack was supported by strong artillery and was conducted at high speed.

Thus, near Oktyabrskiy, of the seven tanks of the 6th Battalion, LAH Panzer Regiment (von Ribbentrop), four were put out of action after moving 220 meters forward. The remaining three, however, took up with the 2nd Battalion of the LAH Panzer Regiment (Stubaf. Martin Gross), which was located 800 meters away.

At distances of between ten and thirty meters, each shot is a direct hit. The Russians could not discern that the German tanks were rolling in the same direction as they, due to the dust and smoke. 19 Russian tanks were already burning as the battalion opened the fire fight. In spite of the crushing superiority (at this time, he had 33 tanks), Stubaf. Gross was able to end the battle successfully. He decided to outflank the attacking enemy on two sides. During the almost three hour battle – one could also call it tank to tank combat – his tanks shot up 62 T-70 and T-34 tanks. Stubaf. Martin Gross and Ostuf. von Ribbentrop were awarded the Knight's Cross for this engagement. (From: Lehmann, R.: *The Leibstandarte*, vol 3. Osnabrueck 1982.)

• • •

The battle in the 4th Panzer Army sector practically came to a standstill. In spite of the superiority of the Russian tank formations, the divisions of the II SS Panzer Corps and the III Panzer Corps did not give up.

They – the officers, non-commissioned officers, men; tankers, riflemen, artillerymen, radiomen, engineers, medics, supply troops, etc. – resisted in spite of the waves of attacking Soviet combat vehicles and deep enemy air strikes and did not give up a meter of ground without exacting a price.

"Operation Citadel" was decided on another front! Soviet armies of both Army Groups "West Front" and "Bryansk front" began an attack against the 2nd German Panzer Army on 12 July and achieved a major breakthrough on the first day that led to the collapse of the entire Army Group Center. The commander of the 9th Army (of Army Group Center), General Model, decided to break off the battle for Kursk and pull his tank forces from the front.

On 13 July, Hitler himself ordered the commanders of Army Groups Center and South to his headquarters in East Prussia and agreed that, due to the breakthrough of Army Group Center and the simultaneous success of the Allied landing in Sicily, "Operation Citadel" had to be suspended. Therefore, the II SS Panzer Corps – the strongest force in Army Group South – had to be withdrawn.

As a result, Field Marshal Manstein had to order the 4th Panzer Army and Army Detachment Kempf to cease further attacks and, from 23 July, to fight a delaying action back to the departure positions.

On the morning of 7/14, Soviet artillery and multiple rocket fire suddenly began in the 167th ID sector, which was predominantly concentrated

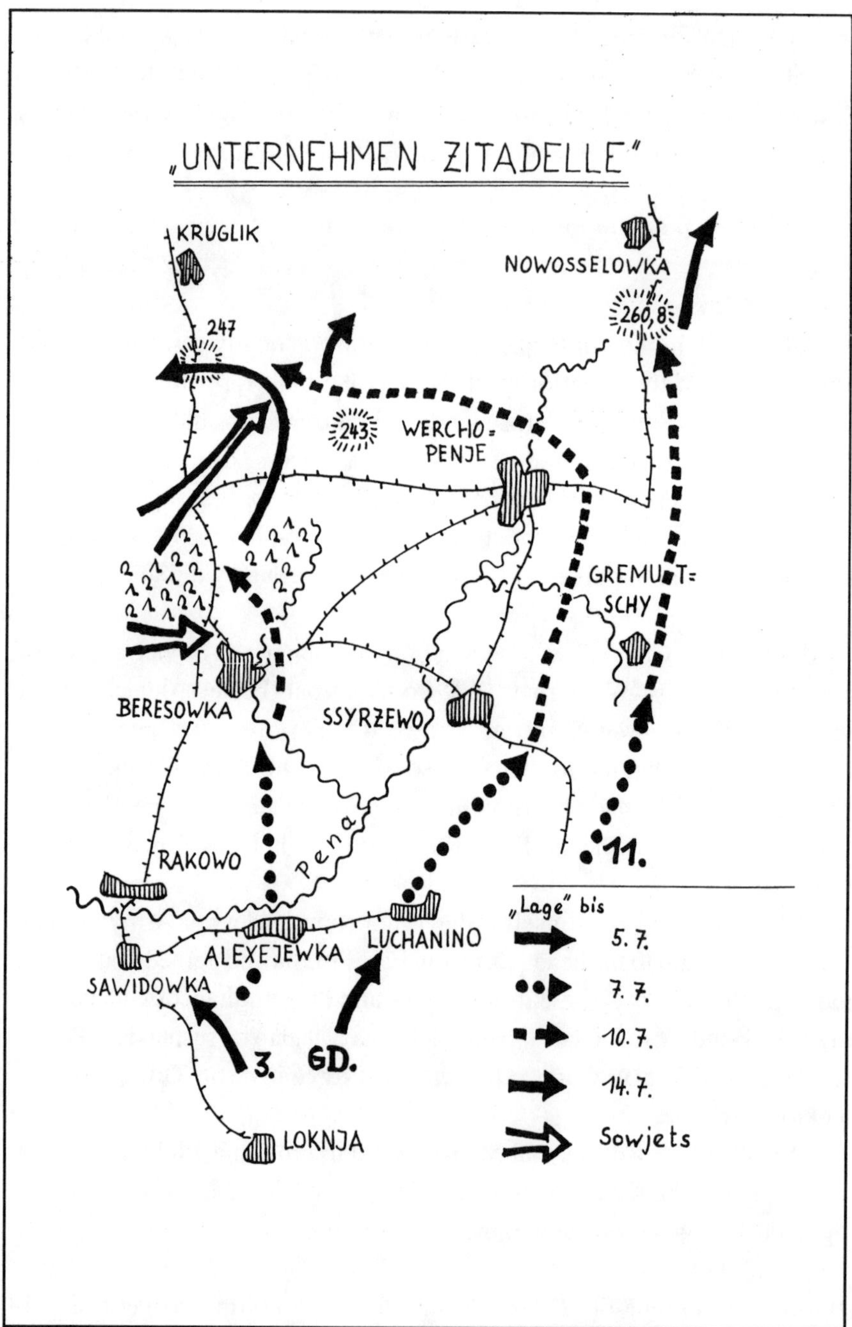

"Operation Citadel"

in the area of the 315th Rifle Regiment and the left flank of the division.

At 0830 hours, the division had to request air support from the SS Panzer Corps to stop an enemy breakthrough near Nepchaevo in the left portion of the 315th Rifle Regiment sector. SS Obergruppenfuehrer Hausser turned down this request on the grounds that a transfer of aircraft at that time was not possible, because there was danger of their being frittered away. Moreover, the enemy was being contained, for the time being; it was not necessary to throw them back any further. However, as it went on the regimental sectors, it went on the entire front of the division, and the clearing of the west bank of the Donets caused unreasonably high losses. Therefore, the commander of the 4th Panzer Army directed that the operation should be pursued only in areas of weak enemy resistance.

A decisive order was received by the 167 ID at 0845 hours. The enemy was tenaciously holding their former positions on the west bank of the Lipoviy Donets, west of Rozhdestvenka, and on the hills west of the Belgorod-Kursk railroad line, when heavy enemy movement in the Shakhovo-Leski-Yablonov area in front of the division's right flank suggested that the bulk of the enemy was threatening to withdraw from the pincer encirclement.

Near Rozhdestvenka, the Soviets undertook a relief attack against the front of the 315th Rifle Regiment, even using infantry forces, but it was repulsed.

Between 1415 and 1515 hours, the division commander visited the 315th Rifle Division command post. Colonel Gronau described the situation:

The enemy attacked through the depression west of Rozhdestvenka near the 9th and 11th Companies. They laid the customary harassment fire on the 10th Company's positions. In the sectors of the 5th and 7th Companies enemy scouts have put out feelers – otherwise, the Russians are 300-400 meters away from our lines. Up to now, attempts to eliminate the enemy mortar, whose fire has been very disturbing, have been unsuccessful.

An attack was planned by the 167th ID from the east bank of the Lipviy Donets to Gostishchevo at 1500 hours. The 7/315 Rifle Regiment was to follow out of the Noviy Losy Bridgehead. In case the enemy was cleared from Gostishchevo, Colonel Gronau would not commit the entire regiment, but would advance to the hills of the western portion of Gostishchevo only with elements of the 2nd Battalion, and the remaining units would take up a line to the northwest at the old main line of resistance. He, therefore, established his sector to be prepared to counter any Russian relief attacks, because the enemy was sure to try to break out by evading maneuver and artillery. (From: Mayerhofer, F.: *History of the 315th Rifle Regiment of the Bavarian 167th ID*. 2nd Edition. Munich 1977.)

• • •

German losses were enormous. For example, here one can see the losses of one division from the first day of the battle to the midpoint of the combat. The 2nd SS Panzer Division "Das Reich" reported:

Date	Dead	Wounded	Missing
7/4-5/1943	67(2)	233(7)	-
7/5-6/1943	43(1)	180(6)	2
7/6-7/1943	18	103(3)	1
7/7-8/1943	50(4)	186(5)	-
7/8-9/1943	22	127(5)	2
7/9-10/1943	16	94(1)	2
7/10-11/1943	29(1)	181(2)	1
7/11-12/1943	41(2)	190(3)	12
7/12-13/1943	17	44	-
7/13-14/1943	58(2)	229(8)	-
7/14-15/1943	26(1)	88	-
7/15-16/1943	58(4)	166(4)	-
7/16-17/1943	10	23(1)	3
7/17-18/1943	1	8	-
7/18-19/1943	-	2	-
15 days of combat	456(17)	1844(46)	23

Dead: 17 Officers 456 Non-commissioned Officers and men
Wounded: 46 Officers 1844 Non-commissioned Officers and men

Missing: 23 Non-commissioned Officers and men
Total losses: 2386 Officers, Non-commissioned Officers and men

During "Operation Citadel", between 5 and 19 July, the II SS Panzer Corps lost a total of 1,447 dead, including 52 officers; 6,198 wounded, including 180 officers; and 138 missing, including three officers. The total losses of the two German army groups committed to "Operation Citadel" came to 3,300 dead, and 17,400 wounded and missing. Included among these were seven division, 38 regiment, and 252 battalion commanders. The final conscription of the German panzer force was destroyed!

Army Group South

DONETS-DNEPR (17 July - 31 December 1943)

The "Red Army" attacked – while "Operation Citadel" was still ongoing – with strong forces against the front of Army Group Center and pressured all of the forces of those German divisions that were still combat capable. The panzer and infantry divisions of Army Group South were no longer in the departure positions they occupied before the battle of Kursk, because the Soviets also launched a major attack here with the goal of destroying the army group.

On 17 July, the Russian Army Groups "Southwest Front" (Army General Malinovski) and "South Front" (General Tolbukhin) began the battle between the Don and the Dnepr, which lasted almost until the end of the year.

On 17 July 1943, the Soviet troops attacked with a seven-fold superiority and with the support of strong air forces – a scarce commodity on the German side – against the edge of the Donets region in the vicinity of Isyum and on the Mius! The 1st Panzer Army (General von Mackensen), in defensive positions around Isyum, was able to maintain its positions in a bitter ten day battle. More then 500 Russian combat vehicles were left behind here as burning wrecks.

On the other hand, the battered infantry divisions of the 6th Army (General of Infantry Hollidt) could not withstand the massive assault. The infantry divisions, which were on the main axis of the attacking Army Group "Southwest Front", broke under the weight of the great attack and had to give ground. Those who suffered most here were the 17th ID (Major General Zimmer), 111th ID (Lieutenant General Recknagel), 294th ID (Colonel Frenking), and the 336th ID (Major General Kunze). The 13th Panzer Division (Lieutenant General von der Chevallerie), which arrived from the Crimea, was inserted as a corset rod. By itself, however, it could not alter the front situation very much.

Since it was freed up by the suspension of "Operation Citadel", the commander of Army Group South transferred the III Panzer Corps (General of Panzer Troops Breith), with the 23rd Panzer Division (Lieutenant General von Vormann) and 16th Armored Infantry Division (Lieutenant

General Count von Schwerin), to the breakthrough area. Shortly thereafter, strong panzer forces of the II SS Panzer Corps followed.

On 30 July, these armored combat groups prepared for a counterattack and, by 2 August, were able to win back the old main line of resistance. During this battle on the Mius, the "Red Army" lost 18,000 prisoners, 700 combat vehicles, and 200 guns.

The situation here was still not alleviated, because the "Red Army" began a new offensive on the left flank of Army Group South. On 3 August 1943, the armies of Army Group "Voronezh Front" and Army Group "Steppe Front" stormed from the north and south of Belgorod against the northern flank of the German army group. Partisan groups behind the front lines disrupted the German railroad traffic for 48 hours. The Russian partisans had blown the most important stretches of track into the air.

The attack objective of the "Red Army" was well selected: The seam between the 4th Panzer Army and Army Detachment Kempf, which was redesignated as the 8th Army on 22 August. On the first day, a gap of nearly 80 kilometers was created in the front line. Therefore, on 5 August, the 53rd Soviet Army recaptured Belgorod. The battered 19th Panzer Division (Colonel Soergel, who died here) was able to fight its way through the enemy back to the west. The 57th (Major General Fretter-Pico), 255th (Major General Poppe), and 332 ID (Colonel Trowitz) also suffered the same fate. They were able to fight their way through with the support of the 11th Panzer Division (Major General Mickl) and meet up with the "Grossdeutschland" Panzer Division (Lieutenant General Hoernlein), which was coming from the north.

The front collapsed further to the south. The 62nd (Lieutenant General Huffmann) and 333rd ID (Major General Menny), which were deployed on the junction with the 1st Panzer Army, could no longer close the gaps. Also, the 9th Panzer Division (Colonel Jolasse), which was immediately committed to this sector, did not alone have the strength to prevent a debacle here.

The 57th Soviet Army now stormed across the Donets and approached Kharkov and Poltava from the east and southeast. The army group transferred all available panzer forces from the III and XLVIII Panzer Corps to this area, which was now taken up by the sudden appearance of the 1st

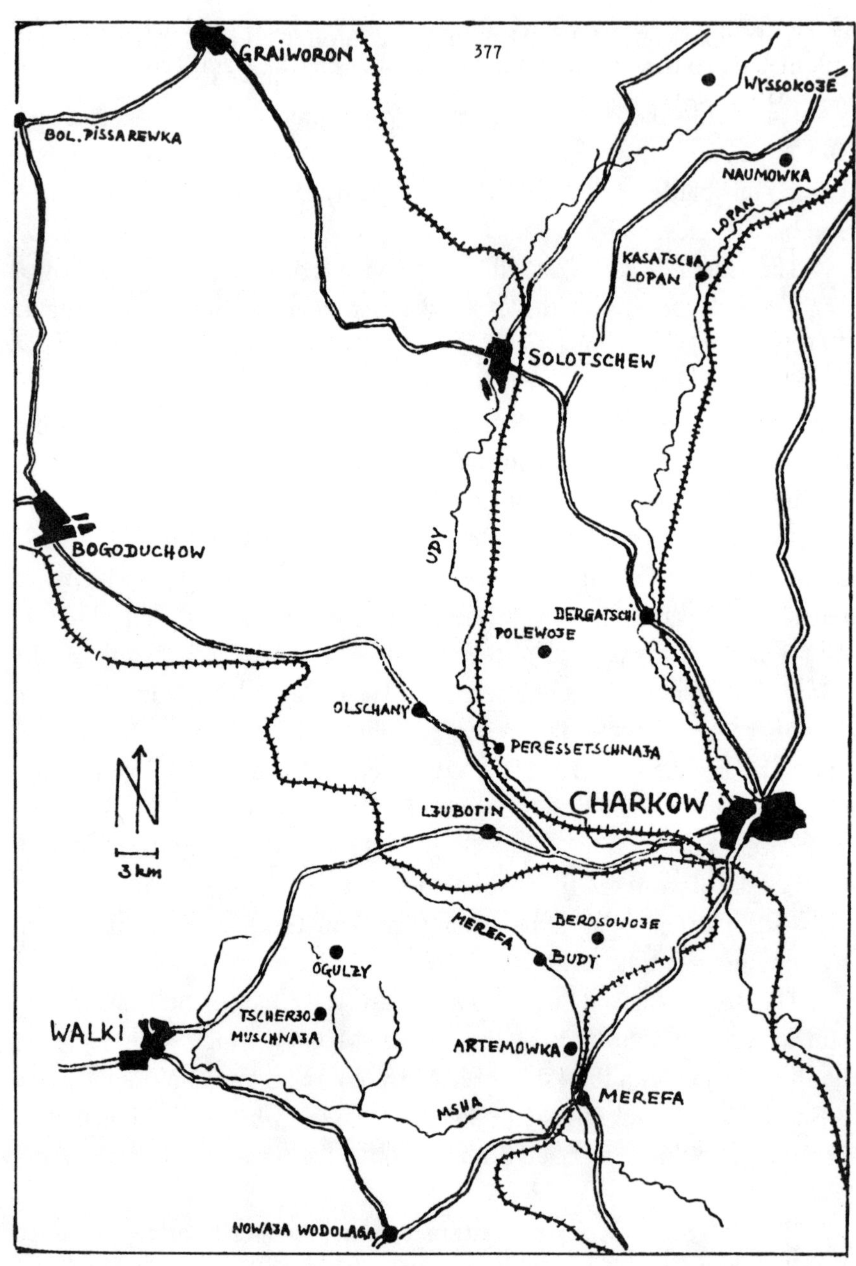
377
GRAIWORON
BOL. PISSAREWKA
WYSSOKOJE
NAUMOWKA
LOPAN
KASATSCHA LOPAN
SOLOTSCHEW
BOGODUCHOW
UDY
DERGATSCHI
POLEWOJE
OLSCHANY
PERESSETSCHNAJA
CHARKOW
LJUBOTIN
3 km
MEREFA
BEROSOWOJE
BUDY
OGULZY
TSCHERJO-MUSCHNAJA
WALKI
ARTEMOWKA
MEREFA
MSHA
NOWAJA WODOLAGA

Soviet Tank Army. They were able to throw the Russians back another 20 kilometers, so that the situation here near Akhtyrka stabilized. On 12 August, Hitler ordered:

> "Kharkov is to be held at all costs!"

The XI Army Corps (General of Panzer Troops Raus) – which took this order to heart – had to establish an all-round defense with its four infantry divisions. It was the soldiers of the 106th (Lieutenant General Forst), 168th (Major General Chales de Beaulieu), 198th (Major General von Horn), and 320th ID (Major General Postel) that had to try to construct a defensive ring around Kharkov with primitive barricades, tank obstacles, and mine fields.

The army group quickly transferred the 3rd Panzer Division (Lieutenant General Westhoven), 6th Panzer Division (Colonel Baron von Waldenfels), and SS Panzer Division "Das Reich" (SS Gruppenfuehrer Krueger) to the city. Therefore, the panzer divisions were ready for mobile combat operations on the wide Ukrainian terrain.

The strong Russian attack forces did not relax on any sector of the front between Belgorod and Mius. While the 1st Panzer Army maintained the front on either side of Isyum opposite the Russian Army Group "Southwest Front", troops of Army Group "South Front" – in all, five armies with 800 combat vehicles – broke through on a 200 kilometer wide front on 16 August against the 6th Army, and achieved a deep breakthrough in the direction of Stalino. Therefore, the southern corps – XXIX Army Corps (Lieutenant General Baron von Mauchenheim), with the 17th, 111th, and 336th ID – was encircled.

Now the battle for Kharkov was coming to an end. The 5th Soviet Guards Tank Army and the 57th Army, followed by the 7th Soviet Guards and 69th Armies, advanced on the important industrial city from all sides.

On the evening of 19 August, the XI Army Corps (General of Panzer Troops Raus), which was in Kharkov, sent to the commander of the 8th Army – which had been taken over by General of Infantry Woehler – the following two radio messages, which described the gravity of the situation:

1.) On 8/19, the corps again defended its positions against a strong attack, which was directed specifically against the left flank. Enemy artillery fire and air attacks on the main line of resistance and inland have become intense.
Enemy situation: The enemy attack has shifted against the left flank of the corps. The enemy attack here, supported by strong artillery fire and tanks, has continued almost without pause. The heavy losses of the divisions deployed here make it possible for the enemy to always locate gaps, through which he attacks and is able to drive the front back. Without a doubt, his objective is to break through the front and encircle Kharkov from the west and northwest. If the heavy losses continue without replenishing the force, the enemy will realize his objectives within the near future.

2.) Combat groups of the 168th ID had to withdraw, sector by sector, from the main line of resistance to a line from the northwest edge of Kuryashi – Hill 194.2 – the northern edge of the woods to the northwest of Gavrilovka, because the enemy is constantly penetrating into gaps caused by the heavy losses and there are no more local reserves at our disposal...

Under continuous heavy artillery, mortar, rocket, and tank fire, and due to the incessant day and night bombardment of the main line of resistance by enemy aircraft and the bitter defense against enemy attack, the regiments, which have been in continuous combat for the past 6 weeks, especially those of the 198th, 168th, and 3rd Panzer Divisions have been bled dry. Not many more major enemy attacks can be withstood in the present positions.

If the enemy launches a major attack, the corps will be broken through, the western flank at Kharkov will be torn apart, and the city will be surrounded.

To prevent this from happening, during the night of 20 August, the left flank had to be withdrawn to a line:
Slope 1 1/2 kilometers south of Losovenka-southwest of Oktyabr-Savchenko-Sinolitsevka-Udy

This line can be held for one to two days by the commitment of an attack reserve, and Kharkov will be spared encirclement. Holding these positions any longer requires the replenishment of the main line of resistance with fresh reinforcements. The corps no longer has such forces at its disposal; on 19 August, it had to commit its final reserves (one company of 150 artillerymen from the 167th ID)...

Commander, XI Army Corps
Ia Nr. 440/43 g.Kdos

Raus

• • •

The army ordered – without consulting the commands in and around Kharkov – the demolition of all important ammunition and supply installa-

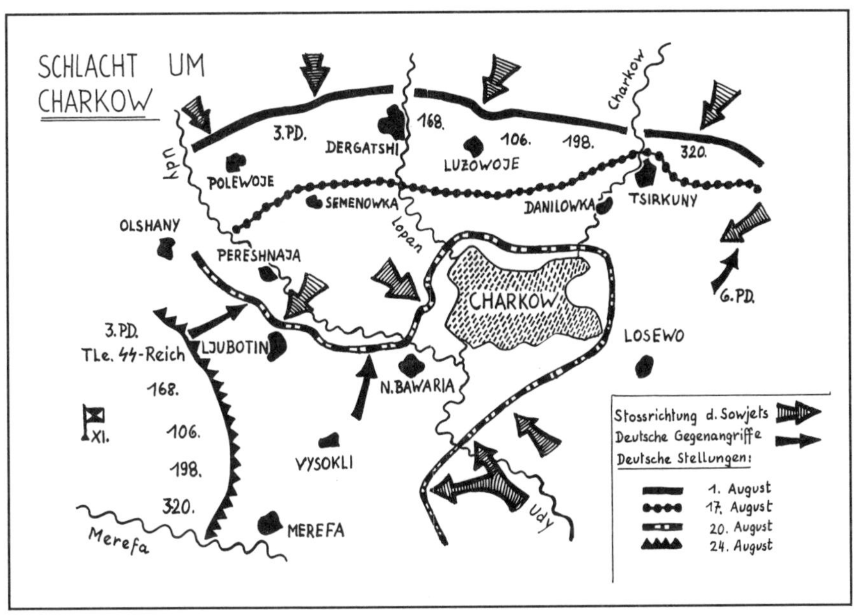

Battle for Kharkov

tions in the vicinity of the city. However, the Russian armies had already crossed the Udy River on either side of Kharkov and were advancing from the south and the north to completely encircle the city.

However, on 22 August, before they could do so, the order to give up Kharkov unexpectedly came. Assault guns and tanks blocked the entrance roads to the north, northwest, and west, while the divisions gathered in long columns behind them. The way to the southwest was still open. In the city itself, partisan groups, which had existed underground, took up their weapons in the attack, and they began firing on several positions. The German engineer demolition troops blew up the most important bridges, installations, and factories. The bulk of the combat troops left the city by midnight; only the rear guards, assault guns, tanks, armored cars, and engineers remained until the morning.

On 22 August, the XI Army Corps evacuated Kharkov as ordered and withdrew on a short front to the west. The pursuing enemy immediately was able to infiltrate the main line of resistance in several locations, but most of them were pushed back again by counterattack. From 25 August, the formations of the XI Army Corps again withdrew to the west. During these days, the weather was warm and sunny and made the movement easier than before.

On 27 August, Hitler – startled by the success of the "Red Army" in the Ukraine – went to his "Werewolf" headquarters in Vinnitsa. Here he summoned Field Marshal von Manstein and demanded that he reinforce or give up the operation. However, Hitler did not want to give up the Donets region and the Crimea and would only agree to construct a so-called "East Wall" – which was later known as the "Panther Defensive Line" – along the Dnepr.

Field Marshal von Manstein did not agree with this half-hearted solution and proceeded, several days later, to the "Wolf's Lair" headquarters in East Prussia with the commander of Army Group Central, Field Marshal von Kluge. Here Field Marshal von Manstein insisted on the withdrawal of the entire army group. However, Hitler was decidedly against this and would only authorize a half solution: Army Group South had to withdraw to the Desna in the north, the 6th Army was to move to the Kalmius sector, and the 17th Army had to vacate the Kuban Bridgehead.

The summer offensive of Army Group South began with a spirited attack by the divisions of the 4th Panzer Army. On 15 July (photograph above), motorized formations reached the city of Voronezh, the important industrial center on the Don.

Meanwhile, panzer and infantry divisions of the 6th Army struggled forward to the Don Basin near Kalach. An armored car races down a dusty road in the almost deserted expanse of the Ukraine. (Photograph from 29 July 1942)

After reaching Stalingrad at the beginning of September 1942, the month long battle for this city on the Volga began. Here, a bitter struggle ensued for each city quarter – the above photograph shows "Red Square" on 22 October 1942 – for each house, even for each floor in the houses. After the lead elements of the Russian armies, attacking on either side of Stalingrad, had met on 22 November near Kalach, the final battle for the 6th German Army and for Stalingrad (today called Volgagrad) began.

The south Stalingrad airfield at the end of October 1942. It could no longer be the salvation of the encircled 6th Army, although the transport aircraft of the Luftwaffe flew in rations and ammunition and flew out wounded practically to the last hour of the battle. The Luftwaffe lost alone in supply flights to Stalingrad 488 aircraft.

The last German position on Theater Square in Stalingrad before winter arrived. To the right in the photograph are the barricades, which the attacking Russian tanks (in the photograph at left, a combat vehicle destroyed in close combat) could not overcome.

The final battle of the 6th Army began at the end of January, as the pocket within the city was split in two. With the surrender of the northern pocket on 2 February 1943, the battle of Stalingrad ended. The photograph shows a group of German general and general staff officer prisoners. The second from the right is General of Infantry von Seydtlitz-Kurzbach, the later founder of the "National Committee of free Germany."

From 22 November 1942 until the beginning of February, the encircled 6th Army lost about 120,000 men in dead, wounded, and missing. An additional 34,000 wounded were flown out by transport aircraft of the Luftwaffe. 91,000 men were taken prisoner. They were collected in a large camp near Stalingrad and then marched into the interior – for many, the march ended in death.

Food issue at a mountain infantry battalion on the northwest slope of the Caucasus – shortly before the order to move off to the Kuban region arrived. The withdrawal of the 17th Army began in mid January in the general direction of the later Kuban Bridgehead.

The photograph – taken on 4/29/1943 – shows a typical German position on one of the many canals in the vast marshes of the Kuban region.

A rest period after defending against an enemy attack in mid summer 1943. The combat group collapsed from exhaustion in a wide trench in the rear area. The weapons are kept in readiness. In the background on the left are two submachine-guns and a light machine-gun.

Fierce combat occurred during the summer months around the harbor of Novorossisk. The photograph, taken on 15 May 1943, shows the capture of two Russian soldiers that had hidden in the thickets.

The construction of a new position for a heavy infantry gun in the thickets of the Kuban lagoons.

The "Kuban Shield." The "Kuban Shield" was instituted on 9/20/1943 for all soldiers of the Wehrmacht that participated in the battle for the Kuban Bridgehead from 2/1/1943. The combat badge was worn on the left upper sleeve of the uniform.

After the German front stabilized at the beginning of 1943, the 4th Panzer Army and the Kempf Army Detachment attacked the Russian troops west of Kharkov on 6 March. The II SS Panzer Corps assaulted the city of Kharkov on 16 March (above photograph). The German attack advanced further and reached Belgorod. Therefore, the departure position for the planned summer offensive – "Operation Citadel" – was captured.

The barren, open terrain southeast of Belgorod – one of the centers of the future great tank battles.

To prepare for "Operation Citadel", the OKH Transferred strong tank forces to Army Groups Center and South. Here, an armored infantry regiment, with its armored vehicles – called Zgkw for short – marches to their assembly area. Army group South took eleven panzer, seven infantry divisions, and three assault gun brigades to the battle for Belgorod.

The battle, which began on 5 July 1943, resulted in an 18 kilometer advance by the southern group after fierce combat and heavy losses. Here, the largest armored battle of the Second World War occurred near Prokhochovka. The photographs show scenes from this battle. After an enormous "Red Army" offensive was turned loose in the Orel Basin on 12 July, "Operation Citadel" was suspended on 13 July. German losses approached 20,720 men.

A German machine-gun position above the lazily flowing Donets (Mid April 1943). The enemy's positions are on the other side of the river.

The major Russian offensive on the edge of the Donets region near Isyum and on the Mius began in mid July 1943. Showing foresight, the German High Command evacuated several terrain sectors. As a precautionary measure, the rear area services transported cattle and heavy equipment to the rear.

The battle in the Donets area and on the Mius ran from 17 July to 2 August. All Russian attacks were repulsed. The enemy lost 700 combat vehicles, of which the majority were assault guns. The assault gun battalions and assault gun brigades belonged to the artillery. Here, 7.5 cm guns were mounted on German "P-III" and "P-IV" chassis. During the war, a total of 10,512 assault guns were produced, of which 6,433 were lost in combat.

The major Russian offensive between Belgorod and Kharkov began at the beginning of August. In a bitterly fought-over village remain only the ruins of the local church and two destroyed "T-34's."

During the middle of August, units of the 4th Panzer Army – here, an assault gun attached to a rifle battalion – were able to push the Russian troops back another 20 kilometers – then the force grew weary.

After bitter combat, our troops evacuated Kharkov on 22 August. The crew of a German tank takes a short breather while the enemy is only several hundred meters away.

The major Russian attack on Zhitomir began on Christmas Eve, 1943. A German combat group takes up defensive positions on the edge of the city.

The German front soldier of 144 – the "Landser" – was no longer triumphant as in the first years of the war. He became hardened and silent, he grew old, and he forgot how to sing. He learned to be silent, to freeze, to starve, and to die. Many of these soldiers no longer had faith in the victory of arms, but did their duty obediently and willingly as no generation of mankind before.

There were no advances in 1944 – only retreat. A last defensive position on the edges of a village somewhere on the border between Russia and Poland. An assault gun, supported by riflemen, is visible.

At the beginning of March, the city of Tarnopol – here in a photograph from February 1944 – a symbol of German resistance, was encircled by the enemy. The brave combat units held it until 15 April!

At the end of January, the German front near Cherkassy was battered and the troops of the XI and XLII Army Corps, located here, were encircled. The crew of a heavy anti-tank gun is under fire from Russian tanks.

In mid February, the encircled troops prepared to break out of the pocket. A field howitzer slid into a ditch and was pulled out by an RSO (tractor/prime mover). About 30,000 soldiers succeeded in breaking out on 16 February; more than 20,000 died or were taken prisoner.

A "Hummel" [Bumble-bee] gun in firing position southeast of Berdichev. The 15 cm howitzer, set on a "P-III" or "P-IV" chassis, was the main weapon of the armored artillery in 1944. The crew totaled up to seven men. and the gun had a driving range of up to 250 kilometers. On 1/1/1945, the Army had 573 such guns available.

At the beginning of March, four Soviet army groups attacked the German positions on a 1,100 kilometer wide front and pushed them back to eastern Galicia. By the end of the month of March, Dubno, Vinnitsa, and Kamenets-Podolsk were all lost. A German motorized column forces its way back through melted snow and mud.

In all of the combat in the east, one must not forget the artillerymen, which – as in the First World War – were the most loyal supporters of the infantry! The photograph shows a heavy field howitzer battery position in eastern Galicia. Often these positions proved to be the last strong point before the front would break.

At the end of March, the entire 1st German Panzer Army of General Hube was encircled north of Kamenets-Podolsk. The army, which had to fight on all sides, maintained its esprit de corps and, on 8 April, broke out of the pocket to the west – with tanks in the lead. The number of wounded was enormous and only a portion of them could be transported on the Luftwaffe aircraft ("Ju-52"). During these weeks, the medical corps deserved undying thanks.

The "Red Army" is now technically superior in weapons to the German Army. Here, one of the new Russian super heavy assault guns is out of commission. The Sergeant Major holds one of the 15.2 cm shells from this gun in his hands.

A battery of light field howitzers breaks through the Russian encirclement at the beginning of April and attacks to the west to the front lines of Army Group North Ukraine.

The situation in Crimea remained unchanged for the first three months. Officers and soldiers of a mountain infantry unit located here soak up some sunshine in the early spring sun.

The guns of the V Army Corps, located on the Kerch Peninsula, were silent – until 7 April, when the major Russian attack began.

The few strong points along the rocky coast – here, the crew of one of these strong points, in the background is a bunker hewn into the rock – could not halt it.

After the front of the V Army Corps near Kerch, and formations of the XLIX Mountain Corps, which was located in the northern and central portions of the Crimea, were broken through in five days, the 17th Army withdrew to Sevastopol on 12 April. The photograph above shows the withdrawal of a motorized column in front of an infantry company on one of the few roads along the coast. The photograph below: Mountain infantry climb up the rocky slope of a fortified position to occupy it.

The Soviets launched a concentrated attack on Sevastopol on 5 may. Seven days later the battle was over. The bulk of the troops fell into enemy hands, only a few could be transported from the fortress on the very small ships – the photograph shows artillery vehicles.

The fronts of the "Red Army" had pushed to the Rumanian and Polish borders by the spring. At many locations the civilians left out of fear for the liberation of their villages and withdrew with the Germans – here, a supply column in retreat.

In May and June, the front in the south remained somewhat stable. There were still troop displacements and evacuations – here, a communications troop is underway – and, as the breakthrough of Army Group Center in June occurred, the southern front was again denuded of divisions.

The 1st Ukrianian Front of the "Red Army" opened the battle against the German troops in the northern Ukraine on 13 July. A heavy battery of an infantry division fires on attacking enemy tanks.

In mid July, large forces of the 1st Panzer Army were encircled in the vicinity of Brody. A heavy anti-tank gun in close combat with enemy tanks.

At the end of the month of August, the 6th Army was encircled for the second time southwest of Kishinev. Only some units could fight their way back. One of these still had a field post office...

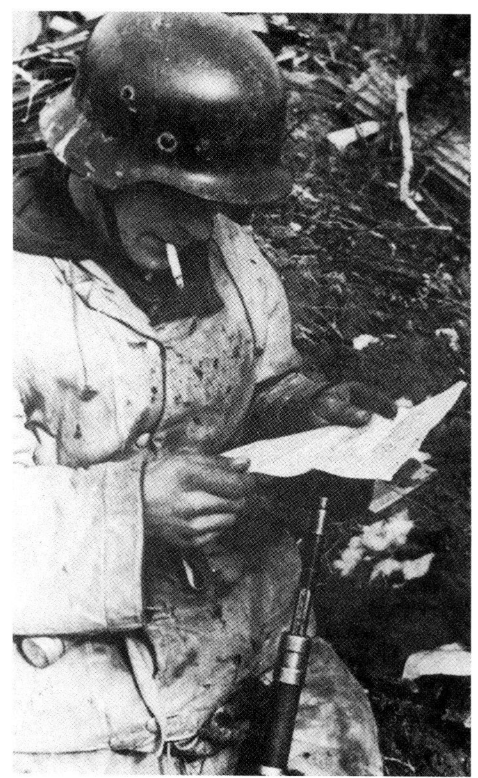

Now the Russian troops were approaching the German homeland. The face of a front soldier is branded by terror, harshness, and also loyalty. They still held the front in the south of the Reich.

Fire and smoke testify to the fact that now the war was shifting onto German territory...

However, before the movement to the rear could begin, the "Red Army" again took the initiative. On 6 September, the Russian Army Group "Southwest Front" broke through the so-called "Tortoise Shell Line" of the 6th Army and penetrated to the south of Pavlograd!

The combat events in the southern sector are mirrored in the radio messages of the 111th ID from 29 August:

0430 hours Radio message to all: Air transport for the wounded will be at the Taganrog West airfield.
0445 hours Radio message from operations officer to the 13th Panzer Division: The 13 Panzer Division will be relieved by approaching troop units. Intent: The 13th Panzer Division will be able to conduct mobile combat on the southern flank.
0540 hours 13th Panzer Division report: Have reached the security positions. The enemy has concentrated in Grekovo Timofeevka, to attack to the south.
0600 hours The 13th Panzer Division was relieved by the 55th and 117th Rifle Regiments on line Nasarov-Karla Liebknekt.
0615 hours two stuka groups attack Malaya Kirsanovka.
0655 hours Radio message to the 111th Anti-tank Battalion: Situation unclear – tank breakthrough northwest of Latonovo.
0730 hours Radio message to the 111th Anti-tank Battalion: 10 tanks and 20 vehicles in the Shirokaya Ravine; buffalos have begun to march with the engineers (buffalo was the code name for an assault gun).
0745 hours Radio message to the 13th Panzer Division: Enemy forces on the rollbahn south of Levinskaya – immediately send an available unit there.
0845 hours Combat group at the division command post. Situation briefing. An assault gun battalion with mounted infantry is sent to the 44th Observation Battalion, which is being threatened by tanks.
0900 hours One stuka group attacks Grekovo Timofeevka.
1022 hours Operations command post. Koshino. There is ammunition there.
1030 hours Group order to all subordinate units: Absenteeism and panic behind the front has been denounced – the General demands the com-

manders ruthlessly rid their units of these unworthy conditions. Cowards will be court-martialed.

1100 hours A new stuka attack on Grekovo Timofeevka.

1154 hours The 55th Rifle Regiment reports an enemy attack along the rollbahn.

1219 hours The 13th Panzer Division is withdrawing.

1230 hours Radio message: 117th Rifle Regiment is on line 115.5-Karla Liebknekt.

1235 hours Radio message: The bulk of buffalos are committed behind the 117th Rifle Regiment (Oppermann) and 55th Rifle Regiment (Herbarth).

1330 hours Enemy on the Mackensen Bridge.

1510 hours 55th Rifle Regiment report: Heavy combat. Request assault guns. 9 enemy tanks with mounted infantry attacking.

1515 hours Air reconnaissance reports 10 T-34 tanks moving to the south from Grekovo.

1530 hours 117th Rifle Regiment received over radio the order to go to the assistance of the 55th Rifle Regiment immediately with all available units.

1540 hours Radio message to the 111th Anti-tank Battalion: Tanks advancing west of Krasnaya Koloniya, make haste.

1550 hours Radio message to the 13th Panzer Division: Strong enemy (1000 troopers, 20 tanks, 40 vehicles) in Shirokaya Ravine north of Novo Troitskiy. Prepare to counterattack to the north.

1615 hours 55th Rifle Regiment reports: Must give up positions, because the buffalos did not come.

1630 hours 2 stuka groups attacked the ravine north of Grekovo-Timofeevka.

1640 hours Radio instructions to 117th Rifle Regiment; 55th Rifle Regiment's left flank needs assistance urgently. Radio instructions to the 111th Anti-tank Battalion: Render anti-tank support to the 55th Rifle Regiment immediately.

1715 hours 117th Rifle Regiment report: 3/111 Engineers rendering assistance to their neighbor. Anti-tank battalion report: Assault guns and elements of the anti-tank battalion are being attached to the 55th Rifle Regiment.

These events alarmed Hitler once again, who, on 8 September – the day the Italians surrendered – went to the Eastern Front for the last time. Hitler now finally agreed to withdraw Army Group South into the "Panther Defensive Line", thereby maintaining contact with Army Group Center on the left flank!

However, it didn't help. The 4th Panzer Army of General Hoth could not maintain contact with Army Group Center. Since 6 September, the army had been broken through at several locations by enemy tanks, was split into three groups, and lost its esprit de corps.

Thanks to the personal leadership of General Hoth, the military skill of his staff officers and commanders, and the combat readiness of all his soldiers, the army was able to withdraw behind the Dnepr in several groups by 15 September.

At this time, Army Group South was ordered to conduct a general withdrawal to the "Panther Defensive Line."

The 6th Army – which was now subordinate to Army Group A (Field Marshal von Kleist) – had to hold open the Kherson and Nikopol crossing sites. The 1st Panzer Army (General von Mackensen) was assigned Saporoshe and Dnepropetrovsk. The 8th Army (General of Infantry Woehler) had to defend Kremenchug and the 4th Panzer Army Kiev.

Now began the hurried withdrawal of both of the army groups in the south of the Eastern Front to and across the Dnepr. It was a complicated operation: in contact with the enemy, on a wide front, across few bridge crossings to the other side of the wide river, to occupy new defensive positions. Almost 200,000 wounded had to be transported. Hundreds of thousands of horses, cattle, and sheep had to be transported safely, and the important war installations of the entire Donets and Ukraine regions had to be made unserviceable.

In spite of pouring rain, the formations in the south were able to reach the "Panther Defensive Line" (which was not a natural defensive line at all!) between Melitopol and Saporoshe, while the center and northern flank of the army group were still in contact with the closely pursuing enemy

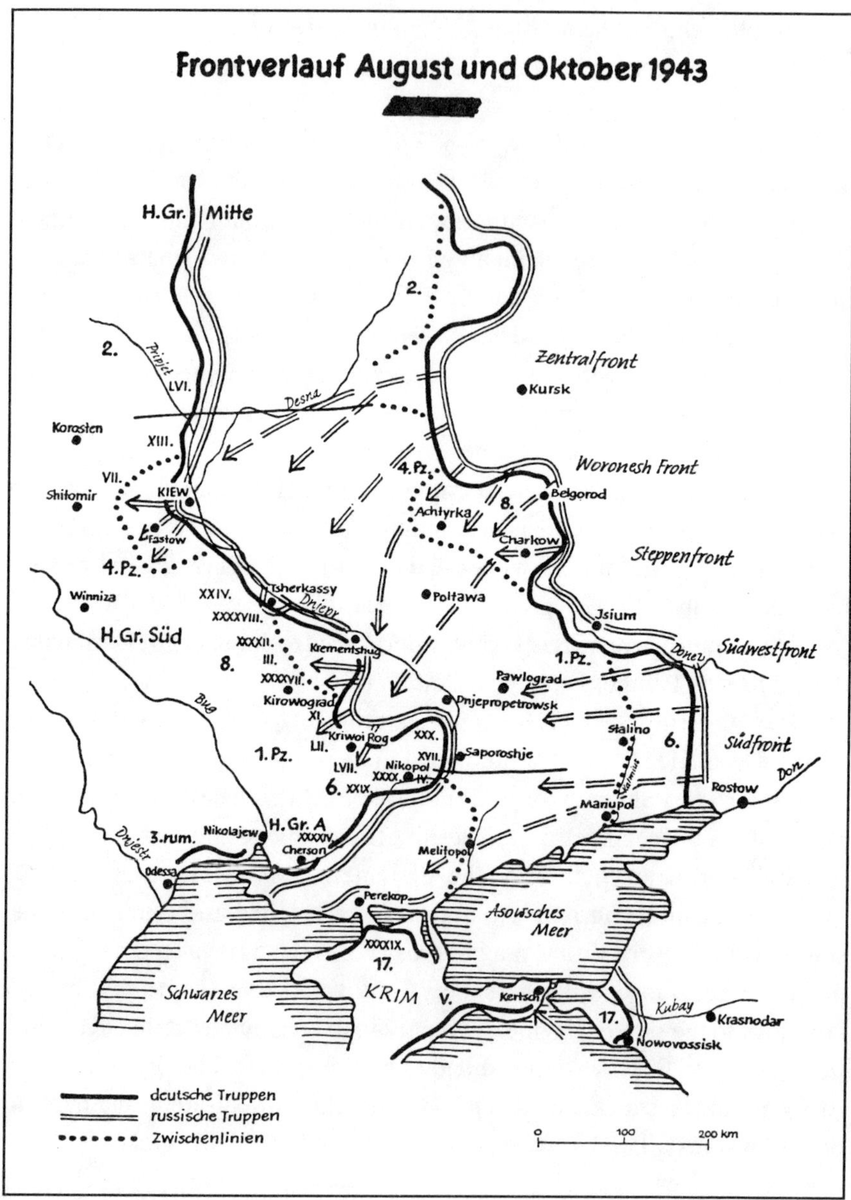

Front line in August and October 1943

armies, who were keeping pace and, in some places, overtaking them.

The Soviet Army Group "Central Front", under Army General Rokossovskiy, did not allow the 4th Panzer Army to stop them, broke through the retreating front in several places, and pushed General Hoth's troops back to Kiev.

An attempt by the 2nd Armored Artillery Battalion and the 38th Armored Engineer Battalion to catch up with the 2nd Armored Infantry Regiment, which was already advancing in the direction of Kiev, was a failure. The enemy forces at the breakthrough site had become too strong in the meantime. Moreover, the swampy terrain along the Desna made it impossible for vehicles to move.

As the first elements of our battalion reached Chernigov, Hungarian Troops in horse carts and a German military police unit approached us in wild flight. They had been assigned as security in Chernigov, which had been the rear operational area. All of the bridges over the Desna were destroyed by these people, without regard for the withdrawing German troops.

Combat Group Colonel Schmidthuber – the commander of the 304th Armored Infantry Regiment – was formed from our division and committed to Chernigov. This included the combat effective elements of our battalion. In Chernigov – an example of the still unknown rich blessings of the Ukraine – we were able to obtain enormous amounts of fine sugar from a supply installation and, from a cold slaughterhouse, quantities of duck, goose, and chicken for the troops. The Landser were astounded, as the good women in the field kitchens allowed them to have as much goose, duck, or chicken as they wished. We lived it up for two days.

Because the enemy, as mentioned above, were unhindered in their march to the west, there was nothing left for the division to do but defend against the Russians in the south and cross the Dnepr in the north, near Lyubekh, and try to outflank the enemy.

The defensive battle was unpleasant, because there were not only regular troops to contend with, but also partisans on the side of the enemy.

There was no continuous front line. The combat effective elements of our battalion were committed with the 2nd Armored Artillery Battalion. 6-8 scout vehicles formed the so-called main line of resistance and had to secure a kilometer wide frontal sector. The 20th and 23rd of September were difficult days of combat near Gushchin and Shukotki. During this time, three of the new vehicles supplied at the beginning of September were captured by the enemy due to the carelessness of Lieutenant Siegwart. Several days later, we had to shoot and destroy our own vehicles, which were now being employed against us by the enemy.

Our superiors still employed the tactic of "scorched earth"; a measure our troops were very much opposed to. But this Führer Directive was only carried out by a few units, since many completely ignored it. It didn't take much thought to realize that by doing this, one was also denying one's self shelter.

The division deployed near Lyubekh and, in the final days of September, the battalions crossed their vehicles over the Dnepr on a combat bridge constructed by our engineers. The crossing was almost interrupted by enemy aircraft. In spite of this, the troop units of the division reached the west bank almost without injury. We were greatly relieved to be free and have this operation put behind us. Colonel Schmidthuber's regiment (304th Armored Infantry Regiment) had secured the crossing against a strong Russian attack.

At the end of September, non-essential and combat ineffective units of the division were transferred to the vicinity of Minsk-Baranovichi; elements of our battalion went to the Nisvich area – 40 kilometers east of Baranovichi – therefore, the bulk of our 2nd Company, part of the 1st Company, 1st Battalion, were placed under the command of Lieutenant H. Bartels. These units were again formed into a battalion on 24 December 1943 in France. (From: Strauss, F. J.: *A Generation's Peace and Wartime Experiences*, (2nd Panzer Division) Neckargemuend 1977.)

• • •

On 21 September, the Russian armies, with the support of air-landed troops, won an 80 kilometer crossing over the Dnepr on either side of the Pripet Estuary. In some places, the Russian soldiers waded through the river in chest high water, or pitilessly drove their cart animals with their harnesses and guns through the water, and established their first bridgehead.

An immediate counterattack by the 7th Panzer Division (Major General von Manteuffel) and the 112th ID (Lieutenant General Lieb) did not penetrate into it. The Soviets advanced further to the west and attacked toward the north against Kiev.

During the following days, the "Red Army" succeeded in establishing additional bridgeheads across the Dnepr. On 22 September, the 3rd Guards Tank Army crossed to the western bank of the river near Pereyaslav-Kmelnitsi. A day later, the important city of Poltava was lost, and the day after that, the Russian 7th Guards Army established an additional bridgehead on the far side of the Dnepr south of Dnepropetrovsk.

By the end of the month, the situation of Army Group South in the center and the north of its front reflected: the 8th Army had fought its way back behind the river between Kremenchug and the south of Kiev; and the 4th Panzer Army was deployed on both sides of the Ukrainian capital, but had lost contact with the 2nd Army of Army Group Center.

During this dangerous period, Field Marshal von Manstein issued an order of the day, on 29 September:

> Soldiers of Army Group South!
>
> After weeks of difficult attacks and defensive battles, the armies of the army group have withdrawn across the Dnepr to again face the enemy in more suitable positions.
>
> The enemy, who has been defeated by you whether in the defense or in the counterattack, could not stop this maneuver. He gained territory, but paid a high price in losses.
>
> That this withdrawal succeeded on a wide front, over few crossing sites, with our most important equipment and while destroying the most important war installations, is the result of the courage of all of the troops that were well led during a critical situation by their commanders, under conditions reflecting an enormous numerical combat superiority in favor of the enemy.

The execution of this especially difficult operation is yet another testimony to the brilliance of the leadership, especially the work of the staff.

My thanks to both the leadership and the troops for their magnificent efforts in this summer's great defensive battle.

That the enemy, in spite of his strength, could not stop us from executing our mission, gives us the opportunity to master new missions.

signed von Manstein
Field Marshal

The "Red Army" now began to attack along the entire Dnepr front. In the north began the first heavy and serious combat for the approaches to Kiev.

• • •

On 25 September, the 593rd Battalion arrived in front of Kiev, where two corps had planned to cross to the other bank on one bridge. They occupied defensive positions near Darnitsa, where, in early 1942, they had hastened to build a training area. The 594th Battalion was nearby. Not only all of the units passed through under the protection of this security, but also countless Russian civilians crossed over the Dnepr bridge into Kiev; engineer troops placed a great many explosives on military targets. The occupied line was to hold until these measures are completed.

At this time, the bulk of the German divisions are on the west bank of the Dnepr. The "Red Army" succeeded in forcing the Germans to withdraw on an almost 1000 kilometer section of the Eastern Front. For the German military leadership, the time had come for their most decisive test of the 2nd World War: they did not succeed. Units of the front that had been broken through in many places traveled the considerable distance in order and always in combat readiness to the rear, across the few serviceable bridges, and across the river to the other side. In all probability, the war in the east had already been decided against the German Reich. At this point in time, the Soviets had already crossed the Dnepr at more than 20 locations, and of these, they established strong bridgeheads at 4 important points – north of Kiev on either side of the Pripet Estuary near Chernobyl, south of Kiev near Kanev, on the Vorskla Estuary, and near Dnepropetrovsk.

True, the Russians had suffered considerable losses, and an air landing operation by their 3rd Guards Parachute Brigade foundered in a small bridgehead near Bukrin (about 20 kilometers north of Kanev), but it must also be considered that they could now recruit all 16-60 year olds in the reconquered territories, mobilize a great mass of manpower, achieve positive results through massing forces, and tip the scales in their favor in the superiority of numbers. Of course, the Germans were also able to take a large number of civilians across the Dnepr with the withdrawing divisions.

The 591st Battalion, moving at high speed (80 kilometers within 24 hours) across the Kiev-Dnepr railroad bridge and Priorka (north of Kiev), shifted to the west bank of the river more than 30 kilometers to the north. They were able to frustrate an enemy crossing attempt in Kasarovichi and force a Russian steamer to change its course.

At 0400 hours on 28 September 1943, the 593rd Battalion was the last German unit to leave the Kiev bridgehead. They crossed over the Reichenau Bridge, over which they had crossed in the other direction almost 1 1/2 years before. The bridge was blown at 0500 hours.

The beginning of October 1943: General Piepenbrink honored the 591st Battalion for its participation in the deployment and emphasized his thanks for its enthusiastic commitment. During the evening they marched off in the direction of Kiev, where the headquarters of the 323rd Combat Group was located in Pshcha Voditsa (the region opposite the Desna Estuary). (From: Schwarz, A.: *Calendar of the 323rd Infantry Division*, Landshut 1966.)

• • •

On 14 October, the battle for the Saporoshe Bridgehead began. Here, the XL Panzer Corps (General of Mountain Troops Schoerner), at the arbitrary decision of its commander, gave up the bridgehead without the final approval of the Führer's headquarters.

The commanding general had acted correctly, for on the next day, the entire Russian Army Group "2nd Ukrainian front", under Army General Konev, with four armies and one tank army, attacked out of the bridgehead near Kremenchug against Krivoi Rog.

The 1st Panzer Army, which was deployed here, immediately counterattacked with the XXIV Panzer Corps (General of Panzer Troops Nehring) and the XLVIII Panzer Corps (General of Panzer Troops Eberbach).

•••

The arrival of new assault formations in the Mishurin Rog area, while there was another breakthrough attempt north of Ivashki, caused an additional crisis for Army Group South. Since 10 October, the LVII Panzer Corps had not given into the undiminished pressure from Konev. However, the 9th Panzer Division counterattack, which was now committed in Omelniktal, was not being executed according to the usual standard. The constant combat since 5 July and the heavy equipment losses, had an alarming effect on the morale of the personnel – each 100-man trench system had to defend a 4 kilometer wide sector! After the loss of their last Panzer III's on 18 September, the division did not have one combat ready tank left!

In their weakened state, they were thrown back into the LII Army Corps sector, defended, occasionally without direction from above, up to the abandoned artillery positions northwest of Pyatikhatka, in and around Losovatka, and parried, with the 16th Armored Infantry Division on the left and the "Grossdeutschland" on the right, an impending breakthrough north of Alferovo, Novo Gurovka, and in the Saksagan sector, with the thinnest crews manning the strong points. The small combat groups, with armored combat vehicles, counterattacked untiringly. On 19 October, the division commander fell, and Colonel Dr. Schulz took command of the 9th Panzer Division.

With the pull out from Pokrovka on 31 October, the division stopped maintaining the combat diary. Since the details of their commitment until the end of the war can only be derived from other sources, it is worthwhile to shed light on the missions, which were so foreign to a panzer division, since the beginning of the defensive battle near Rshev, especially since the beginning of September 1943, in order to clearly detail the war in the east since the autumn of 1942 and the withdrawal from the Mius to the Dnepr basin. For the months after November 1943, the following must suffice for the time being.

On 21 October, the German front south of the great Dnepr bend was also collapsing.

In this see-saw battle the crisis situation increased, and the divisions, hopelessly sinking into the Ukrainian mud, had to exist more and more on their own substance. The 1st Panzer Army persisted, in spite of all of the troubles, and despite increased undermining of their cohesion and resisted enemy efforts to encircle them in the Dnepr basin. The incessant assaults continued against the bitterly fighting formations. The area around Kirovograd and Krivoi Rog remained a hot spot until the New Year. The 9th Panzer Division took shelter from the approaching winter with the XL and LVII Panzer Corps. The vocabulary of the exhausted combatants is sharply defined: Slow withdrawal or avoid contact, halt or break through,

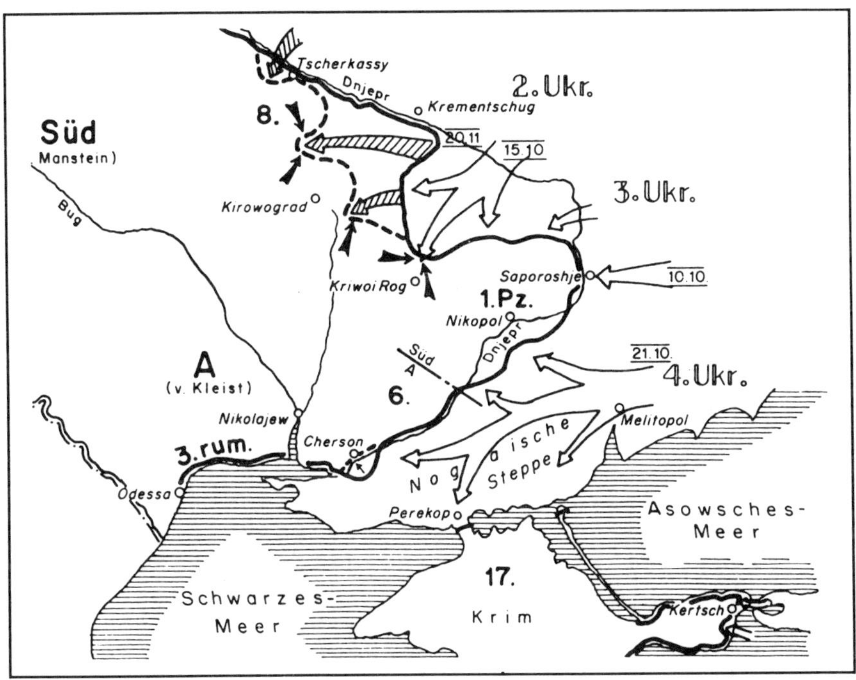

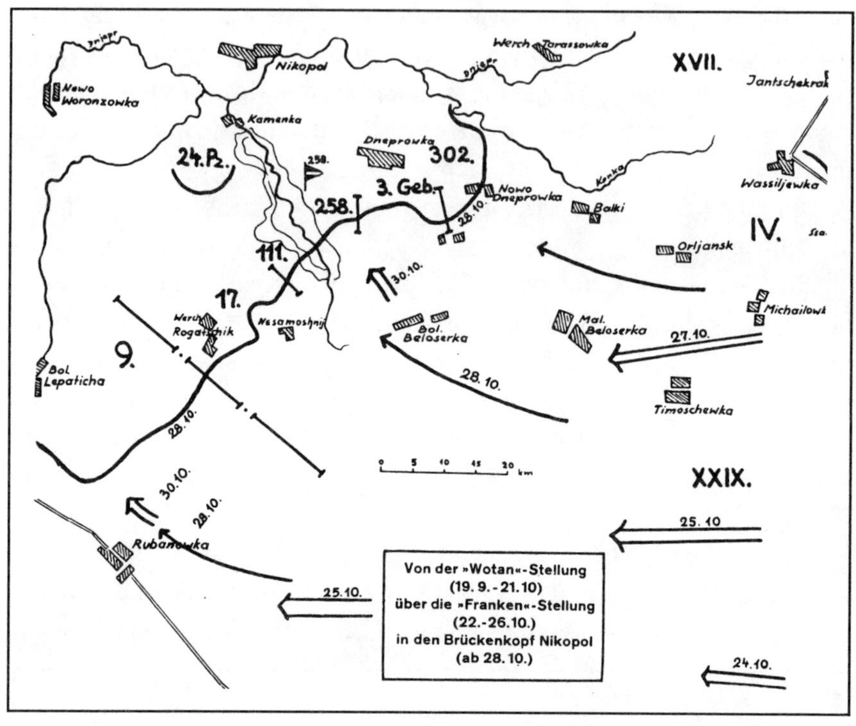

From the "Wotan" Line (9/19-10/21); Through the "Franken Line (10/22-10/26); In the Nikopol Bridgehead (after 10/28)

counterattack, clear up the situation or close the gaps, disengage or repulse, block or obstruct. For the leaders of a panzer division, this was their daily bread. For the troops the only thing that was important was: the overall success of the defense. Under conditions of untold troubles, privations, and hardships, the counterattacks had to be executed on an ever larger scale.

The clear-cut superiority in personnel strength and equipment called forth the necessity to improvise! (From: Hermann, C. H.: *68 Months of War*, (9th Panzer Division) Vienna 1975.)

• • •

The Russian attack was stopped before Krivoi Rog; however, the overall situation worsened from day to day.

On 23 October, the Army Group "4th Ukrainian Front" – on 20 October, the "Red Army" provided new designations for the army groups fighting in the southern sector – began a new attack against the 6th German Army between Melitopol and Saporoshe. The Soviet tank columns quickly broke through the German main line of resistance and their 51st Army captured Melitopol on the second day. The 6th Army withdrew in two directions, to Kherson and Nikopol. Therefore, the Soviets now had room to attack to Perekop and the northern tip of the Crimea.

However, a new portion of the front exploded. On 24 October, Army Group "3rd Ukrainian front" broke through the German defensive positions on either side of Dnepropetrovsk, with support from the "2nd Ukrainian Front." Therefore, the "Panther Defensive Line" was completely torn apart. A retreat began in which everyone ran to wherever he could.

The battle for Kiev ignited at the beginning of November, as the "1st Ukrainian Front", supported by the 2nd Russian Air Army, broke through the German defensive positions north of Kiev. The 88th ID (Lieutenant General Roth) – the commander of which was severely wounded and died a short time later – had to, according to instructions, allow itself to be encircled in Kiev and fought there until 6 November. The VII Army Corps (General of Artillery Hell) and the XIII Army Corps (Lieutenant General Hauffe) blocked the Soviet breakthrough west and south of the city of Kiev. They could not, however, prohibit a breakthrough of General Vatutin's tank forces on Fastov, which fell into enemy hands two days later.

The city of Zhitomir fell on 12 November during the course of the Russian operation; then the enemy attack continued on to Korosten. Here the 8th Panzer Division (Colonel Froelich) and the 20th Armored Infantry Division (Lieutenant General Jauer) proved most successful. The Russian breakthrough finally broke down.

•••

The toughest mission during the retreat fell to the 505th Rifle Regiment. By the end of October, the regiment had left its defensive positions to attack, by order of the corps, to restore contact with the right flank of Army Group Center. Contact was again established at the beginning of

November, but it was again decisively torn apart by the renewed Russian offensive. During the beginning of the withdrawal, the 505th Rifle Regiment received the order from the corps to break off from the corps, with the attached 2/291 Artillery Regiment and the 276th Assault Gun Battalion, to operate independently on the northern flank and to attack into the enemy and deceive him as to the location of the main elements of the corps. The mission was fated to last one day, until friendly reconnaissance established that the regiment to the south was cut off by strong enemy forces that were by-passing Korosten. The commander, Lieutenant Colonel Vogelsang, decided to break out of the encirclement during the night of 12 and 13 November and to reestablish contact with the corps in a 35 kilometer march. The goal was completely achieved and without loss, because it was accomplished without firing a shot. The combat group crossed three large roads in the darkness without being recognized as enemy forces by the Russians located there. All of the wounded were taken along; Lieutenant Colonel Vogelsang was awarded the Knight's Cross.

On 15 November 1943, Germans and Russians ran into each other in total confusion. The city broke out into panic. They turned over the city to the Russians, and the 226th Russian Rifle Division established itself in Korosten. Corp Group C and the 291st ID formed – without contact on the right and left – a defensive line in a half circle around the city, oriented to the north and south, and held the city of Sviagel as a supply base. The roads, of course, passed through a partisan area, so it had to be supplied from the air.

To the north remained an open, but still not fully exploited by the "Red Army", gap of 150 kilometers, which was used as a way to make contact with the partisans, while to the south, the situation was considerably improved by a successful German tank attack on Zhitomir. In this situation, General von der Chevallerie decided on a clever attack on Korosten, which took the enemy completely by surprise. On 24 November, the Corps Group C began to attack in the north and the "Elche" in the south, after a strong artillery preparation, with the support of assault guns. In a few hours, they entered the city at full speed. The surprise of the enemy was fully utilized; the artillery had disastrous effect on the frozen ground; a great number of enemy 7.6 cm anti-tank guns were partially put out of action, and some were undamaged but abandoned by their crews. Subsequently, a diversionary attack from outside and a breakout attempt from the inside of the encircled city were repulsed, and degenerated into house to house combat. (From: Conze, W.: *History of the 291st Infantry Division*, Reprinted. Herne 1984.)

• • •

The front quieted down somewhat. The troop commanders were able to reorganize their formations and to strengthen their defensive positions. The rear area services were able to continue their work. The days again became distinguishable from one another at the front.

After almost eight days, we fell back through Rovenki to Chistyakovo, during which we were bombed several times by aircraft. At the end of August 1943, we were transferred to Blagoveshtashenskoe on the Konka, a tributary of the Dnepr. There was only crushed corn for baking, but we helped ourselves to two tractors to go to a mill house. All we had for fuel was straw. Unfortunately, the meal became too hot during the long transit time, and the gluten of the grain was destroyed. The result of this was that the bread would only rise 10 to 15 cm. However, during these difficult times, we still baked wheat bread for the infirmary.

At the beginning of October, we were transferred through Kamenka, Snamenka, and Nikopol to Novo Voronzovka on the Dnepr. We stayed here until February 1944. At the beginning, the companies obtained oak from the Dnepr Valley to heat our ovens. Therefore, we were not able to produce the proper temperatures in the ovens, for the wood was wet and it boiled inside the ovens. We finally shoved oil cakes between the pieces of wood and the result was that, on the spark catchers of our chimneys formed spark strands that could be seen for great distances at night and, therefore, put us in danger of being observed by aircraft. We had to post extra chimney watches at night.

In the final days of the Nikopol Bridgehead, we issued one loaf of bread to each seven men, because all of the other bakery companies of the 6th Army were out of commission and we were not able to produce any more in our oven. Our company was the only one that had an oven. General Schoerner put six extra tractors at our disposal, so that we could move our oven through Aleksanderstadt to Visunsk. Near Snigerevka, Professor Dr. Richter died from a direct shell hit on his truck. He was well liked by all and nicknamed Uncle Willi. (From: Report of the 302nd Bakery Company. In: Kilgast, E.: *Survey of the History of the 302nd Infantry Division*, Hamburg 1976.)

• • •

The commander of Army Group South (Field Marshal von Manstein) did not give up trying to obtain freedom of movement for his units, in spite of all of the setbacks of the past weeks and months. From the middle of November, the army group commander, with the commander of the 4th Panzer Army – General of Panzer troops Raus had now been named its commander – had worked out a plan to capture Kiev. In spite of the previous defeats, it succeeded in organizing mobile armored forces, thanks to the influx of divisions from the west and from the Balkans, and prepared them for a counterattack.

General of Panzer Troops Balck had taken command of the XLVIII Panzer Corps, which would lead this battle. The corps was subordinated to the newly formed army group of General of Infantry Mattenklott, which also included the XIII Army Corps (Lieutenant General Hauffe).

During the middle of November 1943, the somewhat reconstituted 4th Panzer Army stood as follows (from left to right):

XLII Army Corps (General of Infantry Dostler), with the 454th ID;
LIX Army Corps (General of Infantry von der Chevallerie), with the 291st ID, Corps Group C;
Army Group General of Infantry Mattenklott, with XIII Army Corps (Lieutenant General Hauffe), with the 340th, 327th, 208th ID, 8th Panzer Division;
XLVIII Panzer Corps (General of Panzer Troops Balck), with the 198th ID, 25th Panzer Division, SS Division "Das Reich", 75th, 82nd, 213th ID;

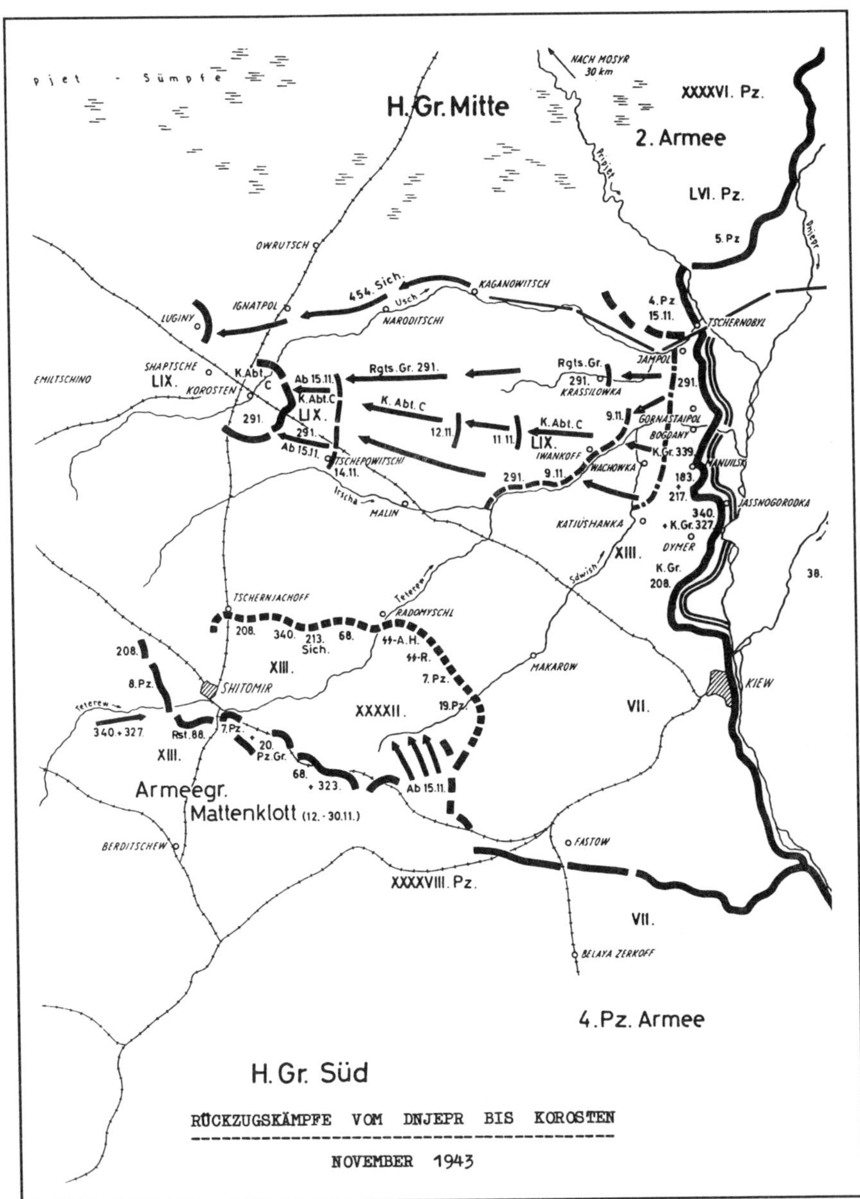

Withdrawal battle from the Dnepr to Korosten November 1943

XXIV Panzer Corps (General of Panzer Troops Nehring), with the 34th, 10th, 168th, 223rd ID, 19th Panzer Division, 112th, 255th ID, 3rd Panzer Division;
Reserve: 4th Panzer Division, SS Panzer Division "Leibstandarte."

This collection of armored forces was, indeed, powerful, but they did not approach the capacity of the panzer troops of the previous years – not by a long shot. The number of tanks by division totaled (in brackets is the number available on 11/20):

SS Panzer Division "Leistandarte"	115	(40),
SS Panzer Division "Das Reich"	136	(22),
8th Panzer Division	66	(7),
25th Panzer Division	63	(10), etc.

The attack with the XLVIII Panzer Corps on the main axis began on 15 November, as the armored forces quickly crossed the Sdvish and attacked

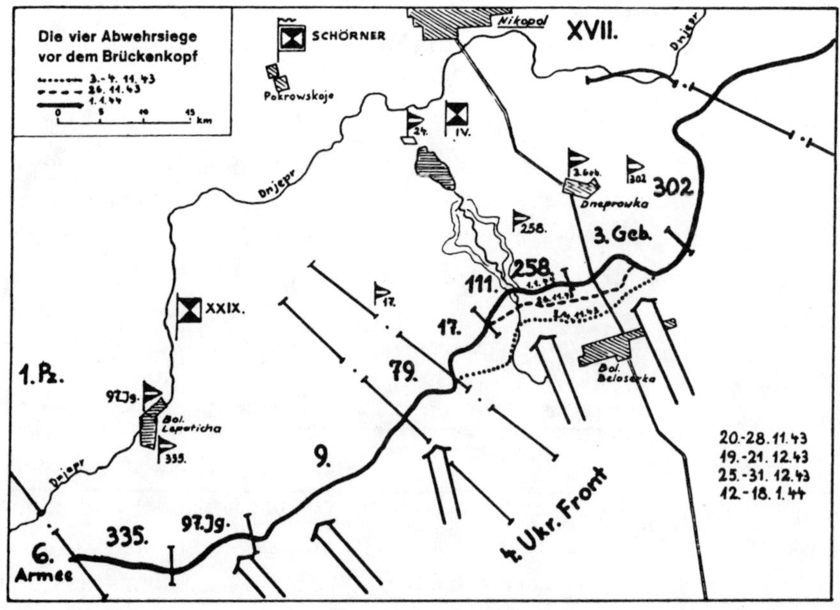

The four defensive victories in front of the bridgehead

into the flank of the 1st Soviet Guards Army. The Russians withdrew before the surprise attack to the north, thereby abandoning Zhitomir, the most important city west of Kiev. The attack of the army group of General of Infantry Mattenklott stopped before Chernyakhov and Radomyshl on the Teterev. The Soviets lost almost 20,000 dead, 4,800 prisoners fell into German hands, 603 enemy tanks, 300 guns, and about 1,200 anti-tank guns were either captured or destroyed.

However, the "Red Army" struck back. On 20 November, Army Group "3rd Ukrainian Front" (Army General Malinovski) opened an offensive against the 1st Panzer Army, which had been commanded by General of Panzer Troops Hube since 29 October, on the lower Dnepr between Nikopol and Krivoi Rog.

The attack of the Soviets was clearly directed at Nikopol, where the German defenders had withdrawn into a bridgehead. Here, the commanding general, General of Mountain Troops Schoerner, issued the following order of the day on 27 November:

•••

"The bridgehead must be held, not only because it has been ordered, but because each enemy breakthrough to the Dnepr threatens to destroy our division.

During the constant decrease of our combat strength, during crises or enemy breakthroughs, during shortages of equipment and ammunition, when the troops are completely exhausted, we must find other means of strengthening our determination and strength:

1. Commanders to the front! All commanders belong at the head of their unit.

Written and telephonic instructions are necessary and obvious formalities. Our essential work begins after that, during the obligatory personal monitoring and execution of the concise and clearly issued order. All officers and staff officials are engaged in this work.

The bearing of the personalities of the generals, commanders, and active officers alone will guarantee continued success. Only by these conceptions of combat, of the high obligation of the German officers, especially in our situation, will the superiority of German leadership prevail over the dull-witted enemy.

Insure that communications equipment is in order, so that the commander can be constantly informed of the situation on the entire frontal sector.

2. Command posts can be relocated only with the approval of the division commanders and commanding general, respectively. The troop stops only when its leader is in the area.

In size, most of the staffs are in blatant disproportion to the combat strength of the troops. In our situation, all staffs are combat troops and will defend themselves to the last man.

3. Our combat strength will quadruple when all of the soldiers in the bridgehead are finally mobilized as fighters. Each division command, therefore, represents a strong last reserve. In each corps and division sector, the rear area troops, supply troops, and camp followers must be monitored daily by special authorities (staff members are always available) in order to weed out troops from your own command.

Using only written orders will not lead to success, only personally seizing the opportunity on the spot, on the road, or in the lay-over towns will."

• • •

The major Russian offensive continued toward Nikopol! Army Group "2nd Ukrainian Front" overran positions of the 8th German Army (General of Infantry Woehler) north of there and gained ground directly east of Kirovograd.

The divisions resisted in spite of terrible losses. Thus, by 20 December, the gaps in the main line of resistance were closed. Only the Russian bridgehead near Cherkassy could not be compressed.

Still, the Soviets did not quit.

The "1st Ukrainian Front", under Army General Vatutin (who later in Kiev fell victim to an attempted murder), conducted a deep breakthrough against the 4th Panzer Army along the Kiev-Zhitomir road. The panzer troops, who fought courageously for four weeks, had to give up Zhitomir and withdraw further.

General Kaellner was as good as his word. With an armored action group – he himself was in a VW amphibious car – he attacked from Brusilov to Lasarevka, opening the route for the 2nd Battalion to retreat. These days, the regiment fought superlatively. In spite of the enormous weight of the enemy attacks, it maintained its defensive positions and only had to leave them when the enemy had broken so deeply through the left and right neighbors that staying any longer in these positions would have been suicide. By evening, the regiment had withdrawn to the northern edge of Brusilov. The enemy slowly advanced across the Savish, in front of our positions. The regiment command post was set up at the previous location of the division main first aid station – Captain Rosenow of the 2/19 Armored Artillery Regiment used it at the same time for his battalion command post. The battalions were reorganized under cover of night. Contact with the supply trains was not available. The rumor was that enemy tank elements had unexpectedly broken through to the combat supply trains.

A small Christmas tree stood in the corner of the regimental command post. Someone stuck some candles on it. That's when we first realized that it was Christmas Eve. For a few minutes, while the candles burned, it was quiet. Soaked, sweaty, and shivering, the men, officers, non-commissioned officers, and soldiers sat and gave thanks. The door opened. General Kaellner entered. He also got caught up in the atmosphere for a moment, torn by the powerful breath of nostalgia. Away with Christmas, away with gloomy thoughts.

The General described the overall situation in broad outline. The enemy had achieved a deep breakthrough into the southern neighbor and was advancing further in the north. Brusilov was no longer held. Therefore, the division was to set out for Kabachin in the early morning.

There, on 25 December, we occupied a hedgehog defense. The snow was changing into rain. The vehicles often got stuck in the mud. The enemy attempted to pursue, but they were beaten back. Just as we pushed him back, the regiment was ordered to withdraw to Romanovka. Here, the enemy also emerged on all sides. Panzer Group Schneider shot up several enemy tanks. Under the cover of darkness we moved to Vilenka. There, we found a unit of combat vehicles. At the division command post, the general clarified the situation. The enemy had already broken through further to the north and south. The division again had to fight its way to the west.

On 26 December we conducted an additional march. The planned route through Toubovka could not be held, because this town was already occupied by strong Russian forces. Near Nikolaevka, the division's march columns, in which General Kaellner was located, suddenly came under attack by strong enemy tank forces from Toubovka. The division immediately took up a hedgehog defense around the town. Panzer Group Schneider from the 27th Panzer Regiment again was able to destroy 20 enemy tanks.

The 1/73 Armored Infantry Regiment was placed in the lead to clear the way to Yelisavetivka. The battalion soon established that the edge of the forest was already occupied by strong enemy forces. In the meantime, General Kaellner had found a new march route. He directed the division in its vehicles over 40 kilometers on a single march route through the Ukrainian forest. Darkness fell, and unremittingly the route traversed the wretched forest paths through gigantic water holes. Super-human efforts were demanded from the exhausted soldiers. Many stuck vehicles had to be extracted, but we still marched. The regiment was the rear guard. As soon as the column would stop for a bit, one could hear in the night the loud rumbling of Russian tanks from the north. (From: Knoblesdorf, O. von: *History of the 19th Panzer Division of Lower Saxony*, Bad Nauheim 1958 - reprinted 1985.)

The "Red Army" finally stopped on the line Belaya Tserkov-Berdichev.

4

1944

CHERKASSY
(28 January-27 February 1944)

At the end of the year, the Soviet Army Group "1st Ukrainian Front" continued their major offensive against the German 4th Panzer Army, breaking through a 30 kilometer wide sector of the front along the Kiev – Zhitomir road. The commander of Army Group South (Field Marshal von Manstein), in view of these developments, transferred the 1st Panzer Army, with four divisions, from their previous sector in the Dnepr Basin to the Uman-Vinnitsa area to attack the Russians, who had broken through, in the flank. However, in the meantime, the Russian advance rolled to the west and the southwest almost without halt. On the fourth day of the new year, the combat vehicles with the "red stars" reached Sarny (Wolhynien) on the old Russian-Polish border for the first time, and on 9 January, Soviet assault troops crossed the Bug and blocked the Lemberg-Odessa railroad line, the main supply route for Army Group South.

As the divisions of the 1st Panzer Army (General of Panzer Troops Hube) arrived, they were directed to the left flank. The 8th Army (General of Infantry Woehler), which was still facing to the east, was being threatened from the rear. For some time, the army stood in a great bend in the front, from Nikopol through Cherkassy up to the area north of Uman. From the right to the left fought the LII Army Corps (General of Infantry Buschenhagen), XLVII Panzer Corps (Lieutenant General von Vormann),

XI Army Corps (General of Artillery Stemmermann), XLII Army Corps (Lieutenant General Lieb), and VII Army Corps (General of Artillery Hell).

Against these positions stormed, at the beginning of January 1944, the "2nd Ukrainian Front", with its tank armies – led by the 5th Guards Tank Army – aimed at the Krivoi Rog-Kirovograd area.

The 2nd Parachute Rifle Division, 10th Armored Infantry Division, and 376th ID were simply overrun by the enemy masses that had arrived on the northern edge of Kirovograd.

• • •

During the day, the commander of the 14th Panzer Division willingly subordinated his formation to the (higher ranking) commander of the 10th Armored Infantry Division. The support and cooperation of both divisions was exceptional. All of the division staffs found themselves in the middle of the battlefield. In this situation, such measures proved appropriate.

At 2300 hours, the commander of the XLVII Panzer Corps was informed that, on 9 January, the 331st Rifle Regiment would attack out of the

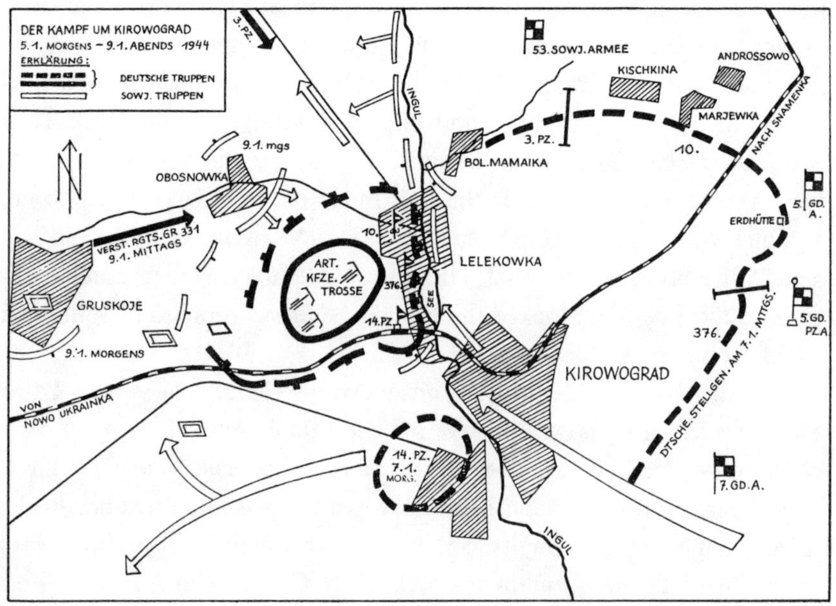

The battle for Kirovograd morning of 1/5 to evening of 1/9/1944

west to relieve the divisions encircled at Lelekovka. On 9 January, an armored convoy succeeded in transporting ammunition to Lelekovka. The enemy ring around Lelekovka tightened. Strong attacks ensued across the entire front, all of them directed at Lelekovka and Kirchenhoehe. They were defended with our last ounce of strength. During the day, heavy artillery fire was placed on Lelekovka and the ravines west of the town, where the artillery of the divisions and the supply lines were located. At the same time, strong air attacks were directed on Lelekovka. In the course of two hours, 14 air strikes thundered over Lelekovka. According to a German observer, the enemy was already flying into the Kirovograd airfield. Also, on 9 January, the German Luftwaffe brought in a small amount of supplies. At 1300 hours, the division reported to the corps by radio: "After reviewing the proposal of the three divisions to close the gap between the 'Grossdeutschland' Armored Infantry Division and the 3rd Panzer Division: This evening, we will withdraw to line Antonovka-Gruzkoe-Alekseevka; Unrein and Schwarz agree. Signed, Schmidt."

At 1600 hours, the corps radioed approval for the withdrawal to the proposed line.

After small local attacks succeeded in masking the withdrawal, all three divisions, on the night of 9 to 10 January, were led out of the Lelekovka pocket without loss. Because there was only one frozen road for supply, the withdrawal of the divisions had to be precisely scheduled. The attack of the "Grossdeutschland" Armored Infantry Division and the 3rd Panzer Division had to be directed against the essential enemy forces.

Only a few enemy tanks vainly tried to stop the breakout of the German divisions from Lelekovka. The 10th Armored Infantry Division withdrew with all of its wounded. No serviceable heavy weapons or guns were left to the enemy. On the morning of 10 January, the division established a security line on the eastern edge of Gruzkoe with a combat group of the 10th Anti-tank Battalion, equipped with self propelled vehicles and 2 cm air defense guns, so that the exhausted infantrymen could grab a short rest. Then, we formed a thin security line on the hills west of Gruzkoe with the 20th Rifle Regiment (on the right) and the 41st Rifle Regiment (on the left). During the day, the 10th Anti-tank Battalion, which was located to the east, was pulled in to the so-called main defensive line. The division command post was set up in Blagodatnaya.

The anticipated attack began at 1000 hours on 11 January along the entire front. The 41st Rifle regiment was pushed back and strongly punished by an attack of 15 tanks, with mounted infantry, which came out of the town of Ovsyannikovka on its left flank. On 12 January, the 20th Rifle Regiment was relieved by the 376th ID. The 20th Rifle regiment, reinforced with a panzer group and the 110th Armored Artillery Battalion, was committed on the left flank of the division and, in a spirited attack, captured the towns of Kulpanka and Alekseevka. During combat on this day, the often successful Captain Herdel, commander of the 2/20 Rifle Regiment, fell. (From: Schmidt, A.: *History of the 10th Division*, Bad Nauheim 1963.)

The army set all available panzer divisions into an immediate counterattack. The 11th (Major General von Wietersheim), 13th (Major General Mikosch), and 14th Panzer Divisions (Major General Unrein) checked the lead Russian tank elements and were able to destroy 150 enemy combat vehicles. As the combat groups of the 3rd Panzer Division (Major General Bayerlein) and the "Grossdeutschland" Armored Infantry Division (Lieutenant General Hoernlein) arrived, the front was stabilized.

The 10th Armored Infantry Division (Lieutenant General Schmidt) and 376th ID, which were encircled by the enemy north of Kirovograd – both were forced to stay put by a "Führer Directive" – could finally break through the Russian lines and make contact with the newly established main line of resistance to the west of Kirovograd. They remained here until the end of the month.

However, throughout most of the main defensive line of Army Group South the activity was still hot. Near Vinnitsa, in the meantime, a further battle developed that could only be quelled by committing the last man – which included supply train drivers, cooks, medics, clerks, radiomen, etc.

• • •

The critical situation was overcome. Nevertheless, by the sensible and quiet behavior of all of the units overrun by the tank attack, they remained calm and resolutely counterattacked. The 3/1 Rifle Regiment, which was on the way to Schastlivaya before the arrival of the tanks, immediately attacked the penetrating, superior enemy and pushed him out of the town. All of the remaining units of the 1st Rifle Regiment, at this time, continued their road march on both sides of Vinnitsa. They still had not arrived.

The 1/22 Fusilier Regiment, which had been relieved from the front that morning and just this moment arrived, attacked the enemy on the southern approach to Losovataya with the support of some "Panthers" and one battery of "Wespen", pushed him out of the town in an extended house to house battle, and beat him back to Korolevka. By evening, the bulk of the tanks were destroyed or captured, and the rest fought their way to the north. Therefore, contact with the front was re-established. The enemy's relief attempt foundered. In order to cut off the retreat route of the enemy withdrawing to the southeast out of the Voronovitsy area, the 16th Panzer Division advanced during the night of 11-12 January to the Vinnitsa-Uman rollbahn. Nevertheless, the bulk of the enemy had made it to safety in the east.

On 1/13, friendly formations were reorganized for the continuation of the attack to the east, with the goal of reaching the Sob sector. The enemy tried to take up the defense and reorganize his heavily battered formations. On 1/14, the division received the order to capture Strutinka and advance on Sob. The town had to be encircled from the north, as the 1st Fusilier Battalion contained the enemy from the north. To obtain more suitable departure positions, the 1st Rifle Regiment and 1st Fusilier Battalion attacked on the evening of 1/13. The 1/1 Rifle Regiment forced a breakthrough in a night attack and captured suitable departure positions near Krutoi Bar in house to house combat. The 1st Fusilier Battalion achieved a similar success north of the town. It overran an enemy battalion in a night attack, took the required high ground, and contained the enemy as ordered. The 22nd Fusilier Regiment was sent forward to participate in the encircling attack on Strutinka.

On 1/14, after an artillery preparation, the 22nd Fusilier Regiment and the 1st Rifle Regiment began to attack with four battalions abreast across

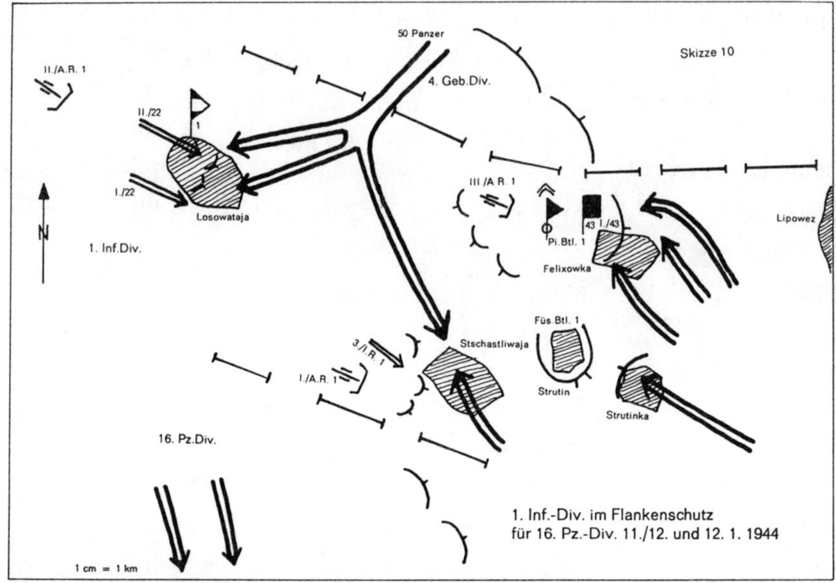

1st Inf Div in flank protection for the 16th Panzer Division 12/1-11/1944

an open plain, and they broke through. Soon the tenaciously defending enemy were turned to flight, after their tanks were forced to withdraw. It was not possible to cross the Sob sector and advance to the east on 1/15. The enemy would obviously be encircled if they tried to hold on to this sector. Under these circumstances, the formations of the XLVI Panzer Corps crossed over to the defense. The division had to defend a 30 kilometer sector. (From: Richter, W.: *The 1st (East Prussian) Infantry Division*, Munich 1975.)

Finally, the Nikopol Bridgehead became active. Here, the 6th Army (General of Infantry Hollidt) had to fend off a week long enemy attack, which broke against the German formations with monstrous weight.

• • •

In mid-January, most of the division was driven out of its positions by a strong frost and conveyed to the Krivoi Rog area in tracked vehicles.

Elements of the 466th Infantry Regiment and the 2/257 Artillery Regiment remained under the command of another division for awhile in the old area. They were released at the beginning of February and marched to their own division. On the way, they were stopped in Nikopol by General Schoerner and employed to reinforce the crews in the Nikopol Bridgehead, who were being hard pressed by the Russians and were soon to be encircled. Here, in heavy combat on the Kamenka, they brought honor onto their division. During the course of February, as the situation called for the evacuation of the bridgehead, the crews were able to fight their way to friendly forces in the west through a small corridor that was covered from two sides by fire of all types of enemy weapons. Therefore, the detached elements of our division fulfilled their special mission and were able to rejoin us near Krivoi Rog after a peaceful march.

Senior Lieutenant Boettcher chatted about his observations at this time, with good natured gallows humor:

> "The withdrawal from the positions around Chumaki, several kilometers distant from Petrovka, passed without incident. To keep Ivan from knowing our intentions, we left a suicide patrol in the defensive

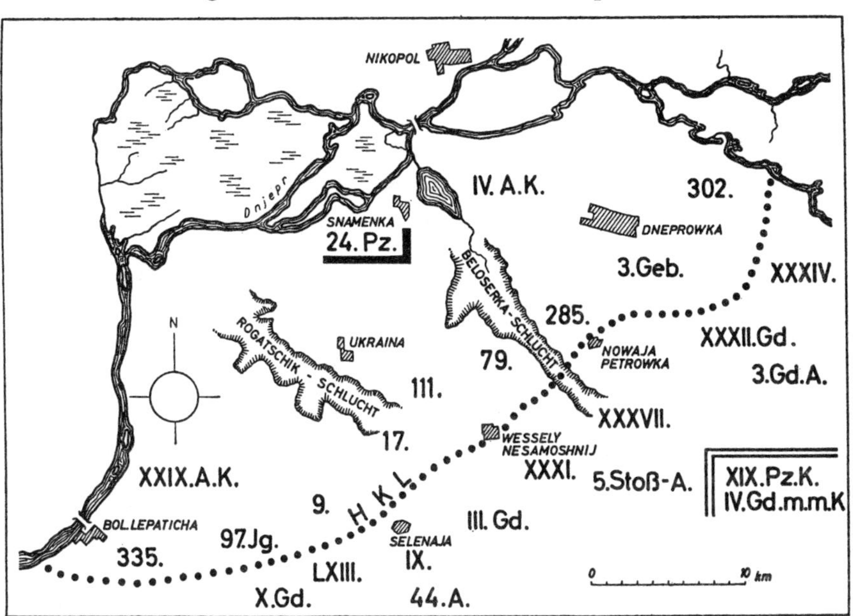

positions (about 10 men for an entire battalion sector) who were to run like the devil after midnight. To their good fortune, Lieutenant Demann of the reconnaissance battalion showed up with vehicles and gave them a lift.

Unfortunately, the regiment, meanwhile, had to give up its portly commander, Colonel Goetz, and received as the new regiment commander Colonel Baron von Grote. We then went to the Nikopol Bridgehead in February 1944. Because of the fun we had, I am sure General Schoerner will never forget us. I am thinking now of the non-commissioned officer in the 3rd Company who, because he was almost completely blind, was being sent home. On the bridge from Nikopol, however, he promptly ran into Schoerner. Because his silk scarf was missing, he was sent back to his company. A few days later, a personal letter came from Schoerner stating that it was no tribute to the 466th Regiment to have such non-commissioned officers in their ranks. Moreover, the letter contained the order that this soldier be punished with ten days extra duty. The letter ended up in the waste paper basket and the non-commissioned officer at home.

Due to the weather, the evacuation of the bridgehead was not very pleasant for man nor beast, and the numerous mud holes on the rollbahn caused considerable losses of supplies. On the other hand, it was so cold that when riding, the boots froze to the stirrup. To orient us during the day we had a Russian youth in whom we believed we could trust. During one night we were surrounded by rings of light from the front and marched according to the compass. Suddenly, near midnight, we heard, in the endless wilderness, the roar of engines on the right. However, instead of the expected Russian tanks, a Sanka appeared and our regimental surgeon, Dr. Kristukat, jumped out. This was not extraordinary, because he was always visiting the forward-most positions. And so it was this time. However, he had no idea of where he was going and swerved into our region with too much faith in God and a full load of wounded who had all turned white as ghosts. Afterward, he popped up in our area, so he must have gotten out of the bridgehead safely." (From: Benary, A.: *The Berlin Bear Division*, (257th ID) Bad Nauheim 1955.)

Finally, at the end of January, the northern flank of Army Group South also participated in a battle "to the last man." The 13th and 60th Soviet Armies began to attack in the direction of Luzk and Rovno from the bridgehead they had established at the beginning of the month. The 13th Soviet Army (Lieutenant General Puchov) overran the makeshift main line of resistance and directly assaulted the important cities in the former Polish border area.

• • •

During the night of 1 to 2 February, the XIII Army Corps was instructed to establish and maintain a new main line of resistance on a line Sdolbuno-the Uscie sector-eastern edge of Rovno-eastern edge of Zolotyov. The forces west of Sdolbuno were organized to protect the southern flank as well as the northern flank.

Then it all happened, as it had to happen:

The development of the situation required the commander of Corps Detachment C to commit his own forces south of Rovno, while the 454th Security Division had the responsibility for the eastern front of the city. Group Pruetzmann was to defend the northern front and northern flank. The command post of Corps detachment C was at Kvasilov on 2/1, the operations detachment was transferred to Dubno, and all elements of the Corps Detachment were so conscious of moving that, whenever possible, they did not pause in the city of Rovno because they did not want to be detained by the commander. The commander of Corps Detachment C saw the main danger to be in the southern flank. The Russians broke through here, near Sdolbuno or further south, so in a short while the entire Rovno combat region would be encircled. In his view, the city of Rovno was already lost. Besides, it had no operational or tactical significance. Also, he was aware that there were already three generals concerned with the defense of the city of Rovno (Koch, Pruetzmann, and Huenten), and the commander of the XIII Army Corps, on the evening of 2/1, expressly charged the commander of the 454th Security Division with the control of combat in the Rovno sector and to the south, allowing the commander of Corps Detachment C to move to the right flank on the morning of 2/2.

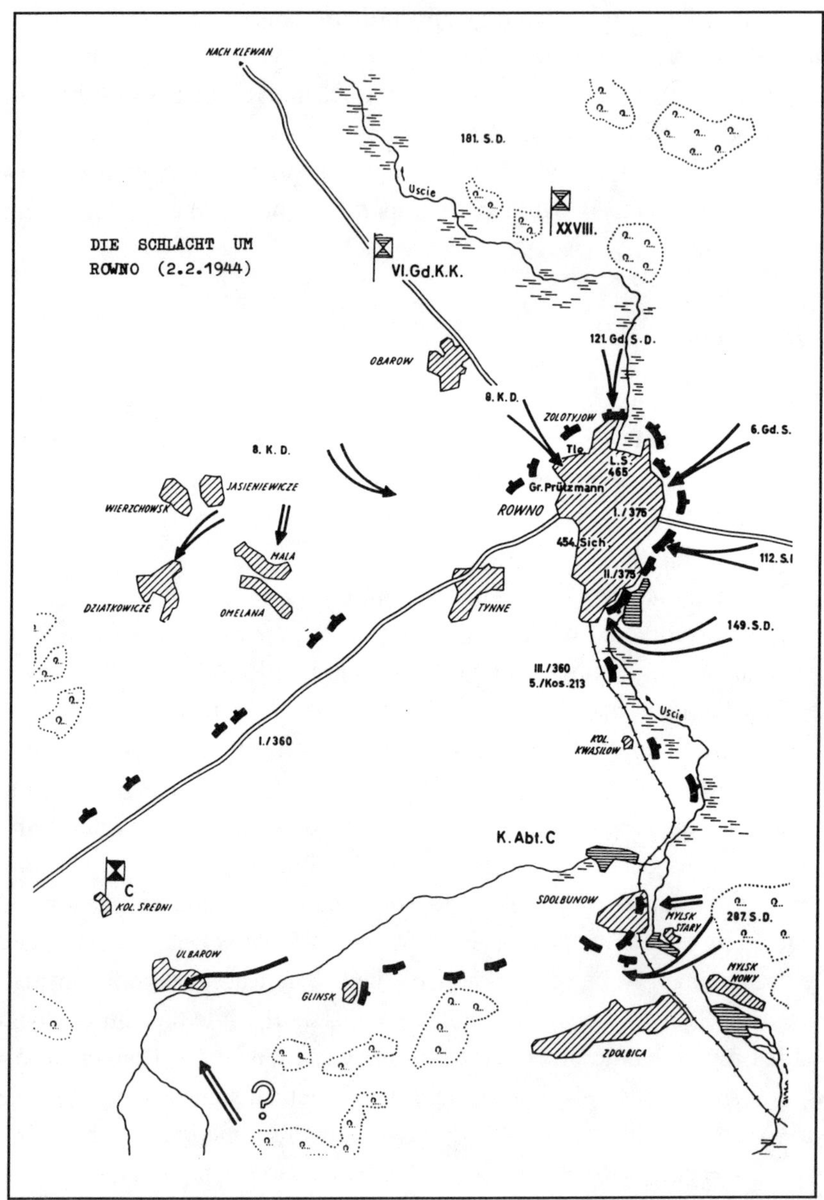

The battle for Rovno (2/2/1944)

Here, I was presented with a deeply moving picture. At one crossing over the Uscie sector, in the vicinity of Kvasilov, which was covered in melting snow and ice, I saw my men returning from the front, wading through it with naked feet. The felt boots had dissolved in the wetness. I left my vehicle and plunged into the knee deep water to meet the men with the result that it brightened a few of their faces, and many even laughed. Witticisms flew through the air. (From: Lange, W.: *Corps Detachment C*, (183rd ID) Neckargemuend 1961.)

• • •

The worst crisis in the Army Group South area of operations developed during the last ten days of January, on and behind the front of the 8th Army. Two strong armored combat groups of the Soviet Army Groups "1st" and "2nd Ukrainian Front", after an hour long barrage fire, tore through the German main line of resistance on the seam between the XI Army Corp (General of Artillery Stemmermann) and the XLVII Panzer Corps (Lieutenant General von Vormann). Here, the 389th ID (Major General Kruse) was separated from the rest and split into combat groups that were pursued by the Russian tank regiments and destroyed.

Because a second attack with the same forces was conducted against the main line of resistance of the XLII Army Corps (Lieutenant General Lieb), the army had to fritter away its only combat reserve. The courageous resistance of the 198th ID (Lieutenant General von Horn) was of no use. The division was blown apart and fell back to the west.

Therefore, the brigades of the 5th Guards Tank Army and the 6th Tank Army had an open route to the west. Their tank wedges advanced one after the other on the second day of the battle and, on 28 January, the lead elements of both armies reached Svenigorodka.

Therefore, the XI and XLII Army Corps were encircled in the vicinity of the city of Korsun! 54,000 soldiers of all ranks, seven infantry divisions, one SS division, and one SS brigade were being compressed by the Russian tank forces.

The Soviet High Command – contrary to all previous operations – stopped both armies to first clear out the new pocket. In the Korsun pocket were encircled: the 57th ID (Major General Trowitz), 72nd ID (Colonel Hohn), 88th ID (Colonel Anders), 389th ID (Major General Kruse), SS Panzer Division "Wiking" (SS Gruppenfuehrer Gille), and the SS Brigade "Wallonien" (SS Standartenfuehrer Degrelle). Additionally, there were elements of the 112th, 255th, and 332nd ID in the pocket.

By a radio message, Hitler forbid the corps commanders in the pocket to break out. There was no way to get to the Dnepr near Cherkassy. The OKH ordered that strong panzer forces were to be collected on the inner flanks of the 8th Army and the 1st Panzer Army, in order to encircle the enemy in a concentrated attack and free the German divisions from the pocket.

On the basis of this "Führer Directive" the commander of Army Group South ordered the assembly of the III Panzer Corps (General of Panzer Troops Breith), with the 1st, 16th, and 17th Panzer Divisions, as well as the SS Panzer Division "Leibstandarte", behind the eastern flank of the 1st Panzer Army in the vicinity of Uman and the alignment of the XLVII Panzer Corps (Lieutenant General von Vormann), with the 3rd, 11th, 14th, and 24th Panzer Divisions, behind the west flank of the 8th Army, south of Svenigorodka. At the same time, both encircled corps had to assemble as many forces as possible on the southern edge of the pocket for an attack to the south.

Naturally, the assembly areas could not be immediately occupied. All of these aforementioned divisions were engaged in defensive combat with superior enemy forces along the entire front of Army Group South. The assigned attack date of 3 February could not be met, because the individual divisions could not break away from the main line of resistance.

Meanwhile, the bitter battle within the pocket continued. Here, men of the rear area services were committed for 24 hours, just like front line soldiers. First of all, they had to protect the 250 kilometer pocket front. The pocket had a total depth of 60 kilometers. The German divisions, regiments, battalions, and even companies resisted the enemy assaults. Since the mud period had set in in the meantime, one had to also overcome the problems caused by the weather.

Losses increased in the first days. The commander of the 88th ID was taken prisoner along with his staff, and Colonel Baermann took command of the division. The wounded could not be tended, because the main first aid station had come under extended bombardment by Russian artillery. Supply to the pocket collapsed. Again, supply had to be conducted by air transports of the Luftwaffe. Because there was a shortage of supply bombs and parachutes during the first days, the pilots landed their heavy "JU-52's" on a temporary airfield south of Cherkassy. They took as many of the wounded as they could out on the return flight. A total of 2,200 wounded soldiers were flown out.

Finally, on 4 February the first panzer divisions began to arrive from the outside in an attempt to open the pocket. Instead of nine, though, there were only three divisions that assailed the strong Russian resistance and the mud. Thus, on the first day, the forces of the 16th (Major General Back), 17th (lieutenant General von der Meden), and 24th Panzer Divisions (Major General Baron von Edelsheim) bogged down in the mud.

Little by little, elements of the 1st (Colonel Marcks), 3rd (Colonel Lang), and 14th Panzer Divisions (Major General Unrein), along with the SS Panzer

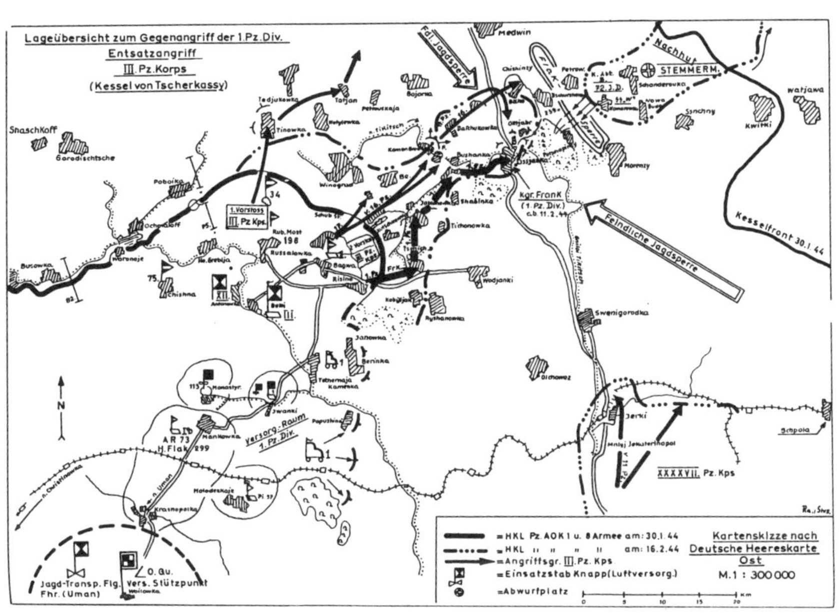

Situation overview of the counterattack of 1st Panzer Division - Relief Attack - III Panzer Corps - (Cherkassy Pocket)

Division "Leibstandarte" (SS Brigadefuehrer Wisch) arrived. The piecemeal attack of these panzer divisions was still able to gain some ground in the direction of the Korsun pocket, but it stopped 15 kilometers in front of the encirclement.

The attack of Armored Combat Group Frank quickly rolled through Chikhovka to the northeast. As the 1st Echelon was engaged by heavy flanking defensive fire from all calibers, from Kobylyaki, Chikhovka, as well as one of the wooded areas to the southwest, the dismounted armored infantrymen immediately attacked.

Under the cover of their heavy weapons, as well as "Panthers", the 2nd Echelon captured Chikhovka at 0930 hours after strenuous combat. The 2/73 Artillery Regiment supported them with vigorous fire and screened the flanks of the panzer wedge. Therefore, all of the anti-tank guns on the left flank were suppressed and eliminated. The Ebelin Battalion pushed the enemy back in the first attack, Kobylyaki was cleared just like Chikhovka, and the first blocking position was set up here.

While Armored Combat Group Frank turned left, the 4/1 Panzer (Lieutenant Wall) entered Chikhovka to the northwest to protect the left flank. In this manner, a deflective barrier was established in front of the neighbor on the left, and units of the 16th Panzer Division destroyed a reinforced Russian infantry battalion that was retreating. After that, the 4th Company took up its armored infantry and followed. In sunshine and spring-like warmth, Colonel Frank set the time for the attack at 0830 hours – this time to the north. Shortly thereafter, the majority of the panzer units began to roll with the company commanders at the head (except for Lieutenant Wall) skillfully guiding their units through the slushy snow dotted with mines. The senior platoon leaders, Lieutenant Mankel and Lieutenant Ciliox, established themselves behind the command tanks of the 1st Panzer Regiment's staff at the head of the "Panthers." The march, with the armored infantry mounted, moved speedily to the northeast past Tikhonovka (on the east) and Yablonovka (on the west). Again, the 1 and 2/1 Panzers formed the "1st Echelon." Near Yablonovka, the forward most tanks shot up several enemy T-34's, then succeeded in capturing this town with the 3/1 Panzer;

the armored infantry cleared out the rest of the enemy. The attack rolled further to the northeast.

The 113th Headquarters Company, which was following in the "3rd Echelon", caught up with the lead elements at 0830 hours north of the Risino-Vodyanika road, and attacked Chikhovka together with the tanks. While under very heavy artillery, anti-tank, and heavy mortar fire, they overcame a very troublesome mine belt without loss; then, at 1000 hours, their armored vehicles came under heavy anti-tank fire from the left flank on the north Chikhovka bridge. Two armored reconnaissance vehicles were lost from direct hits by anti-tank guns! Since contact with the forward echelon of the armored combat group was lost, the 113th Headquarters Company, with elements of the trailing 1st Armored Artillery Battalion, secured Chikhovka, which had become a cornerstone in the security front of the division. The "von Pogrell Group" was relieved by elements of the 1/113 and units of the 1st Armored Infantry Regiment on 2/13/1944.

The attack of the 1st Panzer Division rolled past the enemy occupied forests around Shabinka further in the direction of Gniloi Tikich. Directly west of Bushanka, Armored Combat Group Frank came upon a Russian field position, where Captain Kublitz's battery suppressed and battered the anti-tank gun positions on both flanks. The 2/113 Armored Infantry Regiment, with the support of the closely following guns of the 2/73 Armored Artillery Regiment, rolled over the pockets of resistance of the Russian defensive system and cleared out the covered trenches. In this manner, the armored infantry and artillery took several hundred prisoners. Finally, Bushanka-South fell; Captain Ebeling's armored infantry established a bridgehead over the Gniloi Tikich. At almost the same time, 1230 hours, the reinforced 16th Panzer Division, which was advancing on the left of Armored Combat Group Frank, captured Frankovka on the Gniloi Tikich with the Baeke Heavy Panzer Regiment. (From: Stoves, R.O.G.: *1st Panzer Division*, Bad Nauheim 1961.)

Finally, the 24th Panzer Division arrived on the attack front and was hastily transferred to Nikopol, in order to help prevent a collapse of the front there. In the meantime, the strong Russian forces had compressed the pocket into a 20 x 45 kilometer area. It was a miracle that the troops still held out, even after the daily casualty rate increased to 300 dead and wounded.

• • •

The Walloons marched cross-country. One could no longer know where friend or foe was, because the Soviets would suddenly appear behind the German lines. The dawn broke cold and gray. We were always running into regular soldiers and partisans. The land was crawling with unseen enemies that sallied forth unexpectedly out of the thickets and then vanished into the darkness.

During the entire morning of 9 February, the Belgian volunteer assault brigade "Wallonie" moved on Derenkovets, where the three rifle companies and the heavy machine-gun company assembled to reach their last prepared position northeast of Korsun.

The columns stomped through the mud. Soviet aircraft appeared with the break of day. First they dropped air balloons, which informed the Walloons that they were surrounded. This was not news. Then they demanded that they surrender. The answer was clear: "What happens to us when we stop?" The "Burgundians" have better morale than some of the units in the Wehrmacht, and even the Waffen SS. More than the other encircled troops, they stress that they are "Political Soldiers." The air balloons were popped and dropped into the mud.

In front of the Walloons of the 3rd and 4th Companies, who left their defensive positions in Starosele on foot, a convoy of several hundred vehicles from destroyed units swayed through the mud in confusion and disorder. The horse drawn carts are almost better than the trucks, which sink into the mud up to their axles.

The column slowly moved forward at the speed of one half kilometer per hour. The vanguard, which left on the previous day, had gone a considerable distance. At its head, a staff officer of the "Wallonie" Assault Brigade, SS Hauptsturmfuehrer Anthonissen, rode in a terrain vehicle. Often, he had to get out and help extract his small Volkswagen from the mud or some hole.

Suddenly there was a crack. The Soviets prepared an enormous trap. Are they regular troops? Partisans? Paratroopers? No one can answer these questions. Whoever it is, they are firing from all directions. The head of the convoy was stuck deep in the trap, and new enemies continued to come out of the forest.

"To me!" bellowed Anthonissen. "We must establish a defense! We must not give ground!"

The Belgian officer had a few recruits from the "Wiking" Division. They belonged to those new volunteers that were enlisted from the German minority, living outside of the Reich's borders, Volksdeutsche. During the morning's combat, when their positions were overrun by the Soviets on numerous occasions, they were always hit hard. Moreover, they did not understand what this big SS Hauptsturmfuehrer, with the black-yellow-red arm band of the Kingdom of Belgium, was yelling in French.

SS Hauptsturmfuehrer Anthonissen saw that he had no choice but to take the lead. He attacked the enemy with a machine pistol and a few additional magazines. But the young recruits hesitated. It appeared to them that a counterattack was suicide. So they pulled back onto the rollbahn. Continuously firing from his machine pistol, the Belgian SS commander advanced almost thirty meters by himself. He wanted to save the head of the convoy. Anthonissen was dead before he hit the ground.

Further behind, all of the vehicles and horse carriages had stopped in great disarray. A subordinate commander of the "Wiking" Division assembled all of the vehicle drivers, radiomen, and supply personnel that he could. They formed a combat group to fight their way free.

"Forward!" (From: Mabire, J.: *SS Panzer Division "Wiking"*, Oldendorf 1983.)

Finally – after the German panzer attack bogged down in the slushy snow in front of the strong enemy – on 15 February, Hitler ordered the breakout of "Group Stemmermann", a collection of divisions. At 1100 hours on this day, the commander of the 8th Army (General of Infantry Woehler) ordered:

"The combat capable III Panzer Corps is restricted by weather and supply conditions. Group Stemmermann must lead our forces to a decisive breakout!"

In discussions with Lieutenant General Lieb on the previous day, General of Artillery Stemmermann established a breakout plan. According to this plan, the encircled troops were to attempt the breakout in three attack wedges. In the lead, from right to left, were the Corps Detachment B (Major General Fouquet – who was severely wounded in Russian captivity), 72nd ID (Colonel Hohn), and the SS Panzer Division "Wiking" (SS Gruppenfuehrer Gille), while the 57th (Major General Trowitz) and 88th ID (Colonel Baermann) formed the reserve. The SS Brigade "Wallonien" (SS Standartenfuehrer Degrelle) would be committed depending on the situation. (Corps Group B led combat groups of four additional infantry divisions that were also located in the pocket.)

The heavy weapons and immobile equipment that were not required for the breakout had to be destroyed.

The assembly for the breakout in the Shanderovka area was difficult and costly, but it succeeded in spite of all. On 16 February at 2300 hours, the infantry forces of the three lead divisions set out. The night attack surprised the Soviets to such an extent that the front was broken through and, therefore, two hours later, the tanks, motorized artillery, and supply trains followed. The continuation of the attack was conducted off of the few streets, on poor roads, and through snow and ice. Not a word was spoken, only the clattering of the horses hooves could be heard and the rattle of the few motor vehicles. Thus passed the night.

Contact was lost many times during the night. Then, suddenly, Russian tank fire slammed into the columns. The confusion within the combat groups increased, and control was no longer possible – however, it got worse. The report of an SS man, who was there, reads:

"17 February 1944

At 0200 hours, we were again ordered to dismount.... We slowly moved with our vehicles along the main road. Here, confusion reigned.

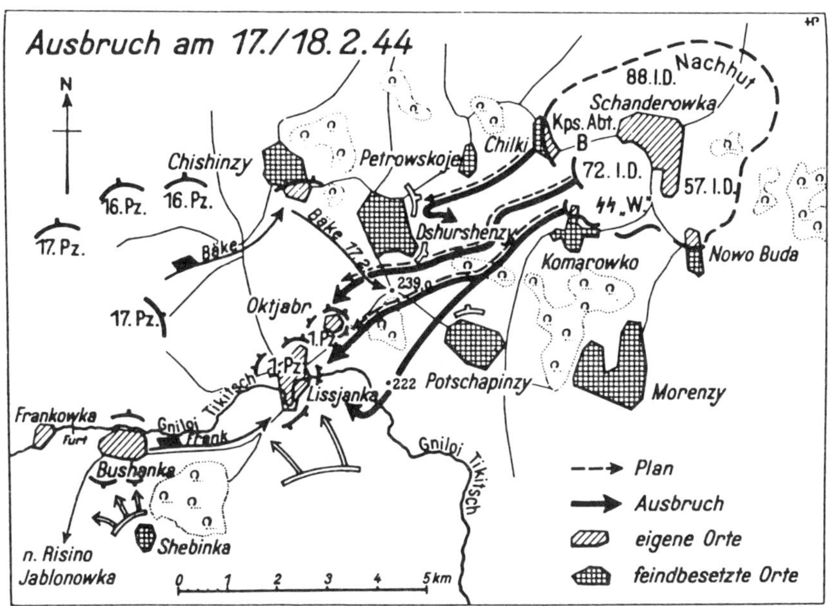

Defensive line of 1st Panzer Army & 8th Army on 1/30/44

In spite of explicit orders to bring only cross-country and indispensible vehicles, here were horse carts, busses, trucks, tractors, and jeeps. We had to forcefully pick our way through them. We inched forward in short bursts. The streets were so jammed that one could move faster on foot. We took account of the situation further on. The situation was desperate. Everybody complained, but, of course, no one did anything about it. I returned to my vehicle and sat down surrounded with boxes and crates. Exhausted, I fell into a half sleep and dozed listlessly. I was disturbed by the rattle of a "sewing machine", and then startled by two dreadful detonations. Dirt and rocks hailed down on our roof and rattled against the side walls. Shortly thereafter, there was another crack. I jumped out. We had a close call: the impacts hit in front of us and behind us, and a horse cart was also hit. The horse wallowed on the blood soaked ground. A truck and a tractor were also hit. Medics were already taking wounded into a house, temporarily bandaging them there and then loading them onto a truck. The frost grew stronger by the hour.

We couldn't move another kilometer until the early morning. As soon as it was daylight, two Russian reconnaissance planes appeared. We dragged ourselves to our feet and into our vehicles. The road we were on went through an extended depression that was completely visible. In front of us was a damaged bridge. We crossed over it one vehicle at a time. However, it took us too long to cross. Behind the bridge, on the flat ascending slope, two endless columns under strong enemy artillery fire were trying to get to the top of the hill.

To escape the fire on the bridge, we turned off the road to the left and trudged through the deep snow across a field into a sector with a brook that had not yet come under fire. We had not passed 200 meters beyond the brook when we were hit again. I don't know how often we had to press ourselves into the snow when the guns roared. Behind us wound the long line of our comrades along the road. Finally, we made it to the hill and took a breather.

A town emerged in front of us; according to the map, it had to be Khilki. The ring of Russians around the pocket stretched four kilometers deep; consequently, we had to go a lot further than Khilki before we met the first German troops!

To the right, a small foot path turned off into a depression, from where we could see a more solid road. Footprints showed that others had been here before us. To avoid a possible Russian fire strike on the main route we turned to the right. However, we had not gone 100 meters when we had another idea; this route seemed too peaceful and quiet. Somehow, it did not feel quite right, and after a short discussion – the others wished to continue on – we turned off the wide route in twos. To this day I still feel something was wrong with the other...

Finally, we reached Khilki. Here, the air was so damned full of smoke that one could not see where one was going. The last German tanks and vehicles, which had been stationed here, were destroyed. The march stopped again up ahead by a hill. We stopped for a moment to collect our strength. Then we came under a hail of machine-gun fire, which hit a horse in the belly. We hit the snow. We crawled into the meager protection of a ground depression as quickly as we could. There was something wrong up ahead – more and more men pushed from

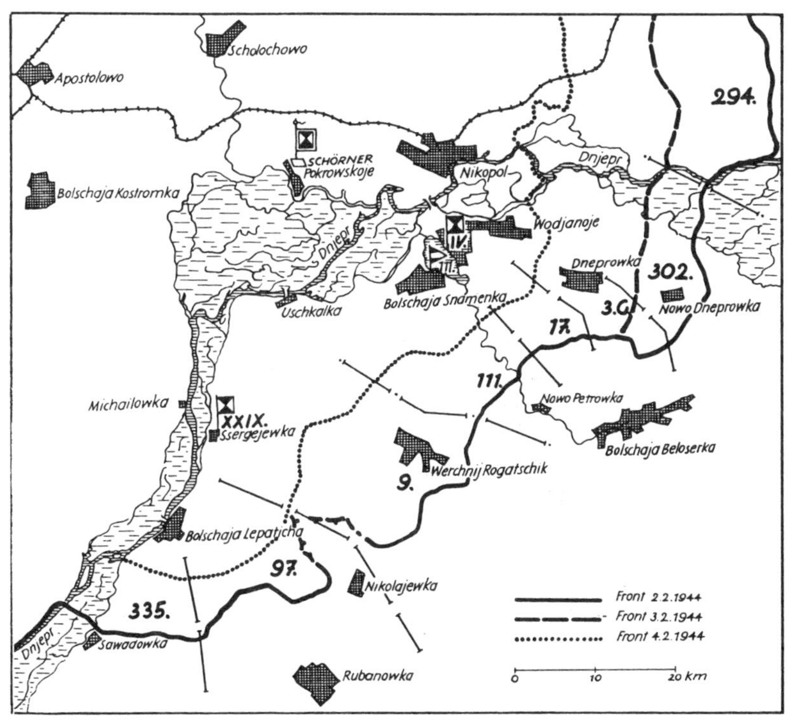
Apostolowo
Scholochowo
294.
SCHÖRNER
Pokrowskoje
Nikopol
Dnjepr
Bolschaja Kostromka
Wodjanoje
IV.
Dnjepr
Dneprowka
302.
Bolschaja Snamenka
3.G.
Nowo Dneprowka
Uschkalka
17.
111.
Michailowka
XXIX.
Ssergejewka
Nowo Petrowka
Bolschaja Beloserka
9.
Werchnij Rogatschik
Bolschaja Lepaticha
97.
Nikolajewka
335.
Dnjepr
Sawadowka
Rubanowka
Front 2.2.1944
Front 3.2.1944
Front 4.2.1944
0 10 20 km

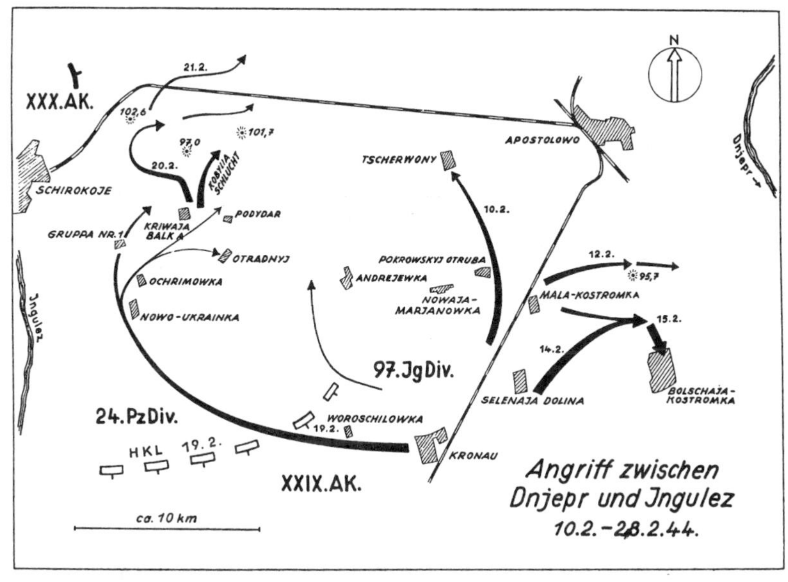
N
XXX.AK.
21.2.
102,6
101,7
97,0
20.2.
APOSTOLOWO
TSCHERWONY
SCHIROKOJE
10.2.
PODYDAR
GRUPPA NR.1
KRIWAJA BALKA
OTRADNYJ
Dnjepr
Jngulez
POKROWSKYJ OTRUBA
12.2.
95,7
ANDREJEWKA
OCHRIMOWKA
NOWAJA-MARJANOWKA
MALA-KOSTROMKA
NOWO-UKRAINKA
15.2.
14.2.
97.JgDiv.
SELENAJA DOLINA
BOLSCHAJA-KOSTROMKA
24.PzDiv.
WOROSCHILOWKA
19.2.
HKL
KRONAU
XXIX.AK.
ca. 10 km
Angriff zwischen
Dnjepr und Jngulez
10.2.-28.2.44.

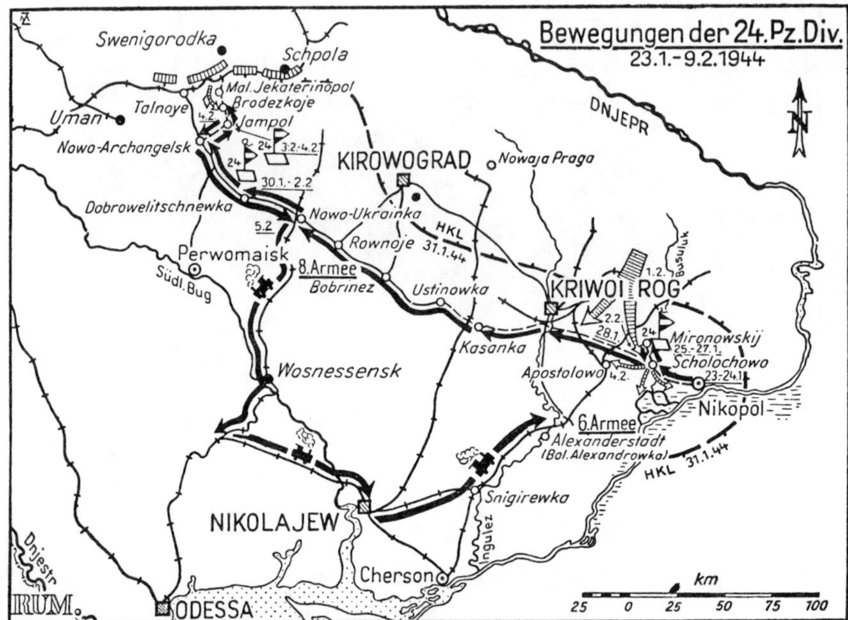

Movement of the 24th Panzer Division 1/23-2/9/1944

behind, but no one ventured over the hill. A disquieting feeling overtook us."

However, they then reached the salvation of the Lisyanka River!

Many dead were left behind. Their bodies were wedged into each other, stuck between exploded vehicles, and laying under dead horse carcasses. Under them was the high ranking officer, General of Artillery Stemmermann.

20,000 exhausted, hungry, and bloodied men arrived behind the III Panzer Corps line – 30,000 were left behind forever.

However, while here on the snowy and muddy fields west of Cherkassy two German army corps were bloodied, the battle continued along the entire main line of resistance of Army Group South.

At the beginning of February, the 6th German Army (General of Infantry Hollidt) had to give up the Nikopol Bridgehead. The divisions of the "3rd" and "4th Ukrainian Fronts" battered the neighboring corps so much that there was danger of cutting off and, therefore, encircling the formations of the IV (General of Infantry Mieth) and the XXIX Army Corps

(General of Panzer Troops Brandenberger), which were located in the bridgehead under the command of General of Mountain Troops Schoerner.

Because the winter battle dragged out until the end of February and because of the heavy demands made on the army group's motorized divisions, it was practically impossible to conduct mobile warfare any longer.

Therefore, on 22 February, the 1st Panzer Army (General of Panzer troops Hube) also had to give up the important iron ore mines around Krivoi Rog, which were lost for the duration of the war.

At this point in time, the Germans could not expect to conduct any more offensive operations. Their losses were enormous. The combat strength of two infantry divisions, including their weapons – as of 19 February 1944 – may serve here as evidence.

Division	Combat Strength	Machine-guns	Guns	Anti-tank
258th	654 men	34	0	0
387th	791 men	51	20	5

In March 1944, the OKH disbanded the following infantry divisions from Army Group South and reorganized them into other units (In brackets are the numbers of the divisions into which the disbanded unit was reorganized.):

38th ID (62nd), 39th ID (106th), 167th ID (376th),
223rd ID (168th), 323rd ID (88th), 327th ID (340th),
328th ID (306th), 333rd ID (294th).

KAMENETS-PODOLSK (28 March-8 April 1944)

The Russian Spring offensive in 1944 began on 4 March out of the Shepetovka. The Army Group "1st Ukrainian Front" (Marshal Zhukov), right off the bat, broke through the seam between the 1st and 4th German Panzer Armies and, in the first days, gained a lot of ground to the east. The attack was aimed at the region around Proskurov and Tarnopol.

Army Group "2nd Ukrainian Front" (Army General Konev) joined the offensive on the following day and, one day later, Army Group "3rd Ukrainian Front" (Army General Malinovski) entered the battlefield.

Therefore, all of the German armies of Army Group South and the 6th Army of Army Group A were now engaged in defensive combat!

The major attack of the "Red Army" expanded in the next ten days to a frontal width of 1100 kilometers, after the last two Ukrainian army groups entered the battle. 17 Soviet rifle, five tank, and one shock army marched irresistibly to the west. They were supported by four air armies, against which the Germans had practically no defense.

The greatest danger arose on the seam between the 1st and 4th Panzer Armies, as the front west of Proskurov practically collapsed. The Russian tanks saw no more enemy in front of them and attacked toward the Seret and the entire area between Kovel in the north and Tarnopol in the south.

The 1st Panzer Army (General of Panzer Troops Hube) was ordered to block the front west of Proskurov, so he sent the very weak III Panzer Corps (General of Panzer troops Breith) there. However, before this "assistance" could arrive, strong forces of the 6th Russian Tank Army broke through the right flank of the 1st German Panzer Army and the left flank of the neighboring 8th Army (General of Infantry Woehler).

The "Red Army" was now able to advance through the gap to the Bug on a wide front. Therefore, the main line of resistance of Army Groups South and A, which stretched from Shepetovka through Vinnitsa to the east of Nikolaev to the Black Sea, collapsed. Therefore, by the end of March were lost: Kherson on the Dnepr Estuary (3/15), Dubno (3/17), Vinnitsa – where Hitler's headquarters was located – (3/20), and Nikolaev (3/28).

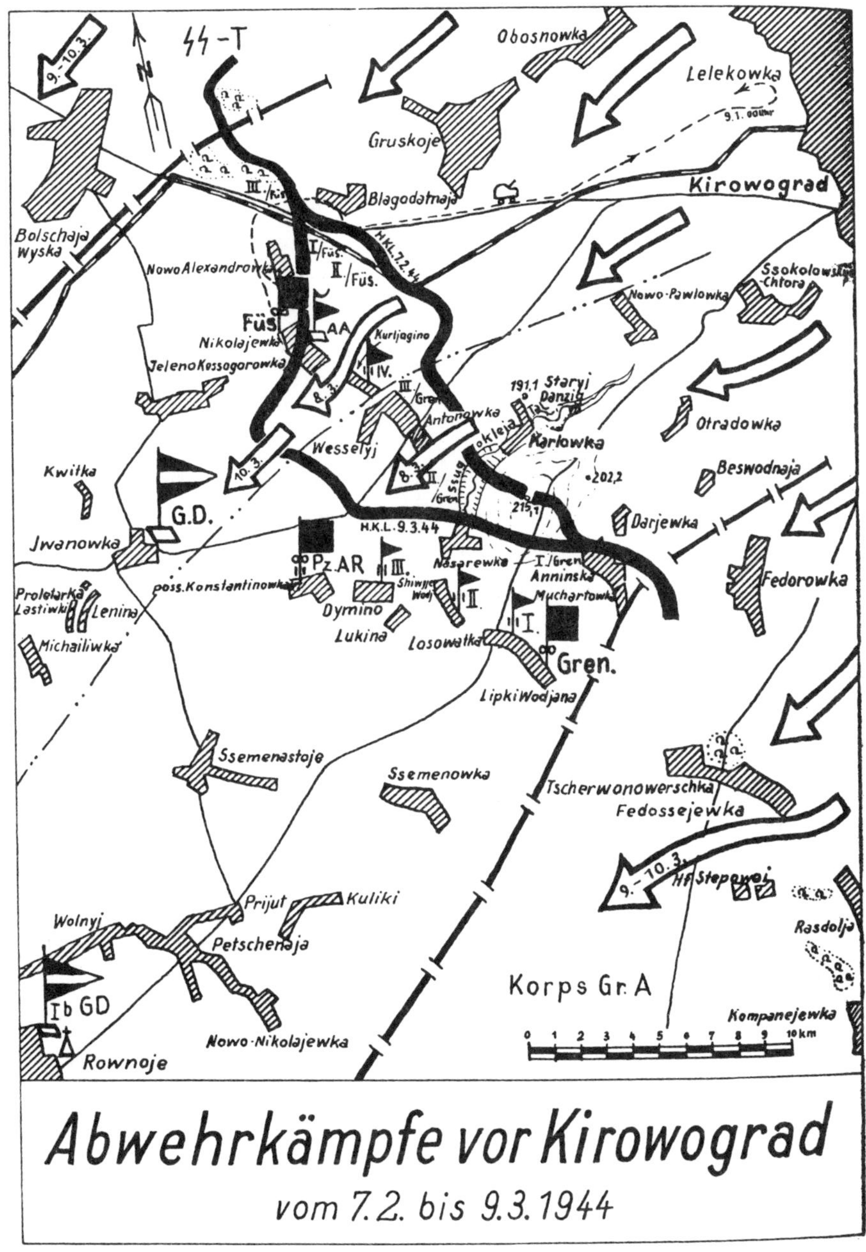

Defensive battle in front of Kirovograd from 2/7 to 3/9/1944

Army Group South

Since November 1943, the city of Kovel – which was in the Army Group Center area of operations – was encircled by the enemy and, after a lengthy and difficult preparation, and with the help of combat groups of the XLII Army Corps (General of Infantry Mattenklott), it was finally relieved on 25 March. The following reports of two infantry divisions may be able to describe the difficult withdrawal battles of the last days of March:

• • •

On 14 March, after a surprise attack by the infantrymen on the bridge at Privolnoe failed, we fought our way, with the other forward divisions, further south on a wide front to the Ingul crossing. We made contact with Group Hoffmann, fought for the Gromokle bridge near Novaya Troitskoe, and turned to the southwest instead of to the west, as was ordered by the army. That evening, the XXIX Army Corps had to report, "that due to the strength of the troop, their extraordinarily low combat effectiveness, and because the ammunition stocks have not been replenished for days, fighting through to Voznesensk – that is, to the west – is out of the question. We wish to change our course to Gurevka."

The breakthrough into the Privolnoe Bridgehead had torn a 6 kilometer gap in the enemy's line. The 258th ID was directed through it, along with other divisions of the corps. They crossed over to cover the Ingul and Gromokle crossings. Under fire from Soviet artillery, tanks, and Stalin Organs from Privolnoe, we succeeded in reaching Konstantinovka early on 15 March. It was pouring rain, and the entire distance was covered over bottomless muddy roads, and the miserable levees, which ran through the almost 100 meter wide swamp to the opposite side of the water and to the bridge, were completely covered in mud. But what could we do? We had to cross! The 478th Rifle Regiment was far ahead, so it established a bridgehead west of the Gromokle streams; the 479th Rifle Regiment had to make several counterattacks during the morning and, therefore, suffered considerable losses. At the crossing site over the Ingul were lined up hundreds of vehicles, the traffic control was unsatisfactory, and all of the drivers were fighting a battle to get ahead of each other. However, they finally succeeded in crossing the majority of the supply trains over the Ingul and Gromokle during the course of that day and night and the following day. Sergeant Major Kemper reported:

> "It began to snow. Russian artillery fired from the north onto the levee and the bridge. The crossing columns sped up. A direct hit threw men, horses, and vehicles into the air like a fountain. The horses balked and plunged – along with their wagons – from the levee and from the bridge into the water... We looked for a way out of the water. There were dead horses and overturned vehicles of all types on the levee. I let the reins loose, and in the next moment, my horse made a great leap: we got onto the levee. We joined up with our battalion on the west bank, and again we were blessed with a little good luck. Later, my battalion commander was criticized for losing the 2nd Company's kitchen and the vehicles: however, we got a new kitchen from somewhere, since we always looked after ourselves. The war continued!"

With luck they made it to the west bank of the Gromokle, but both the men and the horses were exhausted; it continued to rain, and during the evening a dreadful storm arose that even brought snow with it. In Novaya Troitskoe we saw the following: all of the roads on which we had to travel on the next morning, because all of the roads leading to the south were already being threatened by the enemy, were bottomless. (From: Pflanz, H.J.: *History of the 258th ID*. vol 3. Hamburg 1979.)

• • •

The request from the 683rd commander to allow the supply troops to follow directly, because the noise of the engines could be heard for long distances and the situation with the left flank neighbor (3rd Mountain Division) was very unclear, was not answered. We immediately set the assault companies in movement as an advance party; only two groups of infantry engineers were held back to prepare the Stepanovka bridge for destruction.

The commanders of both rifle regiments issue to their subordinate troop units equivalent orders. For the withdrawal, the 682nd Regiment was to assemble in Novakovo and the 683rd Regiment in Stepanovka. The supply troops were to stay away from the enemy for an indicated amount of time. Then, after assembling, they were to follow their regiments.

The diary of the commander of the 682nd Rifle Regiment had this to say about the withdrawal: "Had nice quarters (in Novakovo). The battalions waited until 1830 hours to depart. Engel and Schilling left at 2000 hours. Departed with Moeckl and Ebenig. The roads are covered in mud. The trip went admirably. We arrived in Businovo at 2330 hours. The accommodations are cold, dirty."

The battalions of the 683rd Rifle Regiment entered the assembly area at 2000 hours and began the next withdrawal. The 1st Battalion marched at the beginning of the column. Behind them followed the regimental units, the remaining 8.8 cm wheeled anti-tank gun, and three hornets. The 2nd Battalion, with the rest of the self-propelled guns, brought up the rear. Because it rained hard all night, the streets and roads were bottomless. The soldiers waded through the mud and the water; their boots filled with water.

The columns slowly moved forward. The night was dark, and a wind started to blow. During one of the few short rest stops, which were needed to refresh the exhausted men and horses, the men froze in their wet uniforms and miserable, water-filled boots. During the short time we could stop to rest, we could not sit or lay down because the ground was soaked. In spite of this, the troop's morale is good, and in spite of the loathsome weather and terrain obstacles they, astonishingly, sang out many soldier songs. The successful defense gave us the strength to overcome the problems and apparently also confidence for the upcoming battles.

Unfortunately, the bridge in Stepanovka was only partially destroyed because neither explosives or combustible material nor saws and axes were available. The bridges across the Bolshoi Kuyalnik, directly west of Silovka, were prepared for destruction by the soldiers of the 335th Engineer Battalion. The work will be finished shortly, reported the chief engineer officer, as the regiment crossed the bridge at midnight.

On 2 April at 0300 hours, the 683rd Rifle Regiment reached Koslovka, the first settlement west of the Bolshoi Kuyalnik. After a short rest, the battalions were directed into their defensive sector, the F Line, by the installation commander. The last 8.8 cm wheeled anti-tank gun was given to the 682nd Rifle Regiment. The chief of the hornet company was directed to deploy elsewhere; he received his instructions directly from the regiment commander. The regiment's supply trains were moved back to the next line, the "Panther" defensive line, which extended about six kilometers to the south. Presumably, they were to be withdrawn during the coming night. Units of the "Odessa Bridgehead Front" were to take over these positions. (From: Kissel, H.: *From the Dnepr to the Dnestr*, (335th ID) Freiburg 1970.)

• • •

Since 20 March, the 1st Panzer Army was the center point of combat operations. Here, within three days, the Russian tank armies were able to encircle both flanks and advance in a powerful strike across the Bug to the Dnestr. This river was crossed by the Soviet tank formations near Yampol on 18 March and, a day later, they crossed again near Mogilev-Podolsk.

The 6th Soviet Tank Army, which was advancing in this area, immediately entered the region west of the Dnestr, which was devoid of German troops, while the forces of the 1st and 4th Soviet Tank Armies, which were advancing from the north across the Proskurov-Tarnopol railroad line, also struck south to the Dnestr. Therefore, on 23 March, the 1st German Panzer Army (General of Panzer Troops Hube) was encircled. 24 hours later, Russian tanks stood north of Horodenka on the Dnestr in the rear of the 1st Panzer Army!

The 1st Panzer Army, which still held a front to the east, could, for the time being, prevent an outflanking maneuver in the west only with small armored combat groups of the 1st Panzer Division, while the 6th Panzer Army, which was already south of the Dnestr advancing from the east, could have temporarily prevented it with one combat group of the 75th ID (Lieutenant General Beukemann).

Thus, the Kamenets-Podolsk pocket came into being. It received its name from the city in which General of Panzer Troops Hube set up his headquarters – On 26 March, the city itself was stormed by Russian troops.

The XLVI Panzer Corps – on 23 March, Lieutenant General Shulz took command – stood on the right flank of the encircled 1st Panzer Army. The right flank of the corps – the 75th ID (Lieutenant General Beukemann) and elements of the 18th Artillery Division – fought south of the Dnestr and fell back to the west in front of the superior enemy without maintaining contact with its neighbor. The northern group of the corps fought west of Mogilev-Podolsk against the 40th Soviet Army. From right to left, facing the east, stood the 82nd ID (Lieutenant General Heyne), 254th ID (Major General Thielmann), and the 1st ID (Lieutenant General Grase).

The commander of the 1st Panzer Army ordered the XLVI Panzer Corps to operate as independent corps groups to prevent the enemy from launching further attacks along the north bank of the Dnestr. The corps could never execute this order because it stood without contact on its right and left and was completely incapable of conducting combat operations. Then, the 38th Soviet Army gained room to maneuver on the left flank of the corps and tore a gap of 30 kilometers in the neighboring XXIV Panzer Corps.

Therefore, General of Panzer Troops Hube withdrew the III Panzer Corps (General of Panzer Troops Breith) from his army's west flank. On

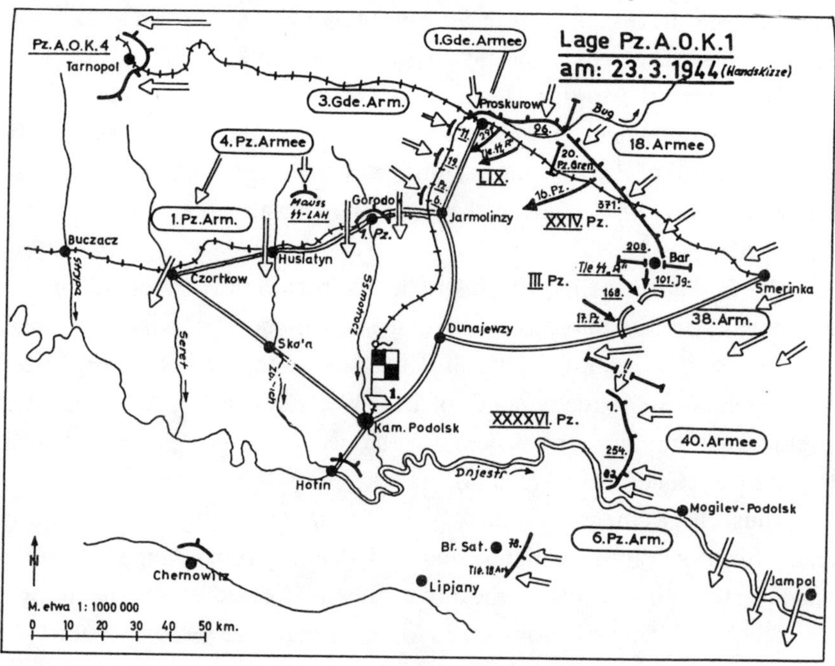

Situation of the 1st Panzer Army on 3/23/1944 (hand schematic)

23 March, the corps had to attack to the southeast with the divisions arriving from the southwest of Bar. Arriving little by little, the divisions – 17th Panzer Division (Major General von der Meden), 168th ID (Major General Schmidt-Hammer), 101st Rifle Division (Major General Vogel), and SS Panzer Division "Das Reich" (SS Oberfuehrer Lammerding) – did not have any initial success.

On the left, the XXIV Panzer Corps (General of Panzer Troops Nehring) fought with its front to the northeast and slowly withdrew to the south. On the day of the encirclement, the corps had at its disposal, from right to left, the 208th ID (Colonel von Schlieben), 371st ID (Colonel Niehoff), 20th Armored Infantry Division (Lieutenant General Jauer), and 16th Panzer Division (Major General Back). They lost the 16th Panzer Division on 24 March when it was withdrawn as the army reserve.

The LIX Army Corps – which was taken over by Lieutenant General Roehricht – was still located north of the Bug near Proskurov and began to pull back across the river with both of its infantry divisions – the 96th ID (Lieutenant General Noeldechen) on the right and the 291st ID (Major General Eckholt) on the left.

During the next night, they went west of the rollbahn to Lekhnovka on the Volkbakh, where lieutenants Lange and Kuehnle defended against an enemy attack with their infantry. During the night, the 283rd Infantry Regiment moved on poor and obstructed roads to Kadievka, north of Yarmolitsny, with a short rest stop in Tatarintsy. The enemy relentlessly pressured the rollbahn. Lieutenant Buelling had to push back those Russians that had penetrated into the northern portion from Kedievka. Lieutenant Lange cleared up a breakthrough at Lenia. The 2/283 Infantry Regiment distinguished itself here, especially the non-commissioned officers Brueckner and Grafe.

At this time, the 96th Infantry Division was fighting its way back from the east into the Yarmolintsy area. The 287th Infantry Regiment hoped to find some respite in Sherovka, but was put on alert in the early afternoon. Captain Grote and his 1st Battalion took up positions at the edge of the forest north of Yarmolintsy and made contact with the 283rd Infantry Regiment to his left. They had to withdraw to the south during the night, so

Grote was also instructed to pull back to the south through Yarmolintsy.

The 27th of March was another difficult day of combat. As the 283rd Infantry Regiment occupied new positions near Novoe Selo, the Russians were already in the town and had to be pushed out in a difficult see-saw battle. The weak regiment, designated the Haufen Regiment, alone suffered 13 dead, and the loss of officers was also high. The 287th Infantry Regiment went to positions on the northern edge of Vyshaya Tomashovka. As the Russians were breaking through near the 283rd Infantry Regiment at 1100 hours, an enemy battalion, with 8 tanks, penetrated the flank and rear of the 1/287 Infantry Regiment. In spite of the lack of anti-tank weapons, Grote's infantrymen distinguished themselves and desperately engaged the tanks in hand to hand combat. Lieutenant Colonel Lorenz desperately clung to a tiger panzer, which could no longer move, and used it in the battle near the threatened command post, driving the tanks away from the 1st Battalion. Additional losses for this battalion included the wounding of two trustworthy company commanders, Senior Lieutenant Hofmann, 1st Company, and Lieutenant Becvar, 2nd Company; the brave Staff Sergeant Sutter fell, and Captain Grote was put out of action for a day by a ricochet, so Captain Schwindt from the 287th Headquarters Company acted in his behalf until 30 March.

To the left, near the 283rd Infantry Regiment, Novoe Selo was lost. The encircled regiment commander was able to fight his way out. The regiment then withdrew to Savintsy. The 1/287 Infantry Regiment, encircled from the left, also had to withdraw its western flank and pull back to the town of Vyshaya Tomashovka. Finally night fell and, as so many times before, they were able to break contact with the enemy.

On 28 March, Major Schlegel was able to assemble what was left of his regiment. At this time, the 287th Infantry Regiment was almost cut off because the order to withdraw was very late in arriving, but it still turned out well. They moved further to the south during the dark, moonless night.

The morning of 29 March found the 1/287 Infantry Regiment and the remainder of the 283rd Infantry Regiment (Major Schlegel), subordinate to Lieutenant Colonel Lorenz, located near Lysogorka and occupying new positions. Then the Russians broke through their neighboring unit at 0700 hours and stood before the regimental command post in Lysogorka with 6 tanks. A withdrawal was impossible, the Russians had already penetrated into the rear of the 1/287 Infantry Regiment and the 283rd Infantry Regiment. With the regiment reserve, the engineer and wheeled vehicles, and all available men from the regiment staff, Lieutenant Colonel Lorenz first blocked and then parried the enemy attack. Even Staff Director Juennemann, who accidentally lingered near the regiment commander, had to grab a carbine and take part in the battle which, by the way, was on his birthday. The "Lame Tiger", which was scrounged two days before by the regimental staff, worked wonders. A T-34, which was being very annoying and could not be taken by the tiger, was destroyed when Lieutenant Colonel Lorenz shoved a hand grenade down the driver's hatch. He, therefore, earned his second tank destruction badge. (From: Pohlman, H.: *History of the 96th Infantry Division*, Bad Nauheim 1959.)

Additional divisions belonging to the corps were already southwest of Proskurov and fought, facing to the west, with strong forces of the 3rd Soviet Guards Tank Army. Fighting here, from right to left, were the 11th, 19th, and 6th Panzer Divisions, under their proven commanders Major General von Wietersheim, Major General Kaellner, and Colonel Denkert. On a fairly cohesive front, these three panzer divisions had lost all contact with the 1st Panzer Division (Major General Marcks), which was on the extreme left flank. These divisions fought in different combat groups separated on either side of the Gorodok with the mission of keeping the Yarmolitsny-Khusiatyn road open to supply traffic. However, strong forces from the 4th Soviet Tank Army had long ago crossed this road and attacked deep to the south. Here, the enemy was opposed only by a conglomeration of security units of the rear services.

On 24 March, as the Russian armored forces approached Kamenets-Podolsk from the north, General of Panzer troops Hube transferred his headquarters to Dunaevtsy, further to the northeast.

By the end of March, the divisions – here arranged from right to left – were only suited for conducting defensive operations. They lacked heavy weapons, artillery, anti-tank guns, tanks, and vehicles, as the following organization chart shows:

75th Inf Div	3 bns	1 lt btry	1 hv btry	0 AT guns	0 tanks
18th Arty Div	0 bns	4 lt btry	8 hv btry	0 AT guns	0 tanks
82nd Inf Div	3 bns	3 lt btry	0 hv btry	1 AT gun	0 tanks
254th Inf Div	2 bns	2 lt btry	0 hv btry	2 AT guns	0 tanks
1st Inf Div	2 bns	1 lt btry	1 hv btry	0 AT guns	0 tanks
17th Pz Div	4 bns	5 lt btry	3 hv btry	0 AT guns	0 tanks
168th Inf Div	6 bns	6 lt btry	3 hv btry	6 AT guns	0 tanks
101st R. Div	10 bns	13 lt btry	3 hv btry	20 AT guns	0 tanks
(including units of the 254th ID and 18 Arty Div)					
SS Reich	1 bn	1 lt btry	0 hv btry	9 AT guns	0 tanks
208th Inf Div	8 bns	2 lt btry	2 hv btry	9 AT guns	0 tanks
20th Arm ID	8 bns	2 lt btry	3 hv btry	10 AT guns	0 tanks
16th Pz Div	5 bns	6 lt btry	1 hv btry	9 AT guns	11 tanks
96th Inf Div	9 bns	5 lt btry	0 hv btry	9 AT guns	0 tanks
291st Inf Div	5 bns	6 lt btry	2 hv btry	6 AT guns	0 tanks
11th Pz Div	2 bns	1 lt btry	1 hv btry	4 AT guns	9 tanks
19th Pz Div	5 bns	2 lt btry	3 hv btry	5 AT guns	0 tanks
6th Pz Div	6 bns	5 lt btry	4 hv btry	4 AT guns	4 tanks
1st Pz Div	5 bns	8 lt btry	3 hv btry	12 AT guns	0 tanks

For the most part, the divisions were completely immobile. The mixing of individual formations decreased their combat strength to even less. Moreover, they were lacking sufficient rations, sleep, and relief. The army transferred its supply base from the Kamenets-Podolsk area to the southern bank of the Dnestr. However, while it was being transported, the Russian tanks were often quicker than the German supply trucks or horse carts.

The topography of the 1st Panzer Division's pocket offered suitable conditions for combat and movement. It was flat, with a few hillocks, and it was criss-crossed by numerous rivers and streams, as well as rich in cover with bushes and patches of forest. The population density was low, and the road network sufficient. It lacked, however, fortified roads. In an east-west direction, north of the Dnestr, ran the Lemberg-Tarnopol-Proskurov-Vinnitsa road and the parallel running railroad line, which was the army's main supply line. After its loss, there were still the fortified roads from Czortkow through Khusiatyn to Yarmolintsy and through Skala,

Kamenets-Podolsk, Dunaevtsy to Bar, as well as the north-south roads from Proskurov through Kamenets-Podolsk, Hotin, and from Tarnopol through Horodenka to Chernovits. South of the Dnestr ran a fortified road and a railroad from Chernovits to Mogilev-Podolsk.

The Dnestr itself was a large obstacle. In this region, it was 150-250 meters wide, with a depth of 2-4.5 meters. The bank was steep and up to 180 meters high. From Ushcziecko on, the bank was flatter and easier to ford. Between Mogilev-Podolsk in the east and Ushcziecko in the west there were no solid bridges. The engineers built a combat bridge near Hotin.

The weather was bad, and the mud period was not yet over. When temperatures vacillated around the freezing point, snow and rain intermixed, and the roads and the terrain became muddy. The best time to overcome maneuver obstacles was at night when the ground froze. During a cold spell in late March there was a snow storm that brought high drifts.

On the evening of 23 March, the commander of Army Group South ordered the 1st Panzer Army:

> "...to stop the advancing enemy forces on both sides of the Zbrucz to the south, free up the Czortkow-Yarmolintsy supply route, and establish contact with the 4th Panzer Army at Seret near Trembowlja!"

The splintered units of the 4th Panzer Army that were still located east of the Zbrucz – combat groups of the 68th ID, 7th Panzer Division, and SS Panzer Division "Leibstandarte" – were placed under the command of Colonel Mauss of the 1st Panzer Army. To the left of this group there were no more German soldiers!

General of Panzer Troops Hube decided to attack to the west, in order to withdraw the northern front of his army and, therefore, greatly shorten the main line of resistance. Engineer units confiscated all ferries and boats on the Dnepr and established a temporary bridgehead near Hotin on the southern bank of the river. Here was located the only bridge in the entire army area, and it was immediately guarded by security units and prepared for destruction by the engineers.

Field Marshal von Manstein prohibited the planned breakout of the 1st Panzer Army across the Dnestr to the south and ordered them to break out to the west! Thus, on 24 March, the commander of the 1st Panzer Army received the order:

"1. The enemy is advancing to the south, with strong tank forces on both sides of the Zbrucz! The next enemy objective is, presumably, the Hotin Dnestr bridge and Uszcziecko, in order to cut the supply of the army.

2. The 1st Panzer Army will break through to the west, screening to the east and north, north of the Dnestr across the Zbrucz and Seret, in order to cut off the enemy attacking to the south and make contact with the 4th Panzer Army.

3. Conduct of Combat:
Group Gollnick (75th ID, 18th Artillery Division, Hotin Combat Command) secures south of the Dnestr.
XLVI, III, and XXIV Panzer Corps attack to the west. The rear guard will remain on the former eastern front. While moving, guard against an attack from the enemy pursuing from the east. The three corps will send out mobile, combat capable advance guards to the Zbrucz that have the mission of establishing a bridgehead over the Zbrucz in the corps lanes and to hold it. The corps will conduct the crossings in their own lanes and establish as many crossing sites as possible.

The mission of the LIX Army Corps and Group Mauss is to cover the northern flank of the Army and then cross the Zbrucz to the west behind the XXIV Panzer Corps."

This army order was canceled on 3/25 and replaced by the following:

"1. Order of the 1st Panzer Army Ia Nr. 741/44 geh. (regarding purpose, conduct of combat, and individual missions) is cancelled.

2. 1st Panzer Army breaks through to the south, across the Dnestr.

Organization:
a) Corps Group Breith, from 3/25 at 2000 hours, consisting of the III and XLVI Panzer Corps.

b) Corps Group Chevallerie, with the LIX Army Corps and XXIV Panzer Corps.

Group Gollnick, with the 75th ID, 18th Artillery Division, and Hotin Combat Command, as well as all of the German forces on the southern bank of the Dnestr.

Missions:
a) Corps Group Breith establishes as large a bridgehead as possible on the northern bank of the Dnestr on a line Kalusik to Brailovka (east of Uszyca)-Glebov-Dzhurshevka-Polniy-Mukarov (north of Dunaevtsy)-Masterovka-Balin-Gumentsy-Uste (west of Hotin). The mission of Corps Group Breith is to defend the bridgehead against enemy attacks and assimilate with Corps Group Chevallerie coming from the north. Units moving to the south bank will immediately reinforce Group Gollnick and become subordinate to it.

b) Corps Group Chevallerie prohibits an enemy breakthrough between Uszyca and Zbrucz to the south and fights a delaying action back to the bridgehead. Enemy forces found on the eastern bank of the Zbrucz, between Corps Group Chevallerie and Corps Group Breith, will be attacked and pushed back.

c) Group Gollnick, in close coordination with elements on the eastern flank of Corps Group Breith, will prevent an enemy breakthrough to the west and to the southern bank of the Dnestr.

5. ...

6. This order will be specially delivered to the force.

On 3/26 this army order was cancelled and replaced by the following:

1. Order of the 1st Panzer Army, Ia Nr. 741; geh. and order of the 1st Panzer Army, Ia Nr. 746/44 geh. regarding purpose, conduct of combat, and individual missions are cancelled.

2. 1st Panzer Army breaks through to the west, screening to the east and north, north of the Dnestr across the lower Zbrucz and Seret and moves to the northwest to establish contact with the combat groups of the 4th Panzer Army (4-5 divisions), which are advancing in the opposite direction out of the area southwest of Tarnopol. The first mission of the army is to cut off the enemy forces, attacking between the Dnestr and the Zbrucz, near and west of Kamenets-Podolsk, from their rear area.

3. Organization (from 3/26 at 2000 hours, the same as in the order from 3/25/44)..."

For this breakout, the army formed two armored assault groups under the command of Generals Breith and von der Chevallerie. Both of the corps' groups had to break through the enemy front to the west, establish a bridgehead over the Zbrucz, and try to make contact with the 4th Panzer Army.

The combat group of Lieutenant General Gollnick had to link up with the breakout south of the Dnepr, where they were to try to cross over the Hotin fortified crossing with all of the security units and formations.

The chief of staff of the 1s Panzer Army, Colonel Wagener, described in his book, "Army Group South", published by Verlag Podzun in 1967, the breakout of the 1st Panzer Army as follows:

"Corps Group Chevallerie, with its panzer divisions (11th, 19th, 6th, and later the 16th Panzer Divisions), was attacking southwest of Yarmolintsy to establish contact with the 1st Panzer Division on the Zmotricz and with Group Mauss between the Zmotricz and the Zbrucz. On the evening of 3/27, the gaps, through which the enemy was attacking to the south, were still not closed. The divisions on the eastern flank of the corps group were withdrawing from the Uszyca sector southeast of Yarmolintsy and in the region south of this town. There was strong enemy pressure from the east.

In the Corps Group Breith area the 17th Panzer Division, 371st, and 1st ID attack on Kamenets-Podolsk from the eastern front was breaking off. During the evening of 3/27, the 17th Panzer Division stood north of Kamenets-Podolsk, where it had thrown the enemy back across the Zmotricz to the west and captured an undestroyed bridge. The 371st ID reached the area 10 kilometers northeast of Kamenets-Podolsk, while the 1st ID was still about 25 kilometers east of the city. The eastern front of the corps group came under strong enemy pressure during the withdrawal from the Uszycz sector.

Group Gollnick, attacking out of the Briczen Sat area to the north, had thrown back the enemy that had been attacking south of the Dnestr to the northeast and, in accordance with an army order from noon 3/27, was about to fight their way back through enemy forces that were already to their west. At the Hotin northern bridgehead tank attacks from the north were parried.

The withdrawal of the rear guard to line "Amalie" (Uszyca-north of Dunaevtsy) was planned for the night of 3/28-29, and it was approved for Corps Group Breith on 3/27 because of strong enemy pressure.

The enemy situation on 3/27, opposite the 1st Panzer Army, reflected the Russian 40th and 38th Armies, with about 8 rifle divisions, south and with 14 rifle divisions north of the Dnestr. The strong points south of the Dnestr were the road to Lipkany (on the Prut) and Hotin, north of the Dnestr, along the approach south to Dunaevtsy."

Opposite the northern front, the Russian 18th Army pursued, without particular pressure, with only three rifle divisions. They had directed the remaining forces to the west, where the 1st Guards Army, with 10-14 rifle divisions, reinforced by the 3rd Guards Panzer Army, set their main emphasis between Uszyca and Zbrucz. They put heavy pressure on the northern front of Corps Group Chevallerie and advanced through gaps there to the south.

In Kamenets-Podolsk the X Tank Corps of the Russian 4th Tank Army (140 tanks) broke through, while their VI Motor-mechanized Corps stood south of Kamenets-Podolsk. Four rifle divisions followed across the Skala, while two brigades of the 4th Tank Army provided the security near the Skala and Husiatyn on the Zbrucz.

The Russian 1st Tank Army, with its three mobile corps, had crossed the Dnestr in the vicinity of Horodenka and set out in the direction of Chernovits, Kolomea, and Stanislau. Four rifle divisions were in movement to the southern bank.

After intercepting a radio message, the Russians expected the German 1st Panzer Army to break through across Hotin to the southern bank of the Dnestr.

In the area of Tarnopol, where the Germans were encircled, the commander of the 1st Panzer Army engaged two superior Russian tank corps and five rifle divisions that were advancing to the west against the southern flank of the German 4th Panzer Army.

On 3/28, in a light frost that somewhat improved the road conditions and isolated snow fall, the lead attack elements began to break through to the west. On this day, in the Corps Group Chevallerie area, they succeeded in establishing contact with the 1st Panzer Division and Group Mauss. Russian fuel supplies captured here made it possible to continue to advance further to the Zbrucz. Corps Group Breith, with the 17th Panzer Division and 371st ID, was attacking Kamenets-Podolsk. The rear guards of both corps reported heavy defensive combat against superior enemy attackers. Air reconnaissance showed that there were no terrain fortifications or field works on the west bank of the Zbrucz. Group Gollnick advanced out of the Hotin Bridgehead to the north, established contact with Corps Group Breith, and reported enemy air supply traffic in the Kamenets-Podolsk area, a curiosity of today's mobile warfare in which a pursuer can also be cut off from his rear area.

The small army staff remained in Dunaevtsy on the first day of the breakthrough, from where they had good radio communications with the corps groups for the entire day. Not to overlook the achievements of the day, but the army leadership was burdened with the concern for the coming night's air supply, which would , hopefully, have the necessary facilities for landing. Only 75 wounded were able to be flown out on the previous night, on 3/27 200, and on 3/26 140 men.

On 3/29, the first important success of the breakthrough operation occurred: The bridgeheads of Corps Group Chevallerie by the Zbrucz and Skala crossed the Zbrucz, and at Skala they did so over an undamaged bridge.

Surprise also appeared to have been achieved. The enemy did not close the encirclement in the west, believing that the Germans would break through to the south and overestimating their success. The bulk of our encircled forces appeared to have actually crossed the Dnepr to the south.

This success was very important for the entire operation. The lead attack elements of Corps Group Breith hung further back on either side of Kamenets-Podolsk, therefore, the enemy did not block this area nor the important road intersections in this corps group's lanes. Corps Group Brieth, with the 17th Panzer Division and the 371st ID, attacked the city convincingly and, in cooperation with units of Group Gollnick, encircled it. The planned commitment of the 1st ID at Kamenets-Podolsk had to be changed due to an enemy breakthrough 15 kilometers south of Dunaevtsy, where they had to be committed in a counterattack. Such a time delay was highly unexpected, because it would be logical to quickly end the battle east of the Zbrucz to bring pressure against the superior troops fighting in the rear of this protected sector.

The shortage of ammunition and fuel held up the entire army area. Reinforced enemy air attacks caused losses.

On the morning of 3/30, the army received the report that, during the night, only 14 Ju's had landed with only 8 tons of supplies. The supply organization did not appear to be functioning properly. Delayed starts were reported due to supplies and loading crews not arriving. The army group would draw attention to the consequences in urgent radio messages.

Corps Group Chevallerie, after defending against an enemy tank attack, returned to the Skala Bridgehead and was advancing to the next sector on either side of the Borszczow. Corps Group Breith maintained the encirclement around Kamenets-Podolsk and attacked the city along the Zbrucz. According to plan, the rear guards of both corps were withdrawn to the "Barbara" Line (Studenica-Dunaevtsy).

On 3/31, the 17th Panzer Division and units of Group Gollnick had also established two bridgeheads across the Zbrucz during the night, directly north and 15 kilometers northwest of its junction with the Dnestr. Corps Group Chevallerie was advancing across the Borszcsow and, with little enemy contact, was able to establish a bridgehead across the Niczlawa, west of the city.

The army leadership, however, could not be happy with all of the tactical successes when the supply situation was not getting any better. Again the air supply failed to appear.

The Kamenets-Podolsk airfield, which lay outside of the encircled city, had just been secured on 4/1 because the resistance line of the rear guards now ran through it. Essentially, we were successful in aerial delivery only west of the Zbrucz.

The enemy situation had not changed with a breakthrough of mobile forces over the Seret, for the infantry divisions took another six days to get to the Seret. The army leadership limited the attack objective on the Seret on purpose, so they were not allowed to attack out of this bridgehead.

The army took nineteen hours to redeploy the command post over poor roads and in constant enemy contact.

The supply situation forced us to consider contingencies in case the planned operation could no longer be guaranteed. So that the previous achievements were not lost, on the code word "Lettow-Vorbeck" the armored combat groups would break through to the 4th Panzer Army, while the infantry divisions would fight their way to the friendly front north or south of the Dnestr. As another contingency, on the Code word "Mackensen" the entire army west of the Zbrucz would turn to the south, in order to cross the Dnestr in the vicinity of Stanislau. These intentions were reported to the army group with the addendum that, if the insufficient air resupply did not improve, it would be necessary to implement one of these two contingencies.

Enemy air attacks persisted all day. The number of wounded had increased to over 3,000, and of these, only 800 were able to be flown out during the night.

On 4/1, the supply situation was substantially improved by the influx of 57 Ju's with 75 tons to Kamenets-Podolsk, so that the anxiety over ammunition was alleviated and only the resupply of fuel was a concern now.

In spite of a sudden worsening of the weather, which included drifting snow, Corps Group Chevallerie succeeded in establishing a bridgehead over the Seret near Lisowce and defending against an enemy counterattack with tanks. The corps group's bridgehead on the east bank of the Zbrucz was withdrawn. Corps Group Breith moved out of their bridgehead on the Zbrucz to the west. They still maintained a narrow bridgehead, however, south of Hotin. The withdrawal of the two corps went as planned. Group Gollnick was subordinated to Corps Group Breith.

Also on 4/2, the persistent snow storm made extraordinary demands on the troops. Their achievements in offense, defense, and movement were exceptional. The achievements of the Luftwaffe were also valued, as they flew constant supply flights in spite of the bad weather. The weather had one advantage, in that the enemy's air activity diminished and the snow drifts hindered the movement of his ground troops. The attack of Corps Group Chevallerie across the Seret had, apparently, advanced into an enemy attack assembly area west of the Seret and located three enemy rifle divisions in an attack assembly area to the south. The enemy's defense of the Seret was nowhere to be found. Air reconnaissance showed, however, that the enemy was driving to the west with strong forces from Yarmolintsy across the Husiatyn. Three to four rifle divisions had already crossed the Zbrucz. The Russian IV Guards Panzer Corps was established in the Czortkow area with 70-80 tanks. An intercepted Russian radio message proclaimed that the "encircled" Russian 4th Panzer Army would soon be relieved from the northwest. The general impression, established through air reconnaissance, was that the Russians intended to overtake the German 1st Panzer Army in pursuit at the Zbrucz or Seret. In the south, the bulk of the Russian 1st Tank Army was widely dispersed south of the Dnestr, while the friendly attack forces were mainly attacking into the rear area, and security units of the Russian 4th and 1st Panzer Armies and uncoordinated defenses. Corps Group Breith was still in the bridgehead east of the Zbrucz.

4/3. The greatest danger threatening the 1st Panzer Army in the following days was from the north. Strong forces were set in pursuit to overtake them from Husiatyn across the Czortkow. There, five to seven Russian divisions, including the probable VI Guards Tank Corps of the 3rd Guards

Tank Army, were pushing south. Other forces had already crossed the Seret on 4/2 and were located west of the Strypa. Recognizing this danger, the commander of the 1st Panzer Army ordered Corps Group Chevallerie to attack north out of their Seret Bridgehead, to block the Seret crossing near Czortkow, and destroy the bridge there.

The friendly maneuver was still going as planned at this time. Corps Group Breith also established a bridgehead over the Seret. A brigade of the Russian 1st Tank Army showed up near Borszczow that had come from the Horodenka area, the first indication of a possible turn around by the Russian 1st Tank Army.

Day by day, more enemy forces were appearing on the rear guard front, and they were directing their attacks on the northern flank of the army. Corps Group Chevallerie had to prevent their operations from the north on either side of the Seret to prevent a new encirclement of the army. The movement lane of Corps Group Chevallerie was, therefore, narrowed, and they were reinforced by an infantry division from Corps Group Breith. It was now desirable to bring both corps onto the same line. However, because Corps Group Breith had the greater distance to travel over poor, obstacle-ridden and jammed roads and cross on the only two available Zbrucz crossings, the planned tempo of the withdrawal could not be maintained, and the rear guard of Corps Group Chevallerie had to remain on the Zbrucz. However, enemy pressure here was so great that the sector could no longer be held unless they sent additional forces from the west. According to the situation on both sides of the Seret, this was not a solution. The immediate withdrawal of Corps Group Chevallerie had to be approved, and the rear guard, upon which Corps Group Breith depended, paid for it.

4/4: A nighttime frost hardened the roads, so that the night movement occurred without problems. Supply no longer gave any cause for alarm becauseit worked itself out. Ammunition and fuel were being supplied to the divisions in sufficient amounts.

Both corps groups were attacking from Seret to the north in the direction of the Strypa sector. Corps Group Breith was dispersed, because its rear guard troops were just now withdrawing to the Zbrucz. The 1st Panzer Division ran into heavy combat in Czortkow, and the 7th Panzer Division was progressing well in its attack against enemy infantry and tanks in the direction of the Czortkow-Buczacz road. By evening, the 6th Panzer Division, the lead elements of Corps Group Breith, were only 10 kilometers from the Strypa sector, and the 17th Panzer Division was approaching Ushcziecko on the Dnestr.

Still nothing was seen nor heard from the combat groups of the 4th Panzer Army, which were attacking in the opposite direction. A radio message from the army group already contained the missions for the 1st and 4th Panzer Armies after they re-established contact. After that, the 1st Panzer Army was to stop the enemy at the Seret, and a later attack to the northeast could then be considered. The army group formed a force group around Stanislau, which had stopped the advance of the enemy south of the Dnepr.

The lead elements of the 1st Panzer Army advanced on to the Buczacz and the main line of resistance of the formations of the 4th Panzer Army. Therefore, the breakout from the pocket was successful. During the course of this battle, the heavily battered army of General of Panzer Troops Hube destroyed 357 Russian tanks, 42 assault guns, and 279 guns.

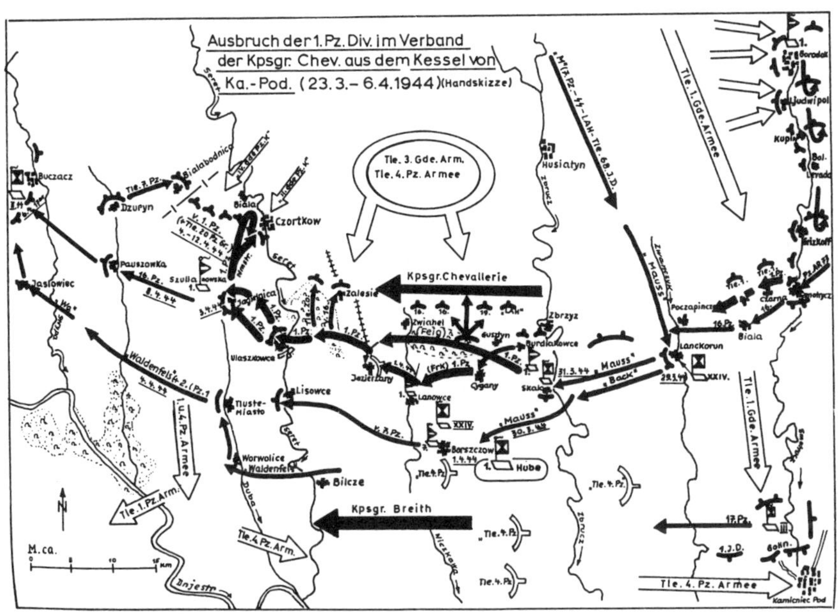

Breakout of the 1st Panzer Division from the Kamenets-Podolsk pocket (3/23-4/6/1944) (hand schematic)

The new commander of the army group, Field Marshal Model, ordered the army to establish and maintain a defensive front along the Seret to Brody. Hitler, in his East Prussian headquarters, promoted the commander of the 1st Panzer Army to General and awarded him the Knight's Cross with diamonds, oak leaves, and swords. On 21 April, General Hube died in an air crash during a return flight to the front.

Hitler did not approve of the overall conduct of the war in the south of the Eastern Front during March and, on 30 March, relieved both army group commanders, Field Marshal von Manstein and Field Marshal von Kleist, from their posts. Army Group South was redesignated Army Group North Ukraine and Field Marshal Model took command. General Schoerner took command of Army Group South Ukraine, the former Army Group A.

The last German strong point on the overall front of Army Group North Ukraine – Tarnopol – likewise fell at this time. The city, which had been encircled since 11 March, was declared a fortress by Hitler, and Major General von Neindorff, commander of the 36th ID, was placed in command of it. The arbitrarily thrown together crews resisted the Russian attack for twelve days, trying to maintain contact with their neighbors. Then, on 23 March, Tarnopol was completely encircled.

The Soviet troops brought in heavier and heavier guns and conducted a regular siege "like in the middle ages." They bombarded Tarnopol until it was ripe for assault and then prepared for the last attack.

On 10 April, the commander of the 4th Panzer Army ordered a relief attempt.

• • •

"Since 4/9, the enemy had been conducting repeated attacks on the Tarnopol fortress with superior forces. The crews defended, with their last ounce of strength, in street battles against the enemy and waited for the first day of their relief attack.

On the first day, using the XLVIII Panzer Corps, the 4th Panzer Army wanted to extract the defenders from the fortifications of Tarnopol and direct the crews back behind the friendly main line of resistance. As they arrived, the crews would be subordinated to the XLVIII Panzer Corps.

On the first day at dawn, the XLVIII Panzer Corps, with the 9th SS Panzer Division and Panzer Formation Friebe, crossed the friendly main line of resistance in the Horodyszcze-Kozlow sector and, after a short artillery preparation, forced a crossing over the Strypa and attacked the enemy penetration wedge a short distance from Tarnopol with sufficient protection for their own flanks.

After reaching the west bank of the Seret near Tarnopol, they covered both sides of Highway IV to the north and south. The extraction of the crews from their fortifications was accomplished under the cover of fire from all of the weapons they brought with them. If they did not succeed in reaching the defensive ring, the crews would have to break out. The XLVIII Panzer Corps gave the order to break out. After guiding all of the crews and all of the wounded to the relieving troops, and after securing the transport of those wounded unable to walk, they slowly withdrew to the Strypa.

All available units of the 359th ID participated in the relief attack. The bulk of the artillery of the 359th ID fired the preparation for the attack and supported the first advance. Fire strikes and assault troop operations were conducted on the 357th ID and 359th ID sectors on the first day to tie down the enemy on the front.

The relief slogan: “No soldier is better than we!”

• • •

In the meantime, the destruction of Tarnopol proceeded. It had not been possible to travel on the destroyed streets since 11 April. Air supply failed because their was no place to drop the supply bombs. The crews withdrew to the west bank of the Seret. The relief attempt of the XLVIII Panzer Corps, with the 355th, 357th, 359th ID, and 9th SS Panzer Division approached to within 10 kilometers of Tarnopol, but they could go no further.

Major General von Neindorff fell in street combat on 15 April. His successor, Colonel von Schoenfeld, in view of the catastrophic situation, issued the order to break out on the next day.

On 16 April, the extraordinary defense of the Soviets, reinforced by the commitment of anti-tank guns and artillery, made itself felt. They conducted strong counterattacks against the lead German elements.

Several, who broke out from Tarnopol, approached the positions of the 357th ID during the morning hours of 16 April, but they could not break out through the Russian main defensive line near Kozowo. During the morning, Panzer Group Friebe assimilated some Tarnopol fighters from the second breakout group. After breaking through the Russian positions, the last group fought their way to Chodaczkow Wielki. The Tarnopol fighters reported that crews were still fighting in the forest south of Janowka. The XLVIII Panzer Corps directed Panzer Formation Friebe to indicate the forward line with light markers.

Air reconnaissance determined that the battle in Zagrobela died out. Nevertheless, the German command still hoped to assimilate a good deal of the Tarnopol fighters.

On the basis of this, the XLVIII Panzer Corps tasked the 9th SS Panzer Division "to support the attack of Group Friebe, in order to assimilate as many of the crews as possible." However, a short while later, the 4th Panzer Army sent an order to the corps describing the mission for 17 April:

> "The corps is to take all appropriate measures to salvage all equipment and all damaged vehicles of the 9th SS Panzer Division and Formation Friebe and withdraw them to the former main line of resistance."

On 17 April, German assault troops set out along the road to Tarnopol and from the line 359-362-Seredynk to the east, in order to pick up as many Tarnopol fighters as they could. After gaining a small amount of ground, the Russians began to counterattack and forced the Germans onto the defense. The Russian VI Guards Tank Corps and two rifle divisions burned the German penetration east of Chodaczkow Wielki. After a bitter battle, the Russians recaptured Seredynk. On 15, 16, and 17 April, the 9th SS Panzer Division and Panzer Formation Friebe destroyed or captured 74 Russian tanks, 84 guns, 21 anti-tank guns, and 12 mortars, the bulk of which fell on 17 April. For his efforts during the commitment of the 2 Regiment, 9th SS Panzer Division Obersturmbannfuehrer Otto Meyer was awarded the Knight's Cross.

In view of the difficult defensive combat, it was believed that not too many more Tarnopol fighters would make it to the German lines. Therefore, maintaining the frontal penetration at Chodaczkow Wielki was senseless and would only lead to unnecessary losses.

At the same time the Russian formations assaulted the penetration, Field Marshal Model visited the command post of the 4th Panzer Army. General Raus briefed him on the relief attack, and both commanders agreed that it was no longer necessary to maintain the penetration. Model stressed emphatically that the 9th SS Panzer Division was badly in need of another mission, and that the division must be withdrawn from this area and assembled in the Brzezany-Podhajce area by 20 April. The withdrawal of the 9th SS Panzer Division began that night. (From: Tieke, W.: *In the Fire Storm of the Last Year of the War*, (9th SS Panzer Division) 2nd edition. Osnabrueck 1978.)

Army Group South

CRIMEA (7 April-12 May 1944)

On 7 April, as Soviet Army Group "4th Ukrainian Front" (Army General Tolbukhin) began a major attack in the Crimea, it signified the final battle for the German southern front. Here, on the beautiful and graceful southern peninsula on the Black Sea, the German Reich's military and political administration had been established since 1942.

The civilian administration was represented by a Gebietskommissar, a former Ostmark Gauleiter, while the Wehrmacht was represented by a high ranking commander.

The Crimea was valued as an important strong point by the German Navy in their battle with the Russian "Black Sea Fleet." The commanding admiral of the Black Sea had had his headquarters in Simferopol since June 1942. The local maritime command resided successively at Yalta, Feodosia, Yalta, Simferopol, and finally in Sevastopol. At times, the Navy had six marine artillery battalions, one marine communications battalion, three marine equipment installations, and one harbor security flotilla.

The good, ice-free harbors of the Crimea were regularly used by submarines, motor torpedo boats, mine sweepers, escorts, landing craft, etc., from the Black Sea until 1944.

This "peaceful" situation changed as the 56th Soviet Army (Lieutenant General Melnik) crossed the Kerch road on 2 November 1943 and pushed the formations of the 98th Infantry Divisions (Lieutenant General Gareis) back to Kerch and Bulganak in ten days.

A few days later, the 18th Soviet Army (Lieutenant General Lesselidze) landed near Eltigen, south of Kerch, and established a three kilometer wide bridgehead. It was only thanks to the energetic defense of the 282nd Rifle Regiment (Colonel Faulhaber) that the two Rumanian divisions, which were located here, were not destroyed. By 11 December 1943, the Russian bridgehead at Eltigen was crushed and removed.

Thus, the situation in the Crimea remained somewhat constant until 7 April 1944, when strong Russian forces entered the Perekop Isthmus and the Sivash Bay to attack the 17th German Army (General Jaenecke).

At this time, the army had the XLIX Mountain Corps (General of Mountain Troops Konrad) deployed on the north coast and the Perekop Isthmus. The V Army Corps (General of Infantry Allmendinger) was before Kerch, along with the 98th ID (on the Left) and the 73rd ID (on the right). To the south they were in contact with the 3rd Rumanian Mountain Division.

The army had the 111th ID as its only reserve. The division was transported by ship from the area south of Nikopol to the Crimea during the end of November/beginning of December.

The entire weight of the major attack of the "4th Ukrainian Front", therefore, fell on the divisions in the north. Here, operated the 50th ID (Lieutenant General Sixt) and the 336th ID (Major General Kunze), as well as the 10th Rumanian ID. The divisions were deployed from left to right in this order. The 50th ID, fighting directly on the Perekop Isthmus, had to give up the city of Armyansk during the first two days, and then, until 12 April, retreated to Karkinskiy Bay. The neighboring 336th ID could not hold out long against the superior enemy forces on the so-called Sivash Bridgehead – in the northern Crimea – and withdrew behind the Chatyriyk to the southwest. The Rumanian mountain infantry, fighting on the right, withdrew on the first day to the southeast, creating a 20 kilometer wide gap in the front, through which the Soviet regiments pushed to the south.

In view of this threatening and critical situation, General Jaenecke withdrew the V Army Corps, which was still near Kerch, to the narrows in front of Feodosia. However, before the corps could establish itself there with its three divisions, the Soviet Coastal Army (Army General Yeremenko) landed with ten divisions! They immediately began to attack and broke through the makeshift German main line of resistance to Feodosia on the first attempt.

Therefore, on the same day, the commander of the 17th Army ordered a general retreat to Sevastopol. The code word "Operation Adler" initiated this withdrawal. Just as they began moving and 200 Russian tanks were observed moving in the direction of Simferopol, the capital of the Crimea, the Führer Directive arrived stating: "Sevastopol must be held!"

The V Army Corps now fought, with both its German and Rumanian divisions, slowly back to the west. Only the coastal route was still clear, because partisan groups had blown all of the bridges and crossroads in the interior. Under very difficult conditions, the divisions had to cover 200 kilometers during their withdrawal. Many vehicles were abandoned due to lack of fuel or were lost to deep Russian air attacks, and the guns they were towing and other heavy equipment had to be destroyed.

The 8.8 cm guns of the 9th Air Defense Division (Lieutenant General Pickert) – the only combat capable unit of the Luftwaffe in the Crimea – had to be utilized as anti-tank guns. Often, the air defenders were the final defense against the enemy.

The weakened troops of both German army corps reached the outermost fortification area of Sevastopol at the same time, on 14 April. They left 13,000 soldiers behind, either as dead, wounded, or as prisoners. At this time, the 17th Army totaled 20,000 men, and they had to defend against 29 attacking Soviet divisions!

The army commander, General Jaenecke, flew to the "Führer Headquarters" to personally request that his troops be evacuated from their fortifications.

On 15 April, the 17th Army stood on a 40 kilometer long main line of resistance, which began in the north 2 kilometers north of Lyubimovka on the Black Sea and ran through Kamyshli directly to the south, to the west of Balakleva, where it again met the sea.

The XLIX Mountain Corps (General of Mountain Troops Konrad) deployed the 50th ID (Lieutenant General Sixt) and the 336th ID (Major General Kunze) on the left sector. The rest of the 10th Rumanian ID and 1st and 2nd Rumanian Mountain Divisions were incorporated into the German divisions.

The V Army Corps (General of Infantry Allmendinger) was east of Sevastopol on the main line of resistance, with the 98th Infantry Division (Lieutenant General Gareis), 111th ID (Major General Gruner, who later fell), and the 73rd ID (Lieutenant General Boehme, who was later taken prisoner by the Russians). Here also, the rest of the Rumanians, the 19th Rumanian ID, 3rd Rumanian Mountain Division, and 6th and 9th Rumanian Cavalry Divisions were incorporated into the German divisions. The army only held two Rumanian corps (the I Rumanian Mountain Corps and the I Rumanian Cavalry Corps) in reserve in Sevastopol.

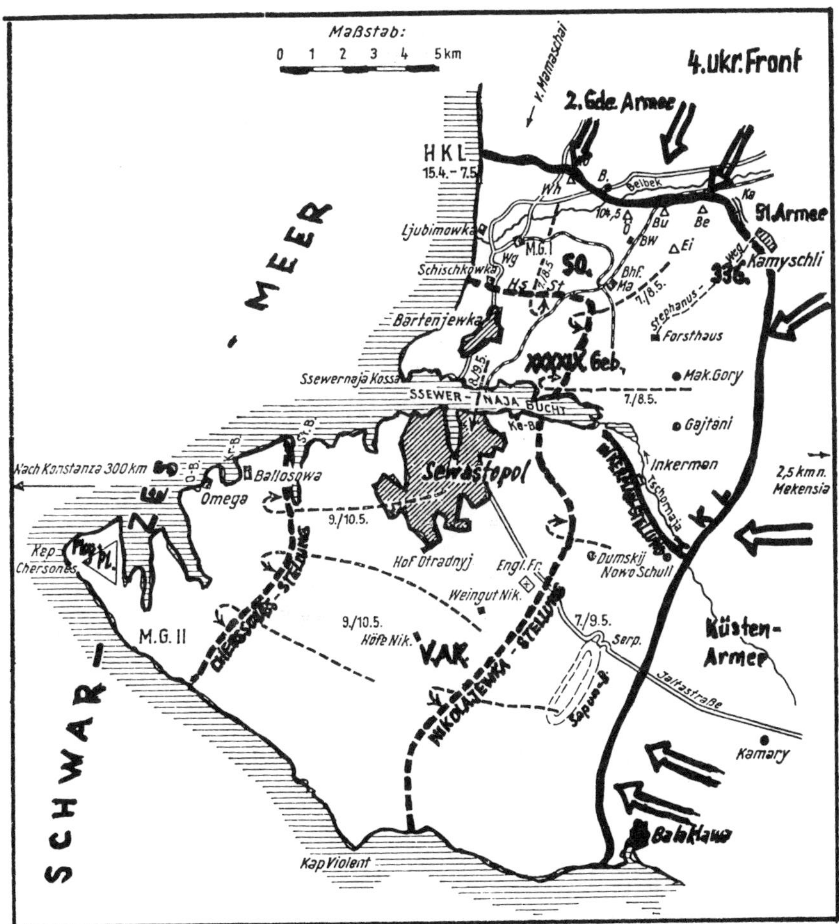

On 15 April, the Wehrmacht High Command reported the efforts to stabilize the front:

> "In the Crimea, German and Rumanian troops withdrew further to the southwest in constant combat with the pursuing enemy. The cities of Feodosia and Simferopol were evacuated. Between 8 and 13 April, formations of the Army, Luftwaffe, and naval artillery destroyed 285 enemy tanks. During heavy combat in the past few days, the combat groups, under the leadership of Major Schroeder and Captain Heidelberg, have especially distinguished themselves."

However, Hitler was not pleased with the recent conduct of the war by the 17th Army and relieved General Jaenecke from his post. General of Infantry Allmendinger was named the commander of the army. Lieutenant General Mueller was flown in from the island of Crete to take command of the V Army Corps. The first order of the new commander read:

"Do not take one step backward in the defense of Sevastopol!"

However, the final battle for Sevastopol had already begun. On 16 April, three Soviet armies - from right to left: the 2nd Guards, 51st Armies and the Coastal Army - began a major attack along the entire front!

The defenders succeeded in defending overall against the massive attack in a day long, costly battle. Local breakthroughs were all removed by counterattacks. The 336th ID defended heroically in the north. The 73rd ID, which was just taken over by Colonel Dorenbeck, fought just as bravely in the south. Here, an assault gun battery, with the infantrymen of the 73rd ID, did not allow enemy tanks to penetrate into the fortifications and frustrated a Soviet breakthrough across the Sapun hills to Sevastopol on 23 and 25 April.

Then the Russians grouped their attack formations around the 2nd Guards Army (Lieutenant General Sakharov) and began to assault with 200 tanks on 5 May!

• • •

On 5 May 1944, the enemy began to attack with unheard of amounts of equipment. For the time being, the main effort was in the northern sector. 400 tubes and numerous rocket launchers fired heavy projectiles and mortars for 48 hours. Then the entire 2nd Guards Army moved forward. The enemy also sent in powerful air strikes, against which friendly fighter aircraft and units of the "Pickert Air Defense Division" had great success. The ground air defenders also defended well against enemy tanks. When compared to the overpowering masses of tanks, these efforts would be totally insufficient.

While the combat was bitter in the north, where losses consumed both combatants, the defenders of the 98th Division had to defend against only weak attacks. At this time, the Bolsheviks did not succeed in breaking through in the north, nor did they on the next day. However, the decisive battle occurred on 7 May. During the early morning, the enemy began to attack in the southern sector from the coast to the Sapun hills with overwhelming amounts of men, equipment, and aircraft. The main line of resistance of the division was covered by smoke and dust for hours. The southern portion of the main defensive line was breached at several locations. The situation developed quickly and menacingly in the area of the neighbor on the right on the Sapun hills. Here, the enemy attacked across the "Serpentine" to the fork in the road southwest of Dumskiy. During the evening, the situation was so serious that the northern sector, which the army considered had to be held at any cost, had to be given up, and this shortened the entire defensive line on the peninsula south of the Severnaya Bay.

The evacuation of the Gaitany positions by units of the 98th ID was accomplished during the night of 7 to 8 May in good order and with few casualties. The mission, to withdraw his regiment through the Inker Mantel into a new sector north of there, was changed by Lieutenant Colonel Goettig.

He suspected that he would not be able to reach positions on a forward slope that was under direct observation from the enemy, and, on his own responsibility, allowed his regiment to enter their new positions by moving along the main line of resistance. The movement of the 289th was completed long before dawn, without interruption and without loss.

In the new "Nikolaevka Defensive Positions" on the west and forward slope of the Inker Mantel, on a line running to the west, the regiment spent a new day in heavy combat. Their command post was located at the previous site of the division command post in the "Engineer Trench", and the 282nd Rifle regiment was in Dumskiy. The division command post redeployed to the "Hof Delgardi", directly south of Sevastopol. (From: Gareis, M.: *The Struggle and Death of the Frankisch-Sudeten German 98th Infantry Division,* Bad Nauheim 1958.)

Two days later, the entire front around Sevastopol burst into flame. On 8 May, the Russian regiments were finally on the Sapun hills. Soviet guns could now range the harbor installations. Hitler finally gave the order to evacuate the Crimea.

On 10 May the enemy, which had been attacking since midday in division strength, was beaten back from the entire front. The 73rd Division destroyed over 20 heavy tanks in its sector. A reconstituted unit arrived from Konstanza and was distributed among the front line companies; officers were also distributed so that all units were now led by officers. The self-confidence of the troops returned, and their morale was high. News arrived in the afternoon that the embarkation, planned for the night of 5/11, had to be postponed because stormy weather prohibited the Navy from bringing their ships in on time. This did not cause any trouble, but gave the last men the uneasy feeling that their resolve would not be enough to counter the enemy's pressure. The front still stood on 5/11. The Russian attack against the Kherson positions, and their attempt to cross the Strelezkaya Bay in boats and establish themselves on the west coast, foundered. At noon, the troops of the XLIX Mountain Corps received the order to embark. After the fall of darkness, the forward positions were manned by only one third of the crews. The units withdrew to the terminal positions on the coast and, from there, the terminal officer directed them to the loading positions on the Kruglaya and Omega Bays for their embarkation onto the ferries. The ferries transported the troops to the German and Rumanian transport ships that were located off of the coast. At midnight, the rear guard also withdrew from its positions and followed them to the loading positions.

The order reached the troops in time so that they could make preparations. The first combat troops of the division were loaded at midnight, because several detours were made between loading positions.

The following description follows a report of the commander of the 123rd Rifle Regiment, Major Teschner. At 1900 hours, the Russians did not appear to notice the beginning of the withdrawal from the Kherson positions. For deception, the regiment employed two assault troops, which were recovered without loss. An enemy counterattack was repulsed. The division's artillery, which was not short of ammunition, fired harassment barrages. Major Teschner, who personally led his rear guard troops, received a report at 2200 hours that there were still no ferries at the loading positions on Omega Bay and that the wounded and the supply trains had been there waiting for 24 hours. He requested permission from the division to postpone the withdrawal of the rear guard in case of an emergency at the embarkation position and, correspondingly, the evacuation of the Kherson position, in order to obtain 24 hours more if he needed it. Wire and radio communications were destroyed, so he dispatched his ordnance officer. An hour and a half later, he returned with instructions to continue the movement as ordered. Just then, the 121st Rifle Regiment reported that they were beginning to embark, so they withdrew their rear guard from their defensive positions around midnight. The neighbor on the right also left around 2400 hours. Major Teschner then gave the order to withdraw and occupy blocking positions, which could protect the loading positions on Kruglaya and Omega Bays from the east. These positions, which offered little cover on the rocky ground, were occupied according to plan and without the Russians following. Major Teschner went personally to clarify the situation. He couldn't find the terminal staff. He had an uncomfortable feeling about the regiment loading positions.

The only ferry that showed up could only take a few hundred men. On the shore it was swarmed over by wounded and supply troops. The situation was the same by the neighboring division. The embarkation by the 121st Regiment seemed to be going better. There were, however, four units awaiting embarkation there.

Despite the desperateness of the situation, those waiting to be picked up demonstrated excellent discipline.

When a ferry arrived in Omega Bay at 0200 hours, they lined up in a column of two and boarded without crowding, and they stopped when the ferry was full. The officers helped several wounded onto the ferry; no one said a word. All was calm, as the officers returned from the ferry to the dock, even though it was announced that this would be the last ferry. The ship departed without being molested. Major Teschner led the remainder to a covered area. (From: *The 50th Infantry Division 1939-1945*, Augsburg 1965.)

• • •

In March, the commanding admiral of the Black Sea immediately deployed those small ships that were located in Rumanian harbors. There were a total of 200 ships – marine barges, landing craft, fishing boats, ferries, etc. – that made their way to the Crimea under the constant attack of Russian aircraft from Konstanza. It took almost three days before the ships fell under Russian artillery fire in Sevastopol.

The first loadings went as planned, even as shells and bombs were falling into the harbor. The soldiers were allowed on the ships with only hand guns, for all of the heavy weapons and equipment were left behind. Many officers and men stepped aside and let the wounded be transported. As soon as the ships were "overloaded" they left Sevastopol. Many did not reach the protection of Rumanian harbors, since they were sunk by Russian bombers or submarines. 8,000 men drowned in this manner.

The last intact companies returned to the Kherson Peninsula after no more ships showed up with German flags. Here they suffered and endured. The chief of staff of the 17th Army, Major General von Xylander, wrote:

> "... Positions were occupied around the piers. The naval evacuation fleet was on its way from Sevastopol, however, the administrative organization of the naval commander was destroyed by the heavy fire. From his command post, he could not monitor the attempts of the ships to approach the piers. During the late evening, the naval commander himself embarked on a ship to personally monitor the arrival of the ships into the harbor. In the rough seas and darkness this could not be done, so the docks remained empty and the troops waited in vain. Some brave marine barge operators risked approaching the docks, loaded their 250 man capacity barges with up to 700 men, and thereby offered proof that it would be possible to gather up the last units with the available ships if the command organization had still functioned. Now, however, 10,000 of our last and best men stood on the docks until morning and waited in vain..."

Since 8 April, during the withdrawal battle, the 17th Army had lost 57,000 men – of which 31,700 were German and 25,800 were Rumanian – as dead or taken prisoner. An additional 20,000 German soldiers were listed as missing!

The 17th Army ceased to exist.

Army Group South

BEFORE THE BORDER (12 May-30 August 1944)

With the beginning of the mud period in spring 1944, the German formations had some time to take a breather. A sudden fall in the temperature turned the streets, roads, meadows, and fields into mud in just a few days. Movement came practically to a standstill – even that of the "Red Army." The attack tempo of the Russian formations decreased noticeably in mid April. The enemy now had to organize their long supply lines.

After the 3rd Rumanian Army gave up Odessa on 10 April, the battle on the Dnestr came to a halt. Army Group South Ukraine (General Schoerner) now had time to fortify its main line of resistance between the Dnestr Estuary and Jassy, and from here along the west bank of the Pruth to Kolomea they constructed trenches and shelters.

After the breakout of the 1st Panzer Army from the Kamenets-Podolsk pocket and the capture of Kovel, Army Group North Ukraine (Field Marshal Model) was able to deploy on a defensive front from Carpathia to the Pripet Swamp. Thus, from the middle of April, a continuous front was established from the Dnestr Estuary on the Black Sea to the impassable Pripet Swamp, where they made contact with Army Group Center.

• • •

"A sunny April day announced the beginning of spring in Wolhynien. The storks arrived, but didn't nest on the roofs like they do at home, but by the dozens in the high trees on the edges of the meadows. Now we can examine the land and the people. East of the Bug is a land removed from the world, with a mixture of Russians and Poles that belonged to Poland before the war. It was first occupied by the "Red Army" after the Polish Campaign in 1939 and still resembles Russia somewhat. For example, the religion still actively follows the Greek-Orthodox traditions.

The villages are intact. Their interiors reflect a childlike joy with their many colored spiraled ornaments, and they are rich in crucifixes and pictures of the saints. On the old Russian festival of Easter, which is celebrated according to the Julian calendar, the churches are full from morning until

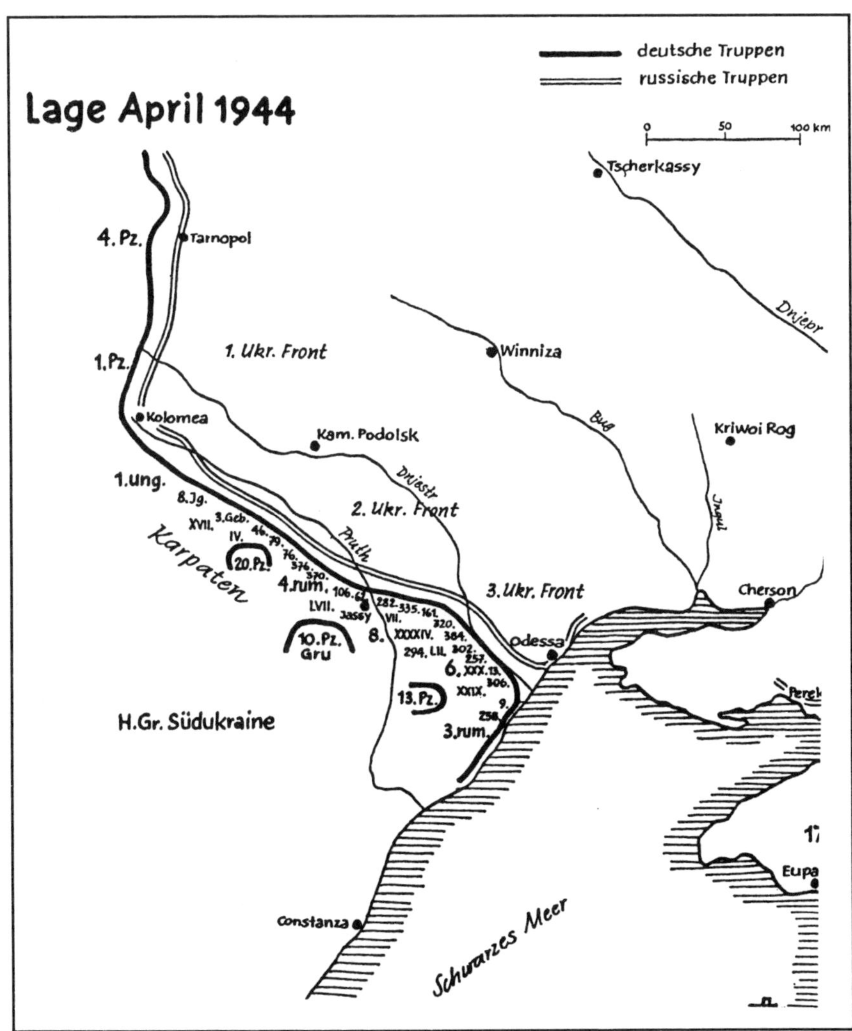

Situation April 1944

night. The vicar is there with his families and cares for his flock. One can still see isolated buildings made out of the ancient Russian cement, which we had not seen in other areas of Russia, where the communists had disallowed this process for the past two decades. On the approaches to the towns and at forked roads stand high double crosses with the slanting crossbeam, the symbol of the Greek-Orthodox faith. Strips of linen flutter in the breeze:

an offering to the faithful from a weaver, since almost every peasant house has a spinning wheel and a loom. We have seen many beautiful patterns of bright and multicolored linen and wool fabrics. The dyes are obtained by the peasants from plants. Through spinning, weaving, and sewing, almost all clothing is homemade – even footwear. We have seen sturdy shoes made from felt. All of this is homemade by the peasant and his wife, and the handiwork and quality is available nowhere else.

The houses are solidly built and they are a little bit cleaner within than the ones we had become familiar with in Soviet Russia. The people differ in two ways: in speech they are talkative, and in bearing they are somewhat "western" (Polish) when compared to the Soviet "culture" – on the other hand, they are apprehensive of the partisan bands in the forests and their uncertain future when the Soviets return.

The fields and forests of this extensive Pripet region are green, and the moors and meadows trafficable. Rest is good for the body and soul and has refreshed us. The division command post and the 5th Artillery Regiment are in Halinowola, surrounded by meadows, forests, moors, and lakes. A land of charm, suitable for horseback riding. On 1 May there will be a hunt, in which 60 riders in the division will participate and the 5th Artillery Regiment Bugle Corps will lead the way.

On another day, the division staff played a merry game of handball: the "command detachment" against the "quartermaster detachment" in the meadow by the town. The game was played so seriously that finally smoke grenades were thrown onto the field and the meadow was covered in a thick white cloud of smoke, in which the players appeared like shadows and searched for the ball in vain." (From: Reinicke, A: *The 5th Infantry Division. 1939-1945*. Reprint, Friedberg 1983.)

• • •

At the beginning of May, the 8th Army (General of Infantry Woehler), which was in defensive positions on both sides of the Jassy, suddenly was pulled into the attack maelstrom of the Soviet Army Groups "2nd" and "3rd Ukrainian Fronts." The superior enemy forces, supported by numerous fighter-bomber and tactical air formations, attacked out of the great bridgehead west of the Dnepr to the Jassy to encircle the German army, which was still in front of the Pruth.

On 15 May, the 8th Army was deployed from left to right, with the following units:

VI Rumanian Corps, with the 101st Rumanian Mountain Division, 7th Rumanian ID, 120th Rumanian Mountain Division, Rumanian Rifle Brigade;
IV Rumanian Corps, with the 18th Rumanian ID, 3rd Rumanian ID;
IV Army Corps (General of Infantry Mieth), with the 79th ID, 11th Rumanian ID, 376th ID;
VII Army Corps (General of Artillery Hell), with the 370th ID, 106th ID, 14th Rumanian ID.

In the rear area, the army had the 198th ID and the 13th Rumanian ID at its disposal.

The 8th Army conducted the defensive battle so that the Soviet troops could not penetrate their positions on any sector and achieve a breakthrough.

The area north of the Jassy was the greatest challenge. The territory won here temporarily by the enemy was cleared and recaptured by the sensible commitment of the reserves – which were received from the army group commander.

Therefore, the "2nd Ukrainian Front" gave up further attack attempts at the end of May.

However, in the meantime the 8th Army commander had worked out a plan that included an offensive operation north of the Jassy with limited objectives.

The attack of units of the 8th Army began completely unexpectedly after a short fire preparation on 30 May. The Wehrmacht's only major offensive operation on the Eastern Front in 1944 thus began. Strong air formations of the Luftwaffe were also gathered and attacked in the early morning hours of the beginning battle, so that for several days they achieved air superiority!

An OKW report on 31 May described this operation:

"In the east, infantry and panzer formations, supported by German and Rumanian tactical and fighter bomber formations, broke through strongly fortified and deeply echeloned defensive positions north of Jassy and threw the Soviets back to the river in fierce combat. The territory won was held against strong Bolshevik counterattacks. Fighters and fighter-bombers destroyed 69 enemy aircraft over this area."

The Soviet formations recovered from their initial surprise and strengthened their resistance. However, the German attack advanced again on the second day of the battle. On this day alone, the Soviets lost 37 tanks, including their newest models, to the 8.8 cm air defense guns and the assault guns. Fighters and fighter-bombers shot up 87 enemy aircraft.

On the third day of the battle, the Russian leadership threw new formations into the battle that were transported from sectors of the front not involved in the attack. Therefore, the 8th Army attack ground to a halt on 2 June. The same combat groups had to withdraw from the superior enemy. However, the army regained its composure during the evening and continued the attack on the next day. Another 23 enemy tanks were destroyed and the excellent high ground northwest of Jassy was regained.

This success was expanded on the next day, as they succeeded in storming the last Russian position on the high ground. The Russians lost another 25 combat vehicles and 33 aircraft. While fighting Russian combat vehicles, Major Rudel from the "Immelmann" Fighter-bomber Squadron distinguished himself, as he destroyed several "T-34's" and assault guns in deep attack.

On 6 June, the 8th Army suspended further offensive operations, since they completely occupied the high ground northwest of Jassy and, therefore, achieved their attack objective. In this manner, the army considerably improved its defensive position.

The next day, mopping up operations were conducted – then the front here quieted down.

During this battle, the 4th Rumanian Army was subordinated to General of Infantry Woehler. On the German side, the XVII, LVII, and von Knoblesdorf Corps participated in the army battle. The divisions that participated were: the 46th ID, 24th Panzer Division, "Grossdeutschland" Armored Infantry Division, and the "Totenkopf" SS Division.

The next weeks were more peaceful. The troops between the Pripet Swamp and the Black Sea had time to erect defensive positions, rear area defensive lines, shelters, and even to construct front recreation centers.

The Wehrmacht reports did not mention the Eastern Front during these days. The Allied invasion in northern France and the combat in Italy were the centerpieces in military events. Typical of the OKW's reports was that of 14 and 15 June:

> "On the Eastern Front, there were no special combat operations to report!"

The two army groups deployed in the south of the Eastern Front again reorganized, regrouped, and reformed their combat forces. The composition of the two major formations reflected:

	South Ukraine	North Ukraine
Corps	11	8
Infantry Divisions	27	20
Rifle Divisions	2	1
Panzer Divisions	5	6
Armored Infantry Divisions	2	1
Mountain Divisions	2	0
SS Divisions	1	3
Parachute Divisions	1	0
Security Divisions	1	1
Foreign Divisions	12 Rumanian	10 Hun

On 10 June 1944, the high command positions were filled as follows (1st name = commander, 2nd name = chief of staff, 3rd name = general staff officer):

Army Group South

Army Group South Ukraine:
- General Schoerner
- Lieutenant General Wenk
- Colonel von Trotha

6th Army:
- General of Artillery Angelis
- Major General Voelter
- Lieutenant Colonel Eisenmann

8th Army:
- General of Infantry Woehler
- Major General Reinhardt
- Colonel Estor

17th Army:
- General of Infantry Allmendinger
- Major General von Xylander
- Colonel Baron von Weitershausen

Army Group North Ukraine:
- Field Marshal Model
- Lieutenant General Busse
- Lieutenant Colonel Willemer

1st Panzer Army:
- General of Panzer Troops Raus
- Colonel Wagener
- Lieutenant Colonel von Graevenitz

4th Panzer Army:
- General Harpe
- Lieutenant General Fangohr
- Colonel Mueller

On 22 June – exactly three years since the beginning of the campaign against the Soviet Union – the Russians began a major offensive against the four armies of Army Group Center. The front of the neighboring army group collapsed within a few days. Hitler relieved its commander on 28 June and named Field Marshal Model as the new commander. At the same time, however, he retained command of Army Group North Ukraine.

Field Marshal Model, with his own rigorous and non-doctrinal conduct of warfare, threw all available forces into the front to prevent a major debacle. Finally, at the end of June he was able to establish a new defensive front behind the Niman.

To stabilize this main line of resistance, he borrowed from the two southern army groups, and, little by little, the XL Panzer Corps and XLIX Mountain Corps, as well as the 3rd, 14th, and 23rd Panzer Divisions, 97th Rifle Division, 304th ID, and "Grossdeutschland" Armored Infantry Division were transferred here and deployed as "corset rods" in the new front of Army Group Center.

On 29 June, in view of the catastrophic situation of Army Group Center, Field Marshal Model relinquished command of Army Group North Ukraine and recommended General Harpe as his successor. General of Panzer troops Balck became the new commander of the 4th Panzer Army.

During these weeks, Army Group North Ukraine discovered a large deployment of the "Red Army" to its front and, from 10 July, established, through air reconnaissance and ground radio reconnaissance, the deployment of strong tank forces in the areas of Tarnopol, Luzk, and Kovel.

On the morning of 13 July, the Soviet Army Group "1st Ukrainian Front" (Marshal Konev) attacked into the seam between the German 1st and 4th Panzer Armies. The superiority of the enemy forces is documented in the number of large formations committed. These were the 1st, 3rd, and 4th Guards Tank Armies; the 1st, 3rd and 5th Guards Armies; and the 13th, 18th, 38th, and 60th Armies – which, with the addition of two cavalry corps and with the support of two air armies, carried the battle forward and later opened up the Carpathians. The superior forces, naturally, could not be restrained by the divisions of the two German army groups that were located on the seam – the 340th ID (Major General Beutlet, who later fell), 361st ID (Major General Lindemann, who was taken prisoner by the Rus-

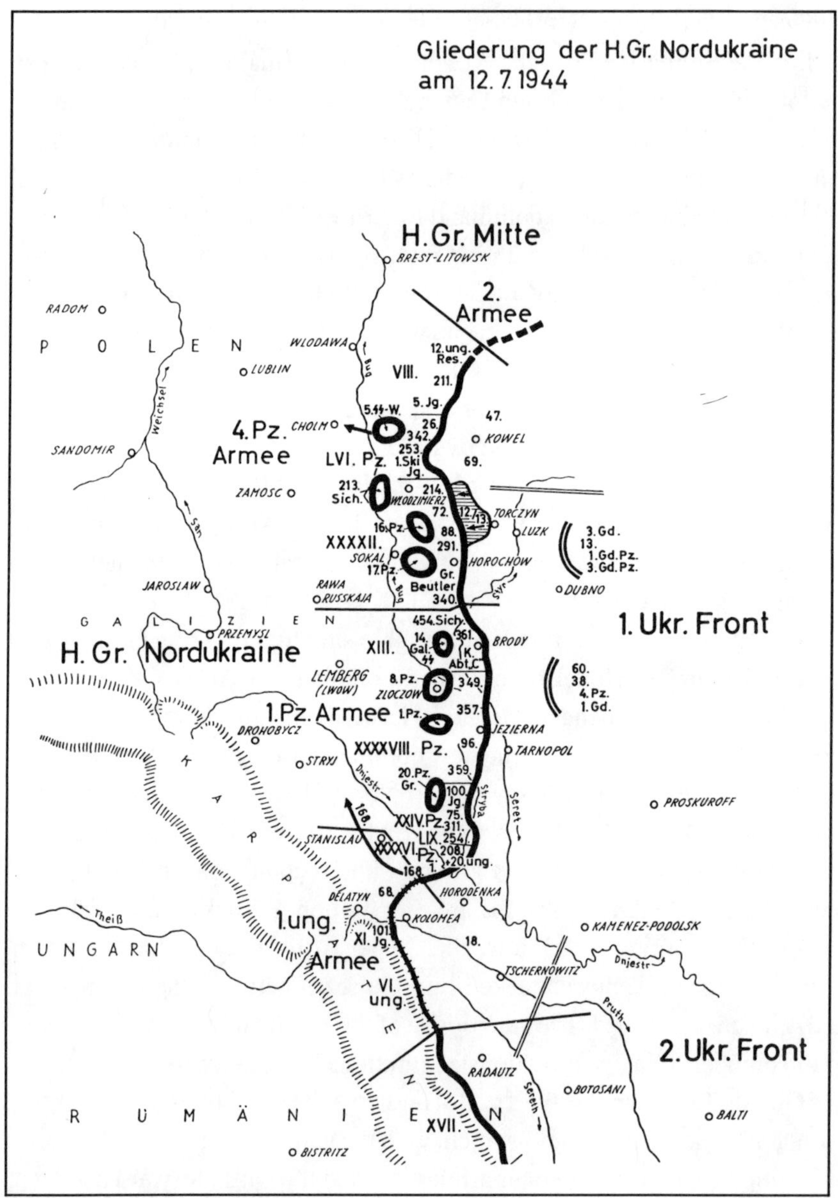

Organization of Army Group North Ukraine on 7/12/1944

sians), and 454th Security Division (Major General Nedtwig, who likewise was captured). The front collapsed on the first day.

The Russian tanks immediately attacked through the gaps toward the west. They succeeded in encircling the XIII Army Corps (General of Infantry Hauffe, who fell a few days later) around Brody with three divisions. In the Brody pocket fought and died combat groups of the 183rd ID (Lieutenant General Lange) – the 183rd ID had combined with units of the 217th and 339th ID's in the winter of 1943-44 to form Corps Group C – 349th ID (Lieutenant General Lasch), 361st ID (Major General Lindemann), 454th Security Division (Major General Nedtwig), and the 14th SS Division (SS Brigadefuehrer Freitag).

The Brody pocket battle ended on 18 July after between 25,000 and 30,000 German soldiers had fallen or been captured. The rest had fought their way through.

• • •

During the afternoon hours of 7/19, the Corps Detachment C issued the order for the attack on 7/20 from the command post to the adjutants of the regiments. The 183rd Rifle Division received the order to advance out of the Bialy Kamien area west of the rollbahn to Poczapy against the Zloczowka sector and, after capturing Belzec and Poczapy, occupy the hills south of there and hold them. The 217th Rifle Division would also advance out of the Czeremosnia area, cross through Hills 366 and Zulice – heavily echeloned to the left – to reach Chilczyce. Corps Detachment C also had at its disposal the 361st Fusilier Battalion deployed on the right of the 183 Rifle Division and the 217th Fusilier Battalion covering the left flank of the 217th Rifle Division.

The 249th Assault Gun Brigade, with a panzer platoon, on which the 1/219 Engineers were mounted, was tasked with crossing the Bug and capturing the high ground south of the river and advancing on both sides of the river to Poczapy to quickly seize the Zloczowka crossing intact and block the Zloczow, Busk road. This armored group was to assemble and prepare in Bialy Kamien.

The operation was very important to the leadership, therefore, the Operations Officer of the OKH published a statement on 7/19. He explained that the situation in the Army Group North Ukraine area of operations was critical. The withdrawal to the Lemberg defensive positions was approved. One hoped that the XIII Army Corps, which was encircled, would be able to fight its way out.

However, one had to believe that, with three Russian tank armies, they would not be able to break out so quickly.

The beginning of the attack on 20 July was set at 0330 hours by the XIII Army Corps. The numerous problems, which under such difficult conditions as were faced here, inevitably occurred, but cannot be described here in detail. Congestion and chaos is typical in a pocket battle. A critical review had recommended that in such cases vehicles not ready for combat should be destroyed away from the streets and roads and that the horses should be put to death, because they would be lost anyway. This is theoretically correct. In practice, it normally is otherwise, as was the situation of 7/22, where just a small fraction of the vehicles made it through the pocket to Zloczow. One also thought of the continuation of the combat after the breakout.

An indication of the problems was the postponement of the beginning of the attack at 0500 hours. The 183rd Rifle Division, with the 351st Rifle Regiment on the right and the 330th Rifle Regiment on the left, had soon overcome limited enemy resistance and reached the northwestern edge of Belzec at 0725 hours.

The 217th Rifle Regiment, on the other hand, ran into strong resistance near Hill 366, where numerous Russian self-propelled anti-tank guns temporarily brought the attack to a standstill. The Russians also committed tanks here. We were able to capture, intact, 5 American self-propelled vehicles. Three were immediately manned by crews whose own heavy anti-tank guns had been destroyed. They shot up three Russian tanks and destroyed two heavy anti-tank guns. 34 prisoners were taken during the battle for Hill 366. However, the rest of the enemy units established a tenacious resistance by 0900 hours. The armored group (249th Assault Gun Brigade and the panzer platoon) was delayed from leaving its assembly area because of strong Russian anti-tank defenses near Hill 366. The attack on

Poczapy had, in the meantime, become a priority, since the 351st Rifle Regiment had already advanced through Belzec to the southeast and ran into strong resistance in the Poczapy direction. (From: Lange, W.: *Corps Detachment C.* (183rd, 217th, 339th IDs) Neckargemuend 1961.)

• • •

In the meantime, Russian Army Group "1st Belorussian Front", which had deployed in front of the seam between Army Groups North Ukraine and Center, broke through the northern flank of the 4th Panzer Army on 18 July. Therefore, the German army group began to retreat to the Bug.

The collapse of the VIII German Army Corps (General of Infantry Hoehne) followed in a few days, after which contact with the left neighboring army – the 2nd Army of Army Group Center – was quickly lost. On 24 July, the 2nd Soviet Tank Army and the 8th Guards Army were able to occupy the Polish city of Lublin.

At the same time, the right flank of the 1st German Panzer Army broke, as Soviet forces tore up the 1st Hungarian Army (General Beregffy) on 23 July and the Hungarian divisions were thrown back into the Carpathian Mountains. At this time, the 68th ID, 101st Rifle Division, and 19th SS Division were subordinate to the Hungarian commander.

The 1st Panzer Army withdrew north of the Carpathians to the Dnestr near Stryj and had to give up Lemberg.

• • •

A Russian tank attack near Horodiszcze was repulsed in the course of a few days. The motorized elements of the division's supply troops counterattacked on 7/23 against lead Russian tank elements advancing in the direction of Siedlce and, in this manner, lost several vehicles. The division's supply troops had lost many officers and men in combat with Polish bands.

On 7/24, the regiment withdrew through Romaszki, Kolombrody, and Kozly to Witoroz (command post), and here occupied a line between Kozly and Korczowka to be able to take countermeasures to the right and the left. The hard-pressing Russian tanks were able to break through the regiment's

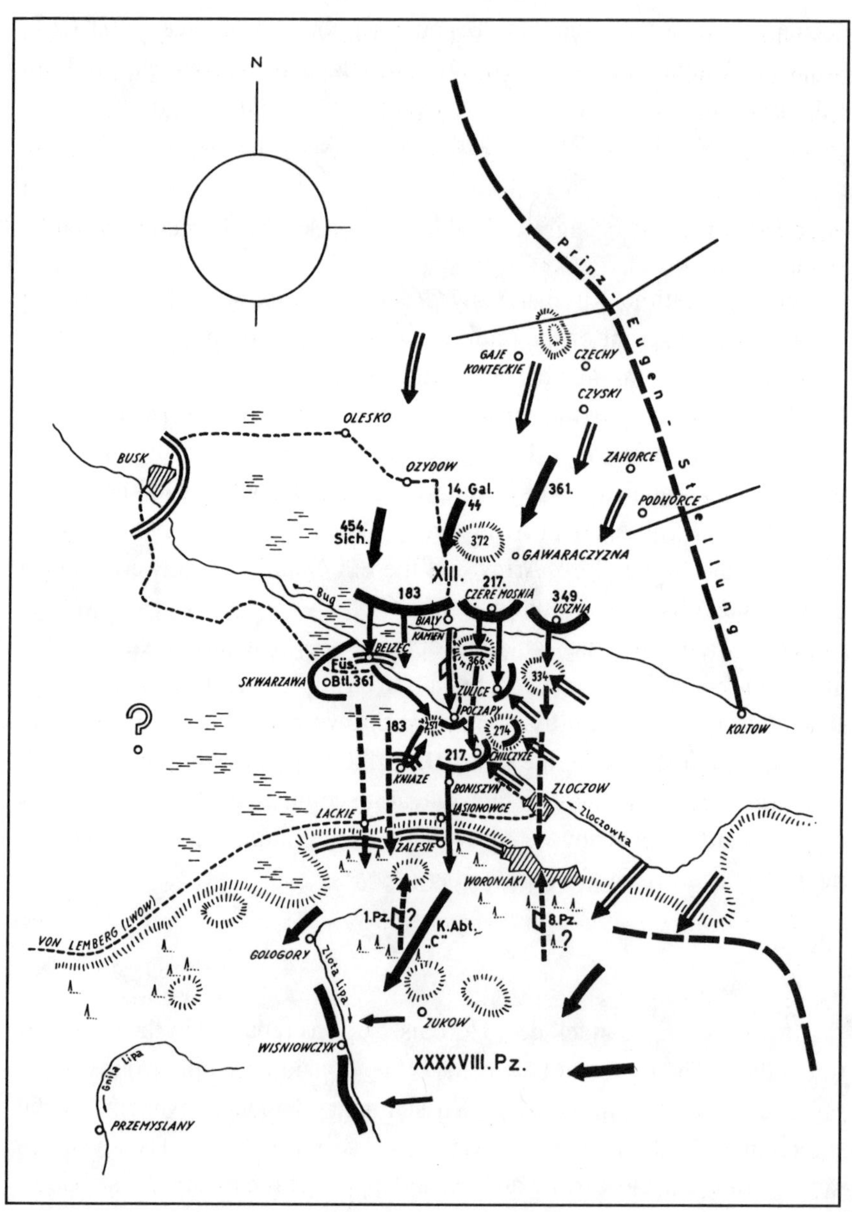
N
Prinz - Eugen - Stellung
GAJE KONTECKIE
CZECHY
CZYSKI
OLESKO
BUSK
OZYDOW
14. Gal.
44
361.
ZAHORCE
PODHORCE
454.
Sich.
372
GAWARACZYZNA
XIII.
Bug
183
217.
CZERE MOSNIA
349.
USZNIA
BIALY KAMIEN
BELZEC
Füs.
Btl. 361
SKWARZAWA
366
334
ZULICE
POCZAPY
KOLTOW
183
274
217.
CHILCZYZE
KNIAZE
BONISZYN
ZLOCZOW
Zloczowka
JASIONOWCE
LACKIE
ZALESIE
WORONIAKI
VON LEMBERG (LWOW)
1.Pz.
K.Abt.
"C"
8.Pz.
GOLOGORY
Zlota Lipa
ZUKOW
WISNIOWCZYK
XXXXVIII. Pz.
Gnila Lipa
PRZEMYSLANY

provisional main line of resistance, by-passing several companies and battering them with concentrated fires, so that their strength had noticeably decreased by the evening. The 14th Company (Lieutenant Schwermann), who was able to save his 7.5 cm anti-tank gun at the last moment before the attack and shot up a tank, joined in the search for fuel, but only found wounded, which he brought to Miedzyrzec under the protection of tanks on the Brest-Litovsk-Warsaw rollbahn.

Although they were able to catch some sleep during the evening and night, in the afternoon of the next day (7/25) the regiment found itself in a hopeless situation, as the 12th Hungarian Division fled its positions, carrying off our lines with them. The planned turning of the left flank was no longer possible. The appearance of the enemy with three tanks in Witoroz made a counterattack necessary, during which the adjutant of the wheeled regiment, Captain Dr. Bernhard, was wounded. In him was also lost an officer with years of experience in the 317th Regiment, who from the first days in the west had gained wide trust on the basis of his abilities and knowledge, as well as his technical and conciliatory deportment.

In the Sokule area, where units were assembling on the order of Lieutenant General Eckhardt, a shell from an artillery attack hit directly next to the jeep of the regiment commander. While Colonel Flinzer and Senior Lieutenant Rose were only slightly injured, the driver, Bachem, and Senior Lieutenant Scheffe, holder of the German Gold Cross and one of the most popular officers in the regiment, were killed.

We exerted ourselves on this same day (7/25) to reach a main line of resistance near Sycyna and Styryniec, south of the Miedzyrzec-Biala Podlaska rollbahn. Between the left flank of the 317th Regiment (command post in the forest northwest of Sycyna) and the right of the 306th Regiment, the 211th Field Replacement Battalion and the cavalry squadron was inserted. The Russians attacked this line fruitlessly for the next few days and engaged the defenders in heavy combat, during which the commander of the cavalry squadron, Captain Berckemeyer, and holder of the Knight's Cross, Staff Sergeant Schneider from the 211th Field Replacement Battalion, fell.

The fact that the 211th ID held these positions near Biala Podlaska for three days against all attacks was, at the time, a double-edged sword. Strong

Russian forces were tied up at these positions. However, because the right neighboring division also was strongly being punished and, together with the 211th ID – detached from Army Group South by the Soviet tank wedge penetrating through Siedlce – a Russian shock army had already reached the sector on the left between Drogiczyn and Janow and began to encircle Brest-Litovsk. They were also making headway along the flanks of our division, bypassing them unhindered and encircling them. Although, on 7/28 the 211th Division quickly crossed the Swory and Makarowka into the area between Lake Huszlew and Kobylany, and occupied the Mszanna line and the gaps in the forest north of here on 7/30, they were, during the evening, still encircled on three sides by an enemy pincer movement into the rear area in the vicinity of Lysow-Losice. (From: Grube, R.: *Memoirs of Operations*. (211th ID) Bielefeld 1961.)

• • •

The "Red Army" extended their successes into Galicia. Now the "4th Ukrainian Front" joined in the great offensive. These new and fresh tank forces drove the 1st Panzer Army and 1st Hungarian Army back to the Beskiden. Meanwhile, the neighboring "1st Ukrainian Front" marched to the San and crossed the river.

General Harpe fetched the freed up 17th Army (General of Infantry Allmendinger) from the Crimea and committed it in this sector as an operations staff. As its forces arrived, they were immediately sent to protect Krakow and prevent the collapse of the two German panzer armies.

In the meantime, the "1st Ukrainian Front" had regrouped and was marching on Kielce with three armies. They had shortly before withdrawn behind the Weichsel and with little trouble encircled the opposing 4th Panzer Army near and west of Sandomir, which prevented the collapse of the entire German Weichsel front. Therefore, at the last moment, they averted the danger to Krakow and the Upper Silesian industrial area.

Shortly thereafter, the army group committed the 1st Panzer Army – General Heinrici took command of this unit on 16 August – to attack the Baranow Bridgehead. The "1st Ukrainian Front" was established here and

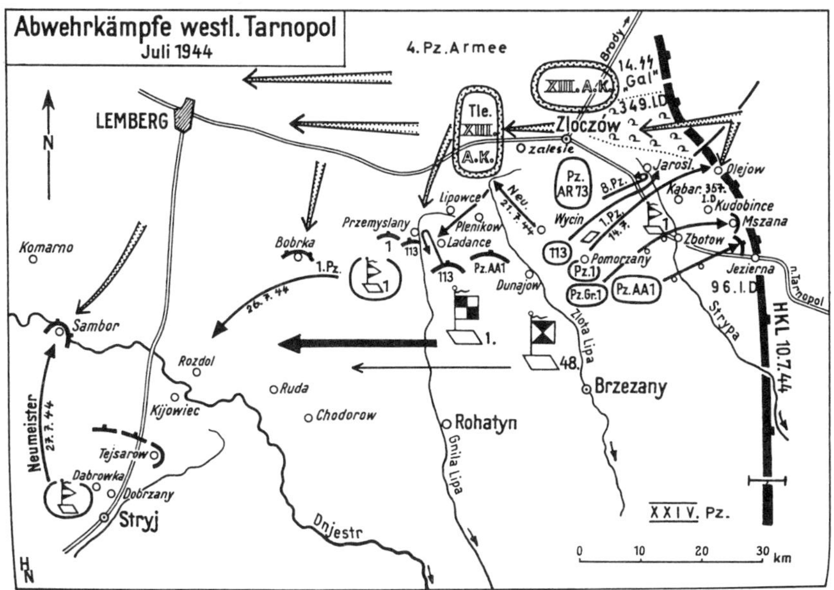

Defensive battles west of Tarnopol July 1944

although it gave up the area, the Weichsel Bridgehead remained, with a length of 50 kilometers and a depth of 30 kilometers.

• • •

The withdrawal to the Bug line was conducted slowly, with local counterattacks, which painted a picture of the enemy situation during the withdrawal. Numerous tanks were shot up, so that the enemy's tank force had considerably diminished. However, as we crossed the Bug near Sokal, it became clear how dangerous the situation really was. On both flanks of the division, enemy lead attack elements were already overtaking us. The division's withdrawal was lagging behind and it was threatened with being cut off. Communications with the corps had been broken; the division had to operate independently. They stuck together closely in all crises and, on many occasions, they [the division] extracted themselves from tight situations, not by defense, but by surprising offensive operations.

Thus, infantrymen of the 505th Rifle regiment, under the leadership of Knight's Cross recipient Major Andree, who was severely wounded several weeks later and died of his wounds, destroyed the guns of an enemy anti-tank battalion by a surprise attack while they were moving on the left flank of the division, or set upon a cavalry division, which was advancing through the woods, and threw it into utter confusion.

On 20 July, the fate of the division hung on a thin thread. The route to the west had shifted. The important breakthrough foundered on the first attempt under heavy enemy defensive fire. Colonel Finger decided to suspend the breakout attempt and, without firm knowledge of the situation, but with good weather, put all of his eggs in one basket, and led his entire division through a thick forest to the northwest to cross over the Wieprz near Szczebrzeszyn, where he assumed the last opportunity for withdrawal would lie. The withdrawal from the sack succeeded completely, and without a fight. We made contact with other troops and reestablished contact with the corps. After the division secured itself south of the Weichsel Bridge near Zawichost in an unpleasant day-long battle to the right of the Weichsel, they crossed the Weichsel at the end of July.

The hope that, on the Weichsel and San a new front could be established and the division would be committed there, was deceiving. The enemy crossed the San and established a bridgehead near Baranow on the Weichsel south of the division sector, which they were able to expand, with the strength of two tank corps. After committing the reserves, the 4th Panzer Army succeeded, during August, in reducing the Baranow Bridgehead and constructing a solid front against the Russian forces that were still there. The German attack resulted in heavy losses of equipment on both sides. At this time, the 291st ID was deployed on the Weichsel Hills near Zawichost, facing the east. At the beginning of August, a bloody battle developed here over a small enemy bridgehead that could not be removed, because all of the attacks of the infantry and engineers broke down under concentrated mortar and artillery fire.

On the other hand, the enemy could not storm the Weichsel Hills, although they continued to commit fresh Russian infantry, including a penal battalion, and were supported by fire from the rear when they withdrew. Enemy losses were unbelievably high. While this battle took place up front, a second "front" developed near the supply trains and division staff, as several enemy tanks with bazookas were disposed of. In the rear area, while the real "front" gradually quieted, a gripping battle occurred, during which otherwise inexperienced fighters blew tanks into the air and mastered commitment during heavy artillery and rocket launcher attacks. At the end of August, the infantry combat and the fire of the heavy weapons diminished. Both sides were exhausted. The Baranow Bridgehead could not be removed. (From: Conze, W.: *The History of the 291st Infantry Division*, Bad Nauheim 1953.)

• • •

Then the Russian and German soldiers dug in to defend on the Weichsel.

Army Group North Ukraine (General Harpe) stabilized its front along the Weichsel – 150 kilometers in front of the Reich's border – with the battle for the Baranow bridgehead. The "Red Army" suspended any further advance here.

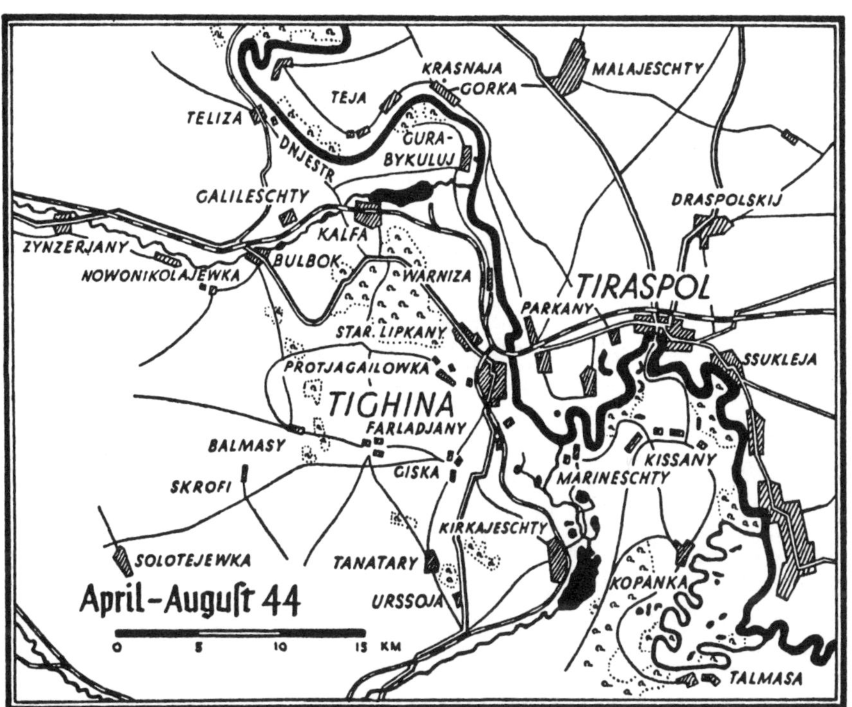

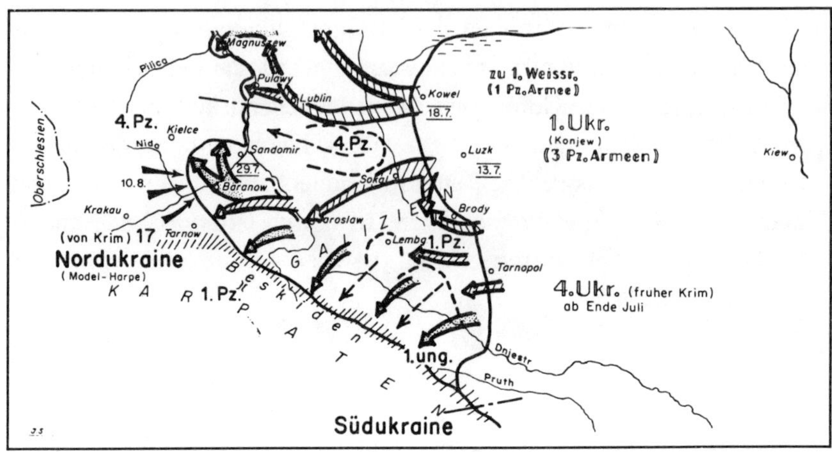

On the other hand, Army Group South Ukraine – led by General Friessner since 24 July 1944 – was pulled into the maelstrom of the collapse. Both Russian Army Groups "2nd" and "3rd Ukrainian Fronts", of Army Generals Malinovski and Tolbukhin, attacked on 20 August with eleven infantry and tank armies, under the protection of two air armies, in the area northwest of Jassy and out of the Tiraspol Bridgehead against the 3rd and 4th Rumanian Armies.

The objective of both army groups was the encirclement of the 6th German Army – which was taken over by General of Artillery Fretter-Pico on 18 July – around Kishinev, between the Dnestr in the east and the Pruth in the west.

The "3rd Ukrainian Front", attacking on the left, threw the 3rd Rumanian Army back to Bessarabia and penetrated with their right flank to the southwest from Kishinev to the Pruth. From the north, the tank troops of the "2nd Ukrainian Front" advanced, which had thrown back the 4th Rumanian Army and units of the 8th German Army.

On 24 August 1944, the lead attack elements of the two Russian formations met and, therefore, the 6th Army – for the second time after Stalingrad – was encircled. Units from the 6th and 8th Armies encircled in the pocket on the Pruth were the IV, VII, XXX, XLIV, and LII Army Corps.

This included the remnants of the 9th, 15th, 62nd, 76th, 79th, 106th, 161st, 257th, 258th, 282nd, 294th, 302nd, 306th, 320th, 335th, 370th, 376th, and 384th IDs, the bulk of the 153rd Field Construction Division, and units of the 10th Armored Infantry Division and the 13th Panzer Division.

The strength of the German soldiers soon diminished under the punishing enemy artillery fire, under the extended deep attacks by Russian fighter-bombers, and under the continuous tank attacks. In some places the smallest combat groups of the splintered divisions defended until the last cartridge, while others surrendered to the enemy completely exhausted, starving, and bloodied.

Major Eckert, who commanded the last combat-capable unit after the beginning of the withdrawal, described the destruction of the 62nd ID as follows:

> "... The control of the army, corps, and division completely broke down. I was ordered by the division to march in the direction of Pruth, cross the Lopuszna to Leuzeni. Since I had to reach Loganesti, I had to come into contact with the Russians. I immediately reported to the division that the Russians had occupied Loganesti.
>
> I had to push the Russians out of this town. I learned from prisoners that the Russians had already captured and occupied Leuzeni and Lopuszna, and with strong tank forces. The division now transferred the command post to me. The order was issued on 8/23/1944 to destroy all documents. At the same time, Major Scheid, commander of the 162nd Artillery Battalion, became the commander of the 179th Regiment, for the time being, because Major von Pritzbuer fell ill and was in a field hospital. The mission included the task of advancing through Lopuszna to Leuzeni with this regiment and the Field Replacement Battalion, as well as the 162nd-Artillery Battalion, and to reach the Pruth. The attack began at 1900 hours. The attack of Major Scheid broke down, and the individual troop units wandered off. At 2400 hours I was ordered by the division to capture Lopuszna in the early morning with the remnants of the Field Replacement Battalion, the division combat school, and the retreating units of Major Scheid, and then attack further to the Pruth.

I succeeded in breaking into the eastern section of Lopuszna three times, but each time the Russian tanks threw me out, destroying my three T-34's by direct hits. My heavy mortar company, equipped with the Russian 8.2 cm, was completely suppressed by anti-tank gun fire. The 162nd Artillery regiment, which did a good job of supporting my attack, was battered by air, artillery, and anti-tank fire. After a murderous 4-5 hour battle we were completely exhausted, and only a few of us reached a large cornfield. This is where I was wounded. Major Scheid, who reported to me during the battle, fell right next to me. At dark, I went with about 60-70 members of the division, from all branches of arms, to a cornfield across the hills. Here I found General Tronnier, with Major von Uechtritz, and about 400-500 members of the division. We assembled all of the stragglers and we agreed to attempt to break through the Russian positions during the night and reach the Pruth." (From: *The 62nd Infantry Division 1938-1944*. Fulda 1968.)

• • •

In a report, the Wehrmacht High Command acknowledged the commitment of the XXX Army Corps (Lieutenant General Postel), with the 15th ID, 306th ID, and 13th Panzer Division, as well as the 661st Army Panzer Detachment (Captain Mergen), who alone shot up 52 Russian tanks in four days. From the ring of the besieger, only units of the 10th Armored Infantry Division (Major General Herold), the 76th ID (Colonel Bruecker), and the 13th Panzer Division (Lieutenant General Troeger) were able to break out and make contact with friendly troops.

The battle for the Kishinev pocket ended at the end of August 1944.

Formations of the "Red Army" had already occupied Bucharest and the entire Rumanian oil region.

While in the south of the Eastern Front, the German and allied armies were being battered by a superior enemy and were fighting for their existence four weeks later, the situation in the area of Army group North Ukraine was "quiet."

Only the Baranow Bridgehead on the west bank of the Weichsel was a thorn in the side of the front. From here, in January 1945, the Soviets let loose their great offensive, which would finally lead the Soviet formations to Berlin.

However, it would still be another eight months before this would happen!

APPENDICES

Appendix 1
THE COMMANDERS OF THE ARMY GROUPS AND ARMIES IN THE SOUTH OF THE FRONT 1941-1944

1941 - 1944

a) Heeresgruppen

Süd	Feldmarschall von Rundstedt
	Feldmarschall von Reichenau (ab 4. 12. 1941)
	Feldmarschall von Bock (ab 18. 1. 1942)
A (ab 7. 7. 1942)	Feldmarschall List
	Adolf Hitler (ab 11. 9. 1942)
	Feldmarschall von Kleist (ab 23. 11.1942)
B (ab 7. 7. 1942)	Feldmarschall Freiherr von Weichs
Don (ab 22. 11. 1942)	Feldmarschall von Manstein
Süd [neu] (ab 14. 2. 1943)	Feldmarschall von Manstein
Südukraine (ab 30. 3. 1944)	Generaloberst Schörner
	Generaloberst Friessner (ab 24. 7. 1944)
Nordukraine (ab 30. 3. 1944)	Generaloberst Model
	Generaloberst Harpe (ab 29. 6. 1944)
Süd [neu] (ab 20. 9. 1944)	Generaloberst Friessner
	Generaloberst Wöhler (ab 24. 12. 1944)
A [neu] (ab 20. 9. 1944)	Generaloberst Harpe

b) Armeen

2.	Generaloberst Freiherr von Weichs
	Generaloberst von Salmuth (ab 15. 7. 1942)
	Generaloberst Weiss (ab 3. 2. 1944)
6.	Feldmarschall von Reichenau
	Feldmarschall Paulus (ab 30. 12. 1941)
6. [neu]	Generaloberst Hollidt (ab 5. 3. 1944)
	General d. Artillerie de Angelis (ab 9. 4. 1944)
	General d. Artillerie Fretter-Pico (ab 18. 7. 1944)
	General d. Pz. Truppen Balck (ab 24. 12. 1944)
8. [neu]	General d. Infanterie Wöhler (ab 16. 8. 1943)
	General d. Geb. Truppen Kreysing (ab 29. 12. 1944)

11.	Generaloberst Ritter von Schobert
	Feldmarschall von Manstein (ab 18. 9. 1941)
	— November 1942 aufgelöst —
17.	General d. Infanterie von Stülpnagel
	Generaloberst Hoth (ab 6. 10. 1941)
	Generaloberst Ruoff (ab 1. 6. 1942)
	Generaloberst Jänecke (ab 26. 6. 1943)
	General d. Infanterie Allmendinger (ab 2. 5. 1944)
	General d. Infanterie Schulz (ab 27. 7. 1944)
1. Panzerarmee	Generaloberst von Kleist
	Generaloberst von Mackensen (ab 22. 11. 1942)
	Generaloberst Hube (ab 6. 11. 1943)
	Generaloberst Raus (ab 22. 4. 1944)
	Generaloberst Heinrici (ab 16. 8. 1944)
4. Panzerarmee	Generaloberst Hoth
	Generaloberst Raus (ab 16. 11. 1943)
	Generaloberst Harpe (ab 2. 5. 1944)
	General d. Pz. Truppen Balck (ab 29. 6. 1944)
	General d. Pz. Truppen Graeser (ab 21. 9. 1944)

Appendix 2
ORGANIZATION OF THE ARMY GROUPS 1941-1943

	Heeres-Gr.	Armee	Korps	Div.
OKH-Reserven zugeteilt bei H.Gr. Süd: H.Kdo. XXXIV. 68. 132. (Südosten Antrsp. 20.6.–4.7.) LI. 79. 95. (Hgr. D, Antrsp. 27.6.–3.7.) 13. noch nicht verfügt: a) bis 4.7. im WK VIII eingetroff.: XXXX.mot. (Antrsp. ab 26.6.) 60. mot. (Antrsp. ab 22.6.) b) nach 4.7. in d. Zufhrg.: 46. H.Kdo. LXV 93., 96., 98., 260., 94. } Hgr. D 183. AOK 2 73. H.Kdo. LXV 5. Pz. WK III 294. H.Kdo. LXV. Zuf. u. U. vor dem 4.7. 2. Pz. WK III c) z.V. OKH i.d.Heimat: 707. WK VII 713. WK XIII	Süd 99. lei.	11. Gen. Kdo. rum. Kav. Korps	LIV.	50. 170.
			XXX.	198. 8. rum. I. D. 14. rum. I. D. 6. rum. Kav. Brig.
			XI.	76. 239. 22. 6. rum. I. D. 5. rum. Kav. Brig. rum. mot. mech. Brig. 8. rum. Kav. Brig.
			rum. Geb. Korps	1. rum. Geb. Brig. 4. rum. Geb. Brig. 2. rum. Geb. Brig. 7. rum. I. D.
			Heeresmission Rumänien	72.
		17. 125. slow. mot. Verb.	Bef.R.H.G. 103	454. Sich. 444. Sich.
			LII.	101. lei.
			XXXXIX. Geb.	257. 1. Geb. 4. Geb. 100. lei.
			IV.	71. 295. 24. 296. 97. lei.
		6. 168. 213. Sich.	XXXXIV.	9. 297. 262. 57.
			XVII.	62. 56. 298.
			LV.	75. 111.
			XXIX.	44. 289.
		Pz. Gr. 1	XXXXVIII. mot.	16. mot. 16. Pz. 11. Pz.
			III. mot.	13. Pz. 25. mot. 14. Pz.
			XIV. mot.	9. Pz. SS „A.H." SS „W"

II. Gliederung am 24. Juni 1942

<table>
<tr><th></th><th>Heeres-Gr.</th><th>Armee</th><th>Korps</th><th>Div.</th></tr>
<tr><td rowspan="11">**z. V. OKH.**
in Zuführung nach dem Osten:
371.
ital. AOK 8 mit ital. II. A. K.
ital. „Ravenna"
ital. „Sforzesca"
ital. „Cosseria"</td><td rowspan="11">Süd
323.
340.
ung. IV.
10. ung. le.
12. ung. le.
13. ung. le.
ung. Pz. Div.
LVII. mot.
V.</td><td rowspan="4">**11.**
Befh. d. Landengen</td><td>LIV.
1/3 46.
im Antransp.</td><td>1/3 132. + 1/3 46.
24.
22. + 1/3 73.
50. + 1/3 46.
4. rum. Geb.</td></tr>
<tr><td>rum. Geb. Korps</td><td>18. rum.
1. rum. Geb.</td></tr>
<tr><td>XXX.</td><td>72.
170.
28. le. + 1 Rgt. 213.
Sich. + 1 Rgt. 444. Sich.
1/3 125.
Stb. Schröder m. 1 Rgt. 444. Sich.</td></tr>
<tr><td>Gr. Mattenklott (XXXXII.)</td><td>Gr. Ritter (Küstensch.)
8. rum. Kav.
10. rum.
19. rum.
rum. schn. Rgt.
Tle. 22. Pz.
2/3 132.</td></tr>
<tr><td rowspan="2">Gruppe v. Wietersheim (XIV. mot.)</td><td>Gr. v. Förster
rum. Kav. Korps</td><td>6. rum. Kav.
5. rum. Kav.
Sich. Rgt. 4
298.</td></tr>
<tr><td>XIV. mot.</td><td>SS „A. H."
2/3 73.
13. Pz.
2/3 125.
SS „Wiking"
slow. Schn. Div.</td></tr>
<tr><td rowspan="4">**17.**</td><td>XXXXIX. Geb.</td><td>4. Geb.
198.</td></tr>
<tr><td>ital. Schn. Korps</td><td>ital. Celere + Bers. Rgt. 6
ital. Torino
ital. Pasubio</td></tr>
<tr><td>LII.</td><td>111.</td></tr>
<tr><td>IV.
1/3 9. i. Ablösung</td><td>94. 2/3 9.
76.
295.
370.</td></tr>
<tr><td>**1. Pz.**</td><td>XXXXIV.</td><td>257.
101. le.
97. le. + wall. Btl. 373
68.</td></tr>
</table>

	Heeres-Gr.	Armee	Korps	Div.
	noch: Süd	noch: 1. Pz.	Gr. Strecker (XI.) / VI. rum.	4. rum. 20. rum. 2. rum.
			Gr. Strecker (XI.)	1. Geb. 1. rum. 454. Sich.
			Gruppe von Mackensen (III. mot.) / III. mot.	14. Pz. 16. Pz. Masse 22. Pz. 60. mot.
			Gruppe von Mackensen (III. mot.) / LI.	384. 62. 44. 71. 297.
		6. 100. le. (+kroat. I.R. 369)	XVII.	294. 79. 113.
			VIII.	305. 389. 376.
			XXXX. mot.	336. 3. Pz. 23. Pz. 29. mot.
			XXIX.	75. 168. 57.
		2. 88. 383. / 2. ung.	III. ung.	7. ung. le. 9. ung. le. 16. mot.
		2. / 2. ung.	VII.	6. ung. le. 387.
		2. / 4. Pz.	XXIV. mot.	377. 9. Pz. 3. mot.
		2. / 4. Pz.	XIII.	82. $^{2}/_{3}$ 385. 11. Pz.
		2. / 4. Pz.	XXXXVIII. mot.	I. D. „Gr. D." 24. Pz.
		2.	LV.	95. 45. SS-Brig. 1 299.

III. Gliederung am 9. April 1943

	Heeres-Gr.	Armee	Korps	Div.
	A	**Bef. d. Krim** (XXXXII.) Abschnitts- Kdo. Auleb Slow.schn.D.	rum. Geb. Korps	1. rum. Geb. Ma. 4. rum. Geb. 2. rum. Geb.
				Ma. 153. F.A.Div.
		Bef. Straße Kertsch	Kdt. v. Kertsch	Tle. 4. rum. Geb. Tle. 5. Lw.-F.
			Kdt. von Taman	1/3 10. rum. Tle. 13. Pz. Tle. 5. Lw.-F.
		17. Ma. 13. Pz. +Tle. 4. Geb.	Gr. Wetzel (V.): Rum. Kav.- Korps	9. rum. K.D. Ma. 6. rum. K.D. +1/3 10. rum.
			Gr. Wetzel (V.)	Ma. 4. Geb. 125. + Tle. 101. Jg. + Tle. 10. rum. 73.+Tle. 6. rum. K.D.
			XXXXIV.	9. + 3. rum. Geb. 97. + Ma. 19. rum. Ma. 101. Jg. + Tle. 19. rum.+Tle. 5. Lw.-F.
			XXXXIX. Geb.	370. 50.
		Bef. H.G. A.		
	Süd **4. Pz.** 387. in Aufst. aus Resten 298., 385., 387. 198. Stab 403. Sich. 1/3 153. F.A.D. i. Abtr.	**6.** 79. 23. Pz. 17. i. Antr.	XXIV. Pz.	Stb. 444. Sich. 454. Sich. 111.
			XXIX.	16. Lw.-F. 16. mot. 336.
			XVII.	294. 306. 302.
			Korps Mieth	304. 3. Geb. 335.
		1. Pz. III. Pz. 19. Pz. 3. Pz. 46. 257. i. Antr.	XXX.	38. 62. 333.
			XXXX. Pz.	7. Pz. SS-„W."
			LVII. Pz.	15. 17. Pz.
		Armeeabt. Kempf SS-Pz. K. SS-„A.H." SS-„R." „G.D." 11. Pz. 168.	XXXXVIII. Pz.	106. 6. Pz. 39.
			Gen.Kdo. z.b.V. Raus	320. SS-„T." 167.
			LII.	332. 57. 255.
		Bef. H.G. Süd		Tle. 213. Sich.

Appendix 3
THE ARMIES WITH THEIR ALLOCATED TROOPS

Armee-Ober-kommando	Ersatz-Wehr-kreis	Höherer Artillerie Kommandeur	Armee-Karten-stelle	Armee-Nachr. Regiment	Kommandeur Armee-Nachschubtrup-pen
2.	IV.	308	540	563	550 u. 580
6.	IV.	306	560	549 u. 648	541
8.	VIII. u. X.	310	590	563	531
11.	V.	ohne Nr.	ohne Nr.	558	587
17.	XII.	304	517	596	591
1. Panzer	X.	311	492	Pz. 1	492
4. Panzer	III.	312	473	Pz. 4	473

Appendix 4
COMMANDERS OF THE REAR OF ARMY REGION 103
Combat Organization 1942

Die Dienststelle »Befehlshaber rückwärtiges Heeresgebiet 103« wurde am 3. 7. 1941 in »Befehlshaber rückwärtiges Heeresgebiet Süd«, am 15. 3. 1942 in »Kommandierender General der Sicherungstruppen und Befehlshaber im Heeresgebiet Süd« umbenannt.

Gliederung am 4. Juli 1942

Stab mit Korps-Kartenstelle (mot.) 532
Sicherungs-Division 213 (Raum Kalitwa-Rossosch-Charkow)
Sicherungs-Division 403 (Raum rückw. Gebiet Heeresgruppe B)
Sicherungs-Division 444 (Raum Mius und Krim)
105. ungarische leichte Division (Raum Ukraine)

Ferner unterstanden der Dienststelle — je nach Bedarf — eine Korps-Nachrichtenabteilung, ein bis drei Sicherungsbataillone, drei bis fünf Ost-Bataillone, mehrere Landesschützenbataillone, je eine Nachschub-, Werkstatt-, Bäckerei-, Schlächterei-, Veterinär-, Baukompanie, ferner je ein Verpflegungsamt, Feldgendarmerieabteilung, Feldpostamt und ein Kranken-Kraftwagenzug.

Appendix 5
INDEPENDENT BATTALIONS, DETACHMENTS AND COMPANIES, WHICH WERE ASSIGNED TO THE ARMY GROUP FOR A TIME
- Randomly Selected -

Heeres- und Armeetruppen an verschiedenen Frontabschnitten

Abschleppkompanie 541, Betriebsstoff-Abfüllkommando 966, Feldausbildungs-Bataillon 336, Feldstrafgefangenen-Abteilung 12, Sturmbataillon 395, Kraftfahr-Abteilung 562, Bewegliche Kfz-Instandsetzungskompanie 142, Radfahr-Sicherungsbataillon 755, Nachschub-Wach-Bataillon 43, Kraftwagen-Transport-Abteilung 566, Zentral-Ersatzteillager 109, Panzer-Zerstörerkompanie 481, Eisenbahn-Bau-Pionier-Bataillon 106, Pionier-Brücken-Bataillon 624, Entlausungsanstalt 58, Kaukasisch-mohammedanisches Legions-Bataillon 805 u. a. m.

Heeres- und Armeetruppen im Kampfraum Stalingrad (Januar 1943)

Schwere Artillerie-Abteilung 430, 616, 631, 733, 800, 849, 851, 855; Bau-Bataillon 16, 110, 540; Brücken-Bau-Bataillon 255, 522, 655; Brückenkolonne 48, 404, 657, 925; Heeres-Fla-Bataillon 602, 608, 614; Bewegliche Kfz-Instandsetzungskompanie 128, 175; kleine Kraftwagenkolonne 795, 829; Straßenbau-Bataillon 521, 540; Werfer-Regiment 2, 51, 53; Heeres-Panzerjäger-Abteilung 521, 611, 670; Sturmgeschütz-Abteilung 245; leichte Beobachtungs-Abteilung 40, 43; Feldkommandantur 249 u. a. m.

Heeres- und Armeetruppen im Donbogen (Januar 1943)

Alarm-Bataillon Charkow; Infanterie-Feldausbildungsregiment 617, 619; Bau-Pionier-Bataillon 133, 135, 246, 419, 523; Eisenbahnbau-Pionier-Bataillon 511; Ski-Bataillon 340; Wach-Bataillon 552; Betriebsstoff-Verwaltungskompanie 561; Frontstammlager 171; Nachschub-Bataillon 619; Festungs-Pionier-Bataillon 30; Radfahr-Aufklärungsschwadron 188; Ortskommandantur I/906; Felddepot Krementschug u. a. m.

Appendix 6
ARMY GROUP FORMATIONS WITH "HIGH DESIGNATIONS"
(Not previously mentioned in Appendix 5)

	Aufstellung
Artillerieverbände	
Artillerie-Regiment 1544	25. 7. 1944
Artillerie-Regiment 1576	25. 8. 1944
Sturmgeschützabteilung 1179	26. 8. 1944
Pionierverbände	
Pionier-Bataillon 1054	1. 10. 1944
Pionier-Bataillon 1573	26. 8. 1944
Bau-Pionier-Bataillon I/999	1. 6. 1944
Landesschützenverbände	
Landesschützen-Bataillon 997	5. 7. 1941
Landesschützen-Bataillon 998	5. 7. 1941
Landesschützen-Bataillon 1012	17. 4. 1944
Sicherungsverbände	
Sicherungs-Bataillon 1018	24. 6. 1944
Sicherungs-Bataillon 1026	1. 8. 1944
Sicherungs-Bataillon 1028	1. 9. 1944
Nachschubverbände	
Versorgungs-Regiment 1579	22. 8. 1944
Kraftwagen-Transport-Abteilung 1021	21. 2. 1943
Turkestanisches Gebirgsträgerbataillon 1001	25. 11. 1942
Ortskommandanturen	
Ortskommandantur 933	7. 11. 1940
Ortskommandantur 934	5. 11. 1940
Ortskommandantur 935	1. 6. 1941

Appendix 7
THE WINNERS OF THE HIGHEST COMBAT AWARDS
(Only the Army Group)

1. Das Eichenlaub mit Schwertern und Brillanten zum Ritterkreuz

Diese höchste Kriegsauszeichnung wurde während des Zweiten Weltkrieges an 27 Offiziere der Wehrmacht verliehen. Für ihre Leistungen bei der Heeresgruppe Süd erhielten zwischen 1941 und 1944 folgende Offiziere diese Auszeichnungen:

Lfd. Nr.	Dienstgrad, Name, Dienststellung	Verleihung
9	Oberst Schulz, Kdr. Panzer-Rgt. 25	14. 12. 1943
13	Gen. d. Pz. Tr. Hube, Oberbefehlsh. 1. Pz. Armee	20. 4. 1944
19	Gen. d. Pz. Tr. Balck, Oberbefehlsh. 4. Pz. Armee	31. 8. 1944

2. Das Eichenlaub mit Schwertern zum Ritterkreuz

Diese Auszeichnung wurde insgesamt 160mal verliehen. Die ersten fünf Träger dieser Auszeichnung der Heeresgruppe Süd waren:

Lfd. Nr.	Dienstgrad, Name, Dienststellung	Verleihung
21	Generalm. Eibl, Kdr. 385. Inf. Div.	19. 12. 1942
22	Generallt. Hube, Komm. Gen. XIV. Pz. Korps	21. 12. 1942
25	Generallt. Balck, Kdr. 11. Pz. Div.	4. 3. 1943
26	SS-Obergruppenf. Dietrich, Kdr. Leibstandarte	14. 3. 1943
27	Oberst Graf Strachwitz, Kdr. Pz. Rgt. »Großdeutschland«	14. 3. 1943

3. Das Eichenlaub zum Ritterkreuz

Diese Auszeichnung wurde insgesamt 882mal verliehen. Die ersten fünf Träger aus dem Offiziersstand und die ersten fünf Träger aus dem Unteroffiziers- und Mannschaftsstand der Heeresgruppe Süd:

1. Offiziere

Lfd. Nr.	Dienstgrad, Name, Dienststellung	Verleihung
34	Generallt. Crüwell, Kdr. 11. Pz. Div.	1. 9. 1941
41	SS-Obergruppenf. Dietrich, Kdr. Leibstandarte	31. 12. 1941
47	Hauptm. Schulz, Kdr. I./Pz. Rgt. 25	31. 12. 1941
49	Major Hoffmann-Schönborn, Kdr. Sturm-Gesch. Abt. 191	31. 12. 1941
50	Oberst Eibl, Kdr. Inf. Rgt. 132	31. 12. 1941

2. Unteroffiziere und Mannschaften

Lfd. Nr.	Dienstgrad, Name, Dienststellung	Verleihung
207	Oberfeldwebel Kohnz, Zugf. 11./Jäg. Rgt. 207	6. 3. 1943
210	Unteroffizier Rietscher, Gruppenf. 14./Gren. Rgt. 513	14. 3. 1943
222	Oberfeldw. Schlee, Zugf. 6./Geb. Jäg. Rgt. 13	6. 4. 1943
245	Oberfeldw. Kruse, Zugf. 7./Pz. Gren. Rgt. 3	17. 5. 1943
474	Oberfeldw. Schwerdfeger, Zugf. 1./Jäg. Rgt. 228	14. 5. 1944

Appendix 8
THE LOSSES OF THE ARMIES FROM 22 JUNE 1941 TO 31 MARCH 1945

Armee	Gefallen		Verwundet		Vermißt		Gesamt	
		davon Offiziere		davon Offiziere		davon Offiziere		davon Offiziere
2. Armee	66 573	2 399	270 819	7 125	50 087	655	387 479	10 179
6. Armee	10 691	321	45 121	1 295	56 471	146	112 283	1 762
8. Armee	45 340	1 585	189 843	4 922	27 245	293	262 428	6 800
11. Armee	konnte nicht ermittelt werden, da diese Armee nach der Eroberung Sewastopols teilweise aufgelöst wurde und der Rest zur Heeresgruppe Nord verlegte							
17. Armee	60 091	1 883	260 432	5 894	70 153	916	390 676	8 693
1. Panzer-Armee	95 665	3 546	382 633	10 509	100 358	1 020	578 676	15 075
4. Panzer-Armee	76 005	2 886	308 007	9 819	68 945	1 236	452 957	12 941

Die 4. Panzerarme war an allen Frontabschnitten zwischen Leningrad und Stalingrad im Einsatz, deshalb verteilen sich die Verluste auch auf alle anderen Abschnitte.

Zu diesen Verlustzahlen sind nicht die Verluste der ganz oder zeitweise unterstellten Heeres- und Armeetruppen gerechnet sowie der landeseigenen Verbände.